Tatsuki Fujimoto

I love *Get Out*!

Tatsuki Fujimoto won Honorable Mention in the
November 2013 Shueisha Crown Newcomers' Awards for
his debut one-shot story *Love Is Blind*. His first series,
Fire Punch, ran for eight volumes. *Chainsaw Man* began
serialization in 2018 in *Weekly Shonen Jump*.

CHAINSAW MAN

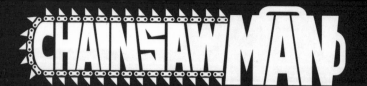

9

SHONEN JUMP Manga Edition

Story & Art **TATSUKI FUJIMOTO**

Translation/AMANDA HALEY
Touch-Up Art & Lettering/JAMES GAUBATZ
Design/JULIAN [JR] ROBINSON
Editor/ALEXIS KIRSCH

Printed in the U.S.A.

Published by VIZ Media, LLC
P.O. Box 77010
San Francisco, CA 94107

10 9 8 7 6 5 4 3 2 1
First printing, February 2022

VIZ MEDIA
viz.com

SHONEN JUMP

RATED T+ OLDER TEEN ratings.viz.com

PARENTAL ADVISORY
CHAINSAW MAN is rated T+ for Older Teen and is recommended for ages 16 and up. This volume contains violence, gore, and brief nudity.

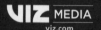

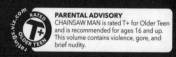

CHAINSAWMAN

9

Bath

Tatsuki Fujimoto

CHARACTERS

Denji

A young man-slash-Chainsaw Devil who carries his partner Pochita inside him. He's always true to his desires. Likes Makima, the first person to ever treat him like a human being.

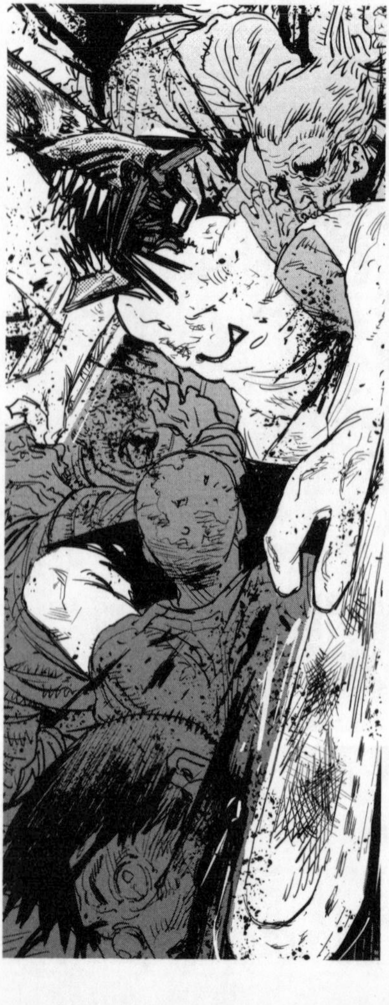

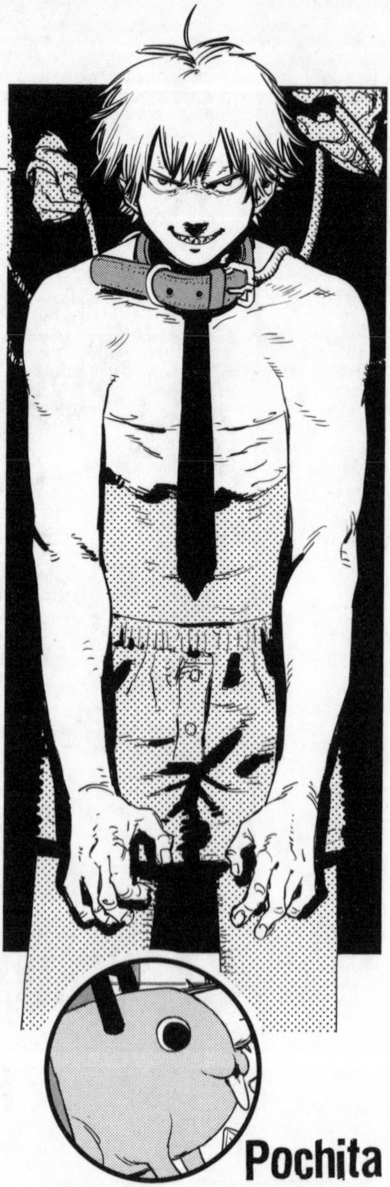

Pochita

Chainsaw Devil. Gave up his heart to Denji, becoming part of his body.

Makima

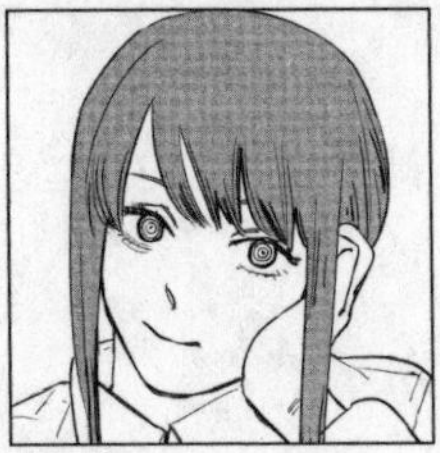

The mysterious woman in charge of Public Safety Devil Extermination Special Division 4. Can smell devil scents.

Aki Hayakawa

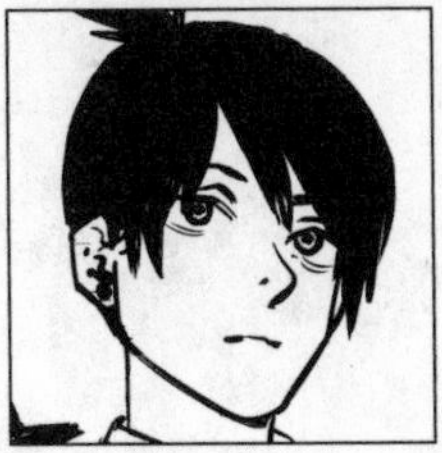

Makima's loyal subordinate and Denji's senior at Public Safety by three years. Contracts: Future Devil, Curse Devil.

Angel Devil

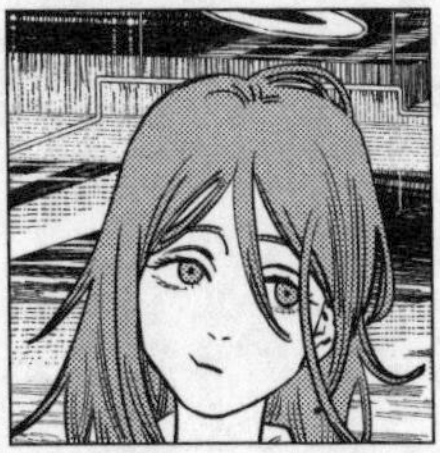

Though not hostile to humans, anyone who touches this devil directly will have their life span siphoned off. Special Division 4 agent.

Power

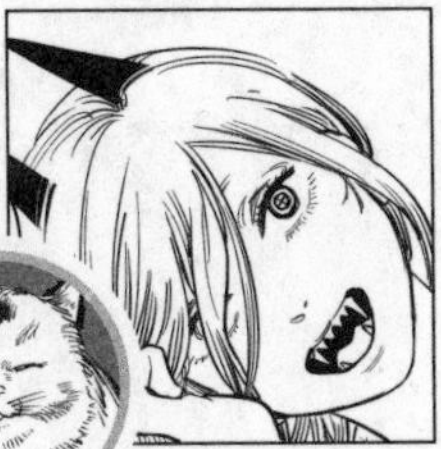

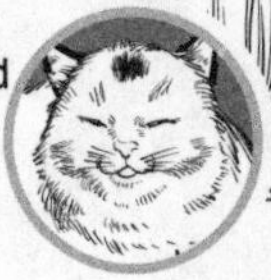

Blood Devil Fiend. Egotistical and prone to going out of control. Her cat Meowy is her only friend.

Future Devil

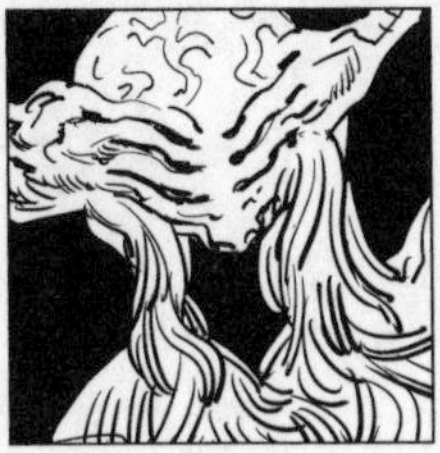

A devil under Public Safety's purview. Pet saying: "The future rules!" Foretold an ominous future when making a contract with Aki.

Kishibe

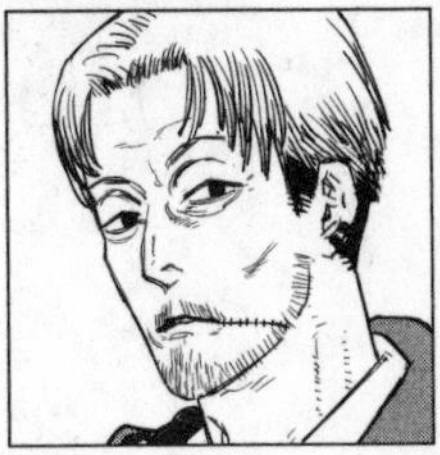

A man with extraordinary fighting ability who belongs to the Special Division. The strongest Devil Hunter. Denji and Power's teacher.

STORY

Denji is a young man who hunts devils with his pet devil-dog Pochita. To pay off his debts, Denji is forced to live in extreme poverty and worked like a dog, only to be betrayed and killed on the job without ever getting to live a decent life. But Pochita, at the cost of the pooch's own life, brings Denji back—as Chainsaw Man! After Denji buzzes through all their attackers, he's taken in by the mysterious Makima, and begins a new life as a Public Safety Devil Hunter.

After the whole wide world figures out Denji's the Chainsaw Devil, assassins from around the globe have assembled in Tokyo to take him out!! As the crazy battle continues, Germany's hit man Santa Claus gets Denji and friends (and enemies too) summoned to Hell, where they're promptly devastated. As it turns out, Santa Claus's true mission was to make a contract with the Darkness Devil and kill Makima all along!! Makima herself shows up and narrowly brings them back from Hell, but Denji is forced into an uphill battle against an immortal, powered-up Santa Claus. He beats back Santa the only way a Chainsaw Man can…by fighting so unintelligently that the power of stupidity actually surpasses the power of darkness. After the battle, Quanxi's assassin group surrenders, only for Makima to mercilessly end their lives…

CONTENTS

Chapter 71: Bath

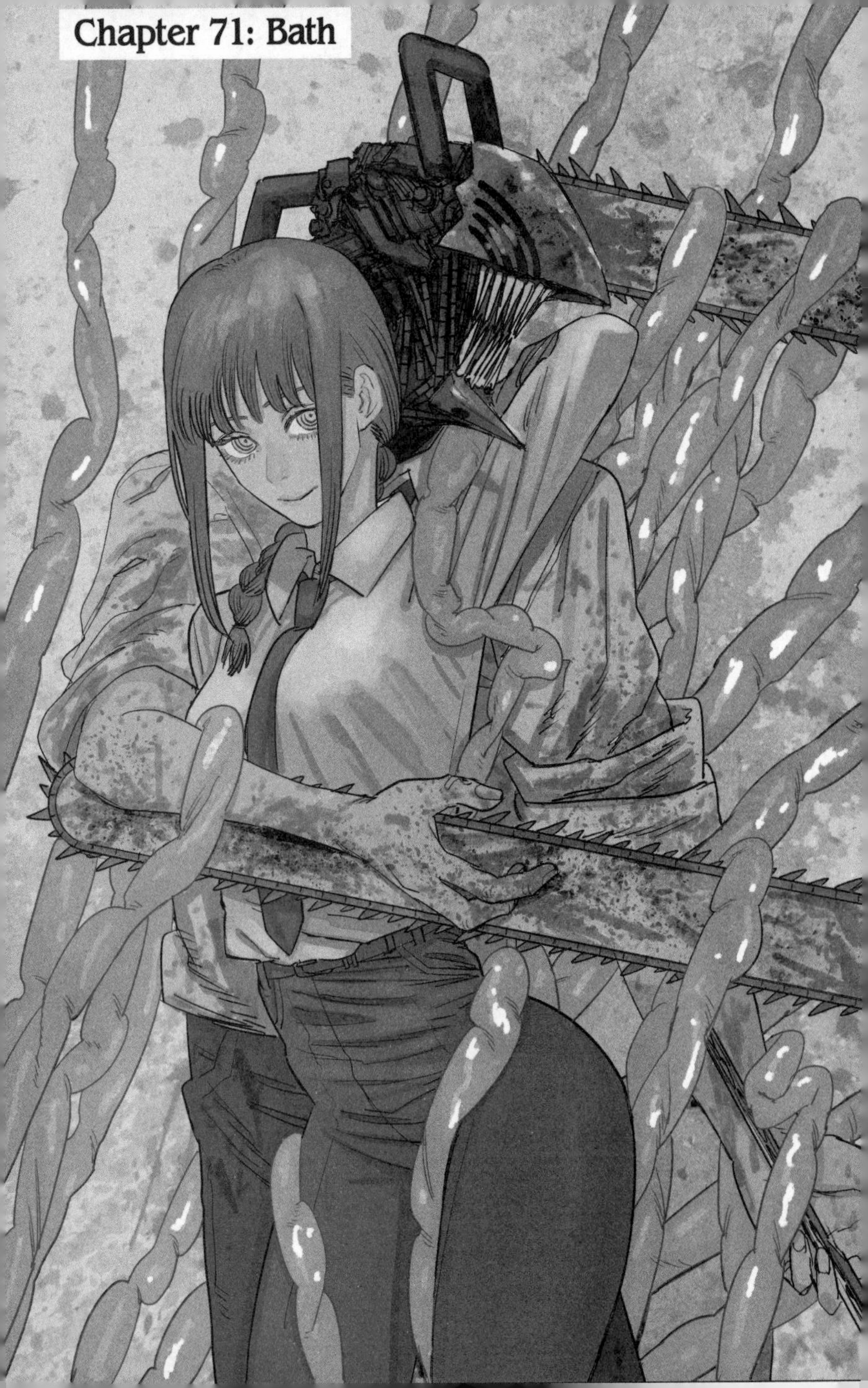

CHAINSAW MAN

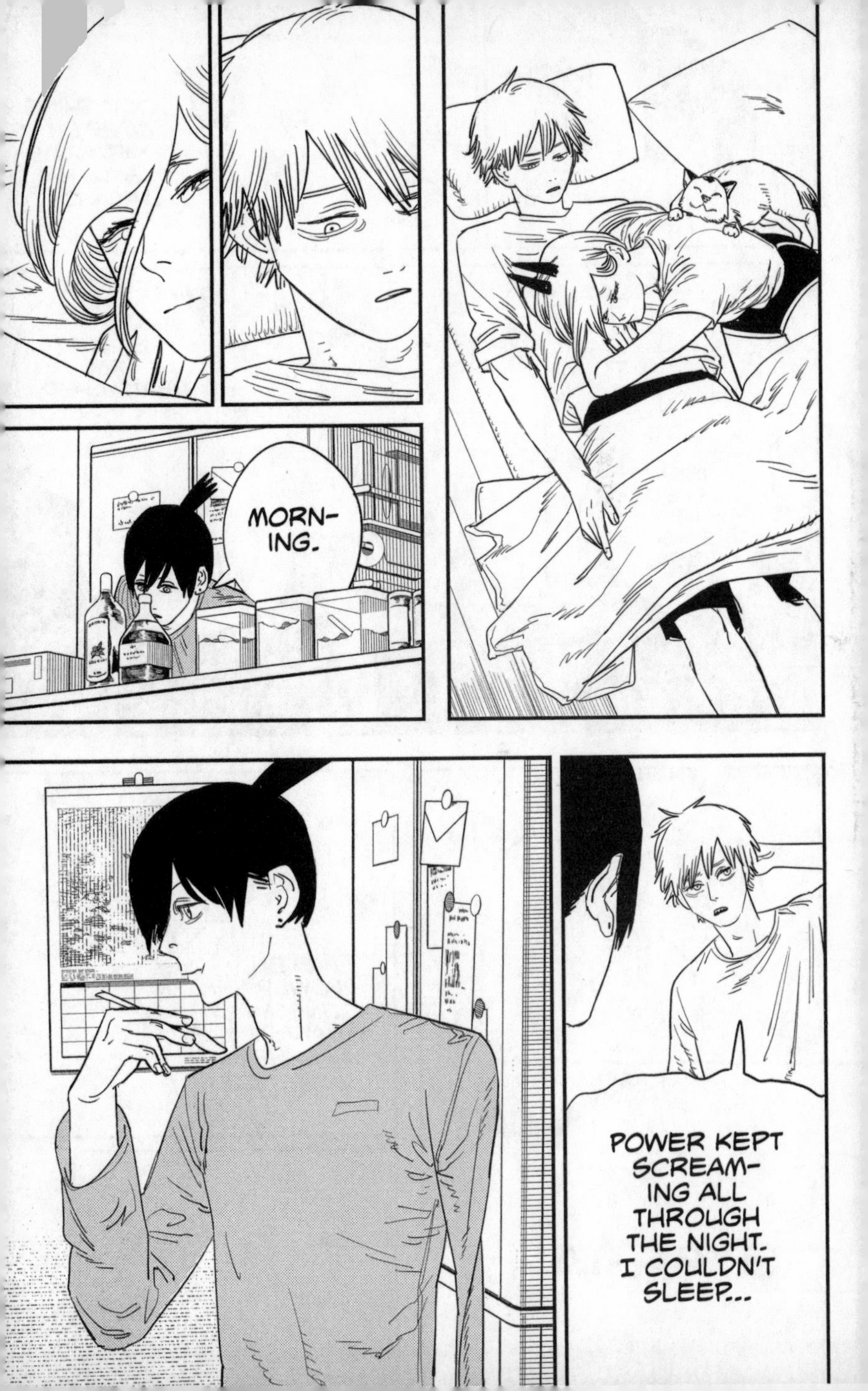
MORN-
ING.
POWER KEPT SCREAM-ING ALL THROUGH THE NIGHT. I COULDN'T SLEEP...

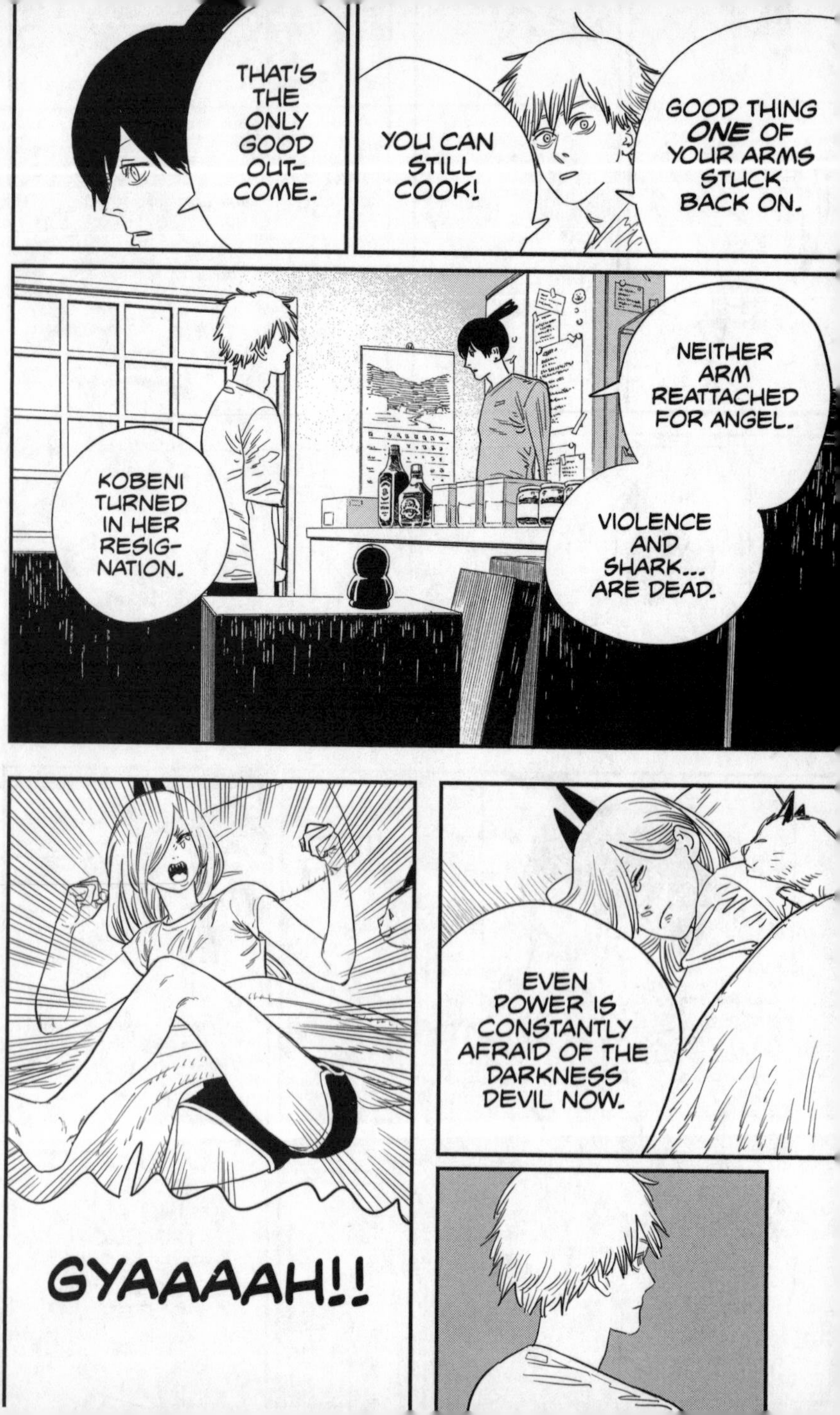
GOOD THING ONE OF YOUR ARMS STUCK BACK ON.
YOU CAN STILL COOK!
THAT'S THE ONLY GOOD OUT-COME.
NEITHER ARM REATTACHED FOR ANGEL.
VIOLENCE AND SHARK... ARE DEAD.
KOBENI TURNED IN HER RESIG-NATION.
EVEN POWER IS CONSTANTLY AFRAID OF THE DARKNESS DEVIL NOW.
GYAAAAH!!

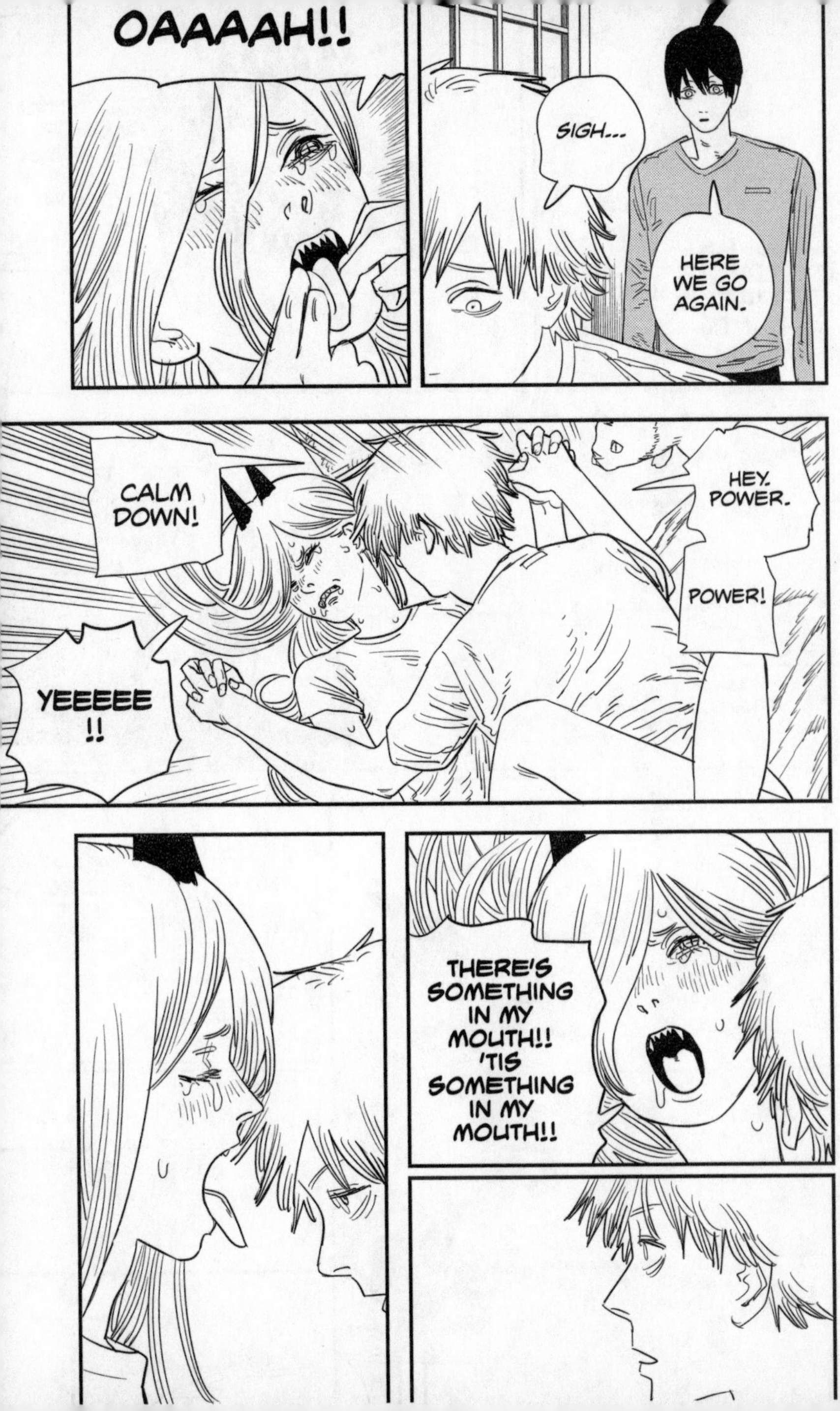
SIGH...
HERE WE GO AGAIN.
OAAAAH!!
HEY. POWER.
POWER!
CALM DOWN!
YEEEEEE!!
THERE'S SOMETHING IN MY MOUTH!! 'TIS SOMETHING IN MY MOUTH!!

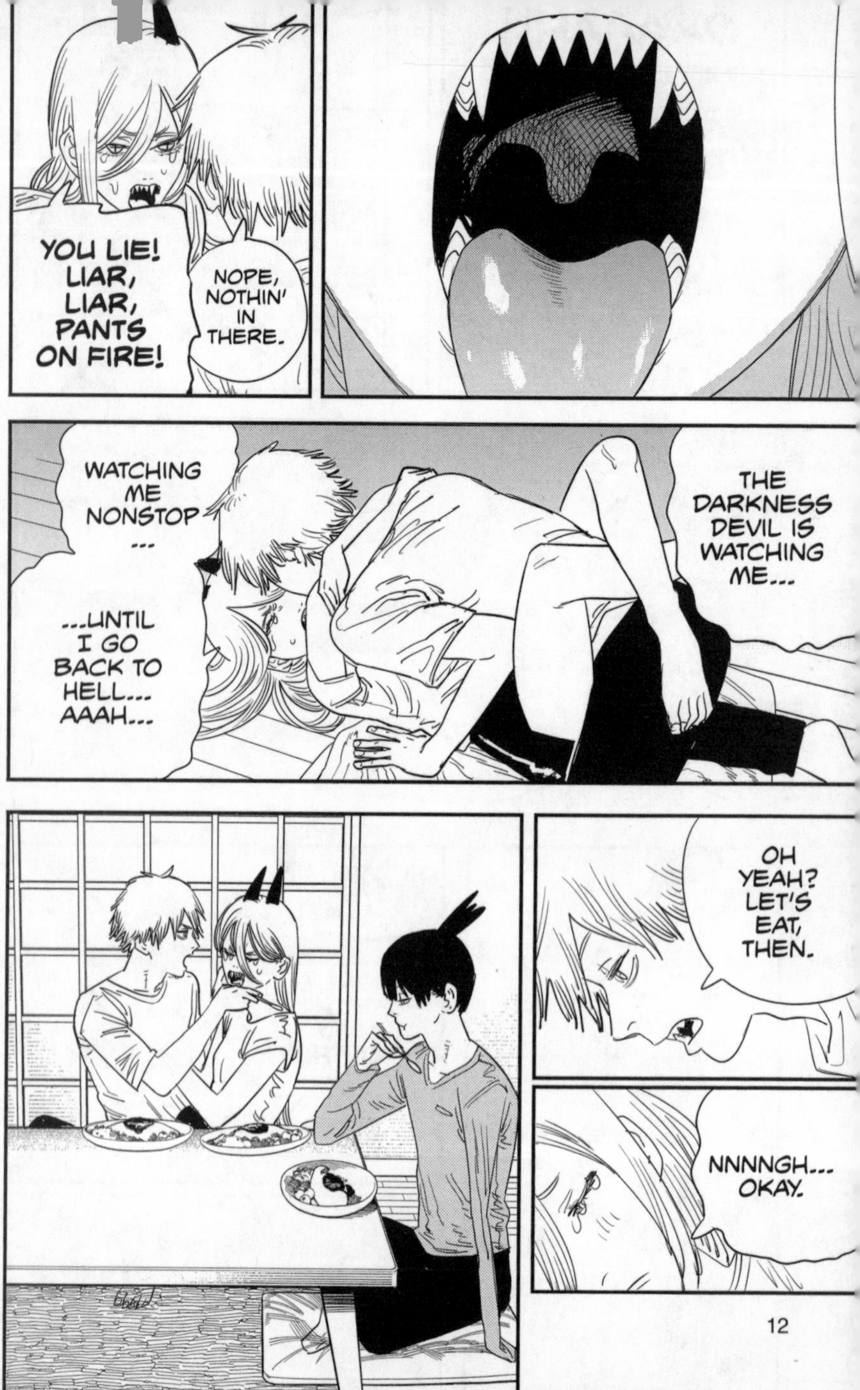
NOPE, NOTHIN' IN THERE.
YOU LIE! LIAR, LIAR, PANTS ON FIRE!
THE DARKNESS DEVIL IS WATCHING ME...
WATCHING ME NONSTOP...
...UNTIL I GO BACK TO HELL... AAAH...
OH YEAH? LET'S EAT, THEN.
NNNNGH... OKAY.

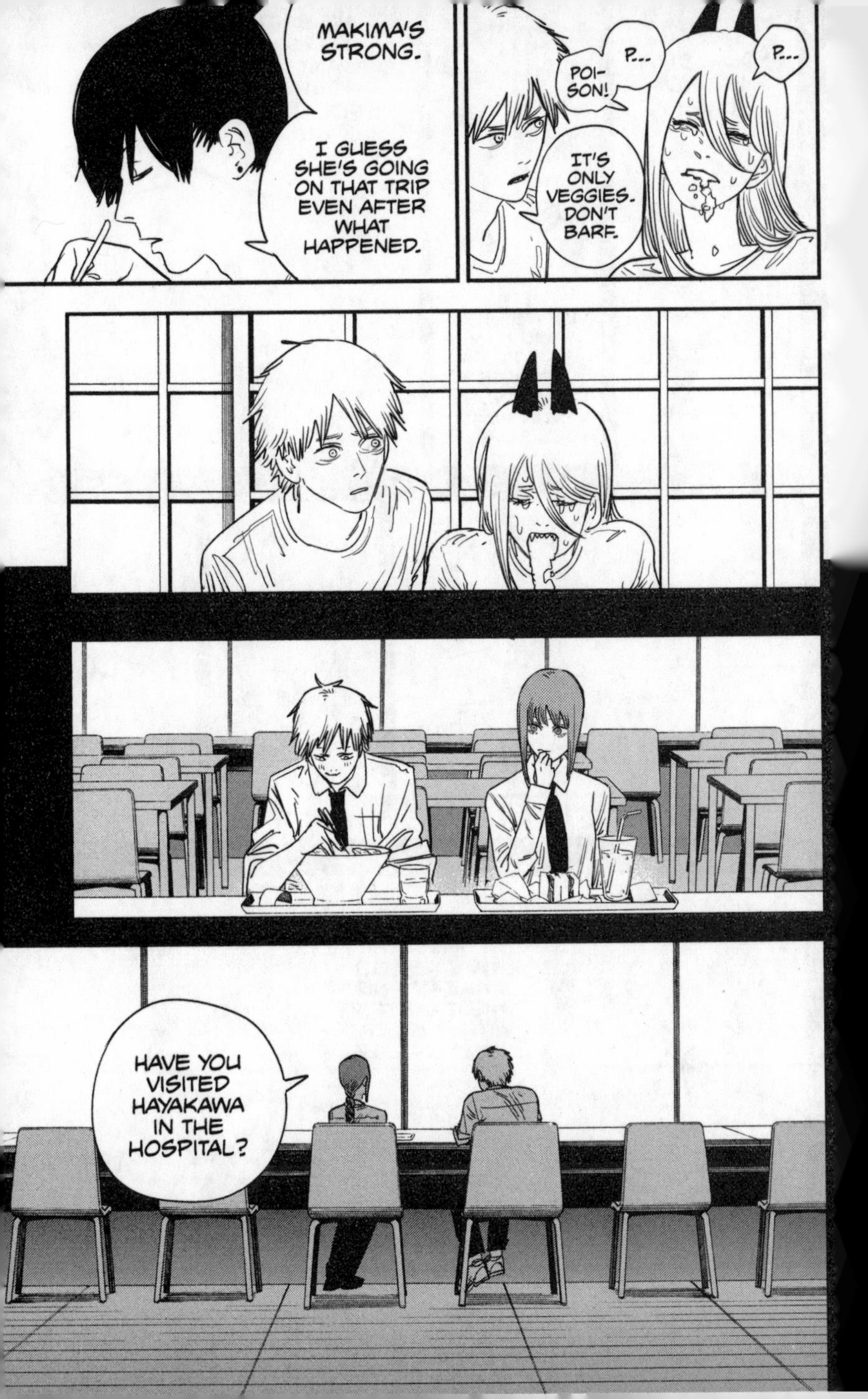
P...
P...
POI-SON!
IT'S ONLY VEGGIES. DON'T BARF.
MAKIMA'S STRONG.
I GUESS SHE'S GOING ON THAT TRIP EVEN AFTER WHAT HAPPENED.
HAVE YOU VISITED HAYAKAWA IN THE HOSPITAL?

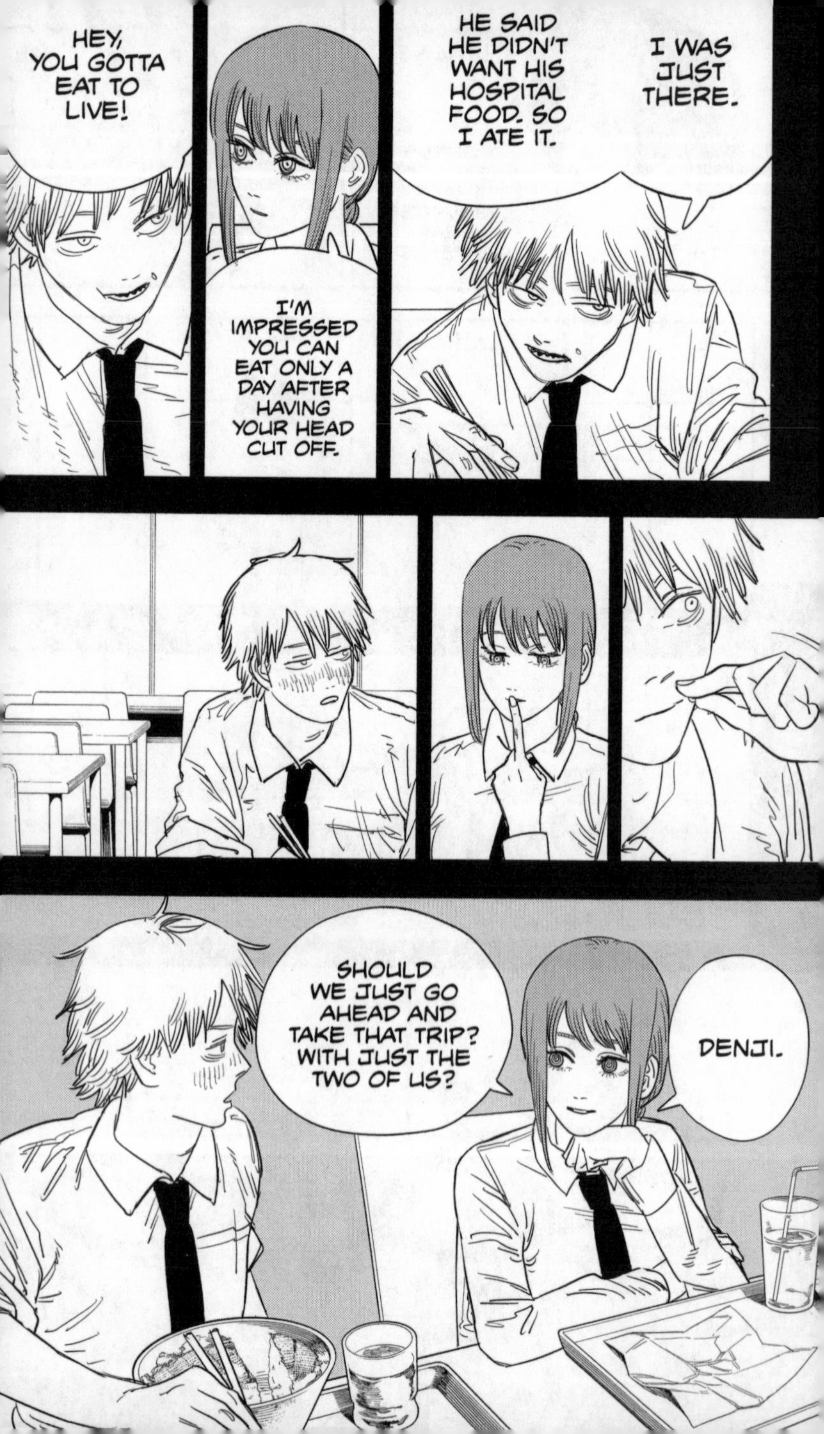
I WAS JUST THERE.
HE SAID HE DIDN'T WANT HIS HOSPITAL FOOD. SO I ATE IT.
I'M IMPRESSED YOU CAN EAT ONLY A DAY AFTER HAVING YOUR HEAD CUT OFF.
HEY, YOU GOTTA EAT TO LIVE!
DENJI.
SHOULD WE JUST GO AHEAD AND TAKE THAT TRIP? WITH JUST THE TWO OF US?

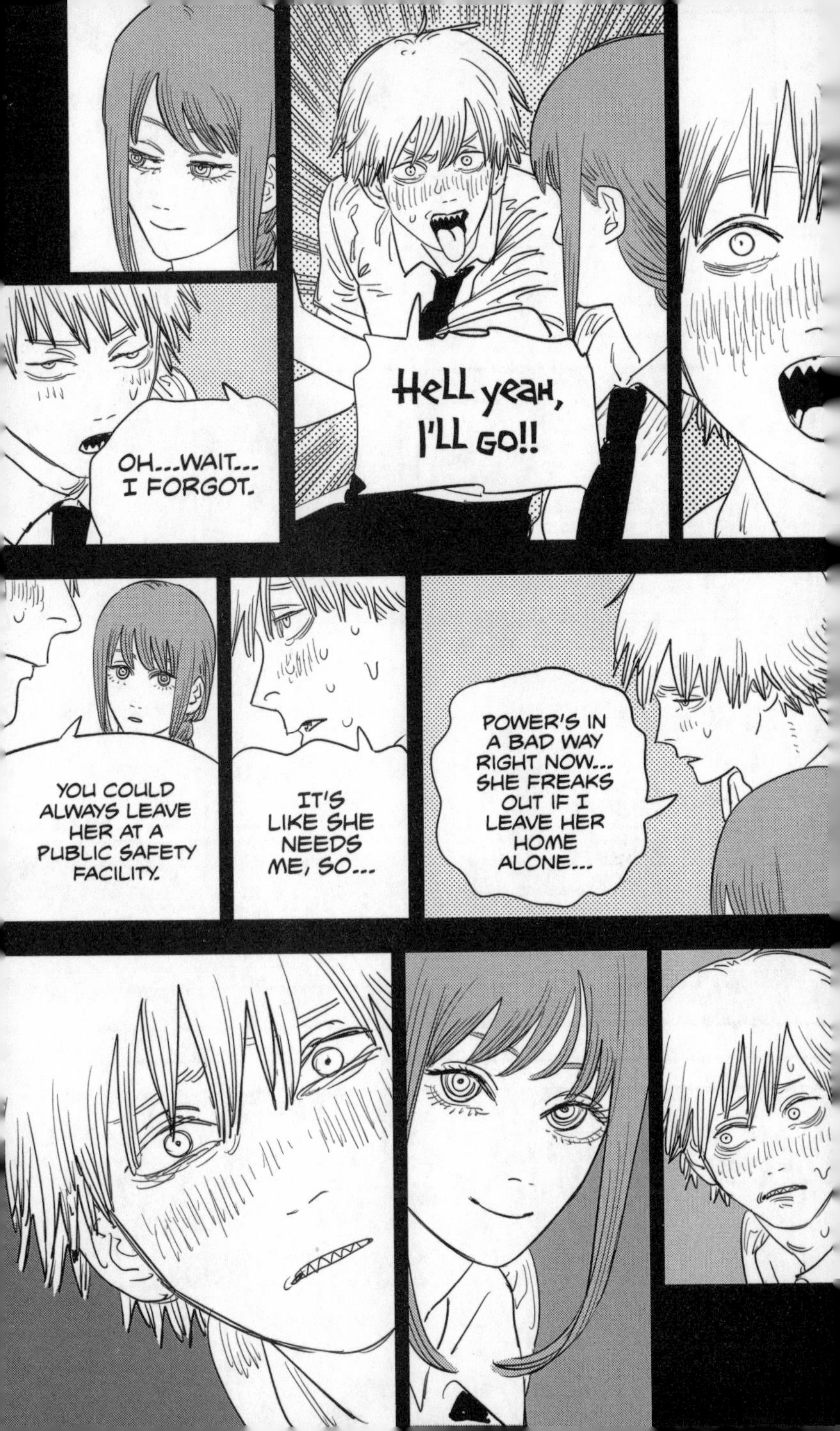
Hell yeah, I'LL GO!!
OH...WAIT... I FORGOT.
POWER'S IN A BAD WAY RIGHT NOW... SHE FREAKS OUT IF I LEAVE HER HOME ALONE...
IT'S LIKE SHE NEEDS ME, SO...
YOU COULD ALWAYS LEAVE HER AT A PUBLIC SAFETY FACILITY.

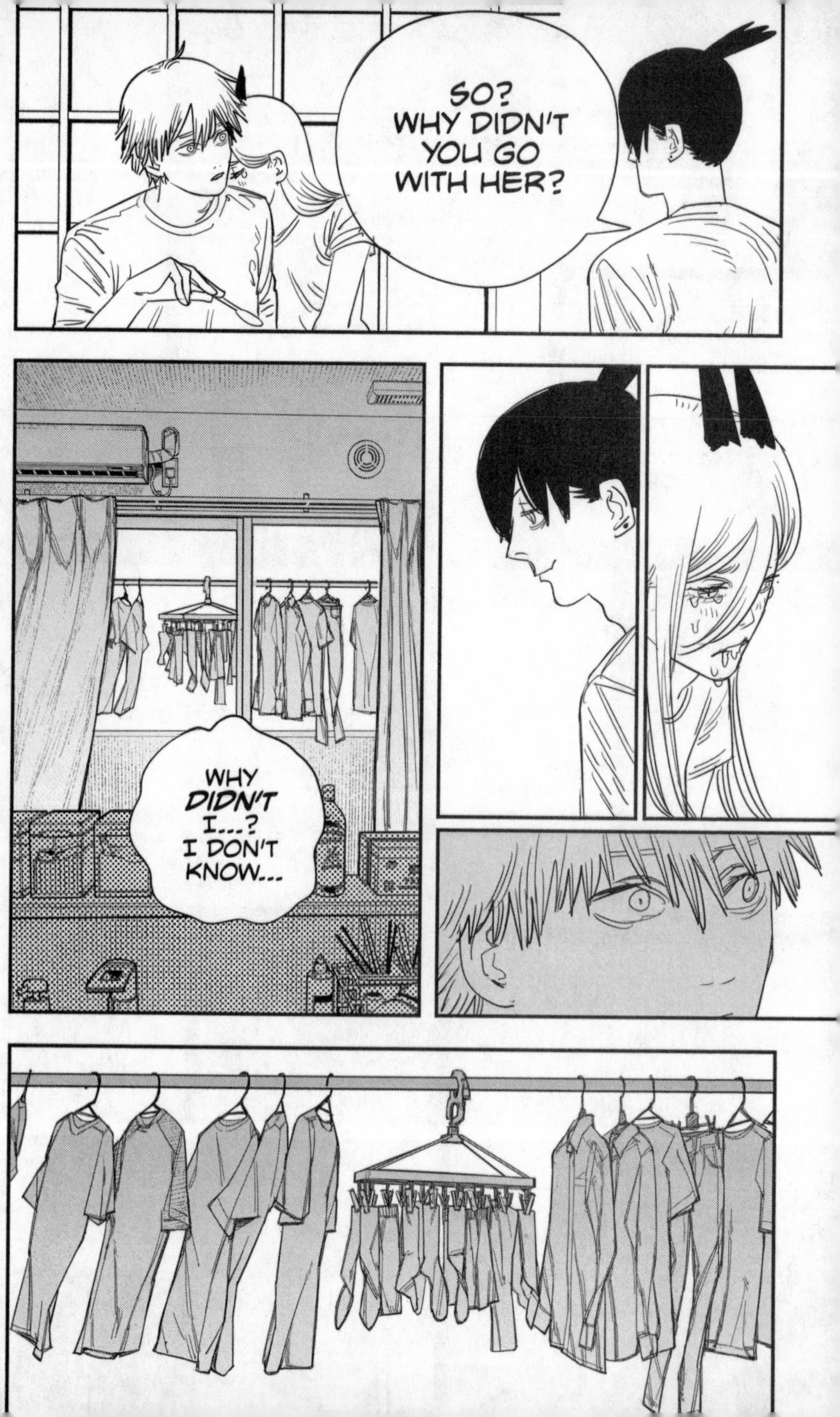
SO? WHY DIDN'T YOU GO WITH HER?
WHY DIDN'T I...? I DON'T KNOW...

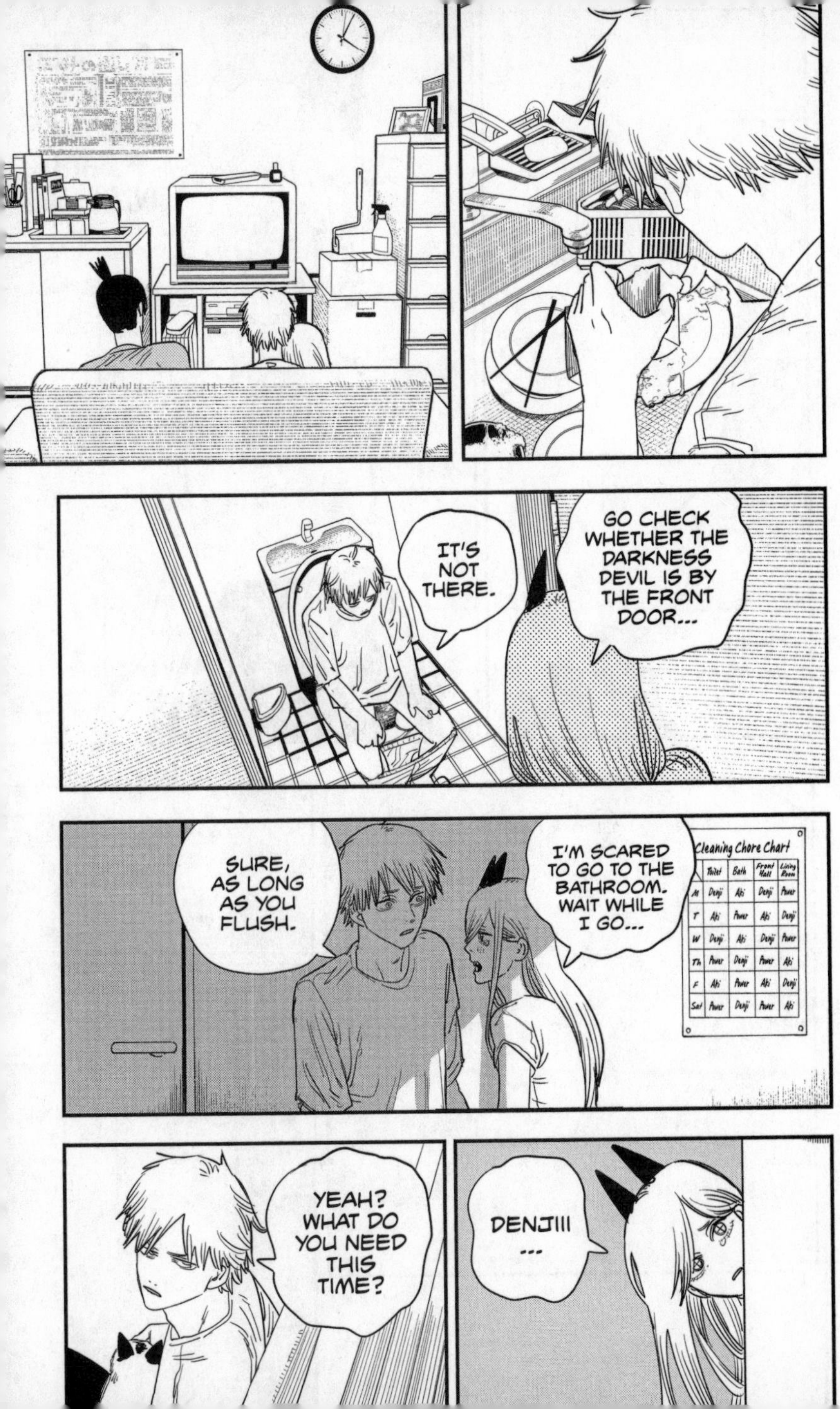
GO CHECK WHETHER THE DARKNESS DEVIL IS BY THE FRONT DOOR...
IT'S NOT THERE.
Cleaning Chore Chart
Toilet Bath Front Hall Living Room
M Denji Aki Denji Power
T Aki Power Aki Denji
W Denji Aki Denji Power
Th Power Denji Power Aki
F Aki Power Aki Denji
Sat Power Denji Power Aki
I'M SCARED TO GO TO THE BATHROOM. WAIT WHILE I GO...
SURE, AS LONG AS YOU FLUSH.
DENJIII ...
YEAH? WHAT DO YOU NEED THIS TIME?

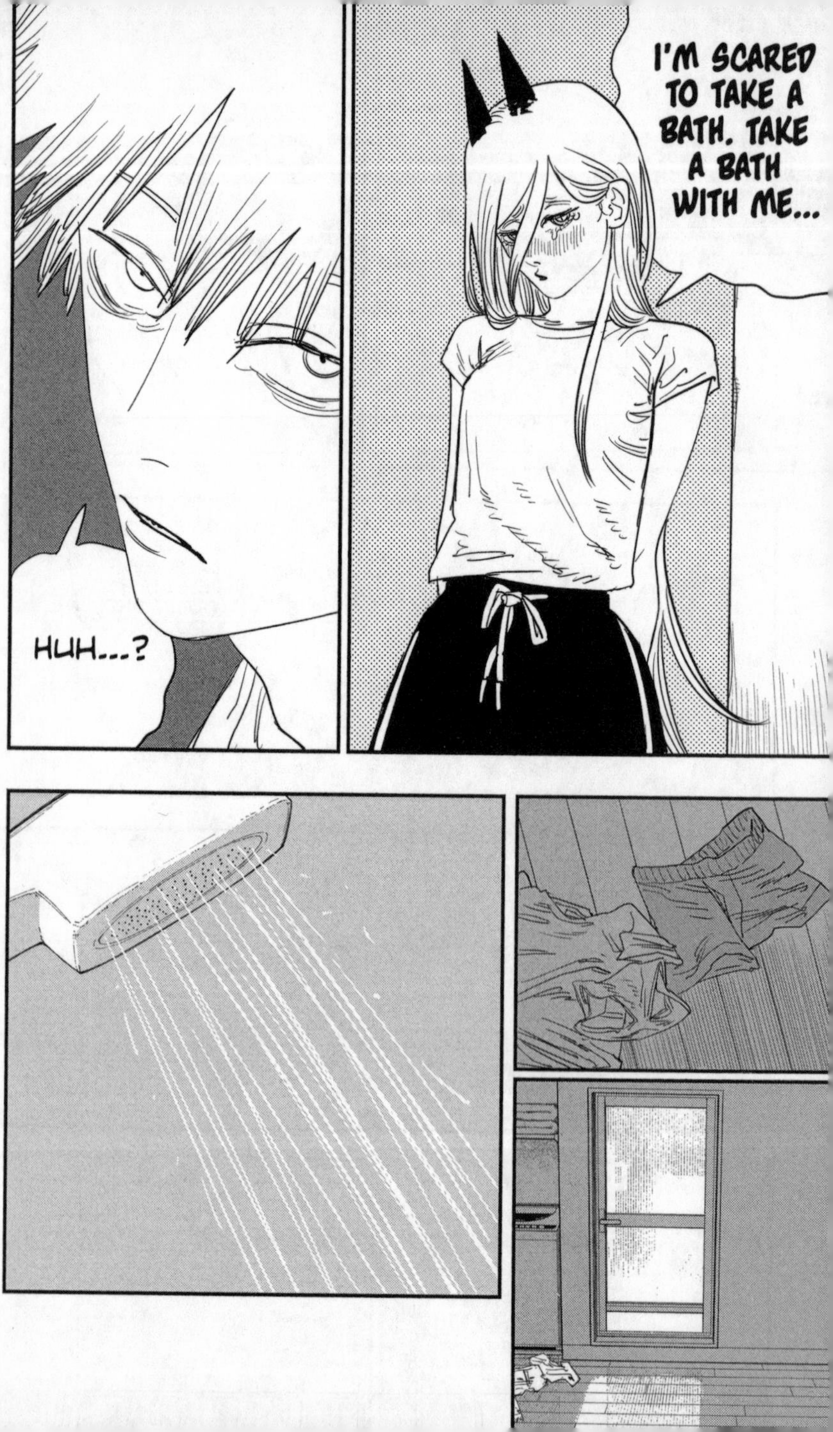
I'M SCARED TO TAKE A BATH. TAKE A BATH WITH ME...
HUH...?

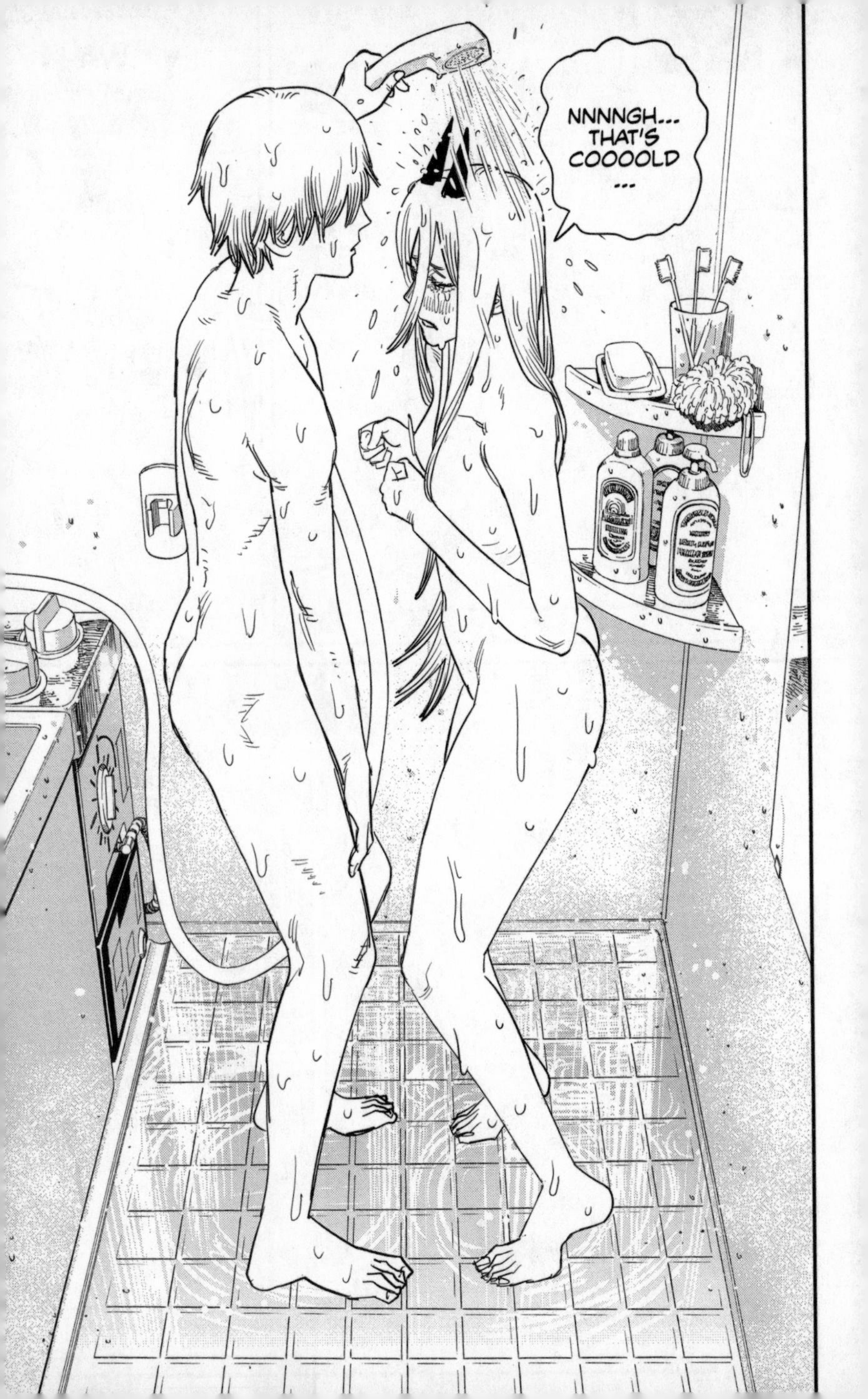
NNNNGH... THAT'S COOOOLD ...

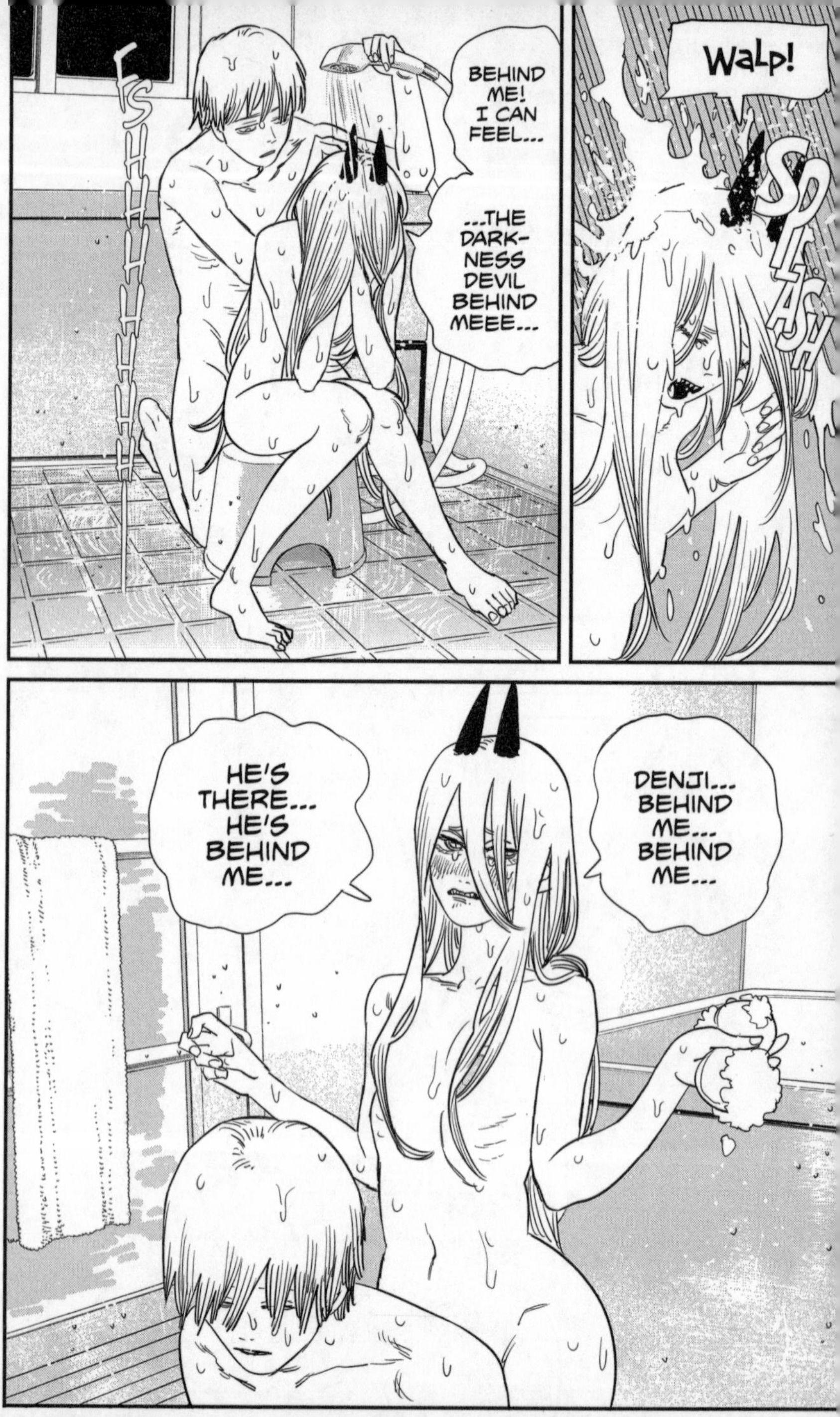
WALP!
SPLASH
BEHIND ME! I CAN FEEL...
...THE DARKNESS DEVIL BEHIND MEEE...
FSHHHHHHHH
DENJI... BEHIND ME... BEHIND ME...
HE'S THERE... HE'S BEHIND ME...

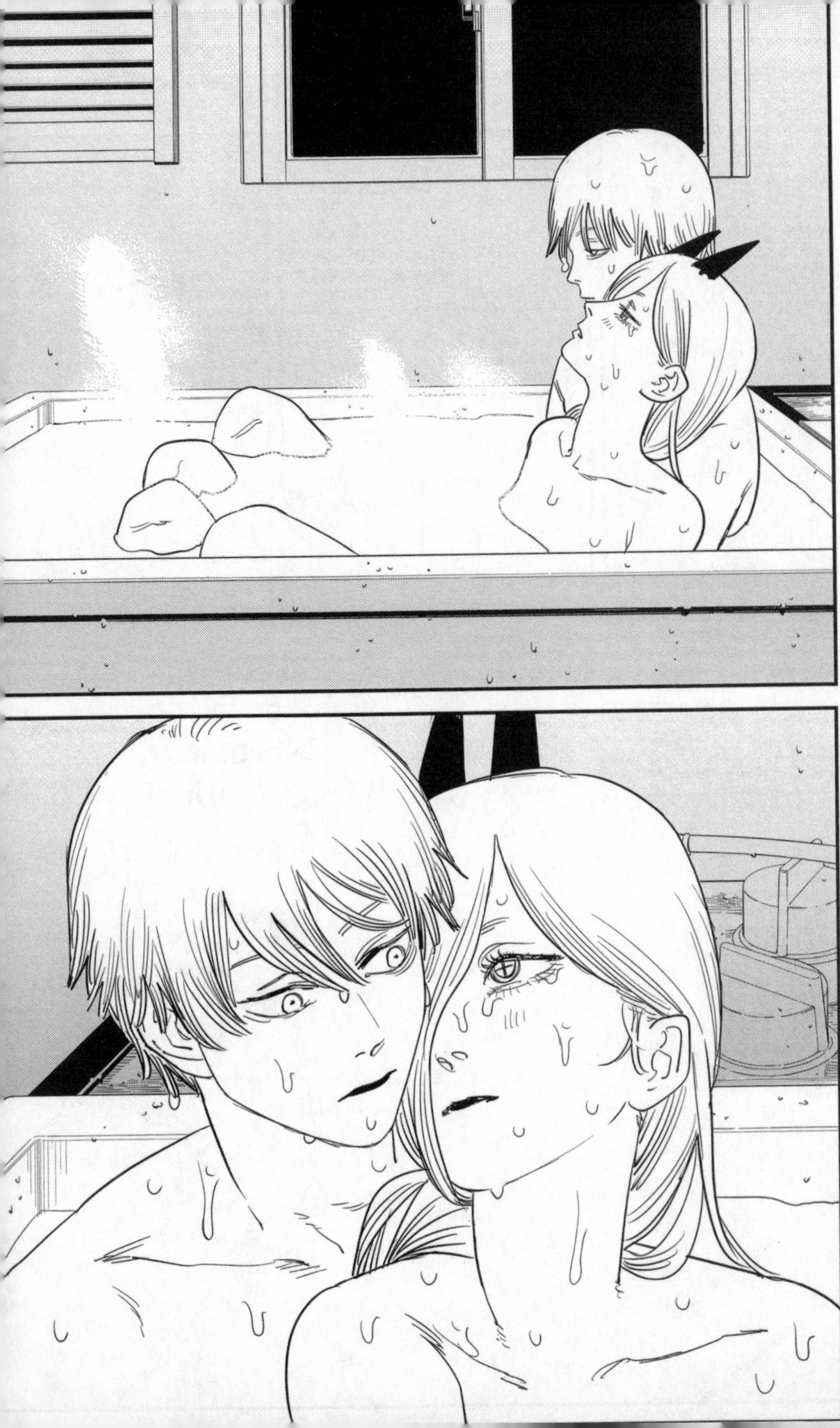

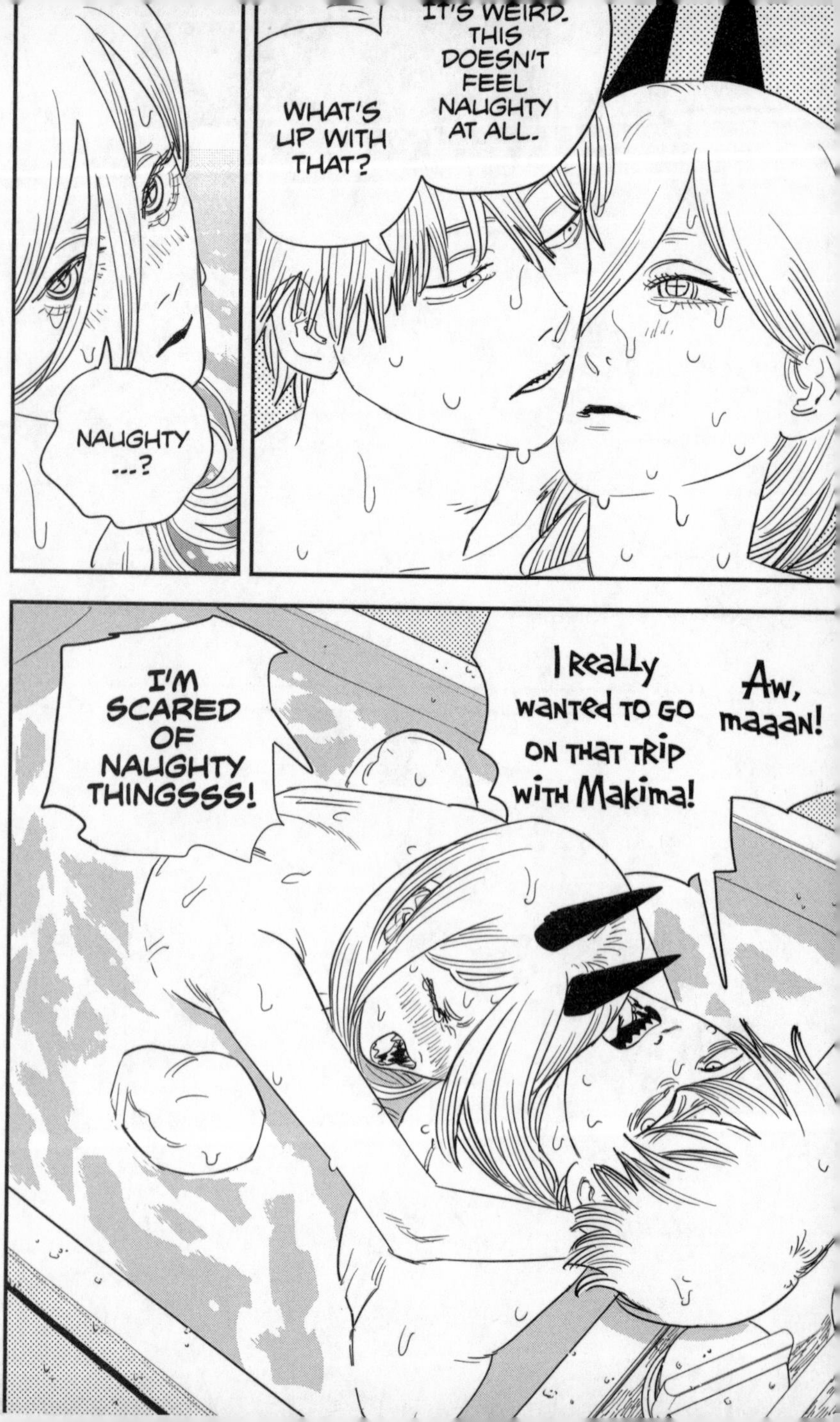
IT'S WEIRD. THIS DOESN'T FEEL NAUGHTY AT ALL.
WHAT'S UP WITH THAT?
NAUGHTY ...?
Aw, maaan!
I really wanted to go on that trip with Makima!
I'M SCARED OF NAUGHTY THINGSSS!

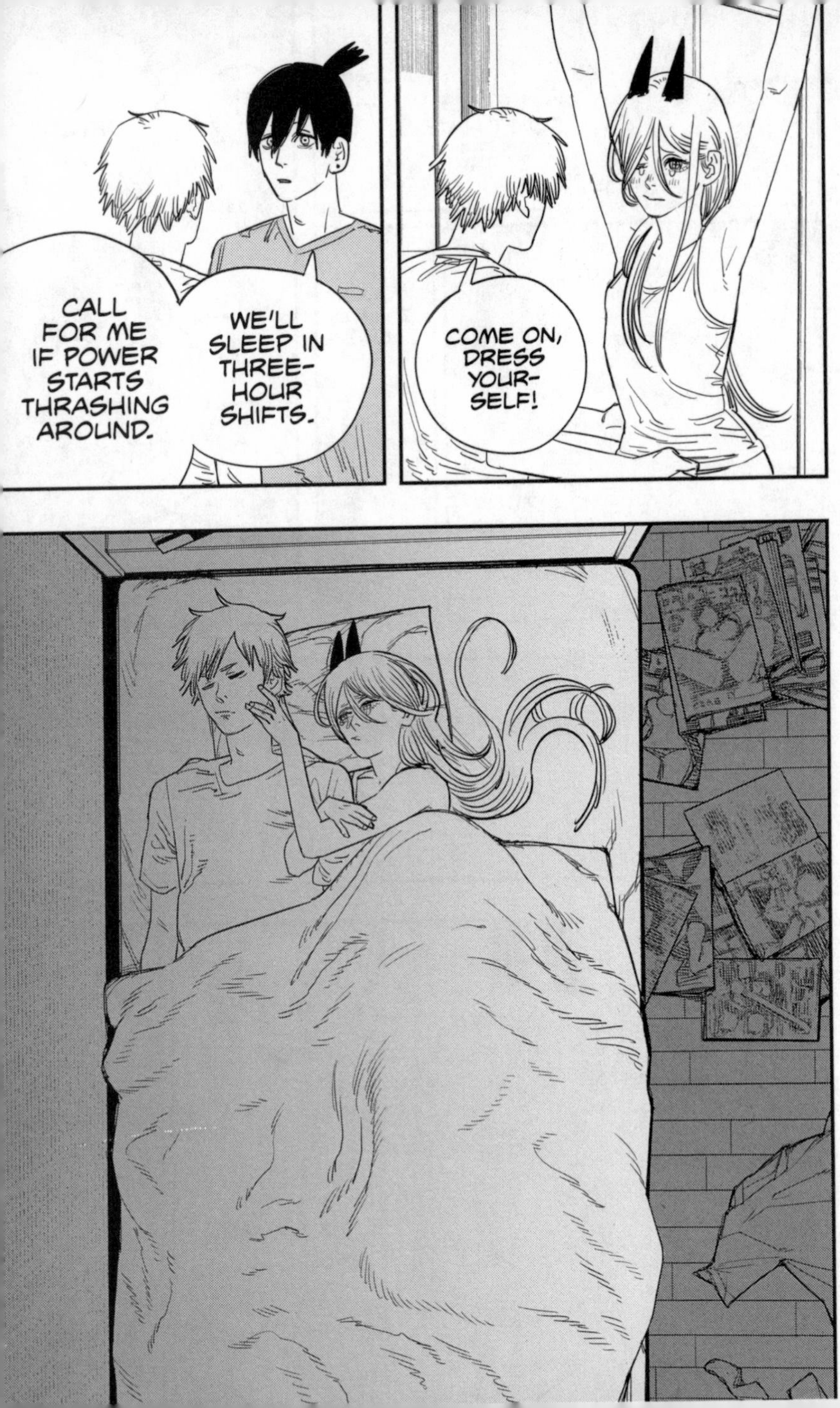
COME ON, DRESS YOURSELF!
WE'LL SLEEP IN THREE-HOUR SHIFTS.
CALL FOR ME IF POWER STARTS THRASHING AROUND.

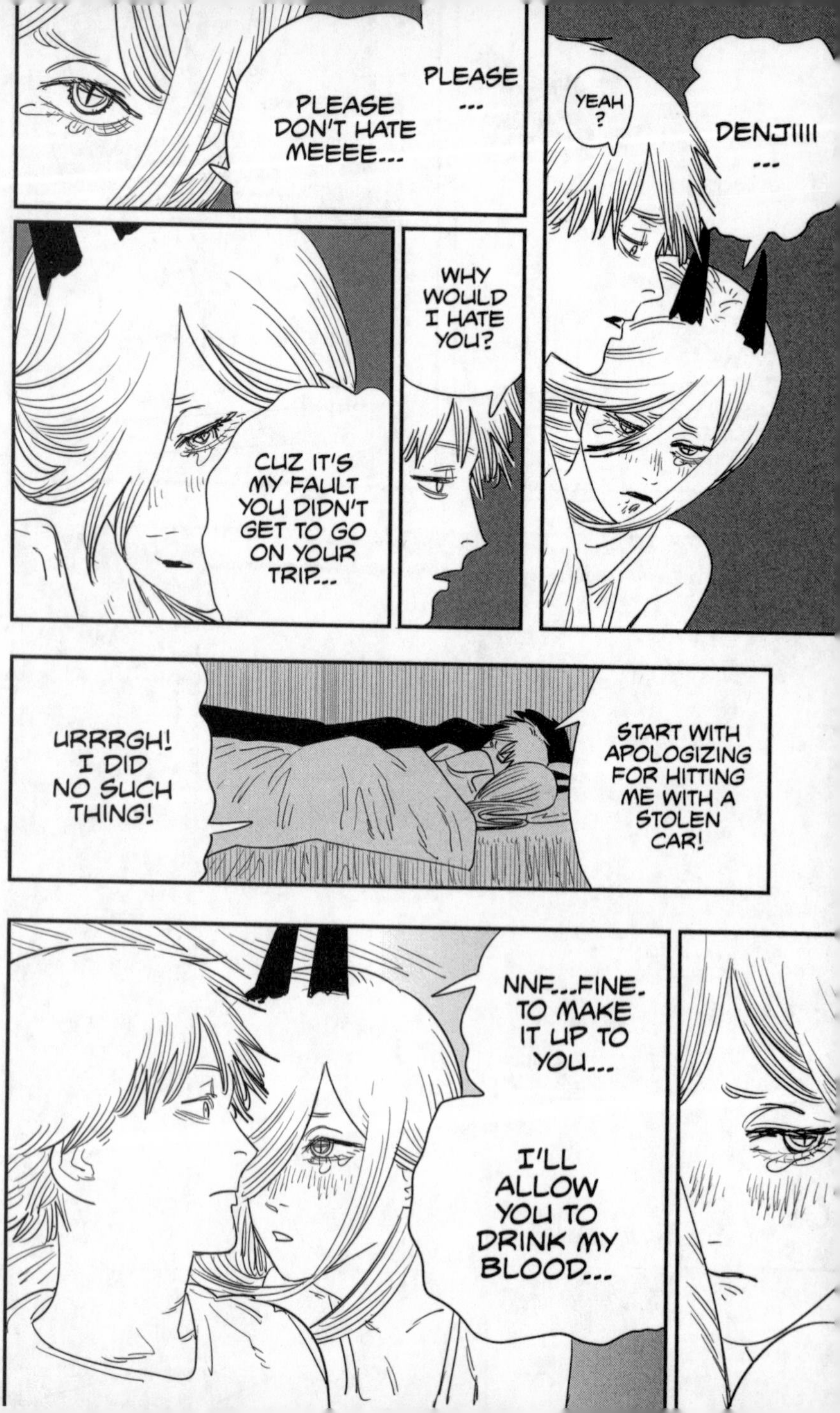
DENJIIII ---
YEAH ?
PLEASE ---
PLEASE DON'T HATE MEEEE...
WHY WOULD I HATE YOU?
CUZ IT'S MY FAULT YOU DIDN'T GET TO GO ON YOUR TRIP...
START WITH APOLOGIZING FOR HITTING ME WITH A STOLEN CAR!
URRRGH! I DID NO SUCH THING!
NNF...FINE. TO MAKE IT UP TO YOU...
I'LL ALLOW YOU TO DRINK MY BLOOD...

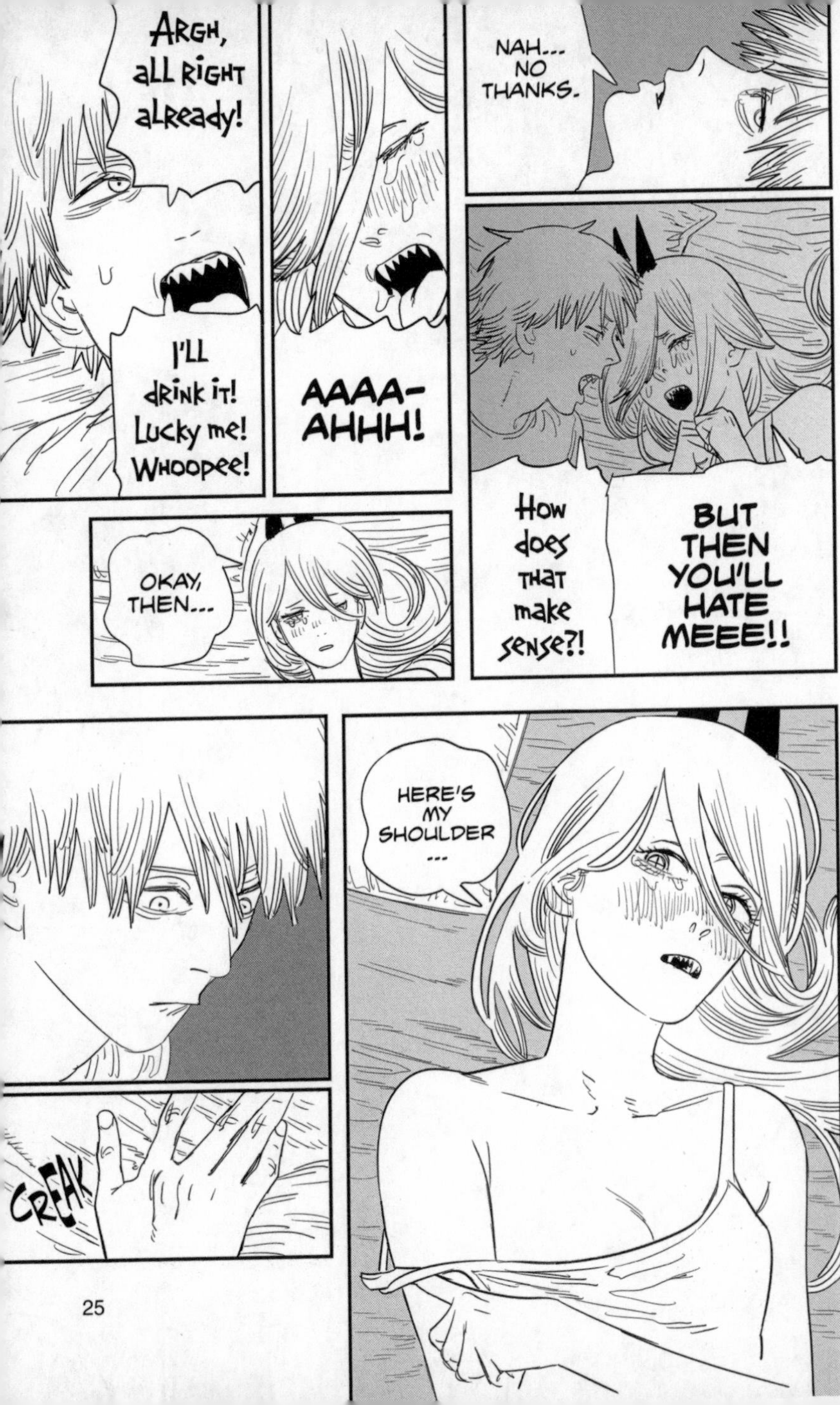
NAH... NO THANKS.
BUT THEN YOU'LL HATE MEEE!!
How does that make sense?!
AAAA-AHHH!
Argh, all right already!
I'll drink it! Lucky me! Whoopee!
OKAY, THEN...
HERE'S MY SHOULDER...
CREAK

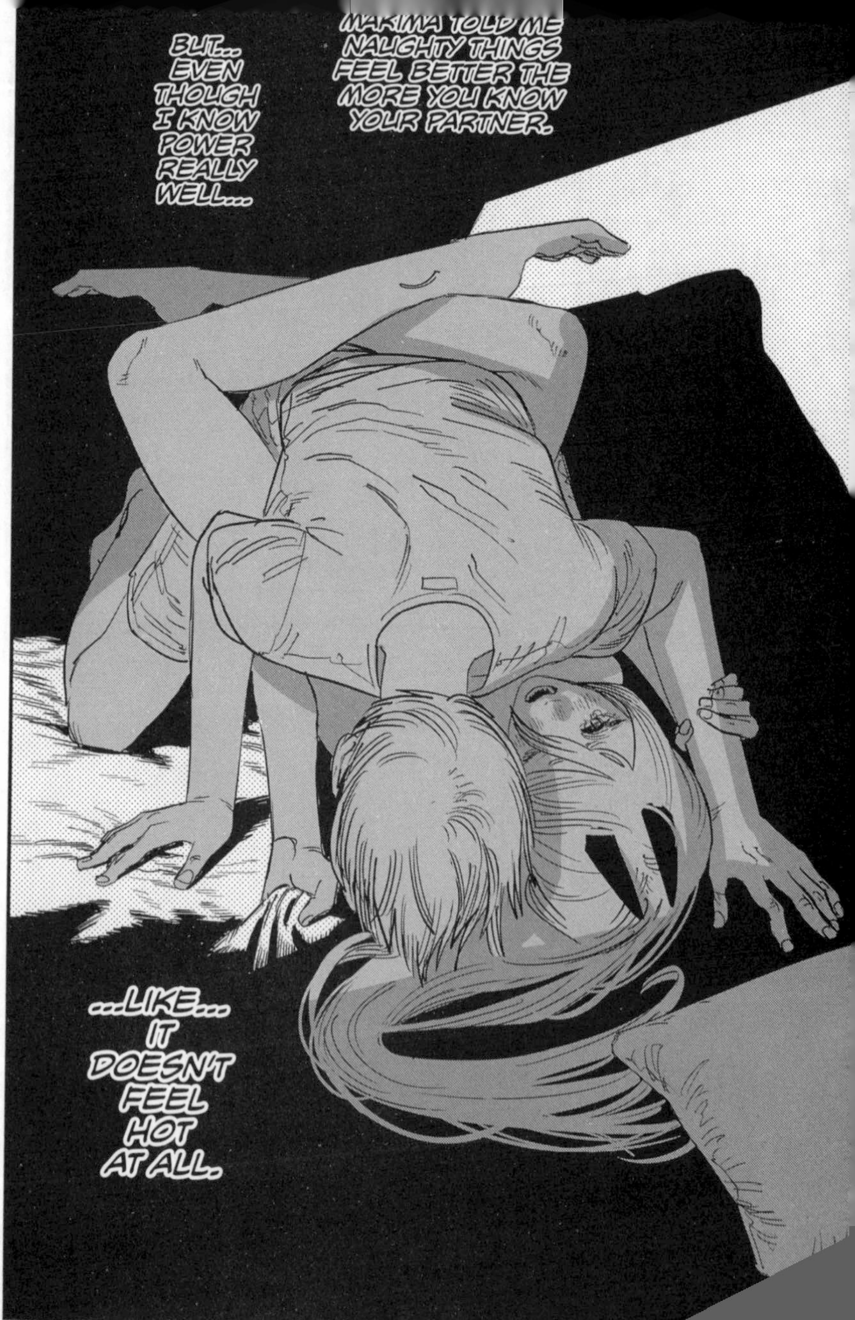
MAKIMA TOLD ME NAUGHTY THINGS FEEL BETTER THE MORE YOU KNOW YOUR PARTNER.
BUT... EVEN THOUGH I KNOW POWER REALLY WELL...
...LIKE... IT DOESN'T FEEL HOT AT ALL.

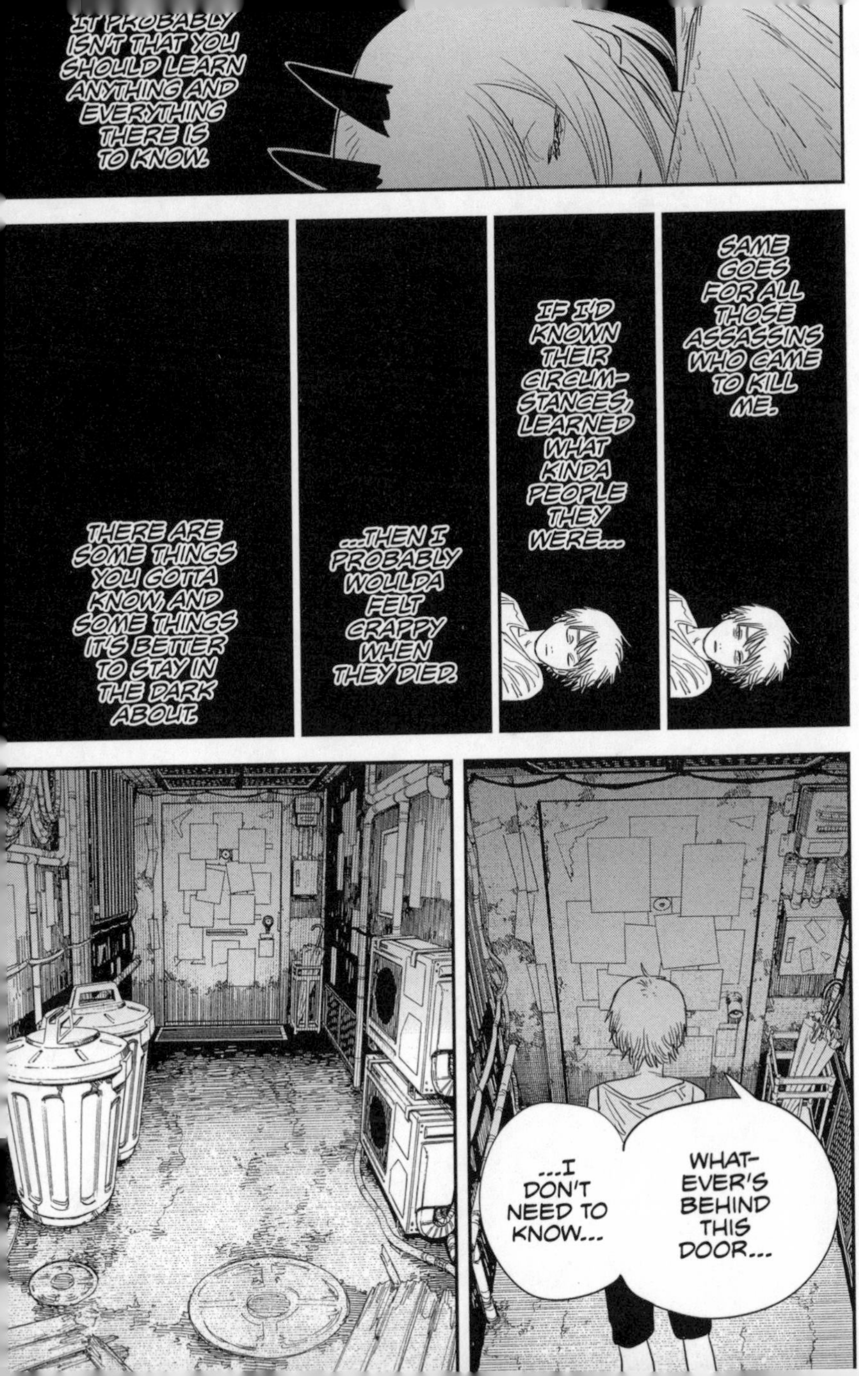
IT PROBABLY ISN'T THAT YOU SHOULD LEARN ANYTHING AND EVERYTHING THERE IS TO KNOW.
SAME GOES FOR ALL THOSE ASSASSINS WHO CAME TO KILL ME.
IF I'D KNOWN THEIR CIRCUM-STANCES, LEARNED WHAT KINDA PEOPLE THEY WERE...
...THEN I PROBABLY WOULDA FELT CRAPPY WHEN THEY DIED.
THERE ARE SOME THINGS YOU GOTTA KNOW, AND SOME THINGS IT'S BETTER TO STAY IN THE DARK ABOUT.
WHAT-EVER'S BEHIND THIS DOOR...
...I DON'T NEED TO KNOW...

Chain saw man

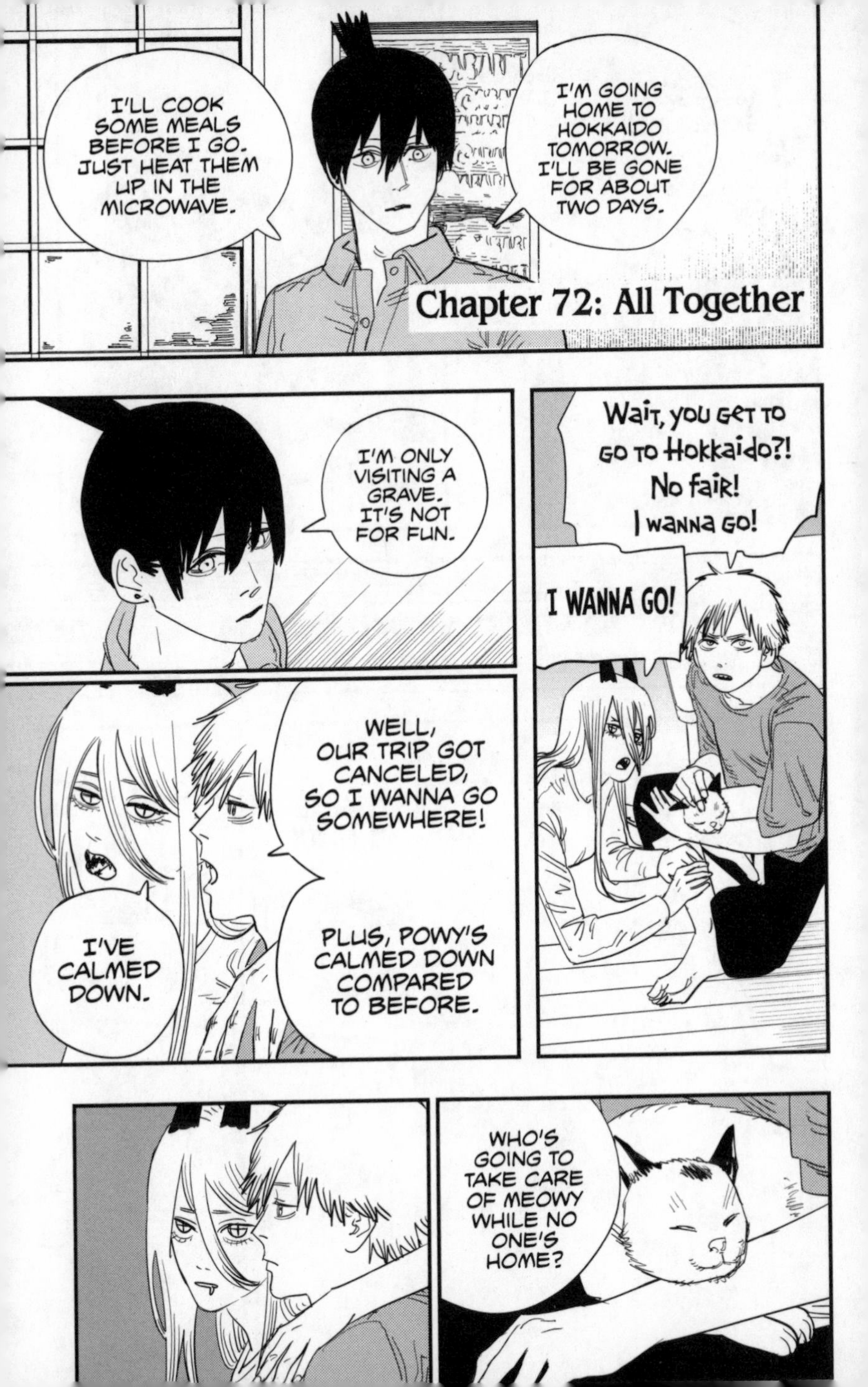
I'M GOING HOME TO HOKKAIDO TOMORROW. I'LL BE GONE FOR ABOUT TWO DAYS.
I'LL COOK SOME MEALS BEFORE I GO. JUST HEAT THEM UP IN THE MICROWAVE.
Chapter 72: All Together
Wait, you get to go to Hokkaido?! No fair! I wanna go!
I WANNA GO!
I'M ONLY VISITING A GRAVE. IT'S NOT FOR FUN.
WELL, OUR TRIP GOT CANCELED, SO I WANNA GO SOMEWHERE!
PLUS, POWY'S CALMED DOWN COMPARED TO BEFORE.
I'VE CALMED DOWN.
WHO'S GOING TO TAKE CARE OF MEOWY WHILE NO ONE'S HOME?

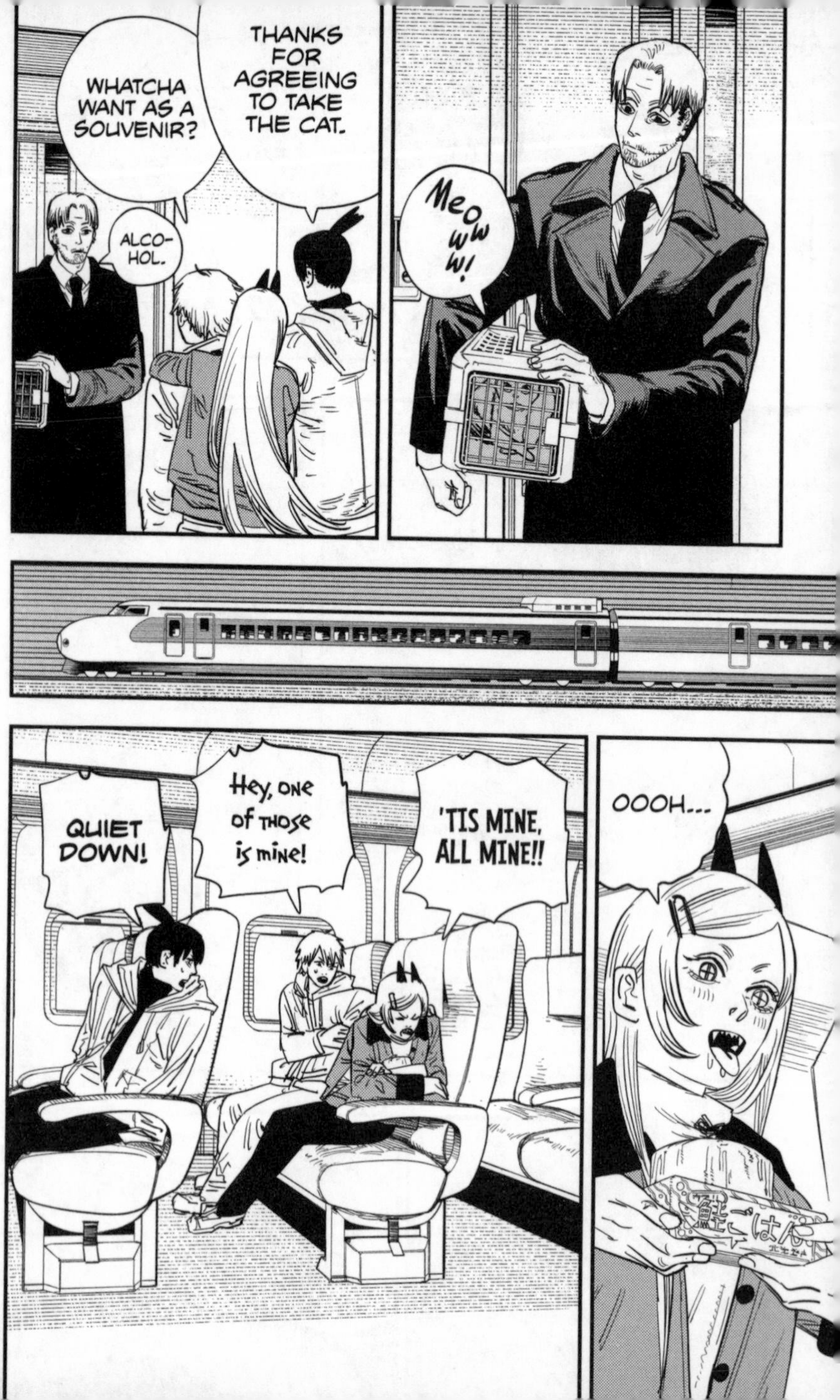

Meowww!
THANKS FOR AGREEING TO TAKE THE CAT.
WHATCHA WANT AS A SOUVENIR?
ALCO-HOL.
OOOH...
'TIS MINE, ALL MINE!!
Hey, one of those is mine!
QUIET DOWN!

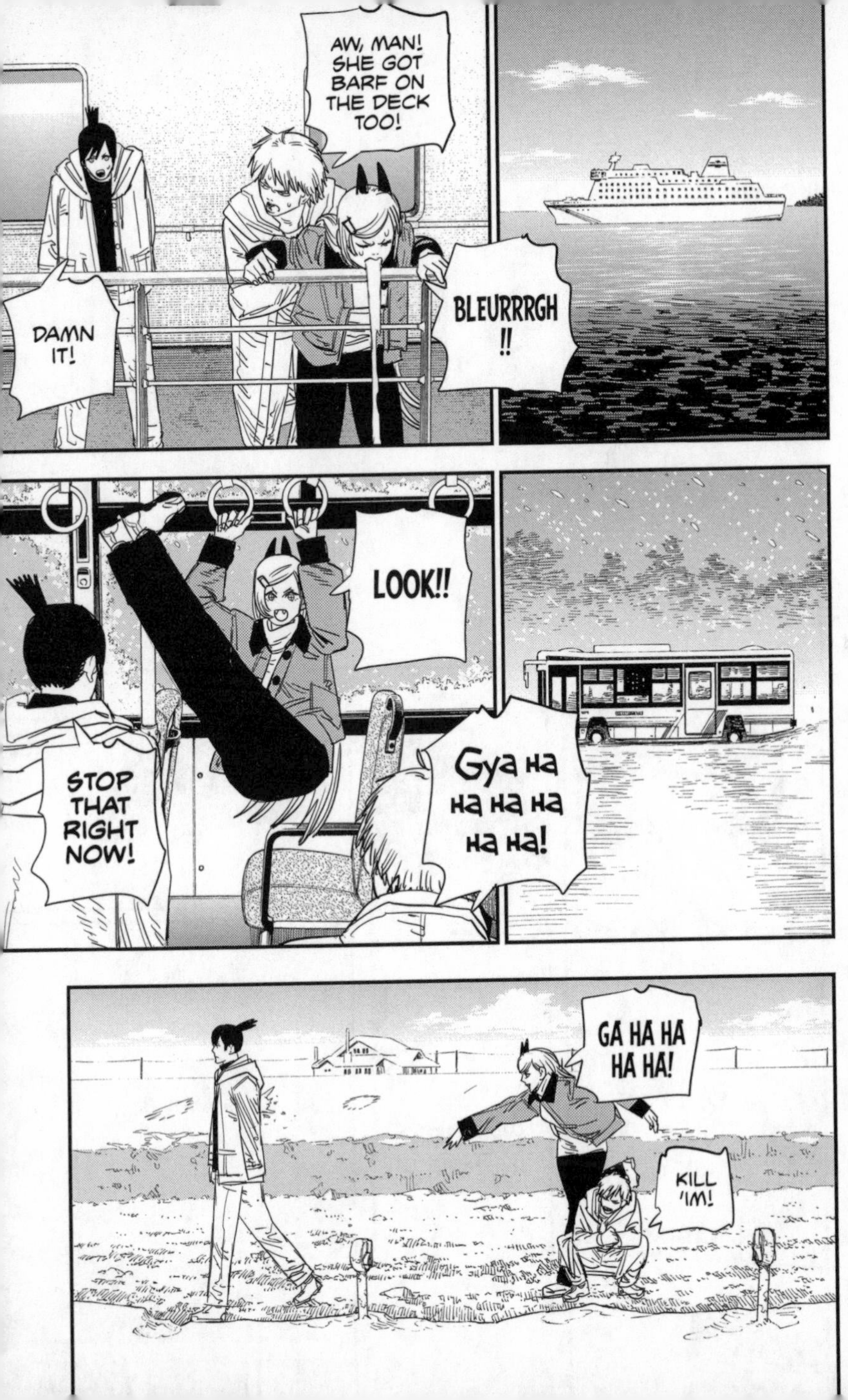
AW, MAN! SHE GOT BARF ON THE DECK TOO!
BLEURRRGH!!
DAMN IT!
LOOK!!
Gya ha ha ha ha ha ha!
STOP THAT RIGHT NOW!
GA HA HA HA HA!
KILL 'IM!

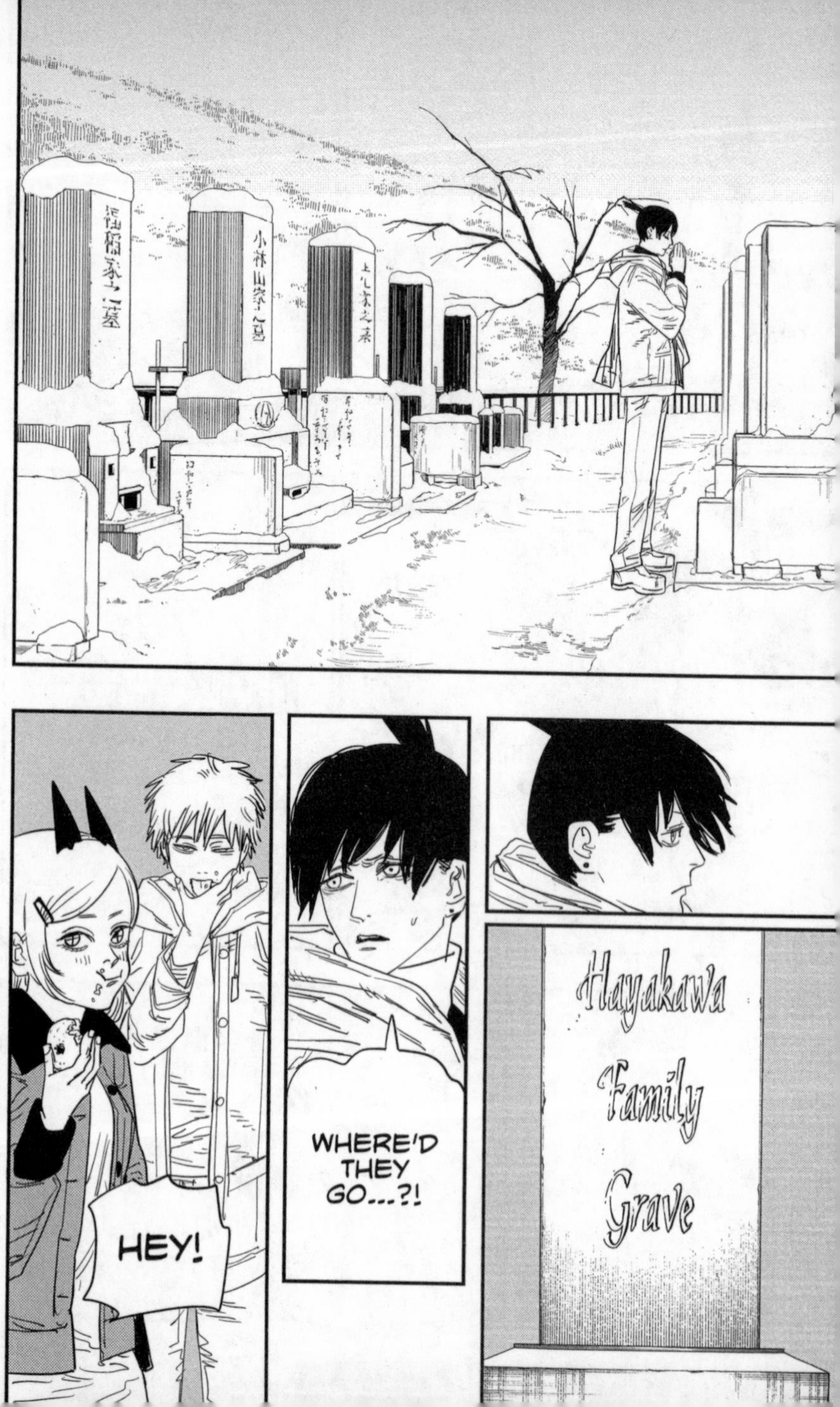
Hayakawa Family Grave
WHERE'D THEY GO...?!
HEY!

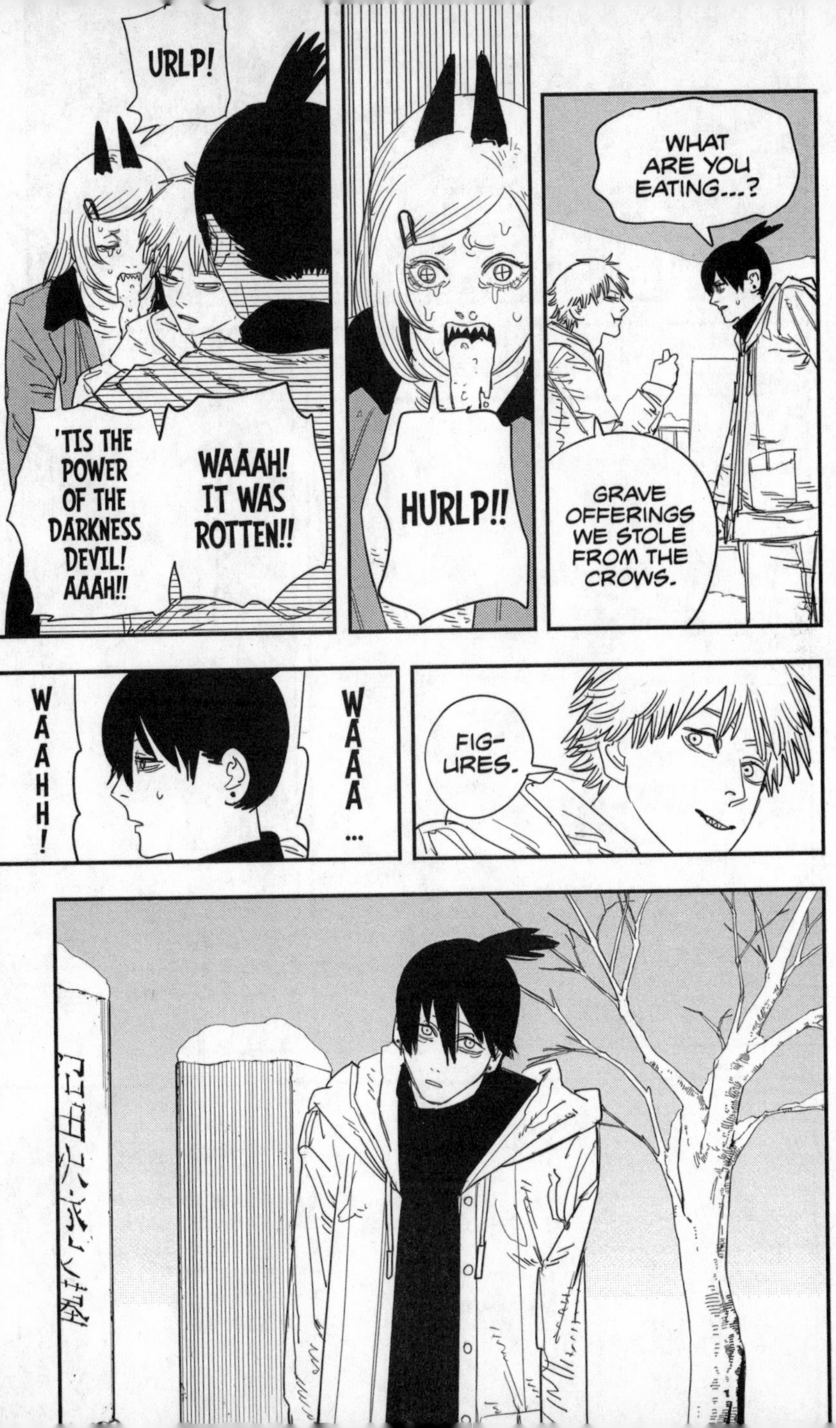
WHAT ARE YOU EATING...?
GRAVE OFFERINGS WE STOLE FROM THE CROWS.
HURLP!!
URLP!
WAAAH! IT WAS ROTTEN!!
'TIS THE POWER OF THE DARKNESS DEVIL! AAAH!!
FIG-URES.
WAAA...
WAAAHH!

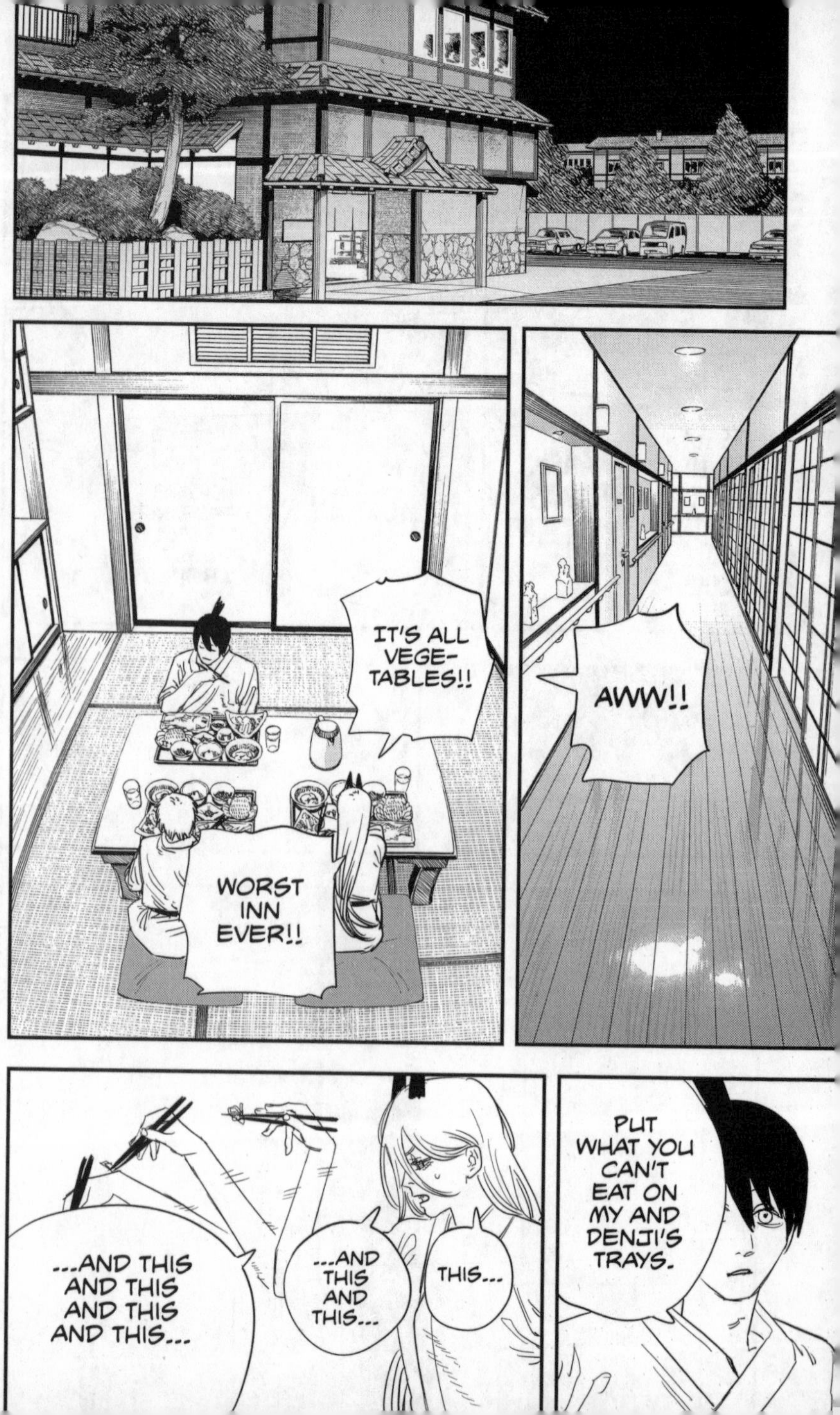
AWW!!
IT'S ALL VEGETABLES!!
WORST INN EVER!!
PUT WHAT YOU CAN'T EAT ON MY AND DENJI'S TRAYS.
THIS...
...AND THIS AND THIS...
...AND THIS AND THIS AND THIS AND THIS...

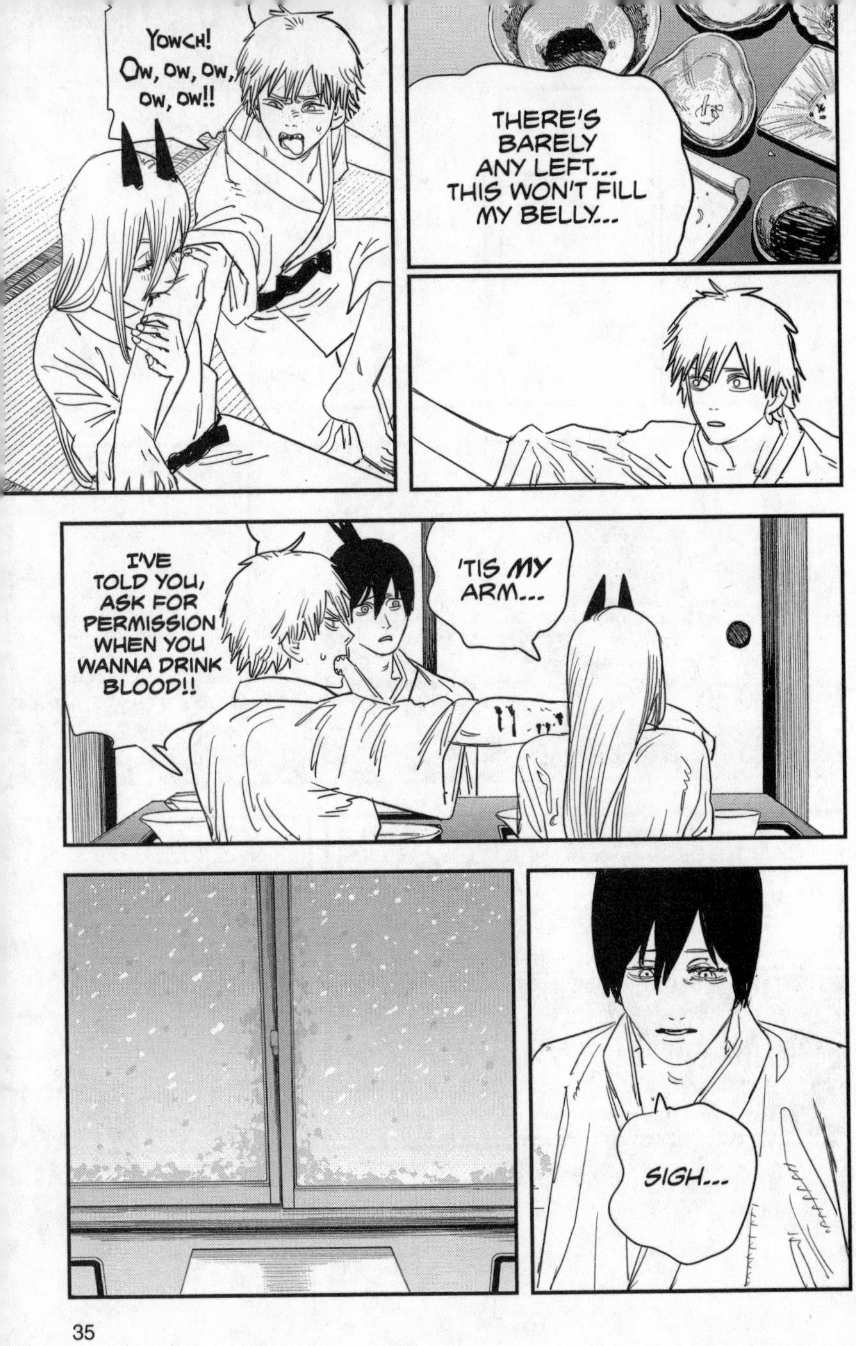
THERE'S BARELY ANY LEFT... THIS WON'T FILL MY BELLY...
YOWCH! OW, OW, OW, OW, OW!!
'TIS MY ARM...
I'VE TOLD YOU, ASK FOR PERMISSION WHEN YOU WANNA DRINK BLOOD!!
SIGH...

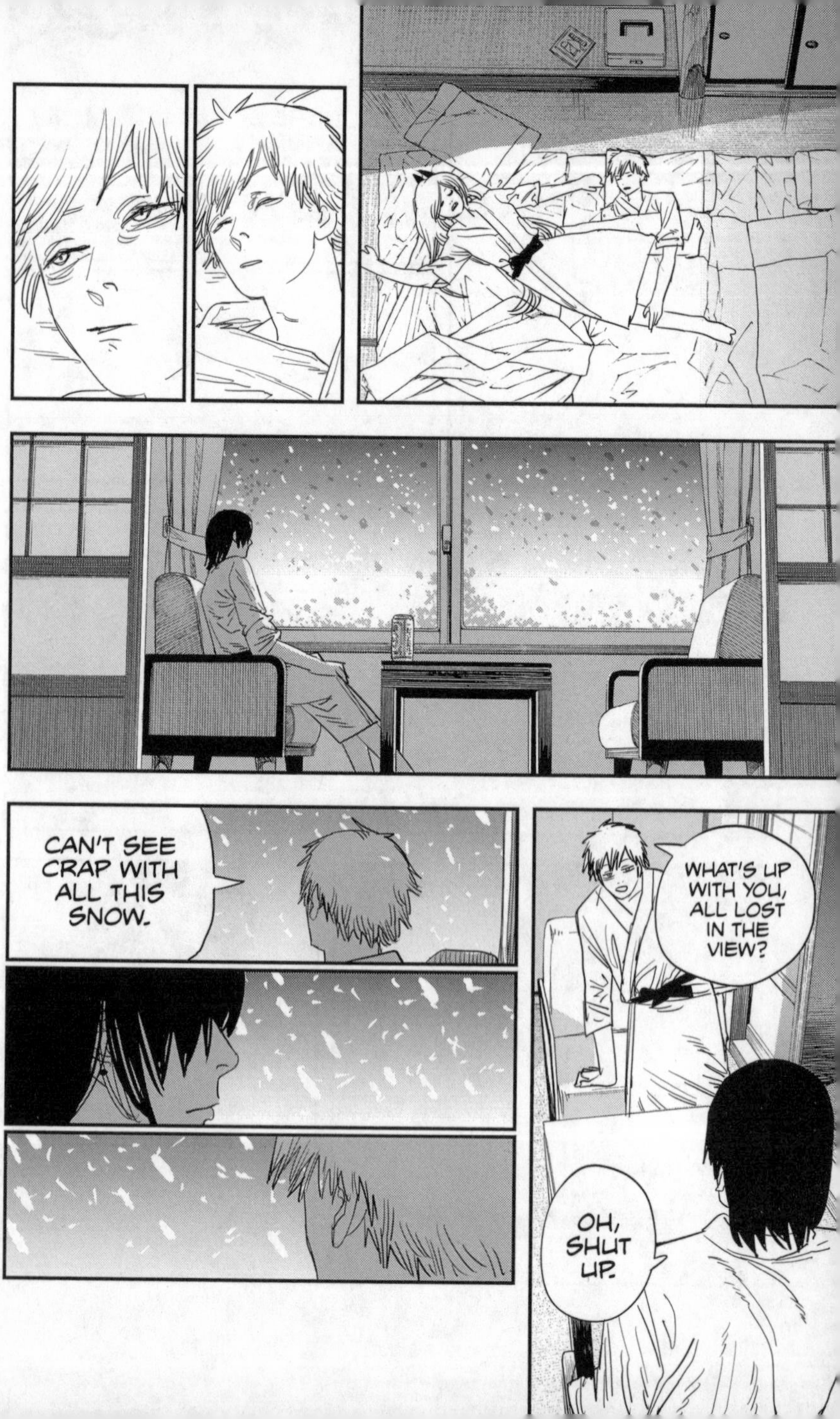
WHAT'S UP WITH YOU, ALL LOST IN THE VIEW?
OH, SHUT UP.
CAN'T SEE CRAP WITH ALL THIS SNOW.

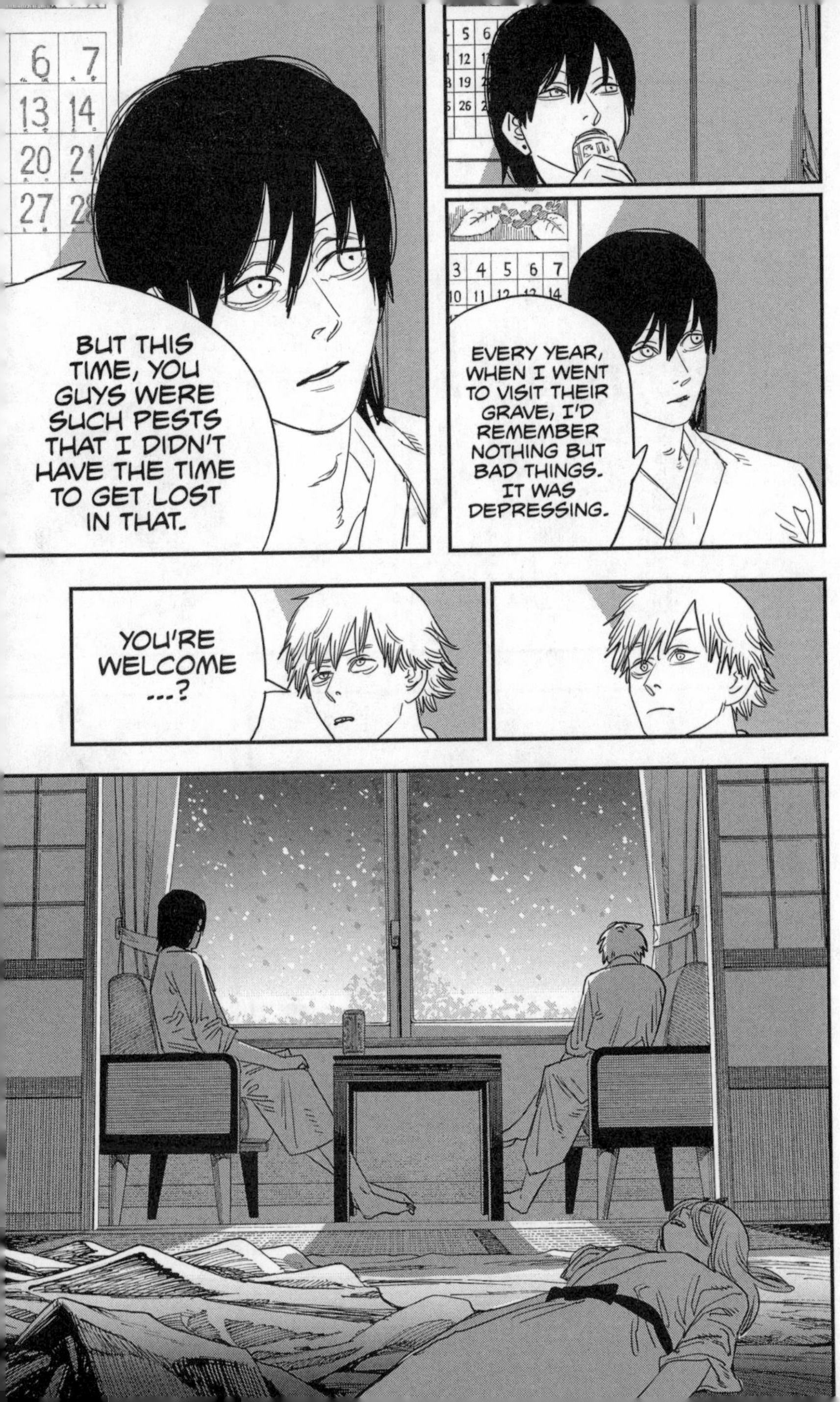
EVERY YEAR, WHEN I WENT TO VISIT THEIR GRAVE, I'D REMEMBER NOTHING BUT BAD THINGS. IT WAS DEPRESSING.
BUT THIS TIME, YOU GUYS WERE SUCH PESTS THAT I DIDN'T HAVE THE TIME TO GET LOST IN THAT.
YOU'RE WELCOME ...?

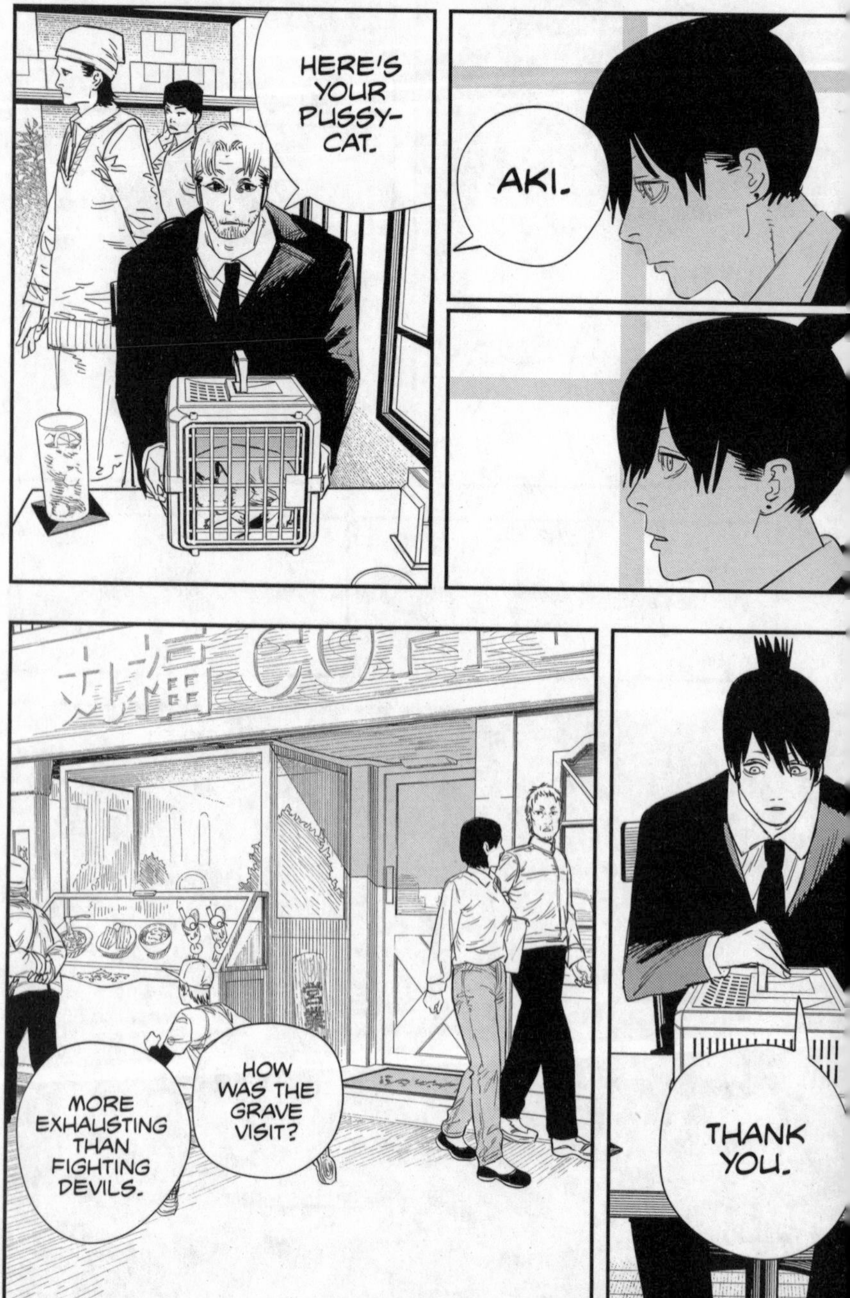
AKI.
HERE'S YOUR PUSSY-CAT.
THANK YOU.
HOW WAS THE GRAVE VISIT?
MORE EXHAUSTING THAN FIGHTING DEVILS.

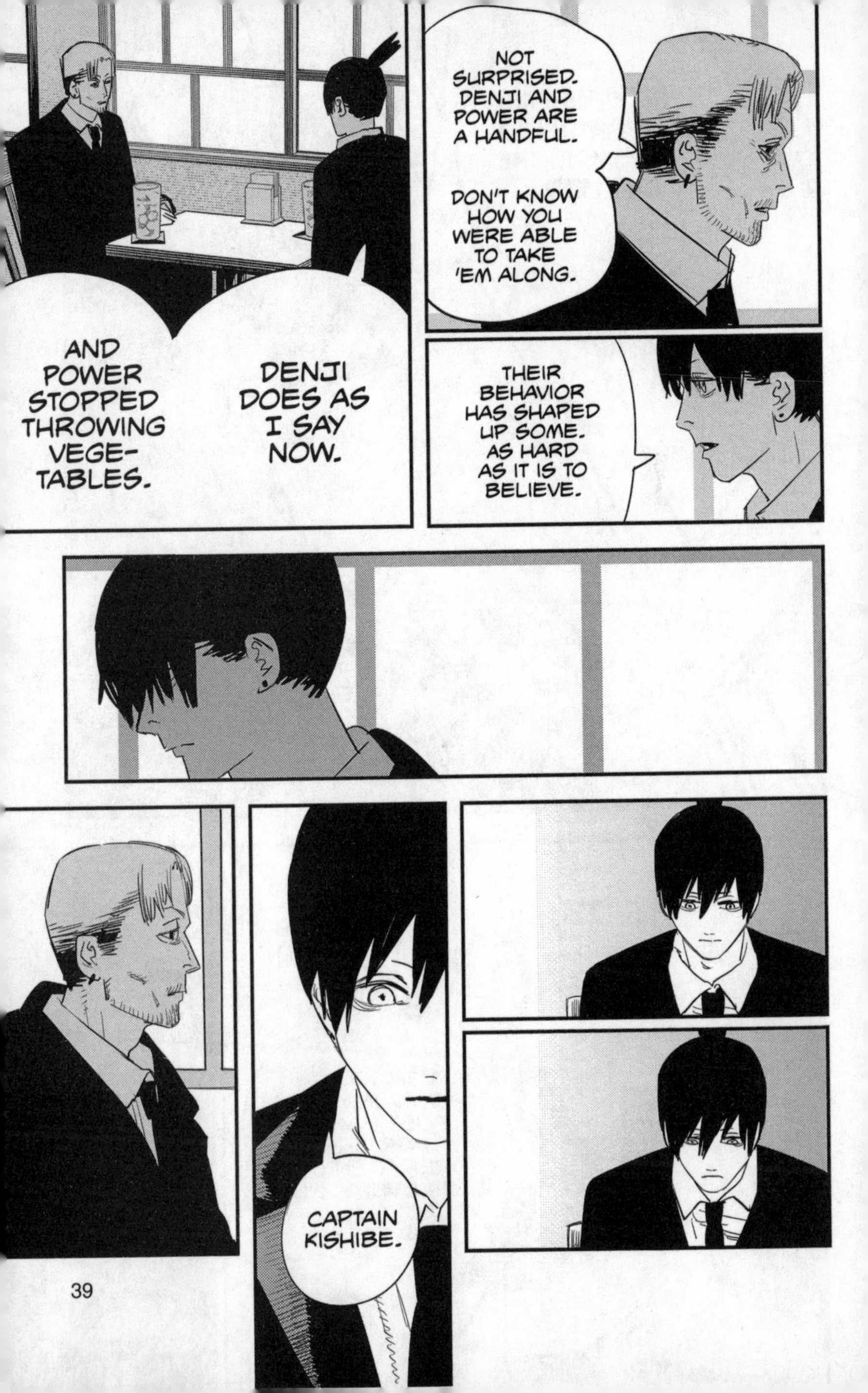
NOT SURPRISED. DENJI AND POWER ARE A HANDFUL.
DON'T KNOW HOW YOU WERE ABLE TO TAKE 'EM ALONG.
THEIR BEHAVIOR HAS SHAPED UP SOME. AS HARD AS IT IS TO BELIEVE.
DENJI DOES AS I SAY NOW.
AND POWER STOPPED THROWING VEGE-TABLES.
CAPTAIN KISHIBE.

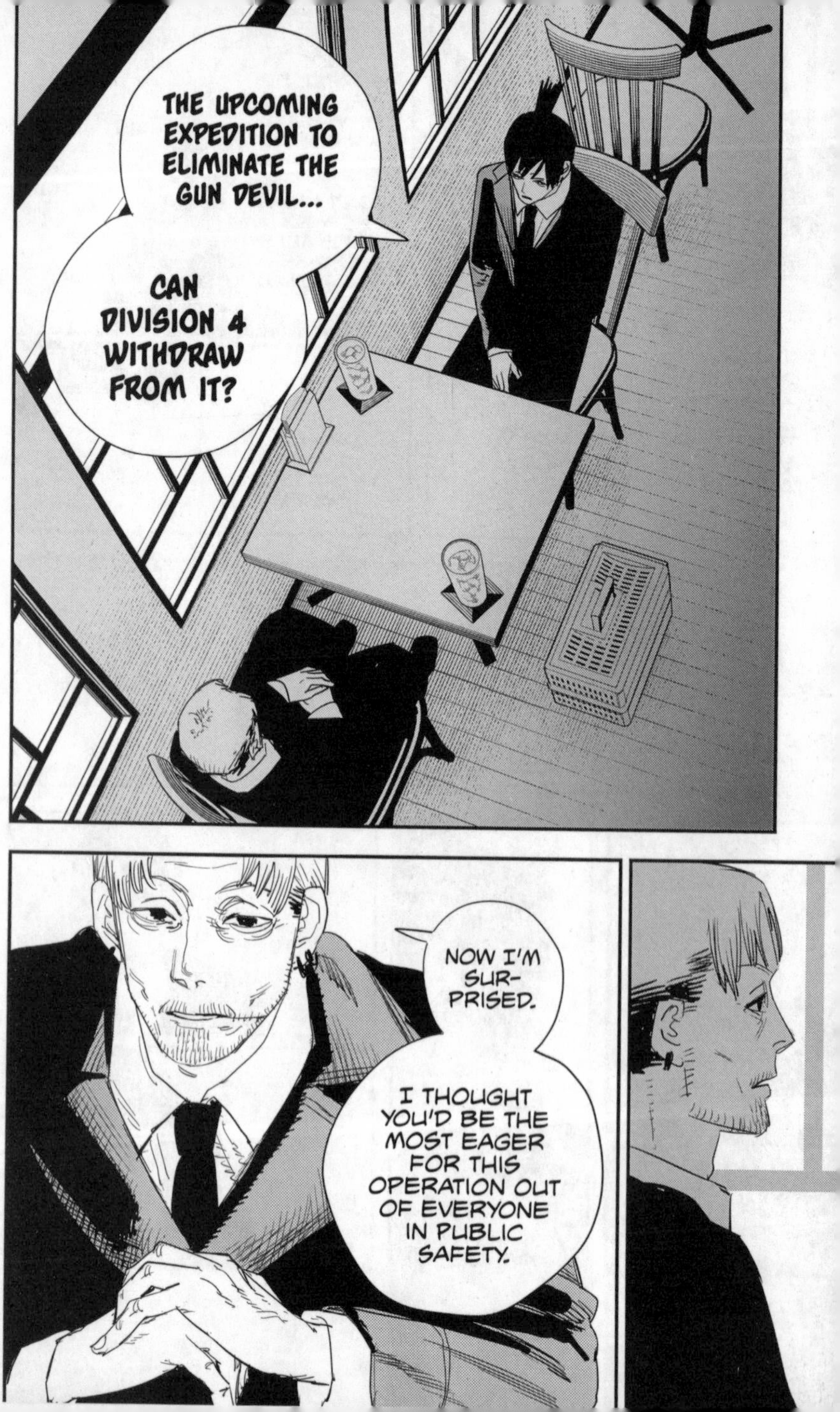
THE UPCOMING EXPEDITION TO ELIMINATE THE GUN DEVIL...
CAN DIVISION 4 WITHDRAW FROM IT?
NOW I'M SUR-PRISED.
I THOUGHT YOU'D BE THE MOST EAGER FOR THIS OPERATION OUT OF EVERYONE IN PUBLIC SAFETY.

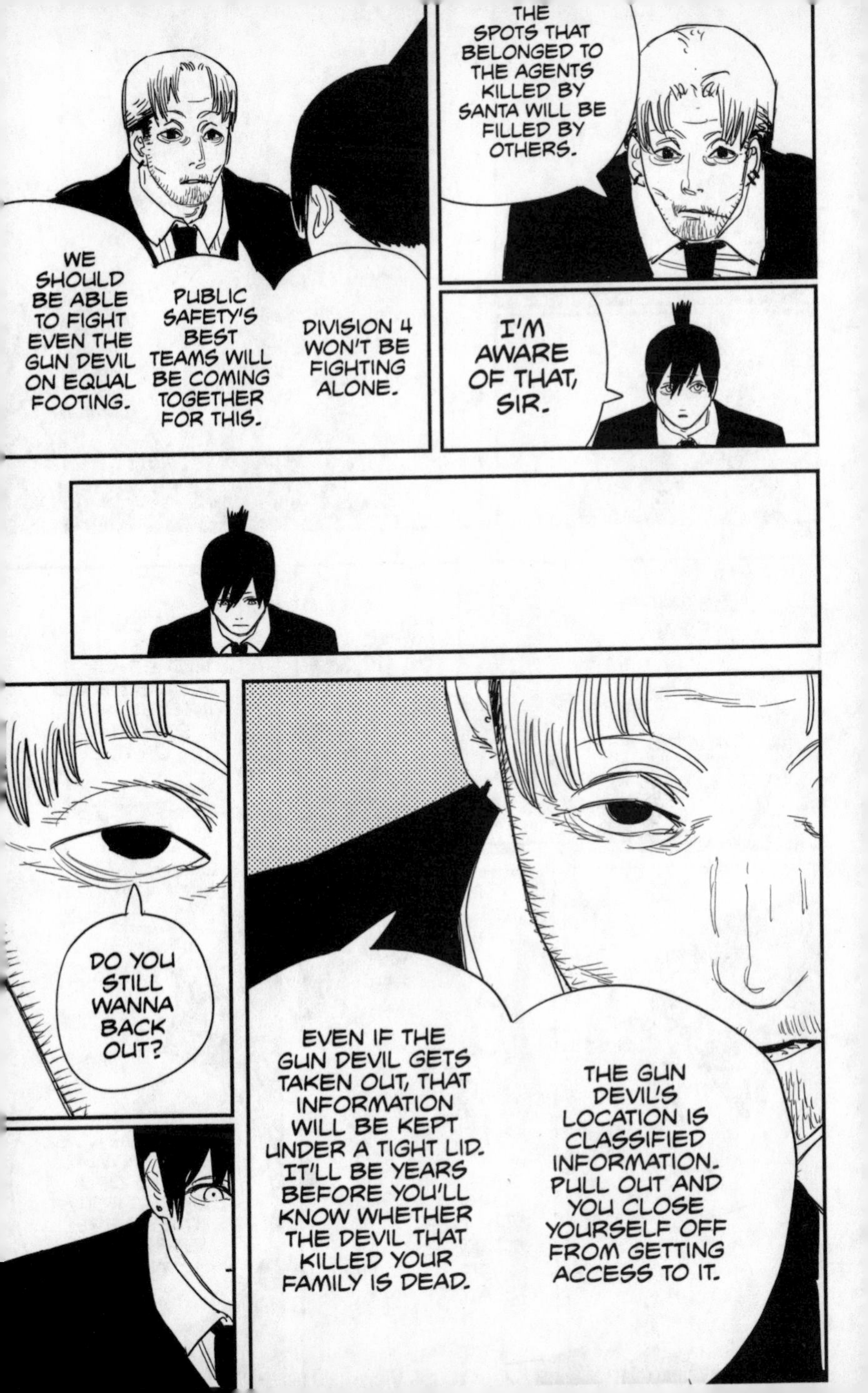
THE SPOTS THAT BELONGED TO THE AGENTS KILLED BY SANTA WILL BE FILLED BY OTHERS.
DIVISION 4 WON'T BE FIGHTING ALONE.
PUBLIC SAFETY'S BEST TEAMS WILL BE COMING TOGETHER FOR THIS.
WE SHOULD BE ABLE TO FIGHT EVEN THE GUN DEVIL ON EQUAL FOOTING.
I'M AWARE OF THAT, SIR.
THE GUN DEVIL'S LOCATION IS CLASSIFIED INFORMATION. PULL OUT AND YOU CLOSE YOURSELF OFF FROM GETTING ACCESS TO IT.
EVEN IF THE GUN DEVIL GETS TAKEN OUT, THAT INFORMATION WILL BE KEPT UNDER A TIGHT LID. IT'LL BE YEARS BEFORE YOU'LL KNOW WHETHER THE DEVIL THAT KILLED YOUR FAMILY IS DEAD.
DO YOU STILL WANNA BACK OUT?

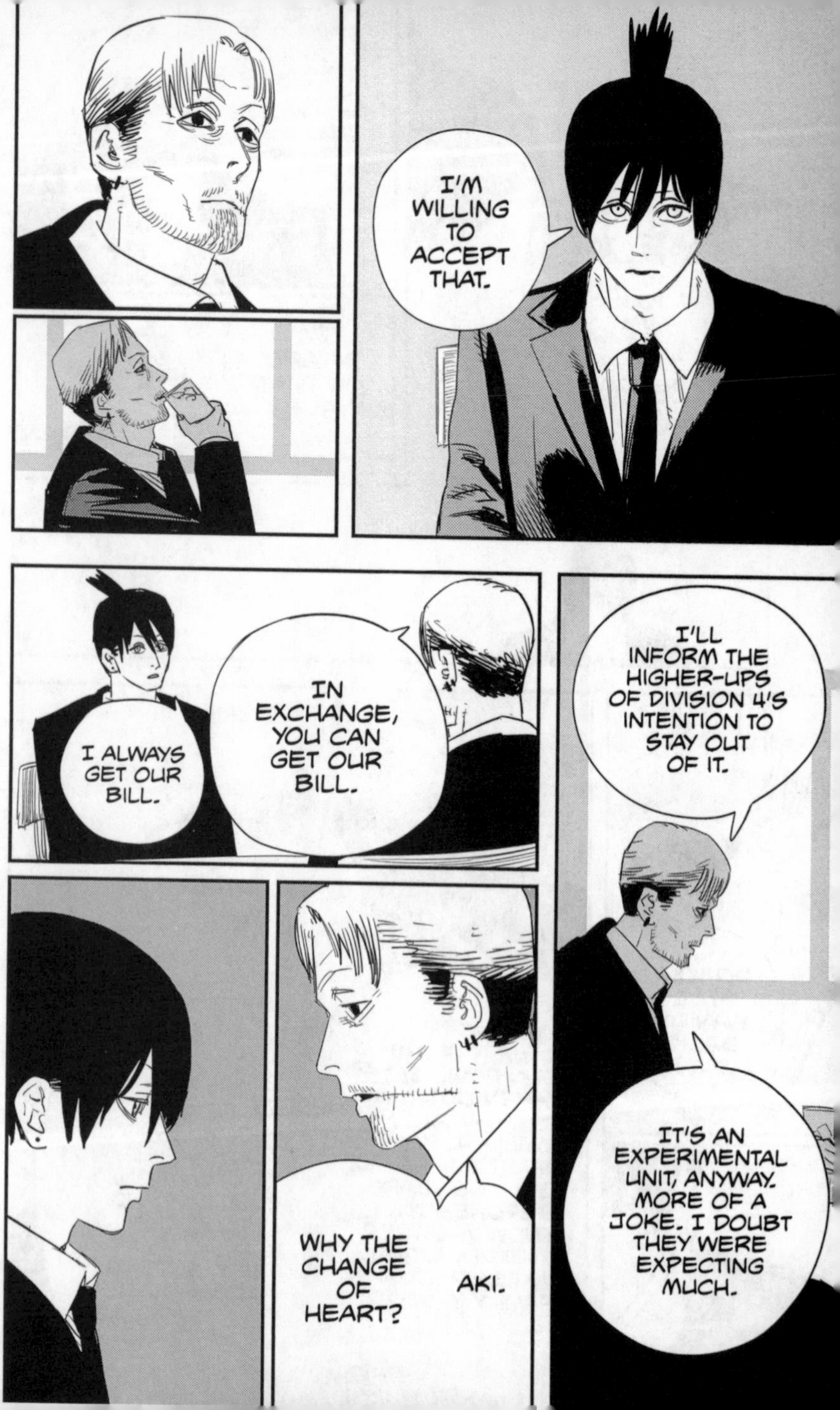
I'M WILLING TO ACCEPT THAT.
I'LL INFORM THE HIGHER-UPS OF DIVISION 4'S INTENTION TO STAY OUT OF IT.
IT'S AN EXPERIMENTAL UNIT, ANYWAY. MORE OF A JOKE. I DOUBT THEY WERE EXPECTING MUCH.
IN EXCHANGE, YOU CAN GET OUR BILL.
I ALWAYS GET OUR BILL.
AKI.
WHY THE CHANGE OF HEART?

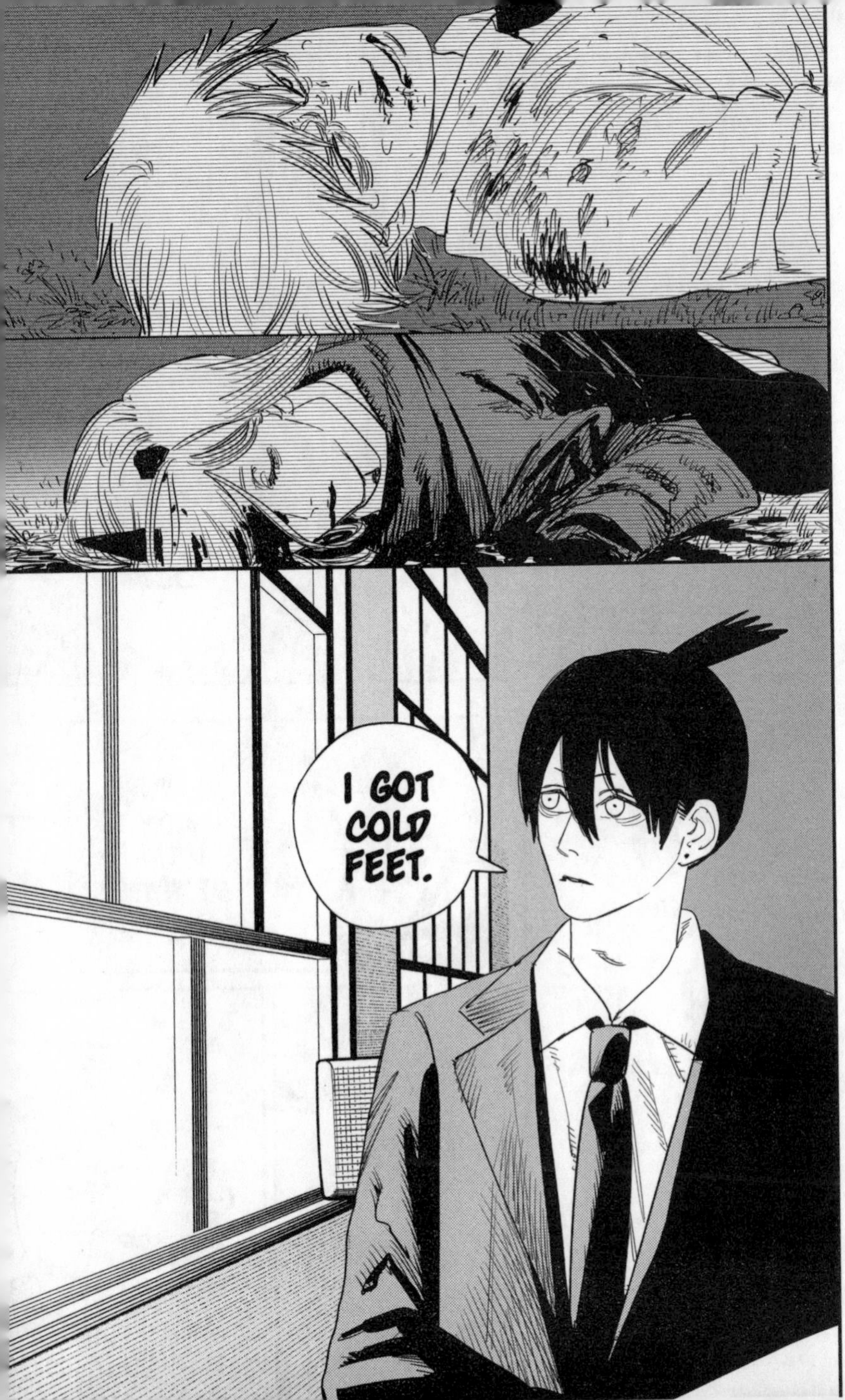
I GOT COLD FEET.

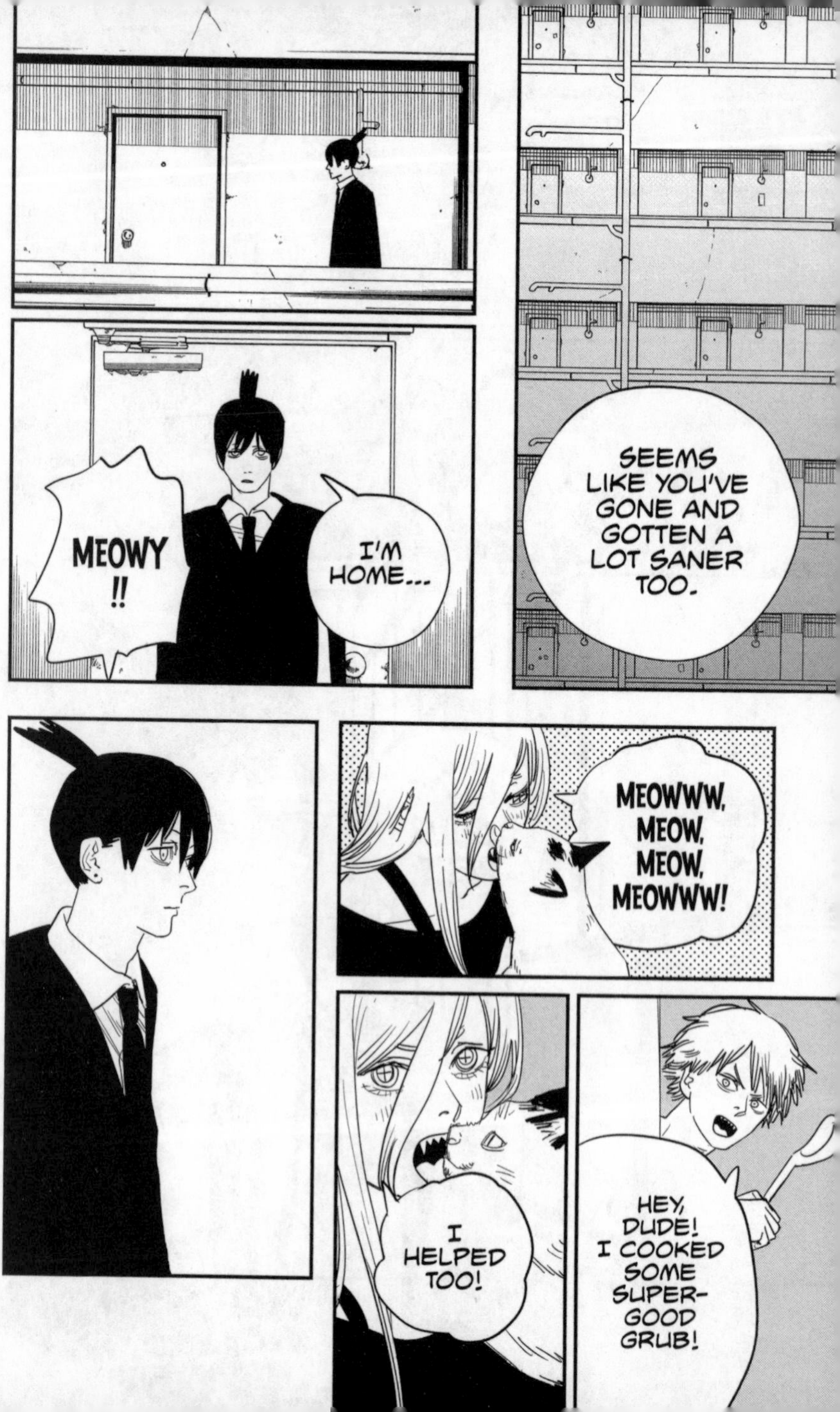
SEEMS LIKE YOU'VE GONE AND GOTTEN A LOT SANER TOO.
I'M HOME...
MEOWY !!
MEOWWW, MEOW, MEOW, MEOWWW!
HEY, DUDE! I COOKED SOME SUPER-GOOD GRUB!
I HELPED TOO!

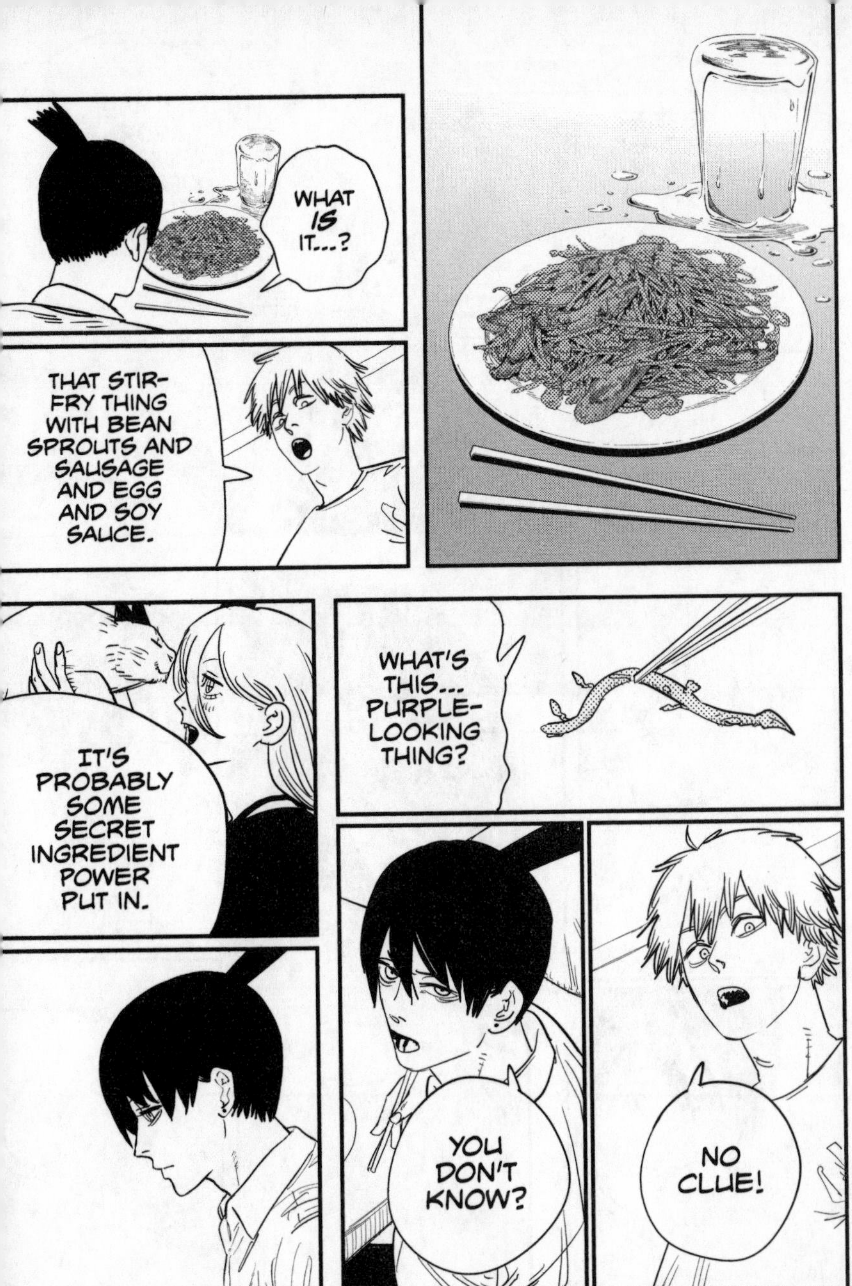
WHAT *IS* IT...?
THAT STIR-FRY THING WITH BEAN SPROUTS AND SAUSAGE AND EGG AND SOY SAUCE.
WHAT'S THIS... PURPLE-LOOKING THING?
IT'S PROBABLY SOME SECRET INGREDIENT POWER PUT IN.
NO CLUE!
YOU DON'T KNOW?

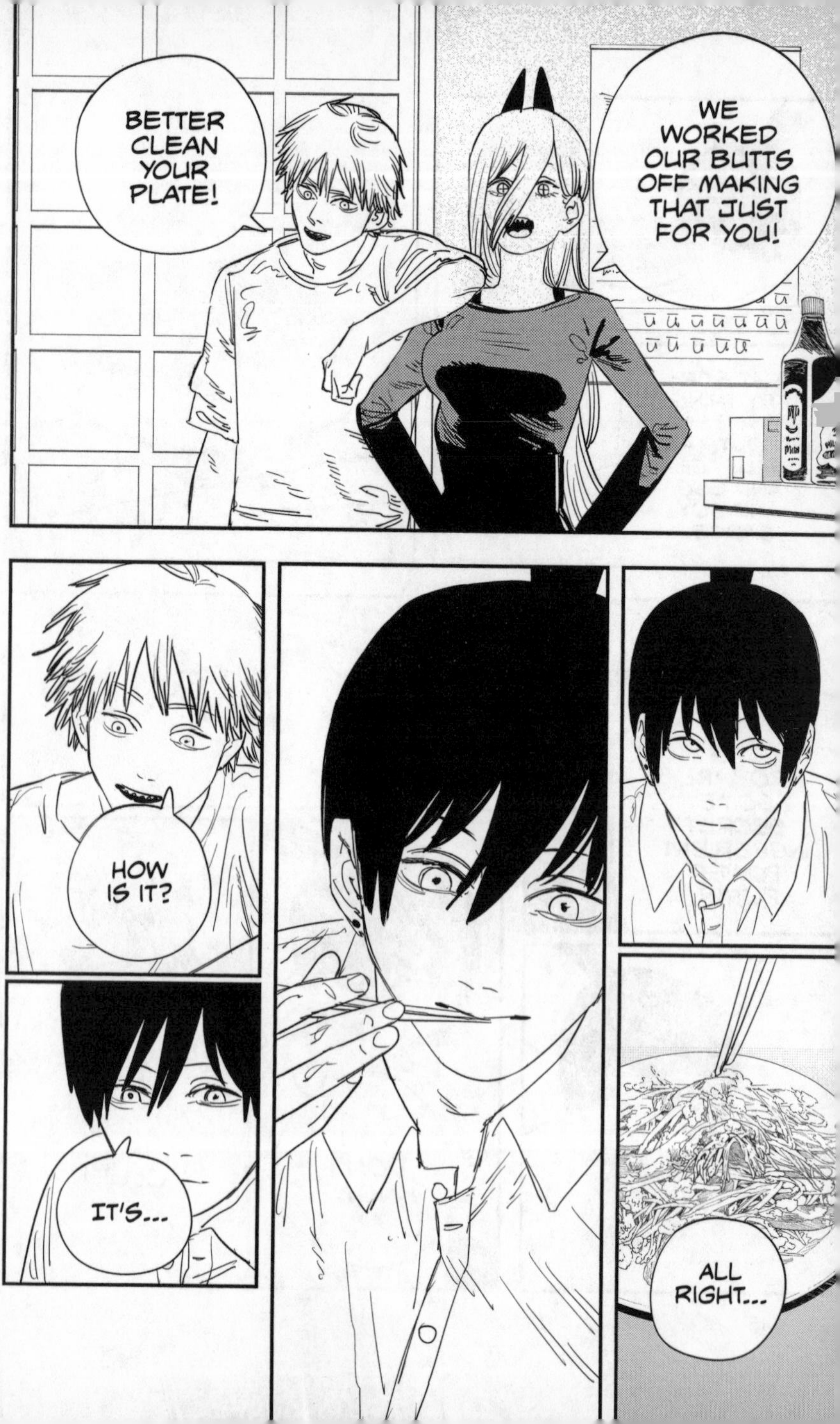
BETTER CLEAN YOUR PLATE!
WE WORKED OUR BUTTS OFF MAKING THAT JUST FOR YOU!
HOW IS IT?
IT'S...
ALL RIGHT...

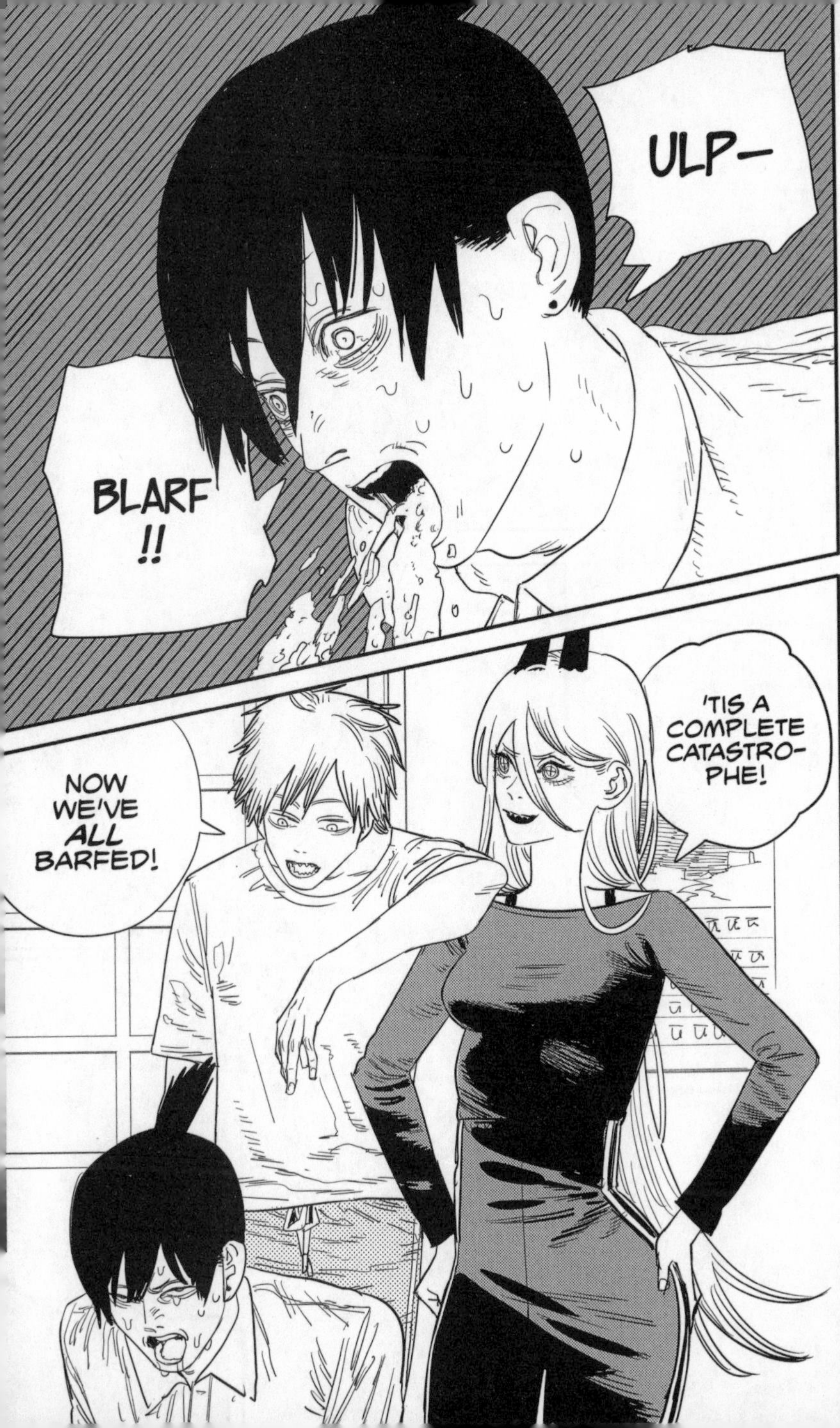
ULP—
BLARF !!
'TIS A COMPLETE CATASTRO-PHE!
NOW WE'VE *ALL* BARFED!

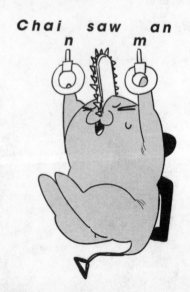

Chai saw an
   n   m

Chapter 73: Everyday Life No More

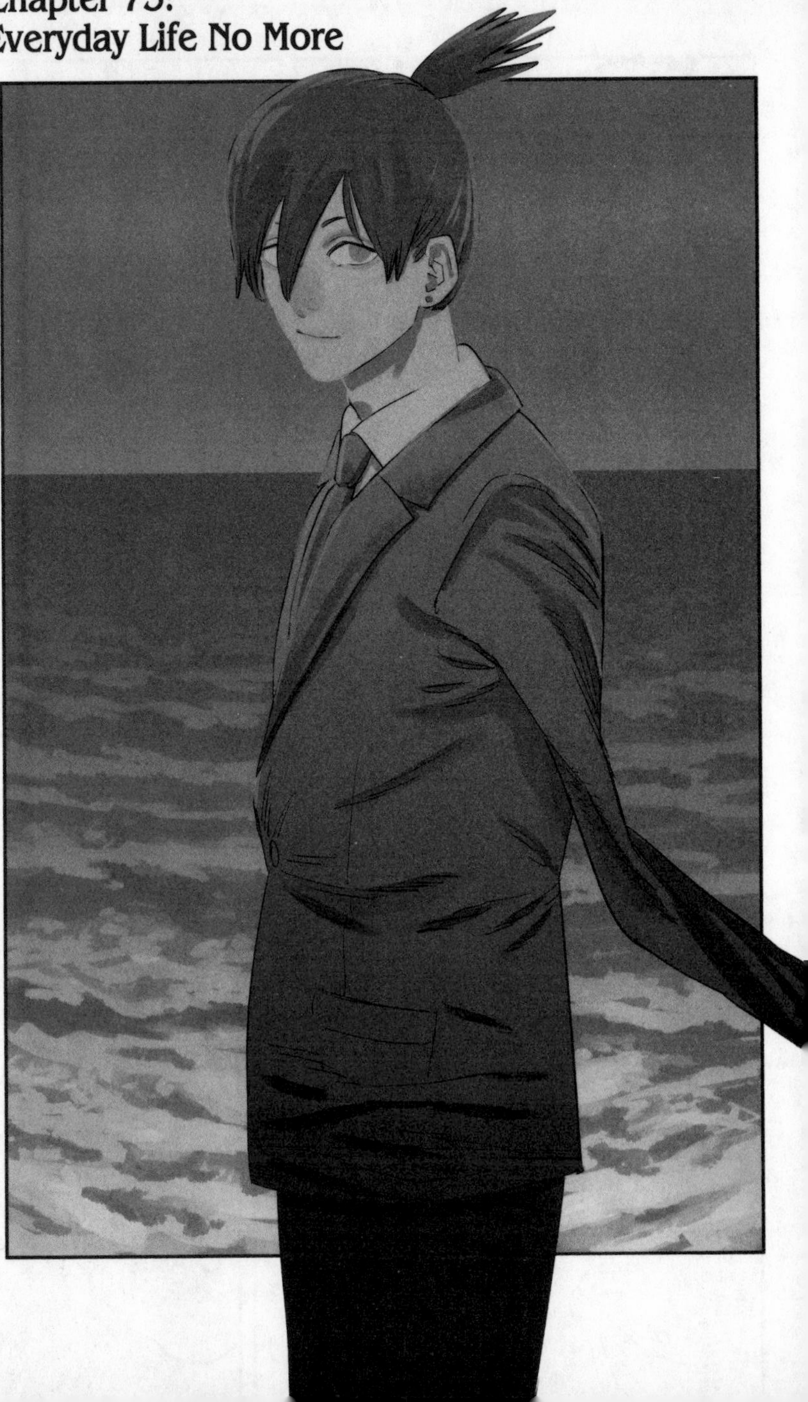

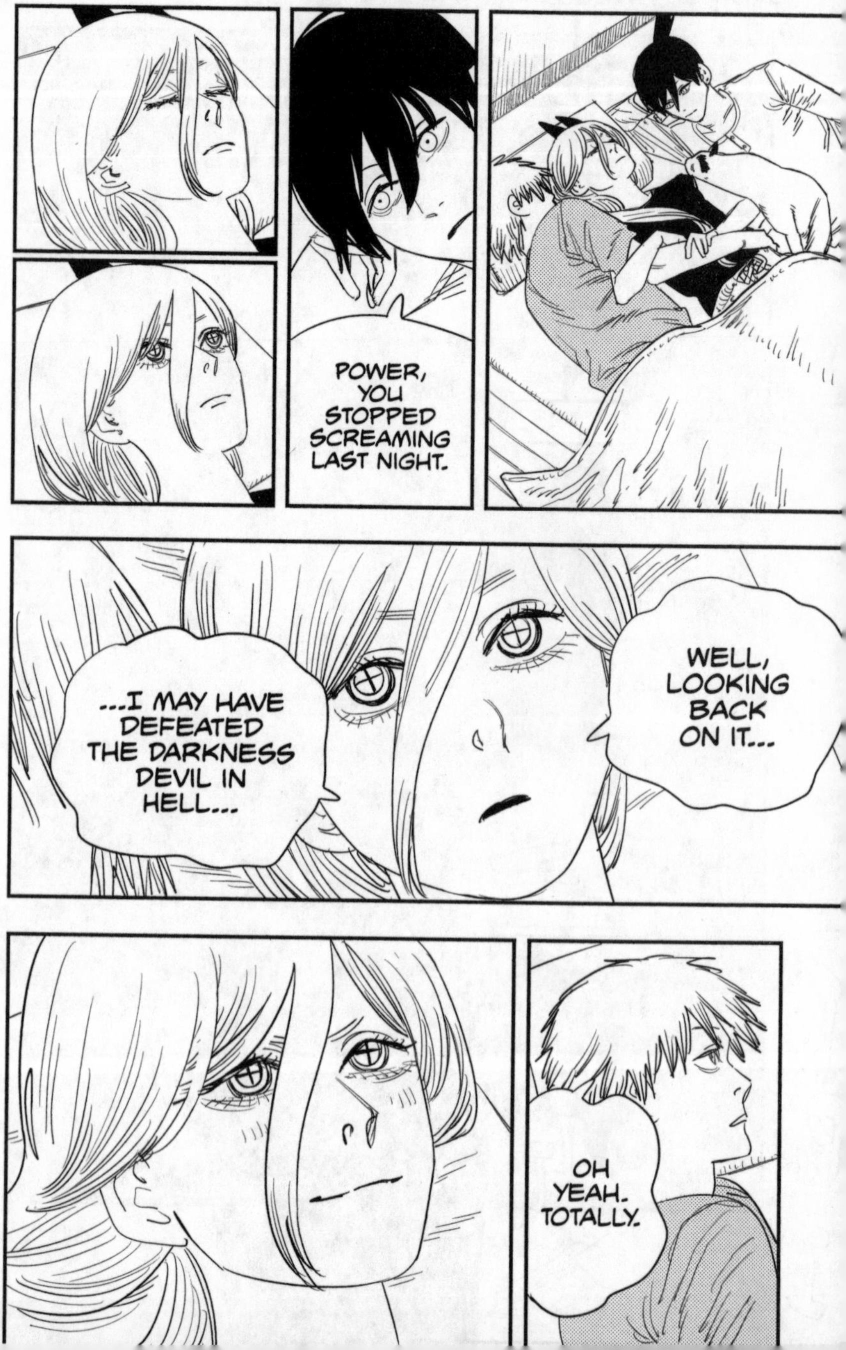
POWER, YOU STOPPED SCREAMING LAST NIGHT.
WELL, LOOKING BACK ON IT...
...I MAY HAVE DEFEATED THE DARKNESS DEVIL IN HELL...
OH YEAH. TOTALLY.

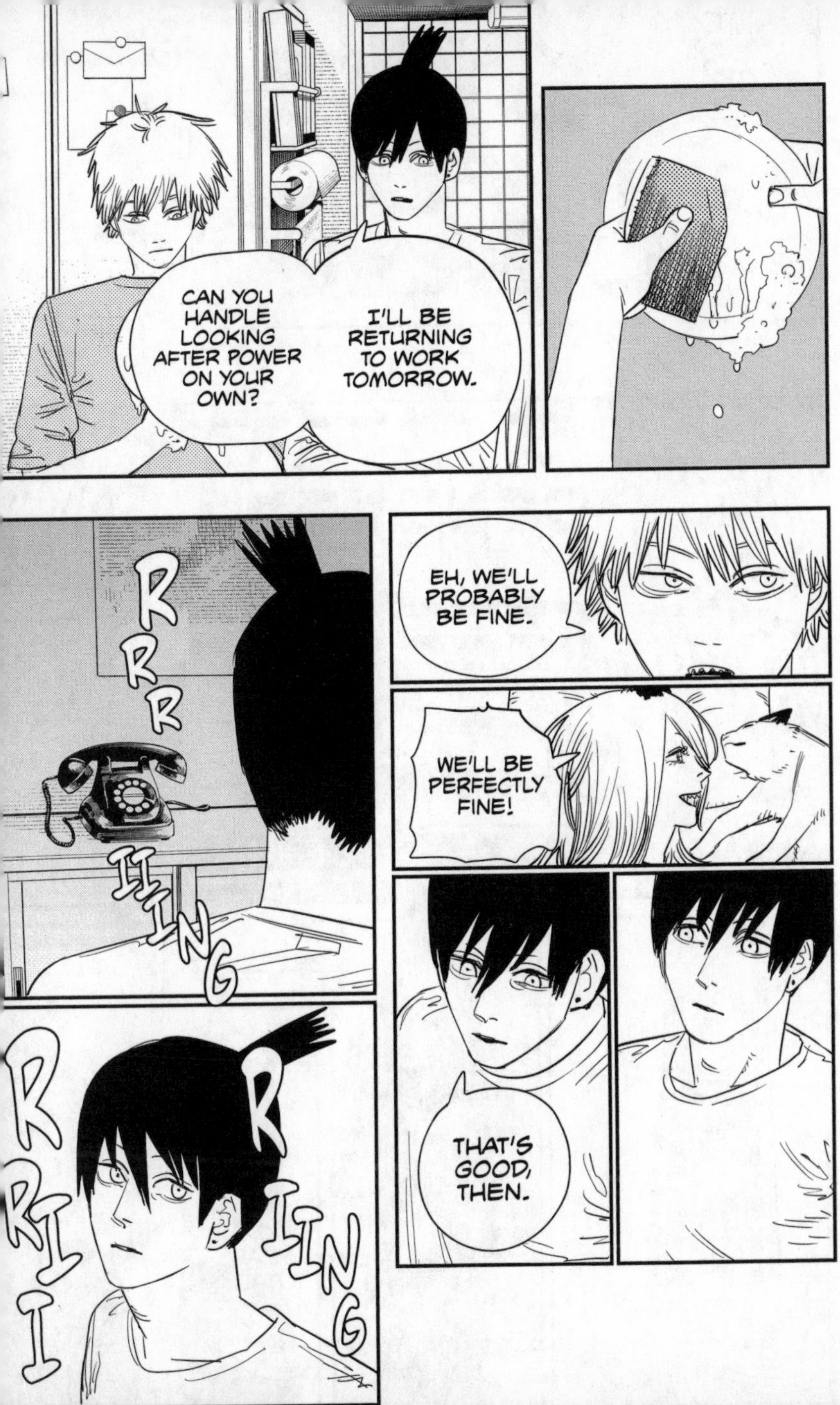
I'LL BE RETURNING TO WORK TOMORROW.
CAN YOU HANDLE LOOKING AFTER POWER ON YOUR OWN?
EH, WE'LL PROBABLY BE FINE.
WE'LL BE PERFECTLY FINE!
THAT'S GOOD, THEN.
RRRIIING
RIIING
RRIII

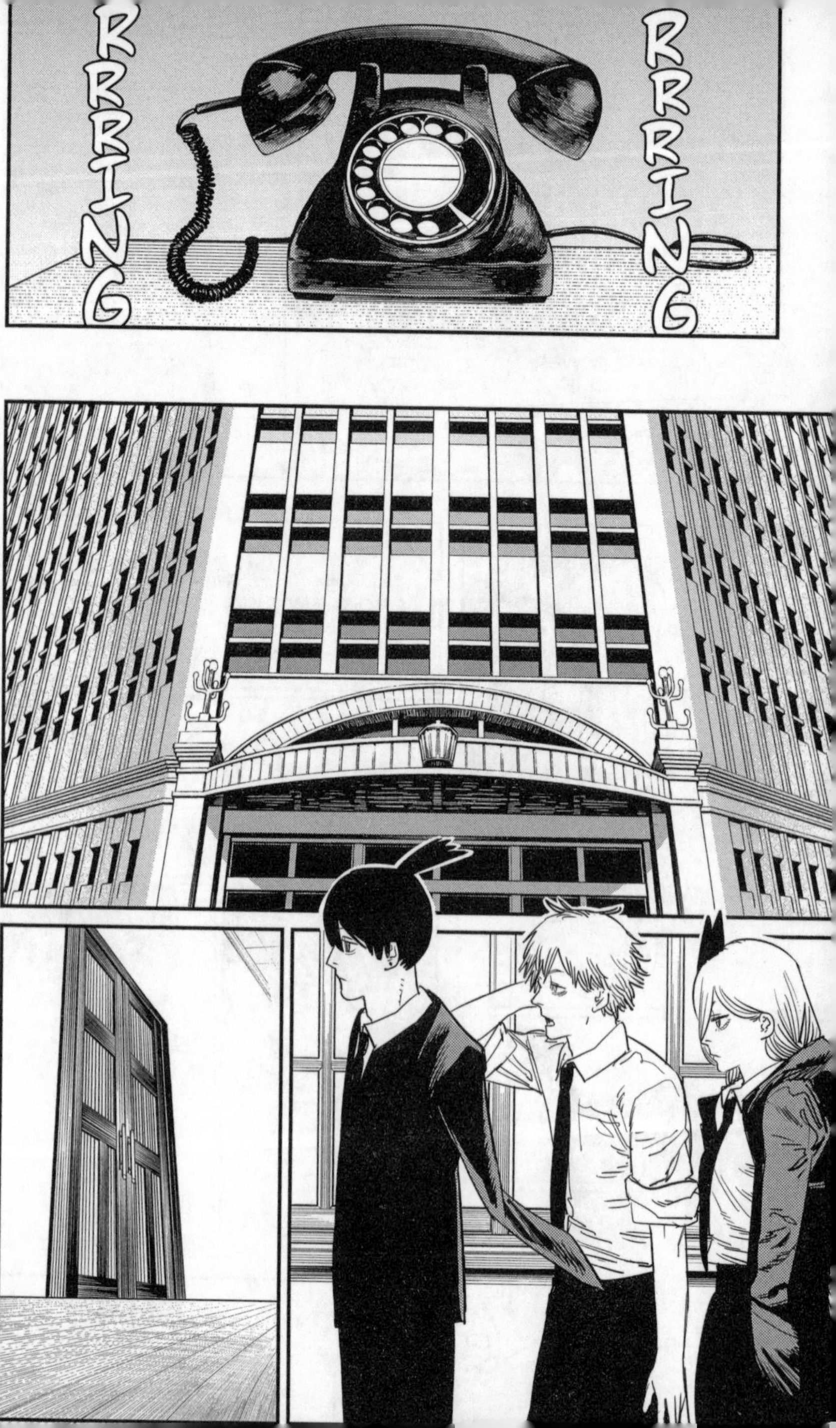
RRRING
RRRING

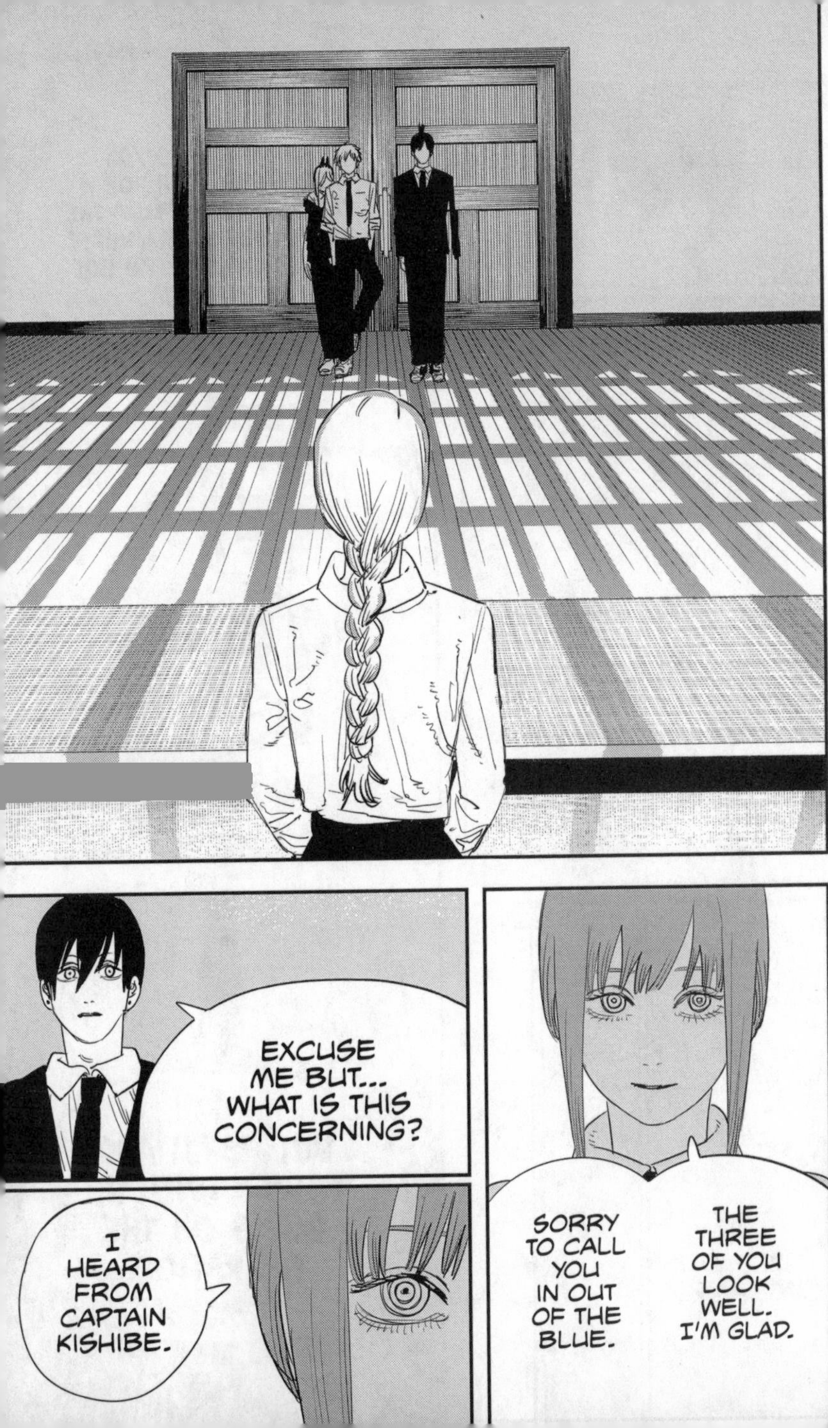
THE THREE OF YOU LOOK WELL. I'M GLAD.
SORRY TO CALL YOU IN OUT OF THE BLUE.
EXCUSE ME BUT... WHAT IS THIS CONCERNING?
I HEARD FROM CAPTAIN KISHIBE.

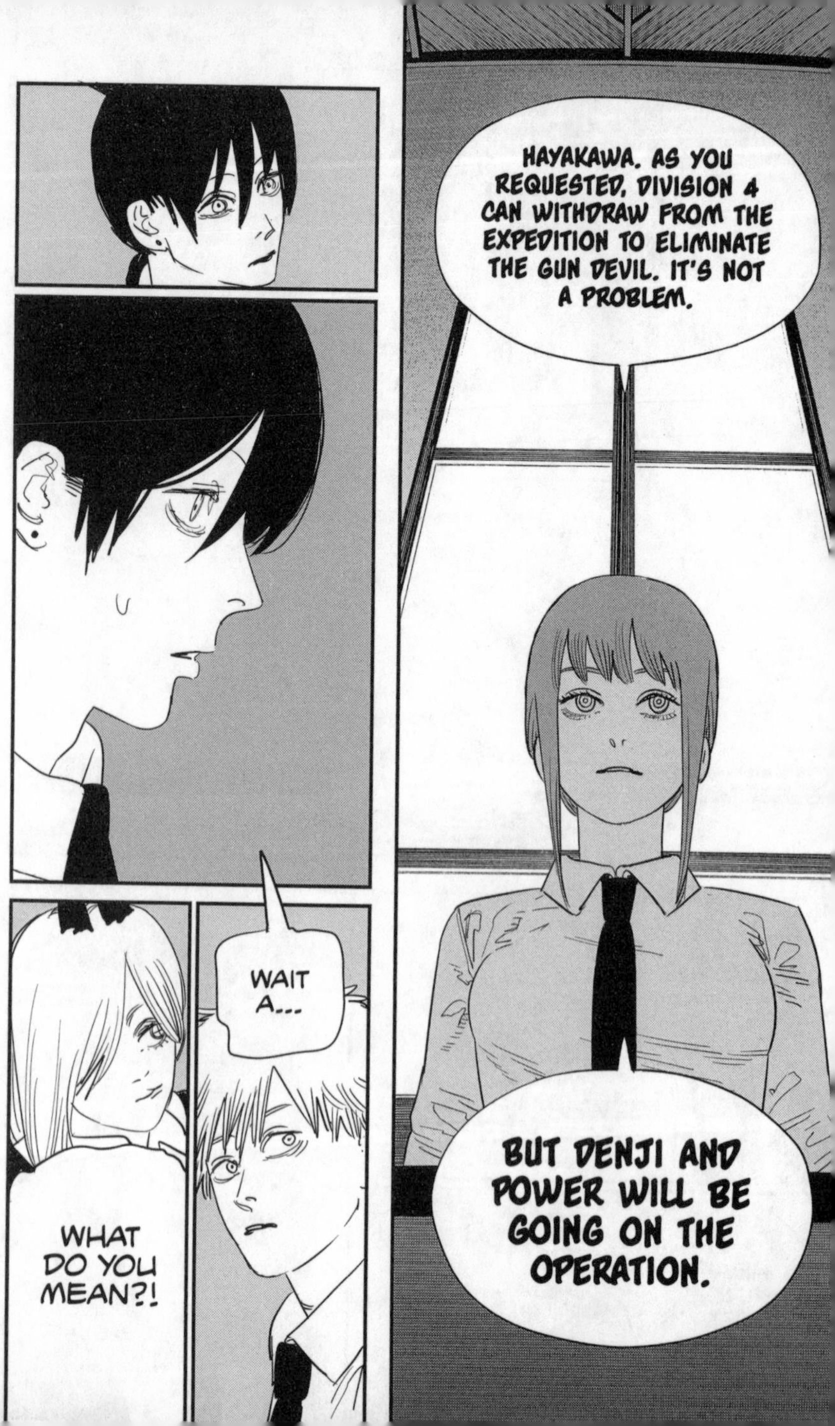
HAYAKAWA. AS YOU REQUESTED, DIVISION 4 CAN WITHDRAW FROM THE EXPEDITION TO ELIMINATE THE GUN DEVIL. IT'S NOT A PROBLEM.
BUT DENJI AND POWER WILL BE GOING ON THE OPERATION.
WAIT A...
WHAT DO YOU MEAN?!

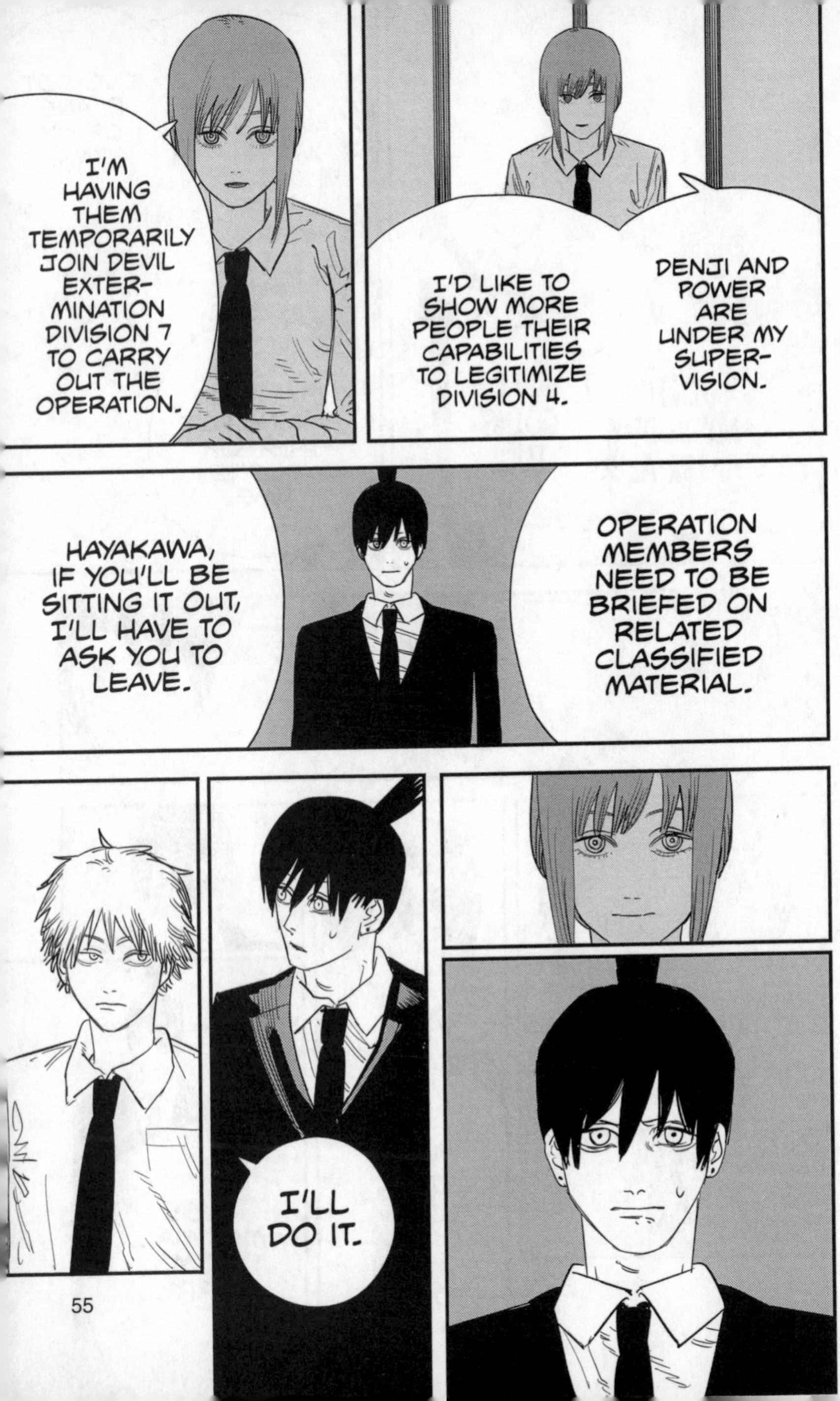
DENJI AND POWER ARE UNDER MY SUPER-VISION.
I'D LIKE TO SHOW MORE PEOPLE THEIR CAPABILITIES TO LEGITIMIZE DIVISION 4.
I'M HAVING THEM TEMPORARILY JOIN DEVIL EXTER-MINATION DIVISION 7 TO CARRY OUT THE OPERATION.
OPERATION MEMBERS NEED TO BE BRIEFED ON RELATED CLASSIFIED MATERIAL.
HAYAKAWA, IF YOU'LL BE SITTING IT OUT, I'LL HAVE TO ASK YOU TO LEAVE.
I'LL DO IT.

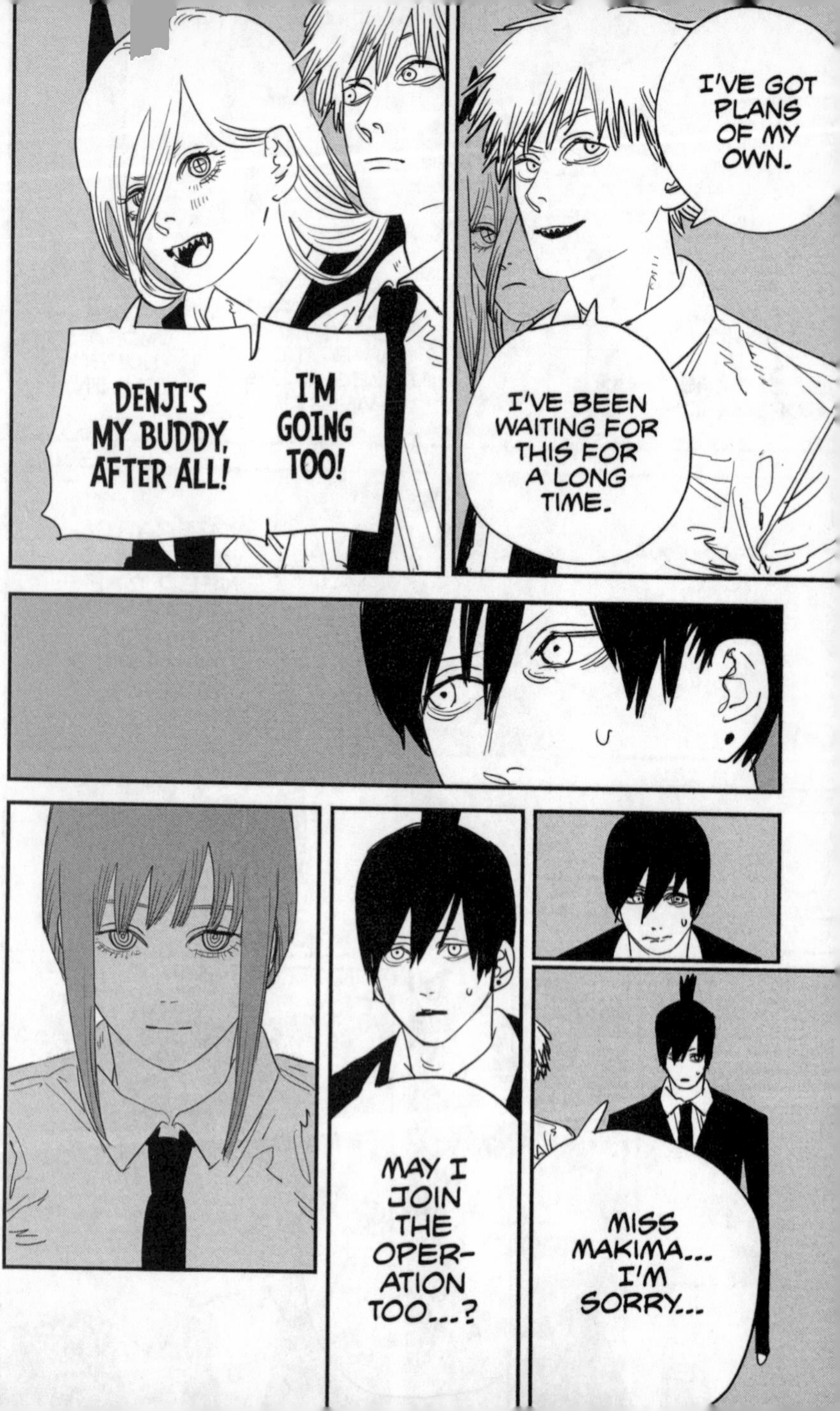
I'VE GOT PLANS OF MY OWN.
I'VE BEEN WAITING FOR THIS FOR A LONG TIME.
I'M GOING TOO!
DENJI'S MY BUDDY, AFTER ALL!
MISS MAKIMA... I'M SORRY...
MAY I JOIN THE OPERATION TOO...?

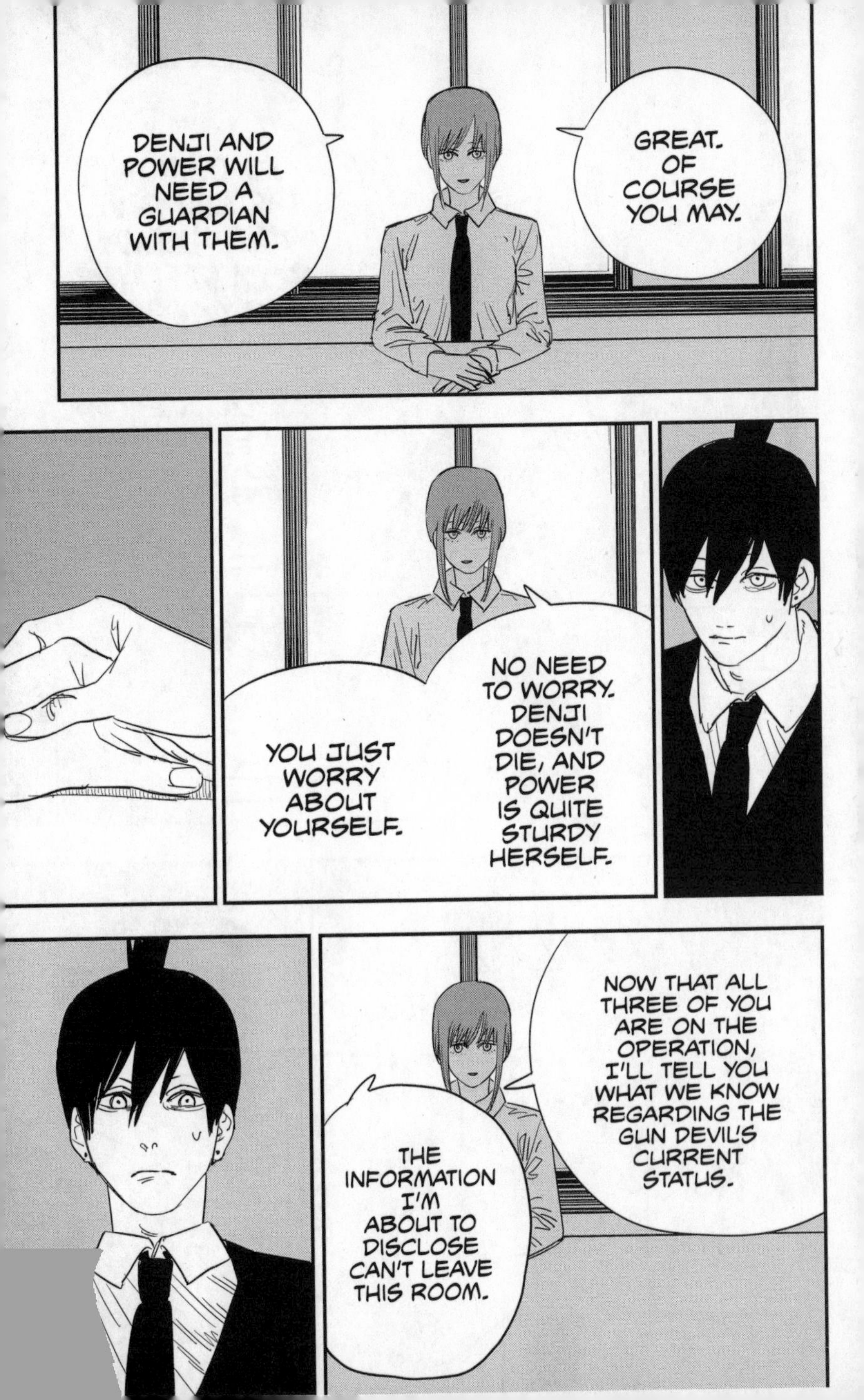
GREAT. OF COURSE YOU MAY.
DENJI AND POWER WILL NEED A GUARDIAN WITH THEM.
NO NEED TO WORRY. DENJI DOESN'T DIE, AND POWER IS QUITE STURDY HERSELF.
YOU JUST WORRY ABOUT YOURSELF.
NOW THAT ALL THREE OF YOU ARE ON THE OPERATION, I'LL TELL YOU WHAT WE KNOW REGARDING THE GUN DEVIL'S CURRENT STATUS.
THE INFORMATION I'M ABOUT TO DISCLOSE CAN'T LEAVE THIS ROOM.

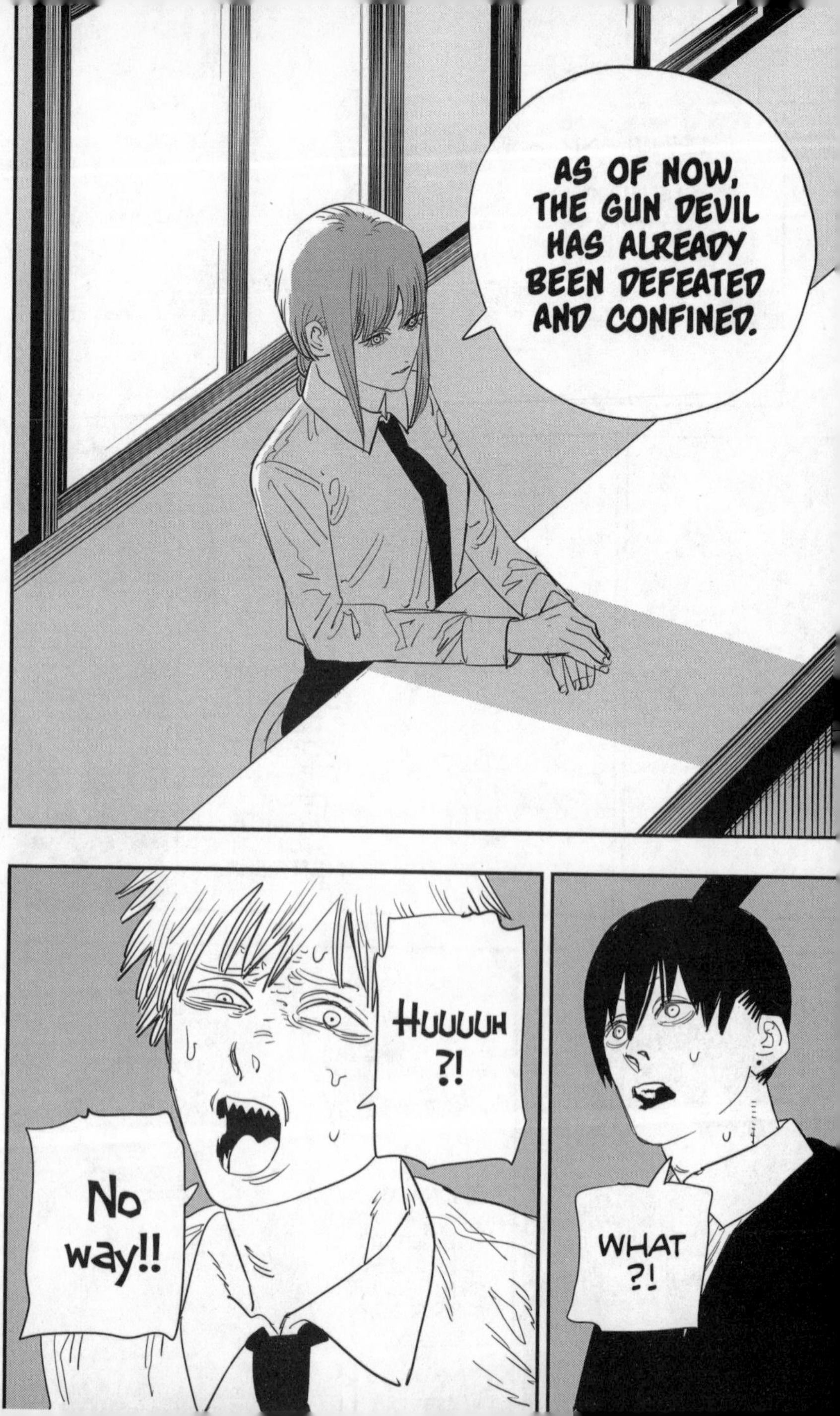
AS OF NOW, THE GUN DEVIL HAS ALREADY BEEN DEFEATED AND CONFINED.
WHAT ?!
HUUUUH ?!
No way!!

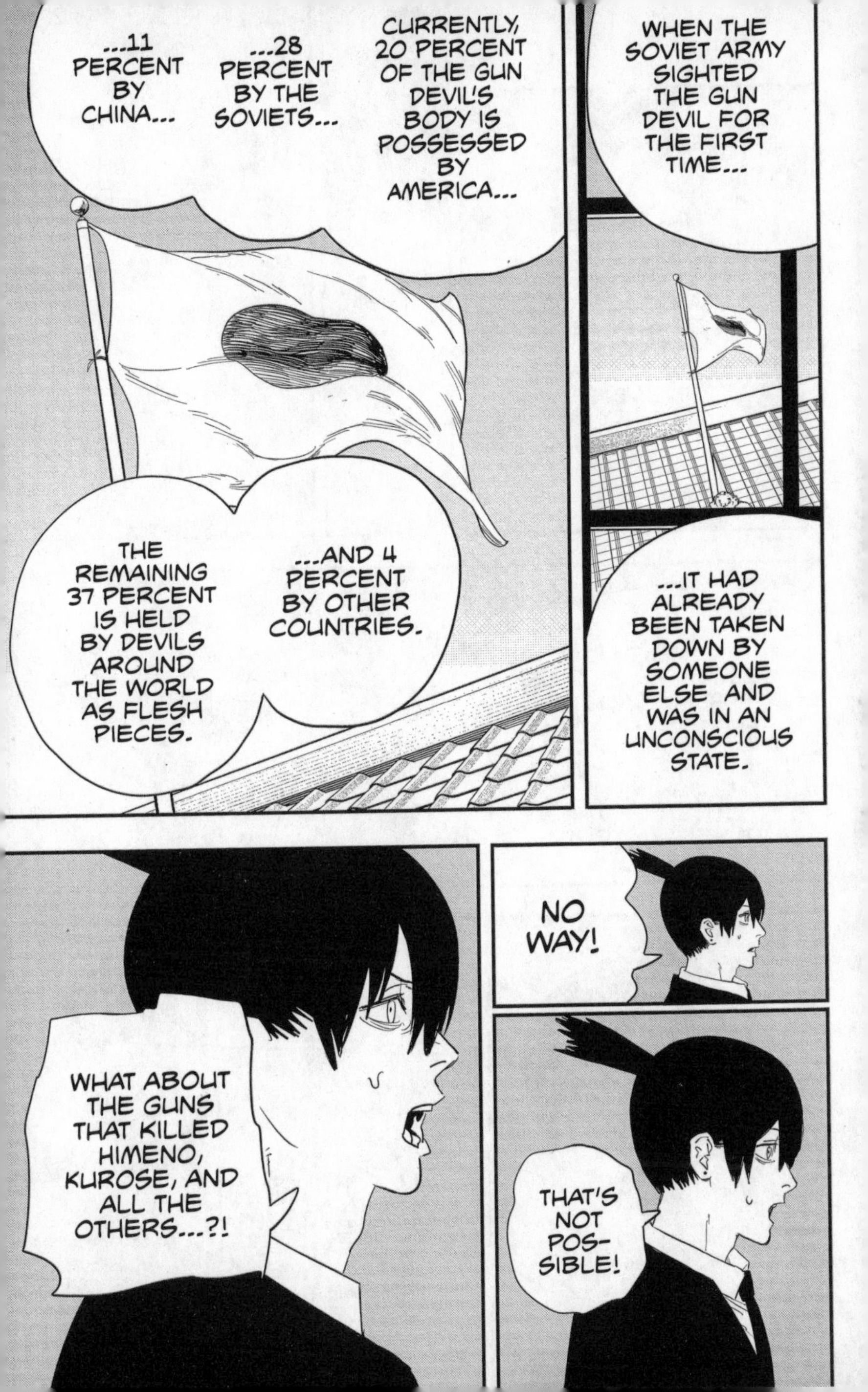
WHEN THE SOVIET ARMY SIGHTED THE GUN DEVIL FOR THE FIRST TIME...
...IT HAD ALREADY BEEN TAKEN DOWN BY SOMEONE ELSE AND WAS IN AN UNCONSCIOUS STATE.
CURRENTLY, 20 PERCENT OF THE GUN DEVIL'S BODY IS POSSESSED BY AMERICA...
...28 PERCENT BY THE SOVIETS...
...11 PERCENT BY CHINA...
...AND 4 PERCENT BY OTHER COUNTRIES.
THE REMAINING 37 PERCENT IS HELD BY DEVILS AROUND THE WORLD AS FLESH PIECES.
NO WAY!
THAT'S NOT POS-SIBLE!
WHAT ABOUT THE GUNS THAT KILLED HIMENO, KUROSE, AND ALL THE OTHERS...?!

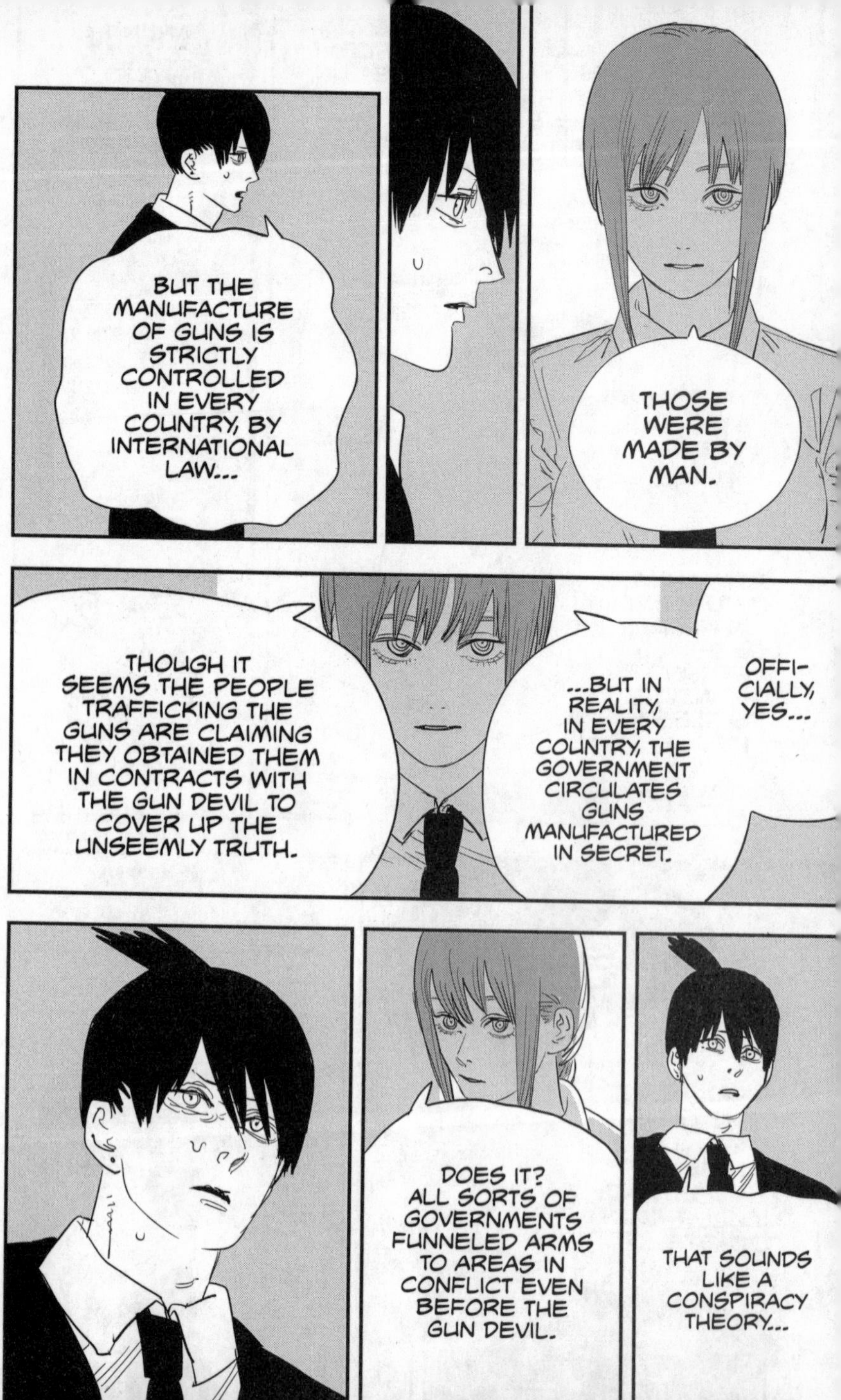
THOSE WERE MADE BY MAN.
BUT THE MANUFACTURE OF GUNS IS STRICTLY CONTROLLED IN EVERY COUNTRY, BY INTERNATIONAL LAW...
OFFI-CIALLY, YES...
...BUT IN REALITY, IN EVERY COUNTRY, THE GOVERNMENT CIRCULATES GUNS MANUFACTURED IN SECRET.
THOUGH IT SEEMS THE PEOPLE TRAFFICKING THE GUNS ARE CLAIMING THEY OBTAINED THEM IN CONTRACTS WITH THE GUN DEVIL TO COVER UP THE UNSEEMLY TRUTH.
THAT SOUNDS LIKE A CONSPIRACY THEORY...
DOES IT? ALL SORTS OF GOVERNMENTS FUNNELED ARMS TO AREAS IN CONFLICT EVEN BEFORE THE GUN DEVIL.

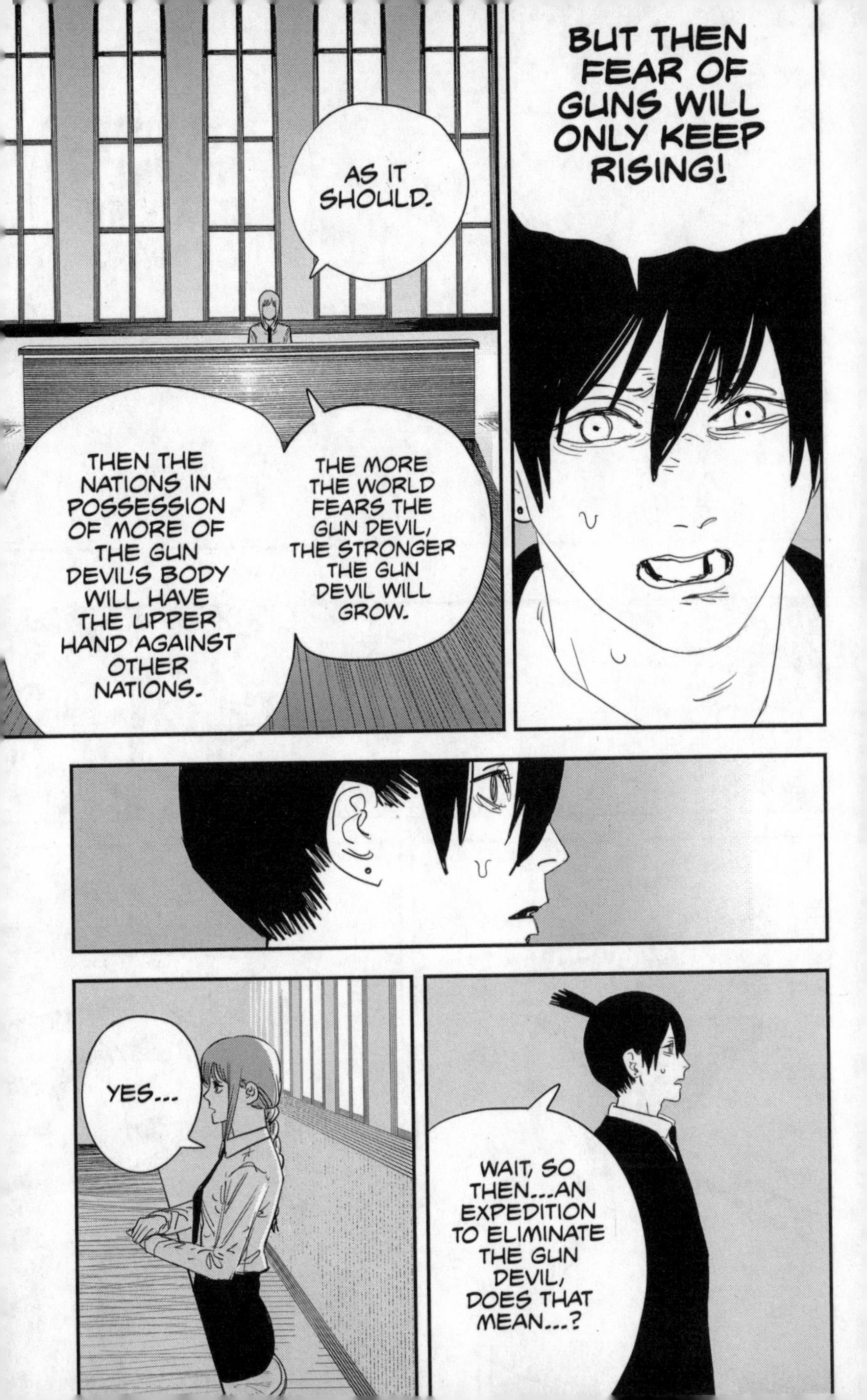
BUT THEN FEAR OF GUNS WILL ONLY KEEP RISING!
AS IT SHOULD.
THE MORE THE WORLD FEARS THE GUN DEVIL, THE STRONGER THE GUN DEVIL WILL GROW.
THEN THE NATIONS IN POSSESSION OF MORE OF THE GUN DEVIL'S BODY WILL HAVE THE UPPER HAND AGAINST OTHER NATIONS.
WAIT, SO THEN...AN EXPEDITION TO ELIMINATE THE GUN DEVIL, DOES THAT MEAN...?
YES...

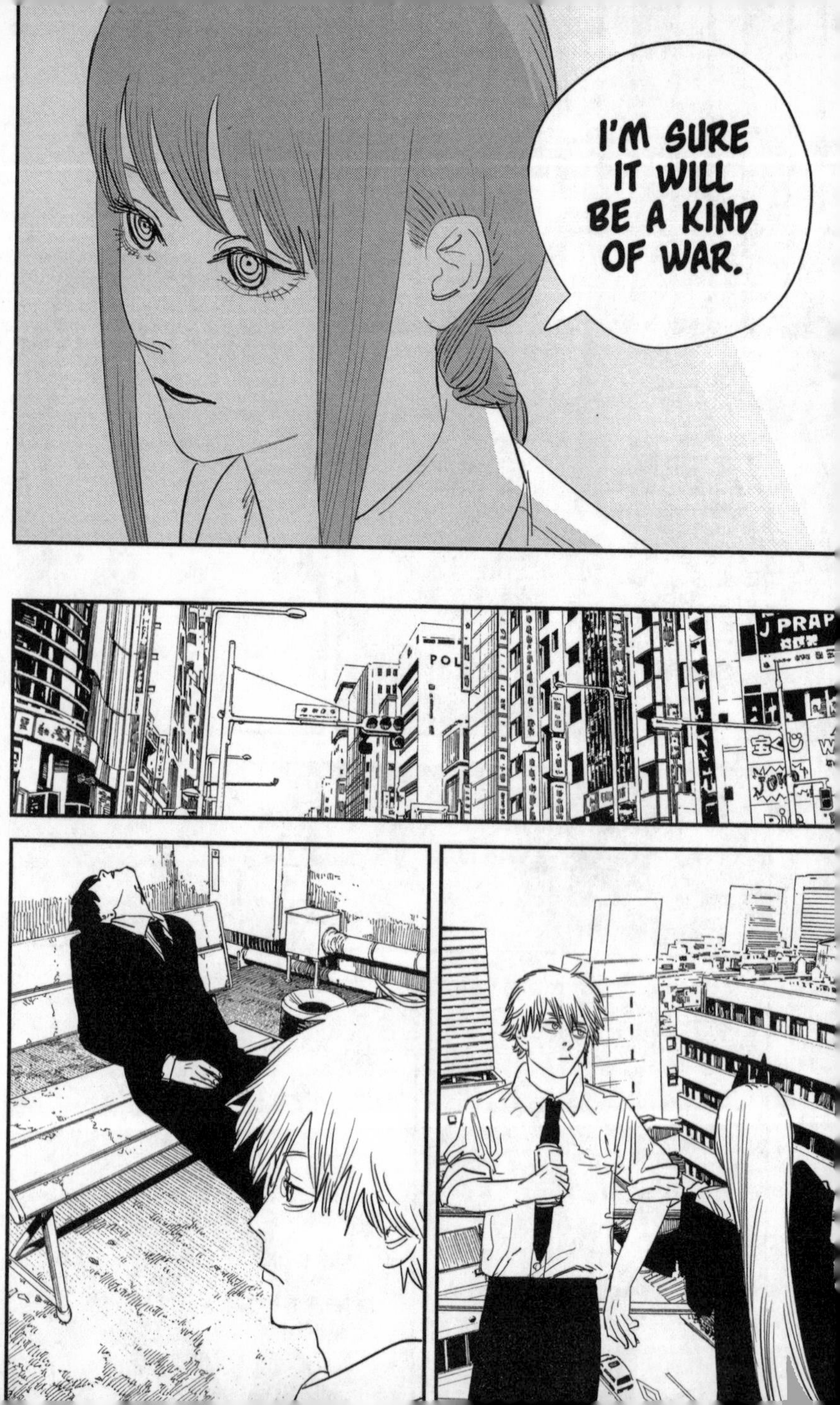
I'M SURE IT WILL BE A KIND OF WAR.

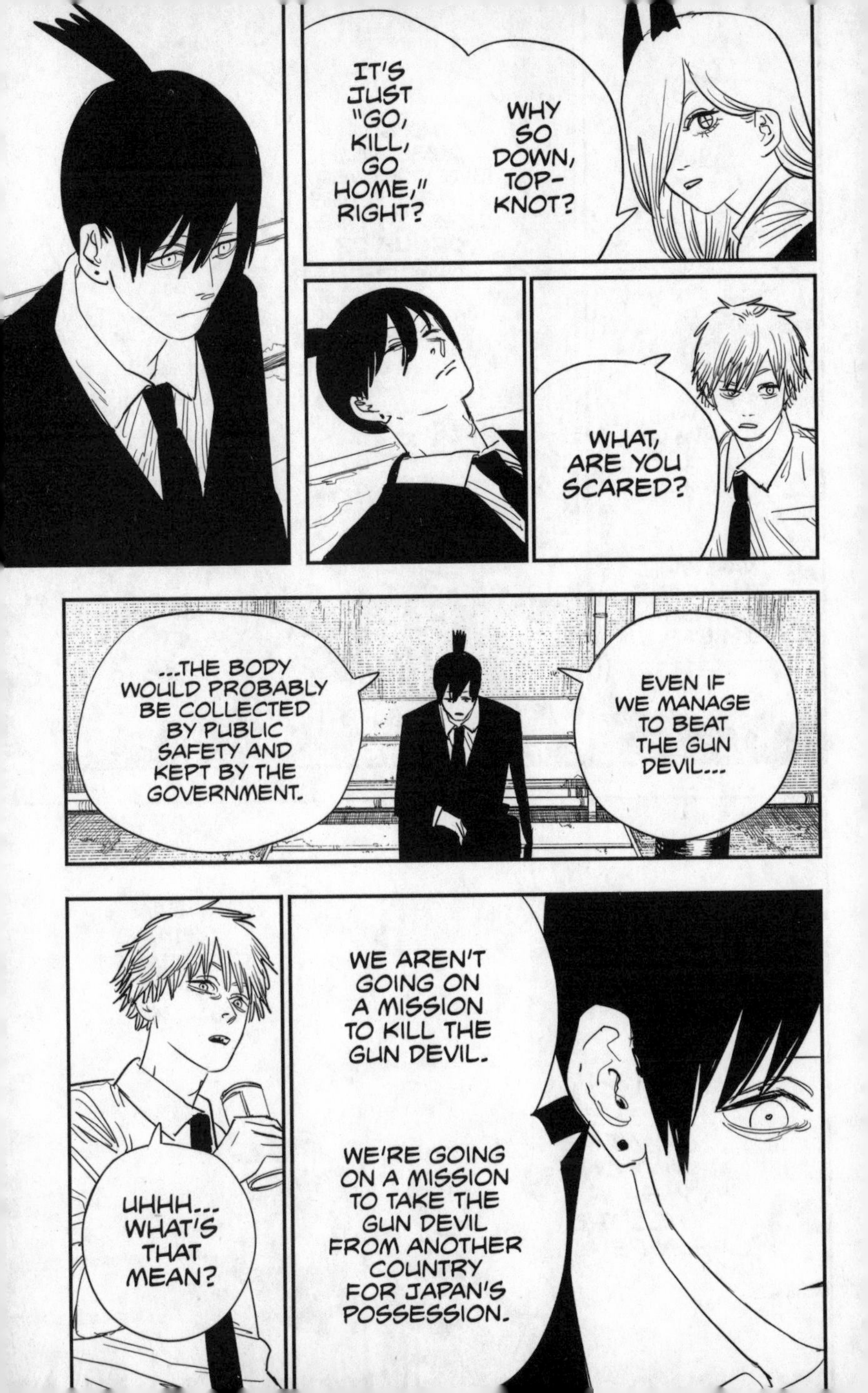
WHY SO DOWN, TOP-KNOT?
IT'S JUST "GO, KILL, GO HOME," RIGHT?
WHAT, ARE YOU SCARED?
EVEN IF WE MANAGE TO BEAT THE GUN DEVIL...
...THE BODY WOULD PROBABLY BE COLLECTED BY PUBLIC SAFETY AND KEPT BY THE GOVERNMENT.
WE AREN'T GOING ON A MISSION TO KILL THE GUN DEVIL.
WE'RE GOING ON A MISSION TO TAKE THE GUN DEVIL FROM ANOTHER COUNTRY FOR JAPAN'S POSSESSION.
UHHH... WHAT'S THAT MEAN?

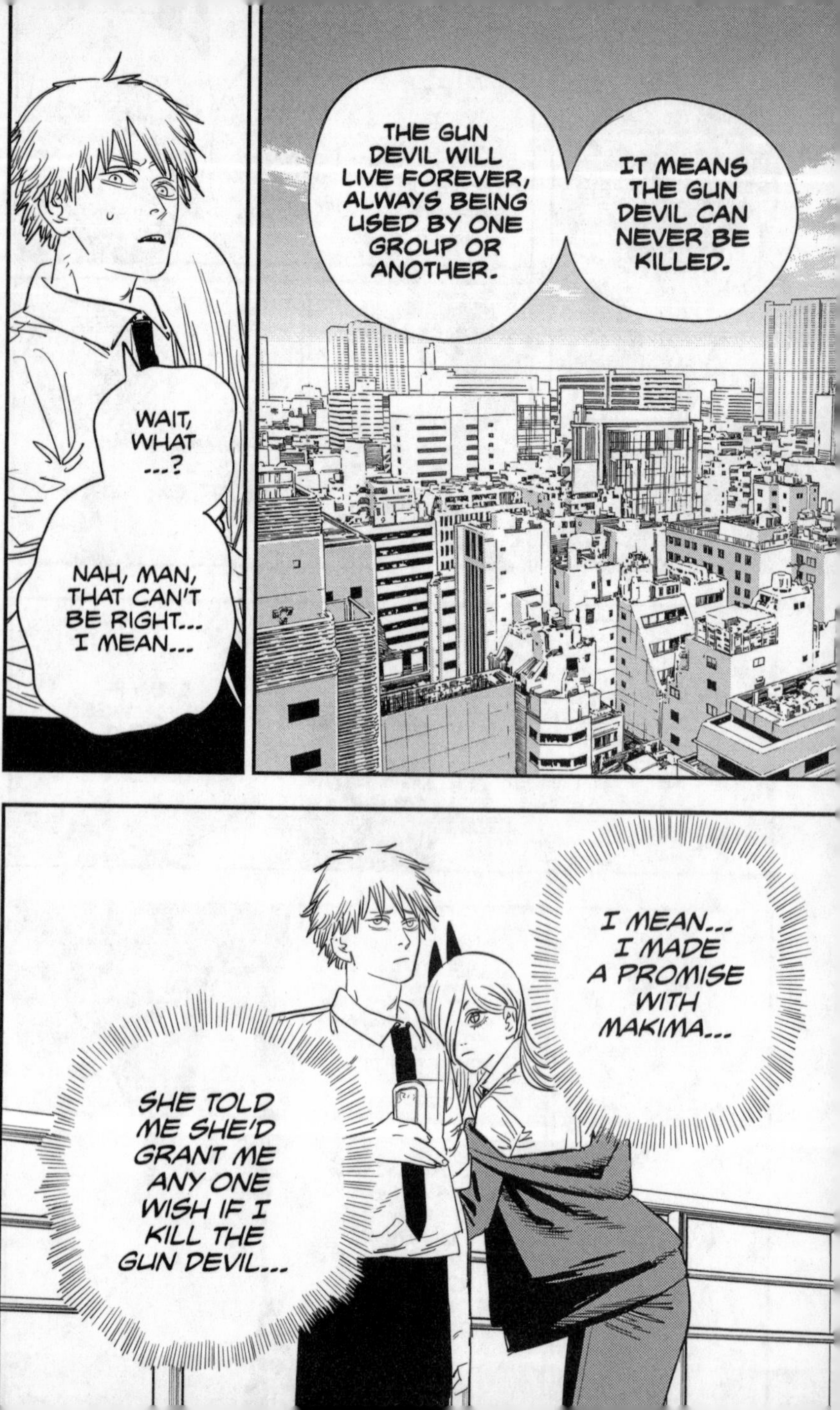
IT MEANS THE GUN DEVIL CAN NEVER BE KILLED.
THE GUN DEVIL WILL LIVE FOREVER, ALWAYS BEING USED BY ONE GROUP OR ANOTHER.
WAIT, WHAT ...?
NAH, MAN, THAT CAN'T BE RIGHT... I MEAN...
I MEAN... I MADE A PROMISE WITH MAKIMA...
SHE TOLD ME SHE'D GRANT ME ANY ONE WISH IF I KILL THE GUN DEVIL...

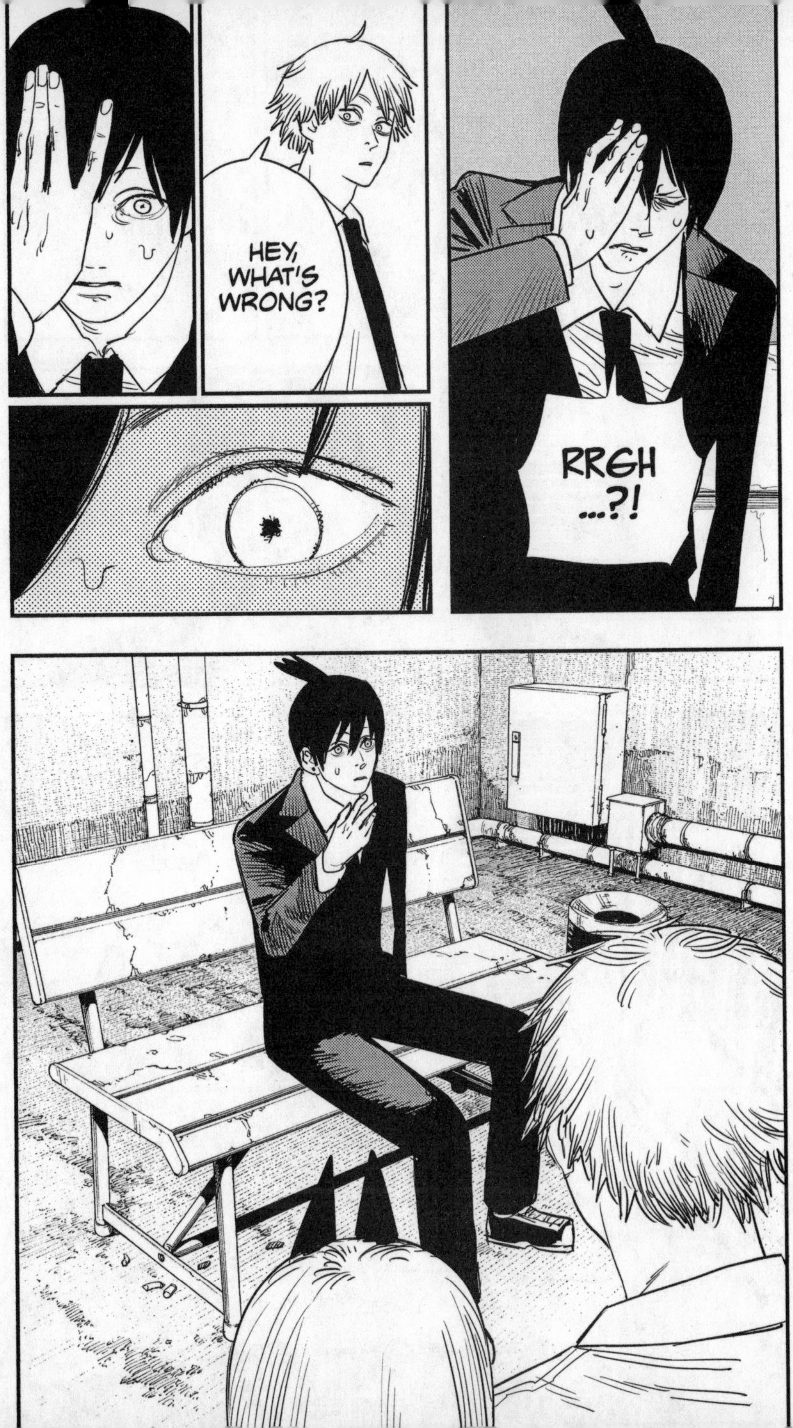
RRGH ...?!
HEY, WHAT'S WRONG?

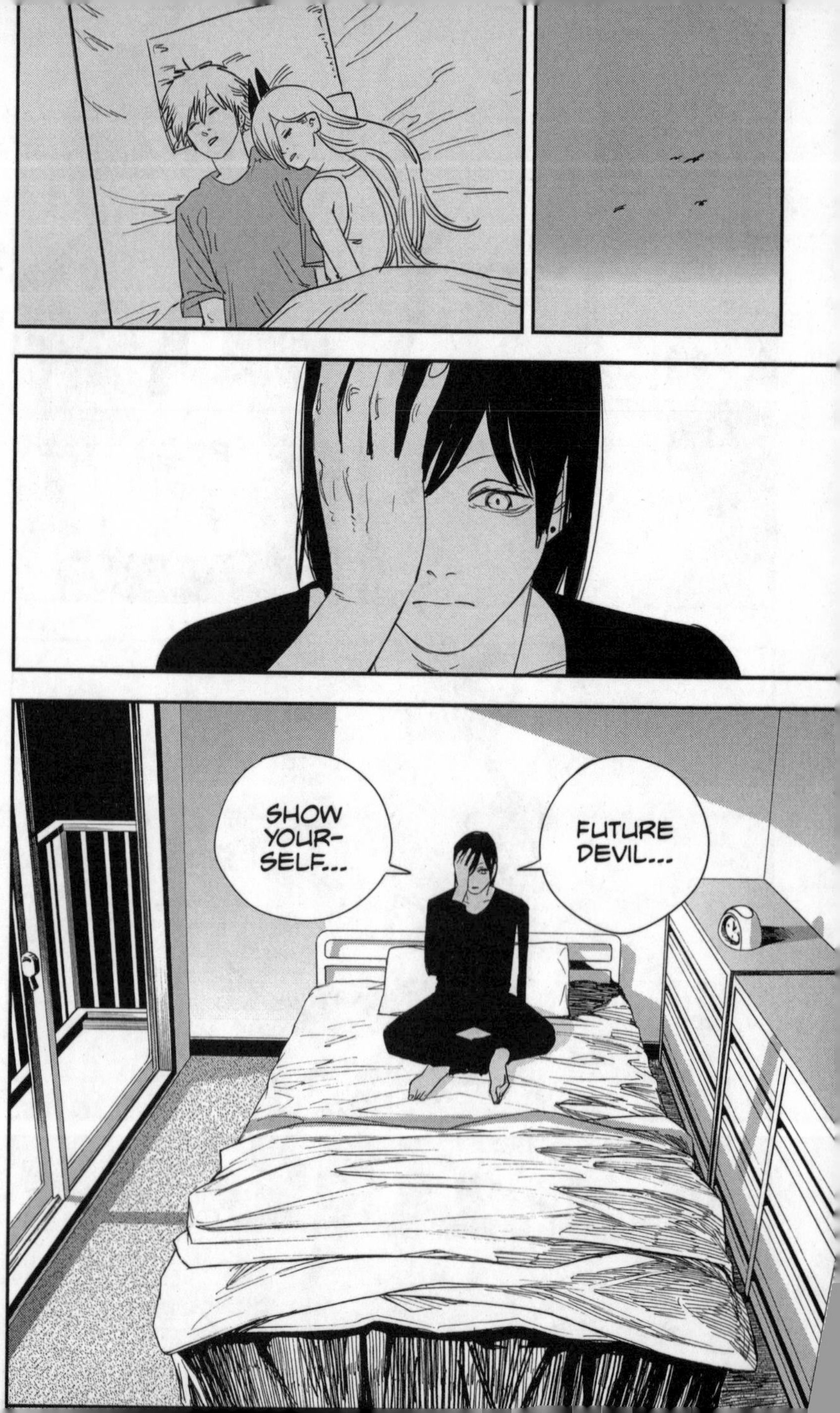
FUTURE DEVIL...
SHOW YOUR-SELF...

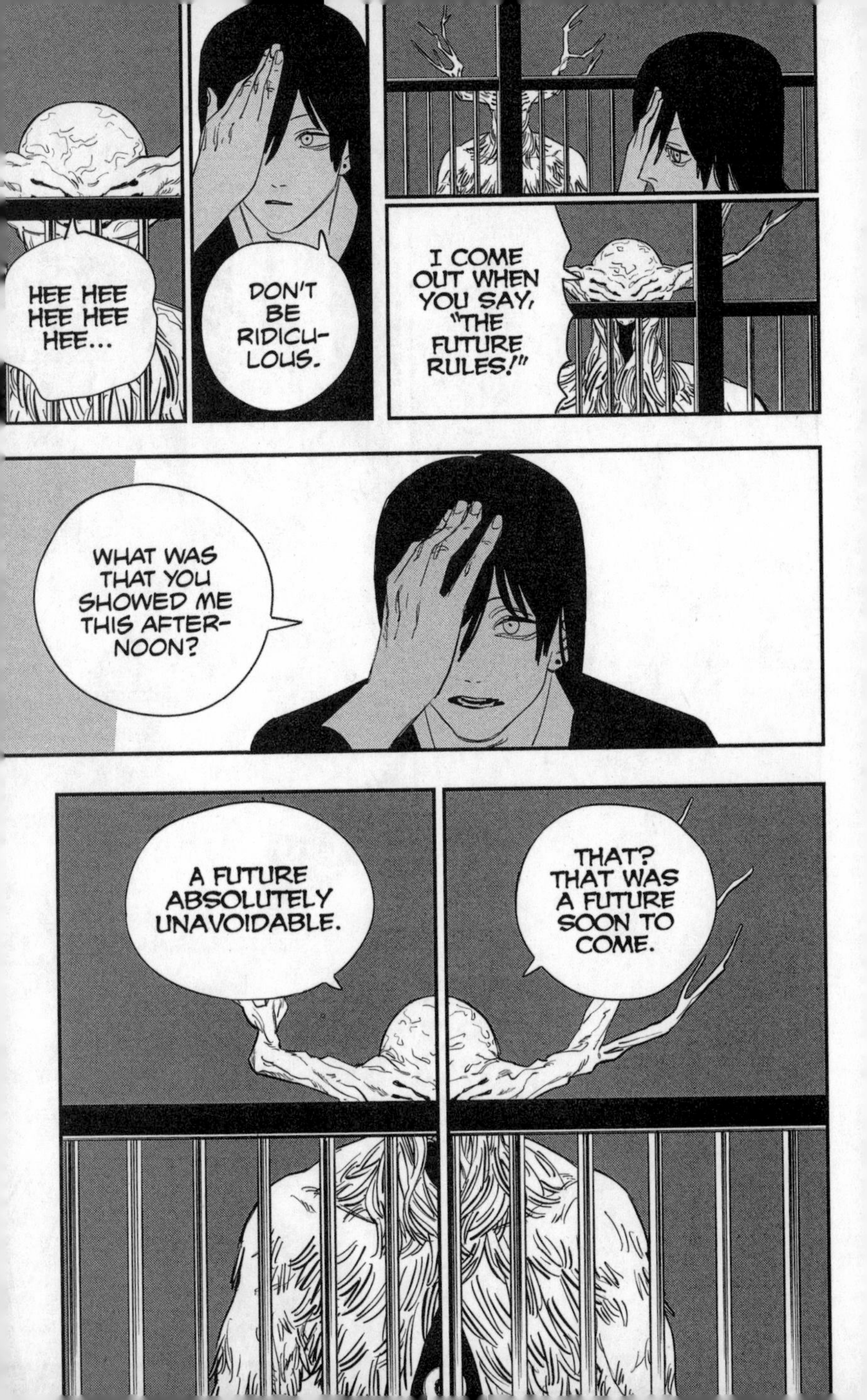
I COME OUT WHEN YOU SAY, "THE FUTURE RULES!"
DON'T BE RIDICULOUS.
HEE HEE HEE HEE HEE...
WHAT WAS THAT YOU SHOWED ME THIS AFTERNOON?
THAT? THAT WAS A FUTURE SOON TO COME.
A FUTURE ABSOLUTELY UNAVOIDABLE.

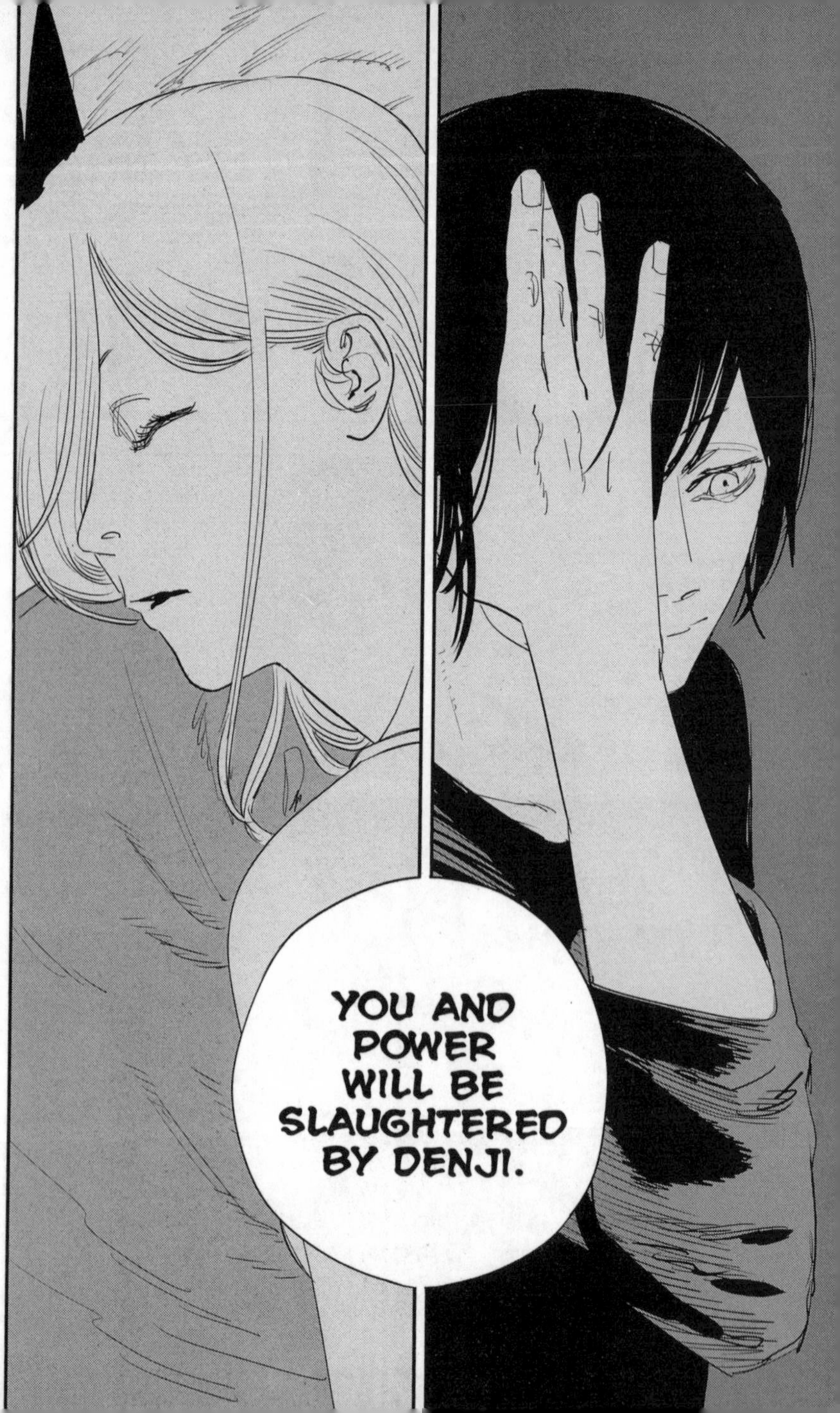
YOU AND POWER WILL BE SLAUGHTERED BY DENJI.

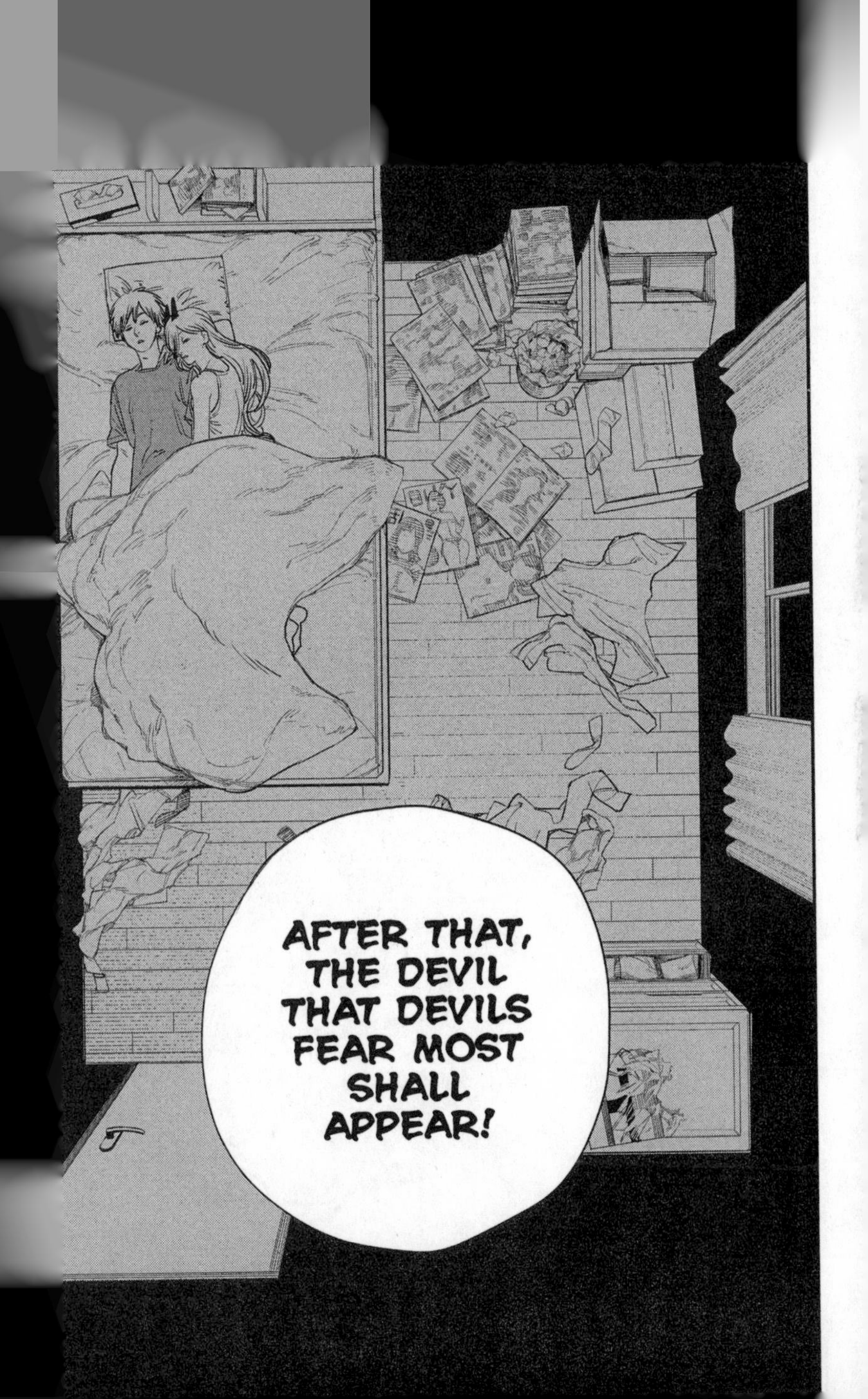
AFTER THAT, THE DEVIL THAT DEVILS FEAR MOST SHALL APPEAR!

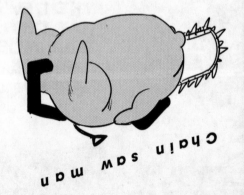

Chain saw man

Chapter 74: What the Waves Say

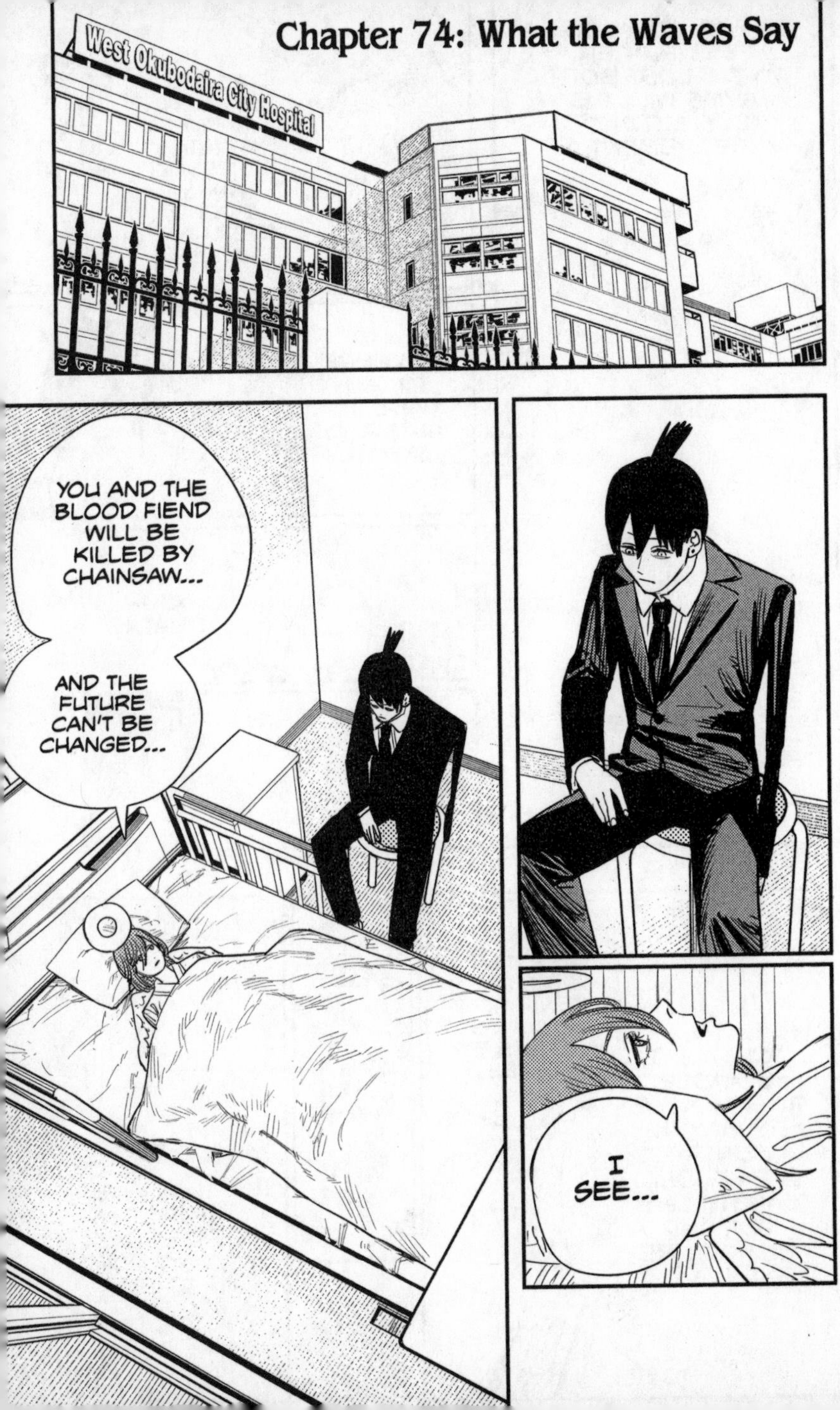
West Okubodaira City Hospital
I SEE...
YOU AND THE BLOOD FIEND WILL BE KILLED BY CHAINSAW...
AND THE FUTURE CAN'T BE CHANGED...

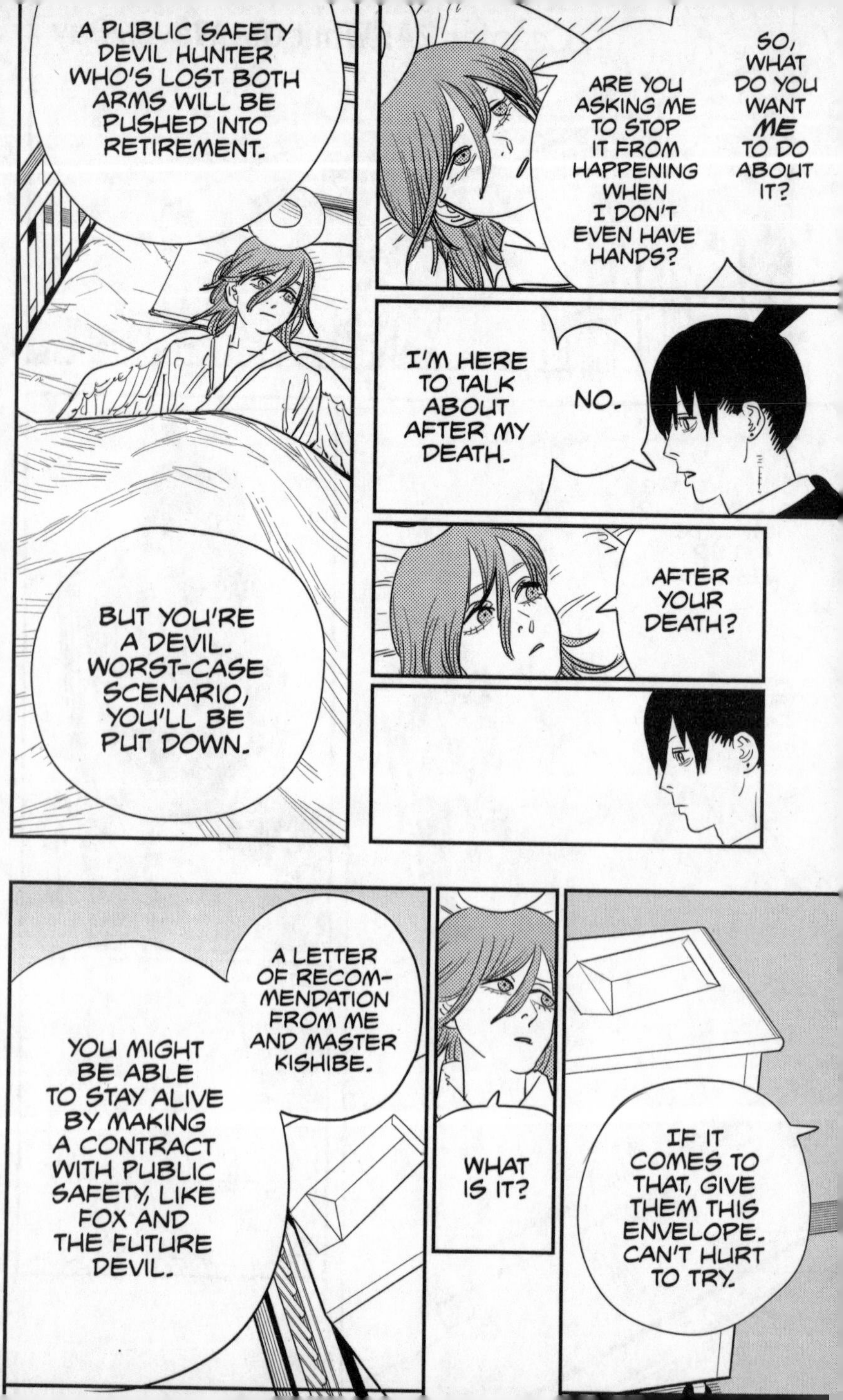
SO, WHAT DO YOU WANT ME TO DO ABOUT IT?
ARE YOU ASKING ME TO STOP IT FROM HAPPENING WHEN I DON'T EVEN HAVE HANDS?
NO.
I'M HERE TO TALK ABOUT AFTER MY DEATH.
AFTER YOUR DEATH?
A PUBLIC SAFETY DEVIL HUNTER WHO'S LOST BOTH ARMS WILL BE PUSHED INTO RETIREMENT.
BUT YOU'RE A DEVIL. WORST-CASE SCENARIO, YOU'LL BE PUT DOWN.
IF IT COMES TO THAT, GIVE THEM THIS ENVELOPE. CAN'T HURT TO TRY.
WHAT IS IT?
A LETTER OF RECOM-MENDATION FROM ME AND MASTER KISHIBE.
YOU MIGHT BE ABLE TO STAY ALIVE BY MAKING A CONTRACT WITH PUBLIC SAFETY, LIKE FOX AND THE FUTURE DEVIL.

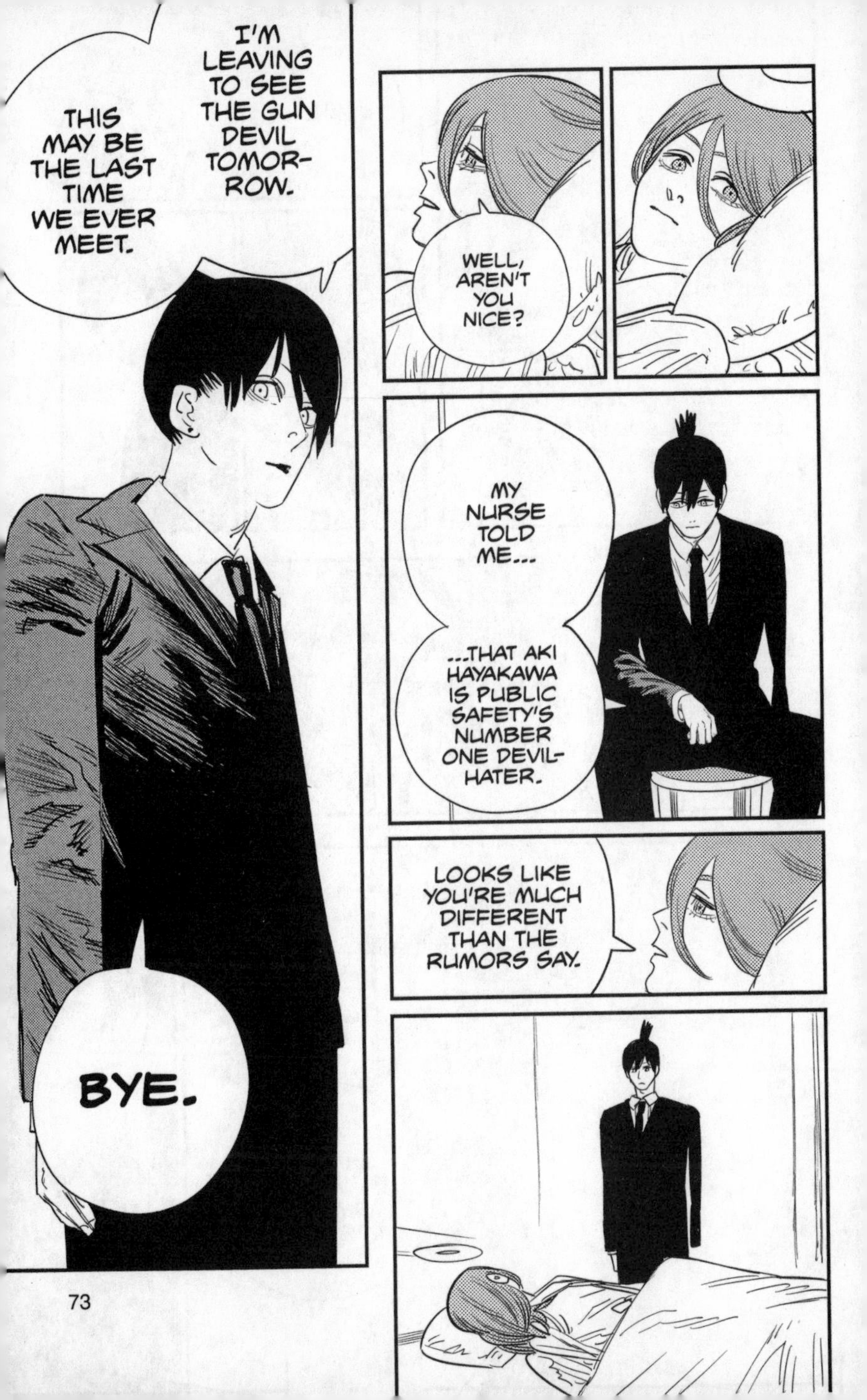

WELL, AREN'T YOU NICE?
MY NURSE TOLD ME...
...THAT AKI HAYAKAWA IS PUBLIC SAFETY'S NUMBER ONE DEVIL-HATER.
LOOKS LIKE YOU'RE MUCH DIFFERENT THAN THE RUMORS SAY.
I'M LEAVING TO SEE THE GUN DEVIL TOMORROW.
THIS MAY BE THE LAST TIME WE EVER MEET.
BYE.

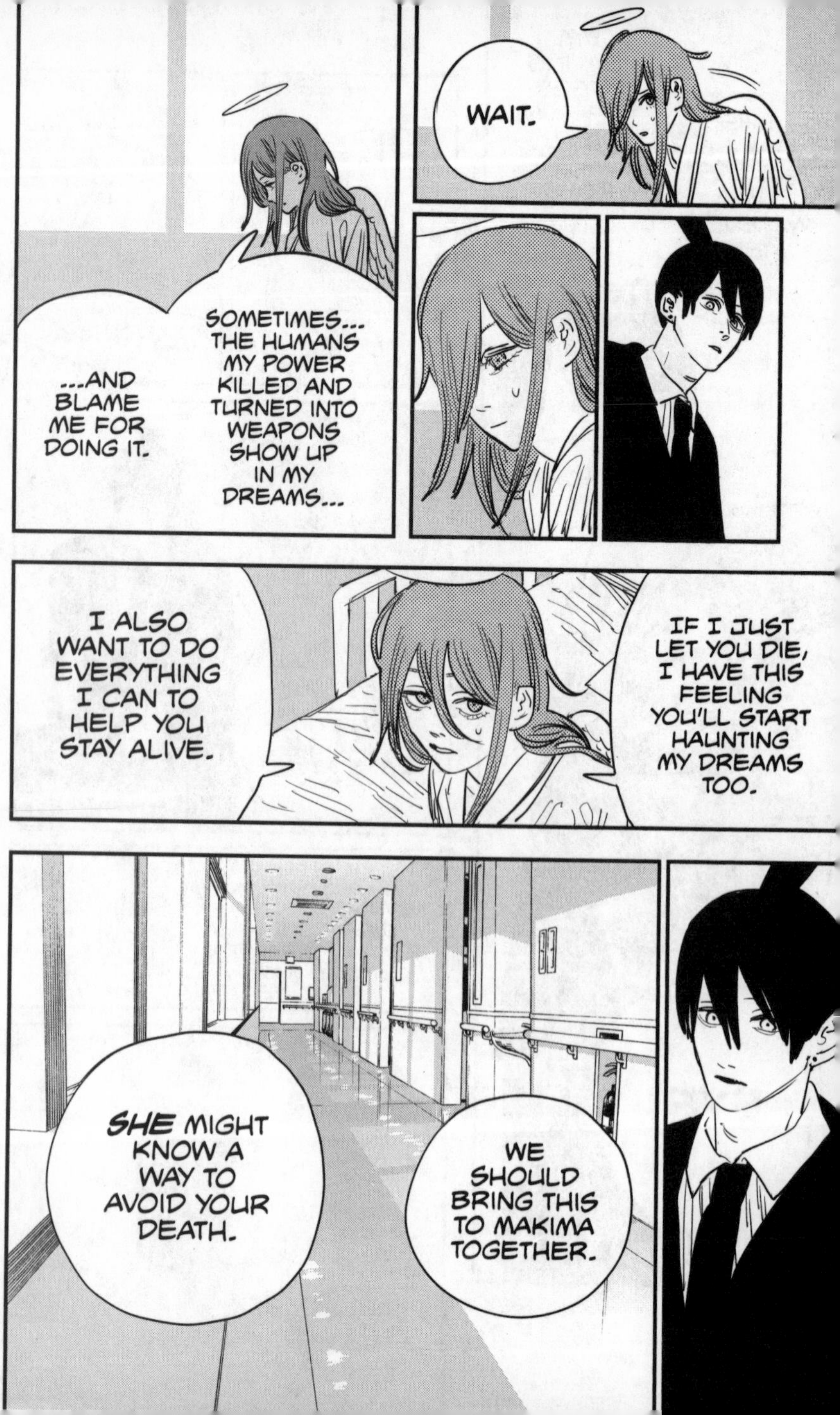
WAIT.
SOMETIMES... THE HUMANS MY POWER KILLED AND TURNED INTO WEAPONS SHOW UP IN MY DREAMS...
...AND BLAME ME FOR DOING IT.
IF I JUST LET YOU DIE, I HAVE THIS FEELING YOU'LL START HAUNTING MY DREAMS TOO.
I ALSO WANT TO DO EVERYTHING I CAN TO HELP YOU STAY ALIVE.
WE SHOULD BRING THIS TO MAKIMA TOGETHER.
SHE MIGHT KNOW A WAY TO AVOID YOUR DEATH.

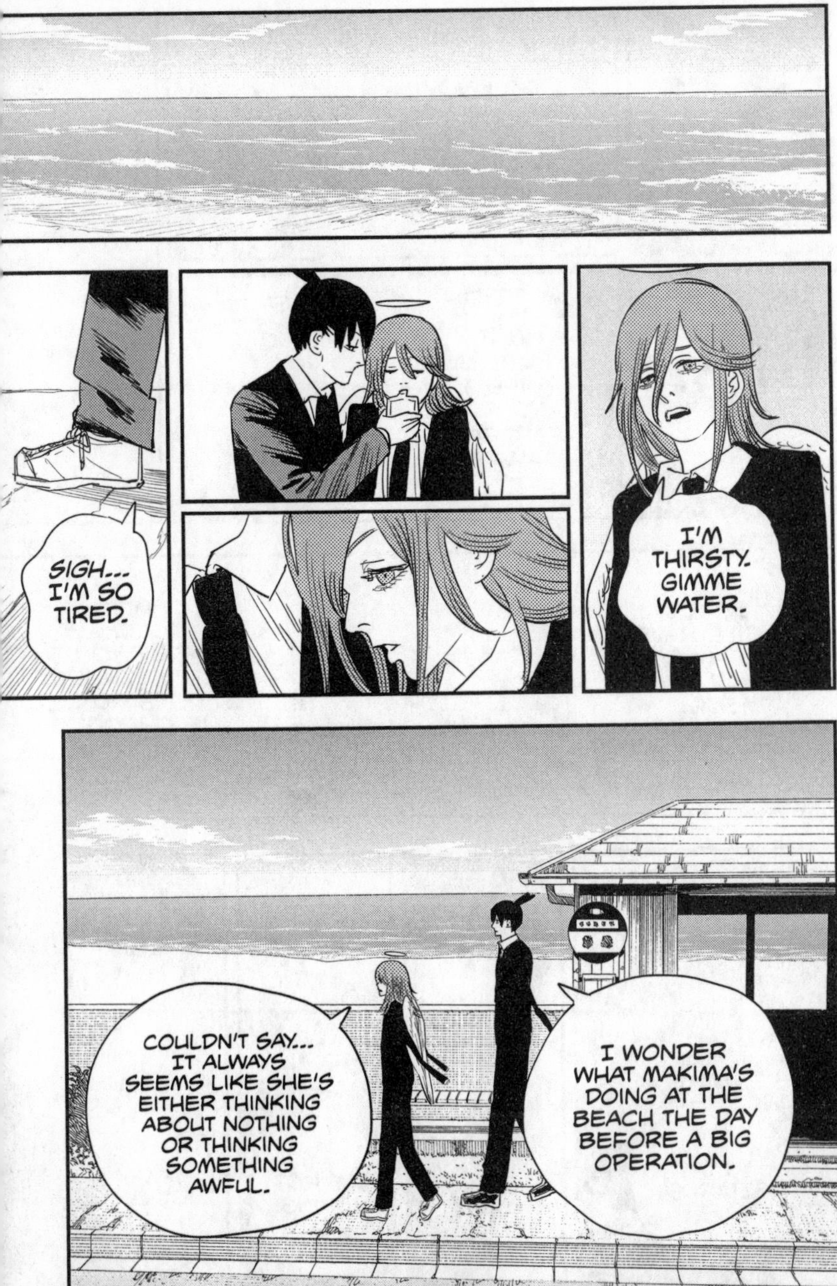
I'M THIRSTY. GIMME WATER.
SIGH... I'M SO TIRED.
I WONDER WHAT MAKIMA'S DOING AT THE BEACH THE DAY BEFORE A BIG OPERATION.
COULDN'T SAY... IT ALWAYS SEEMS LIKE SHE'S EITHER THINKING ABOUT NOTHING OR THINKING SOMETHING AWFUL.

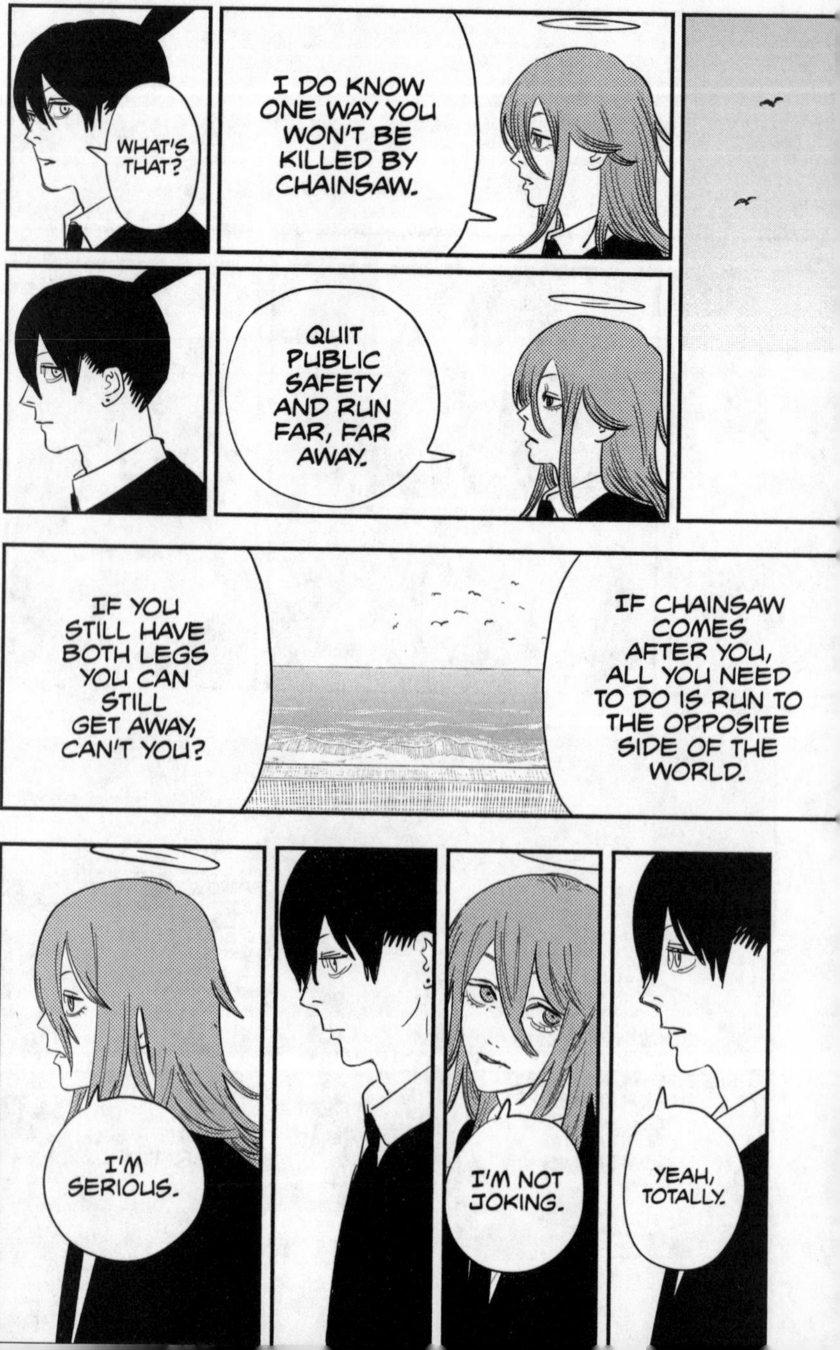
I DO KNOW ONE WAY YOU WON'T BE KILLED BY CHAINSAW.
WHAT'S THAT?
QUIT PUBLIC SAFETY AND RUN FAR, FAR AWAY.
IF CHAINSAW COMES AFTER YOU, ALL YOU NEED TO DO IS RUN TO THE OPPOSITE SIDE OF THE WORLD.
IF YOU STILL HAVE BOTH LEGS YOU CAN STILL GET AWAY, CAN'T YOU?
YEAH, TOTALLY.
I'M NOT JOKING.
I'M SERIOUS.

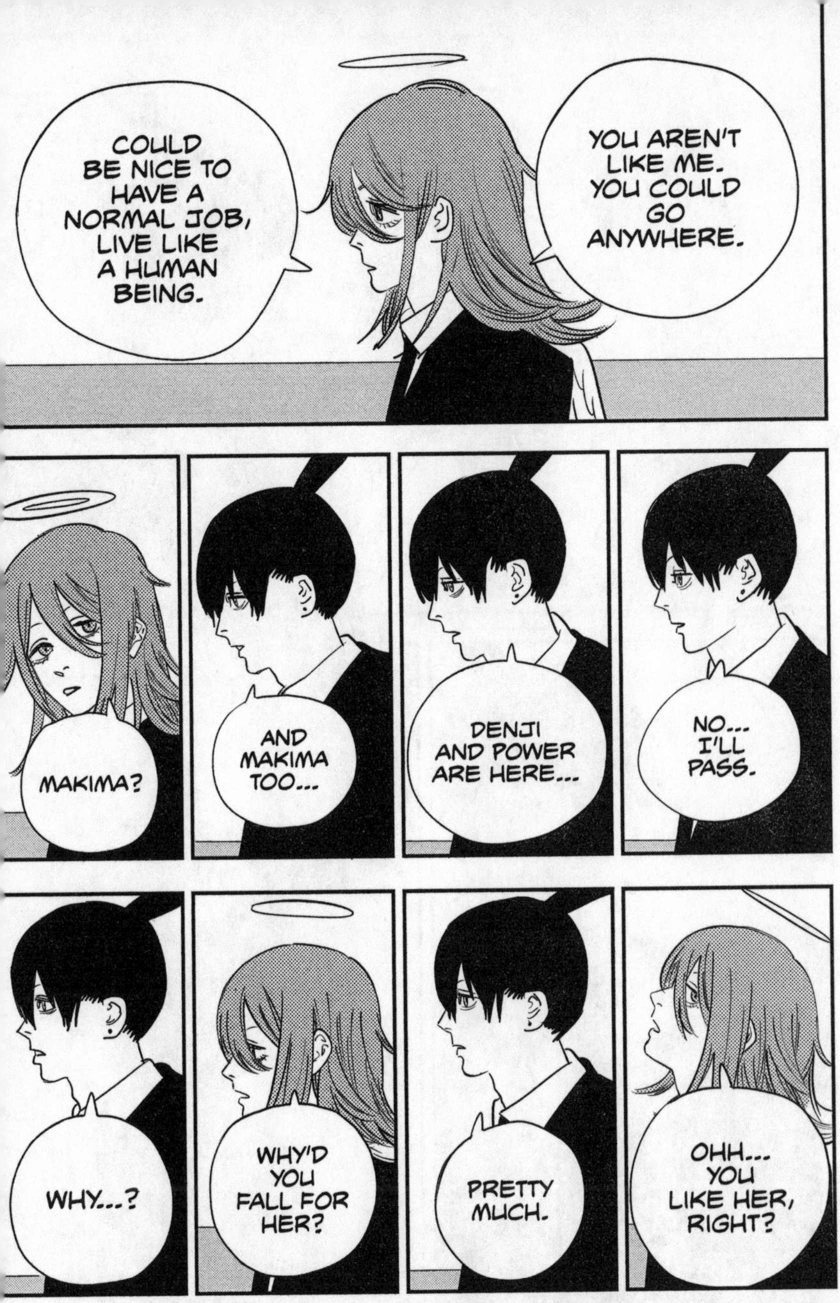
YOU AREN'T LIKE ME. YOU COULD GO ANYWHERE.
COULD BE NICE TO HAVE A NORMAL JOB, LIVE LIKE A HUMAN BEING.
NO... I'LL PASS.
DENJI AND POWER ARE HERE...
AND MAKIMA TOO...
MAKIMA?
OHH... YOU LIKE HER, RIGHT?
PRETTY MUCH.
WHY'D YOU FALL FOR HER?
WHY...?

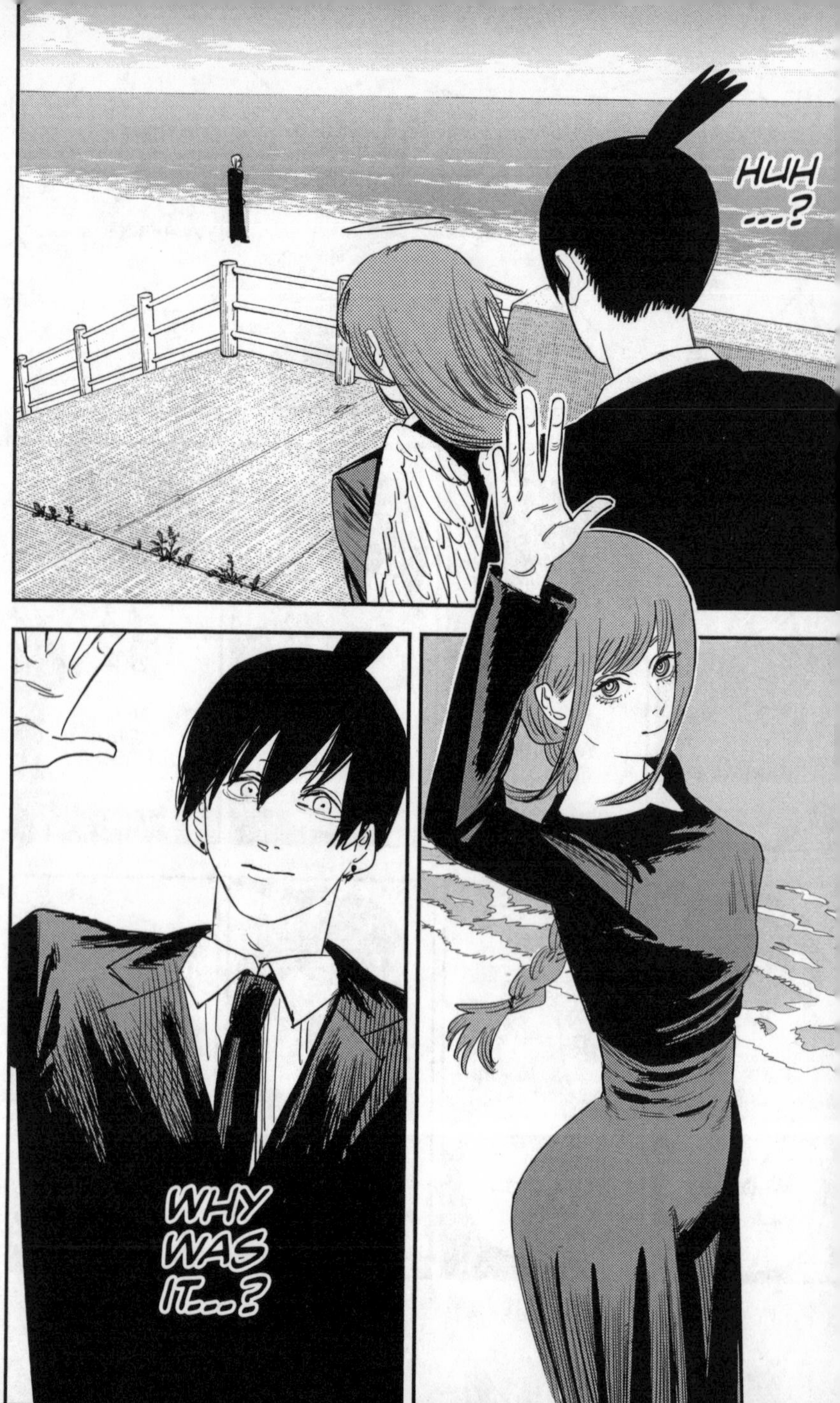
HUH ...?
WHY WAS IT...?

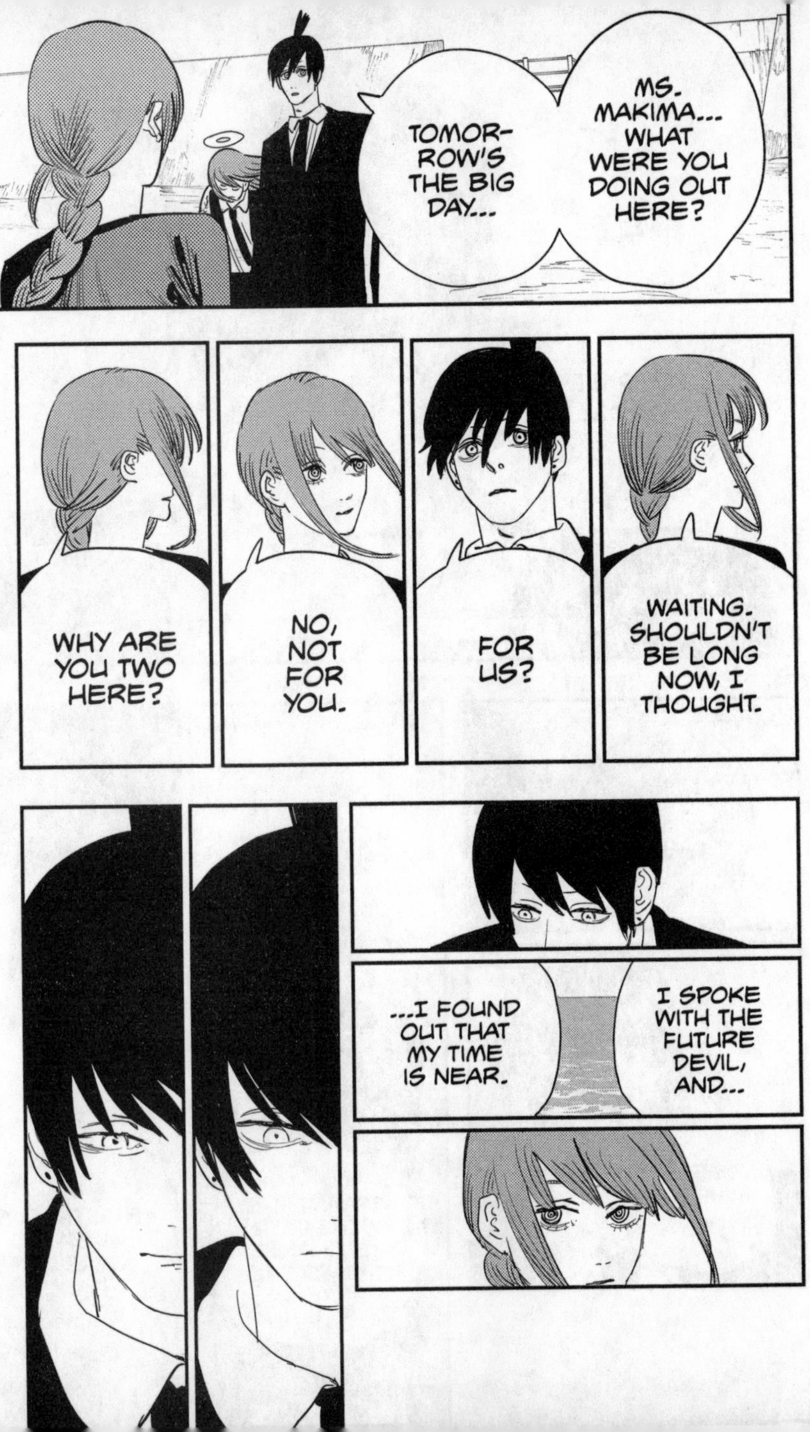
MS. MAKIMA... WHAT WERE YOU DOING OUT HERE?
TOMOR-ROW'S THE BIG DAY...
WAITING. SHOULDN'T BE LONG NOW, I THOUGHT.
FOR US?
NO, NOT FOR YOU.
WHY ARE YOU TWO HERE?
I SPOKE WITH THE FUTURE DEVIL, AND...
...I FOUND OUT THAT MY TIME IS NEAR.

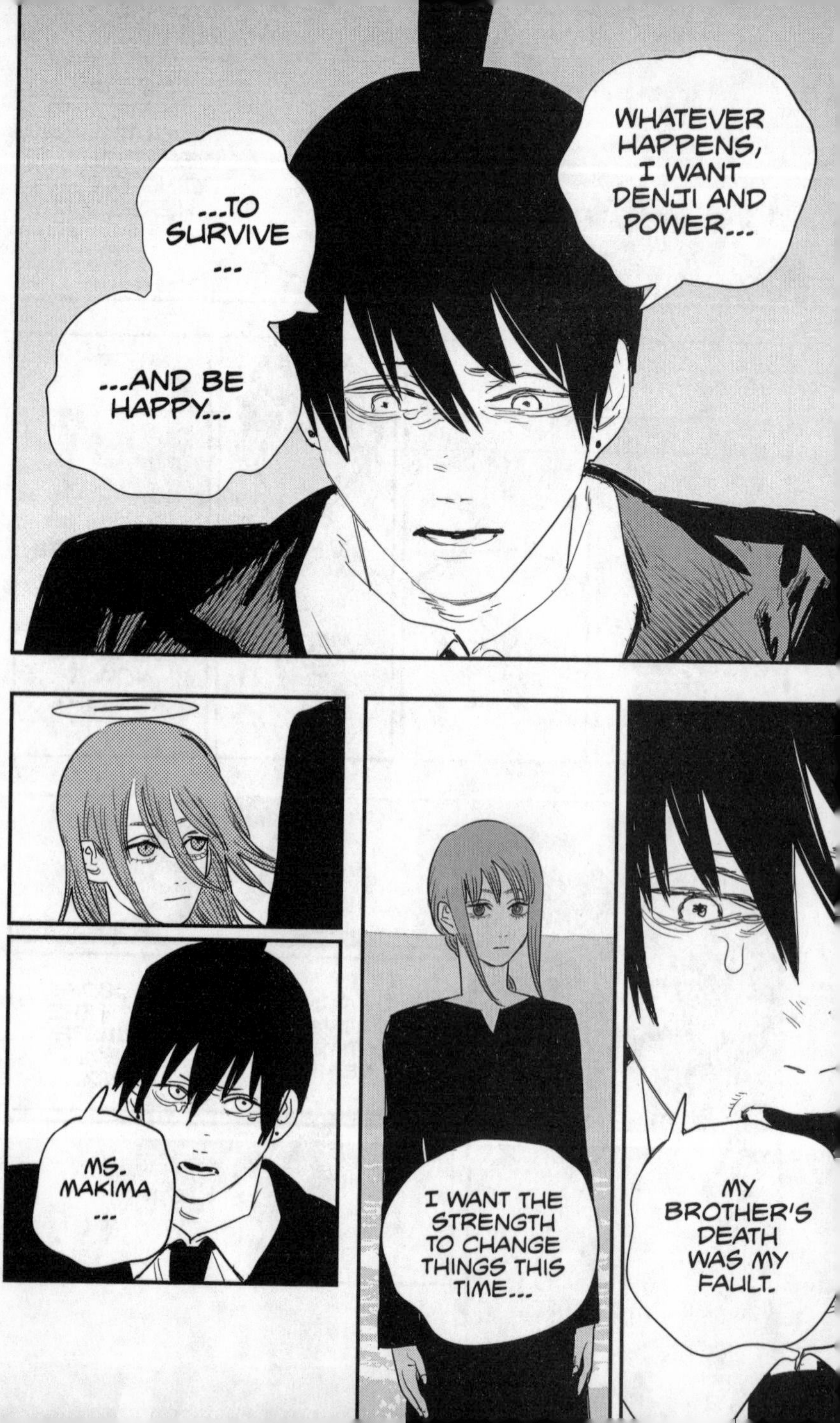
WHATEVER HAPPENS, I WANT DENJI AND POWER...
...TO SURVIVE ...
...AND BE HAPPY...
MY BROTHER'S DEATH WAS MY FAULT.
I WANT THE STRENGTH TO CHANGE THINGS THIS TIME...
MS. MAKIMA ...

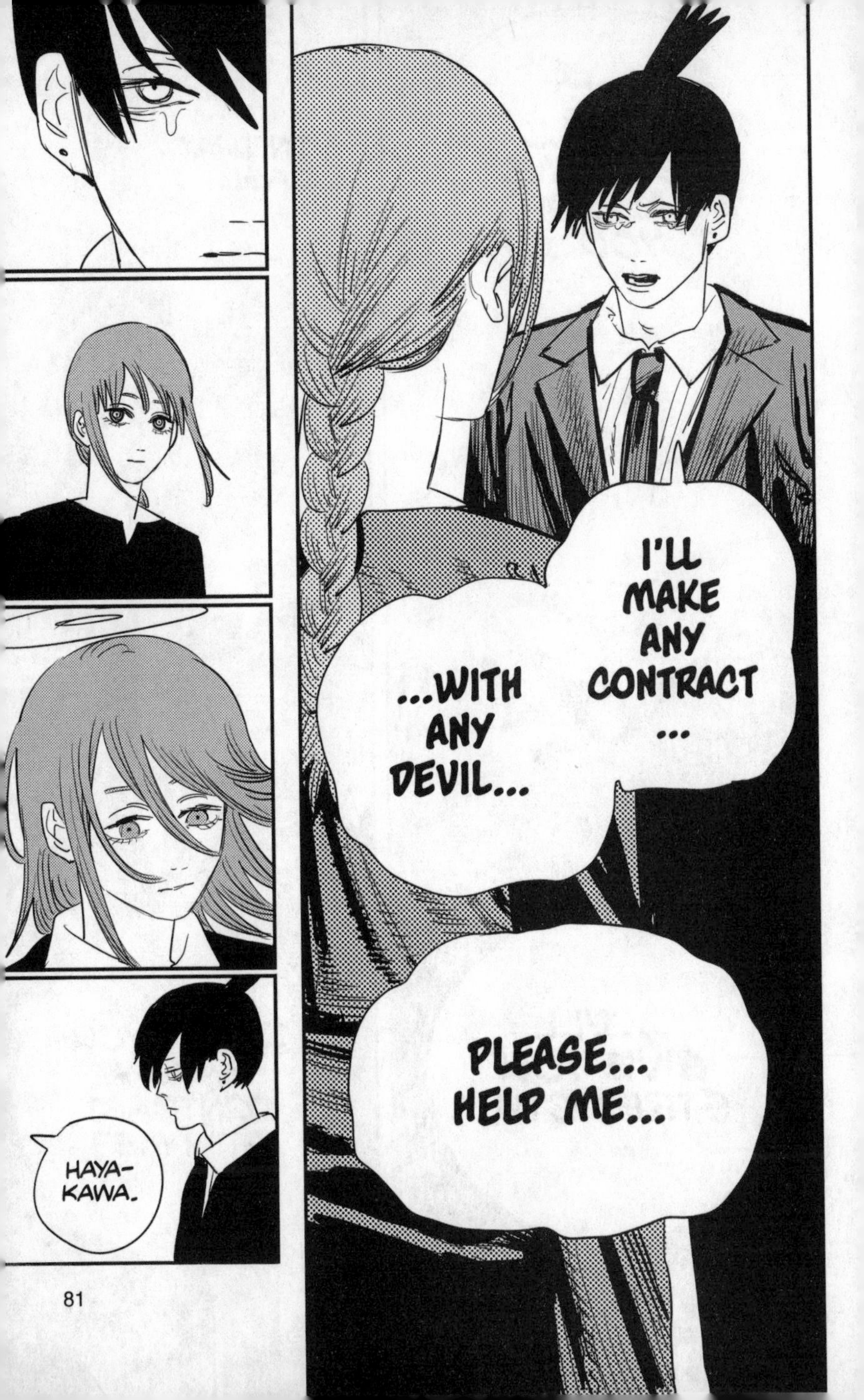
I'LL MAKE ANY CONTRACT...
...WITH ANY DEVIL...
PLEASE... HELP ME...
HAYA-KAWA.

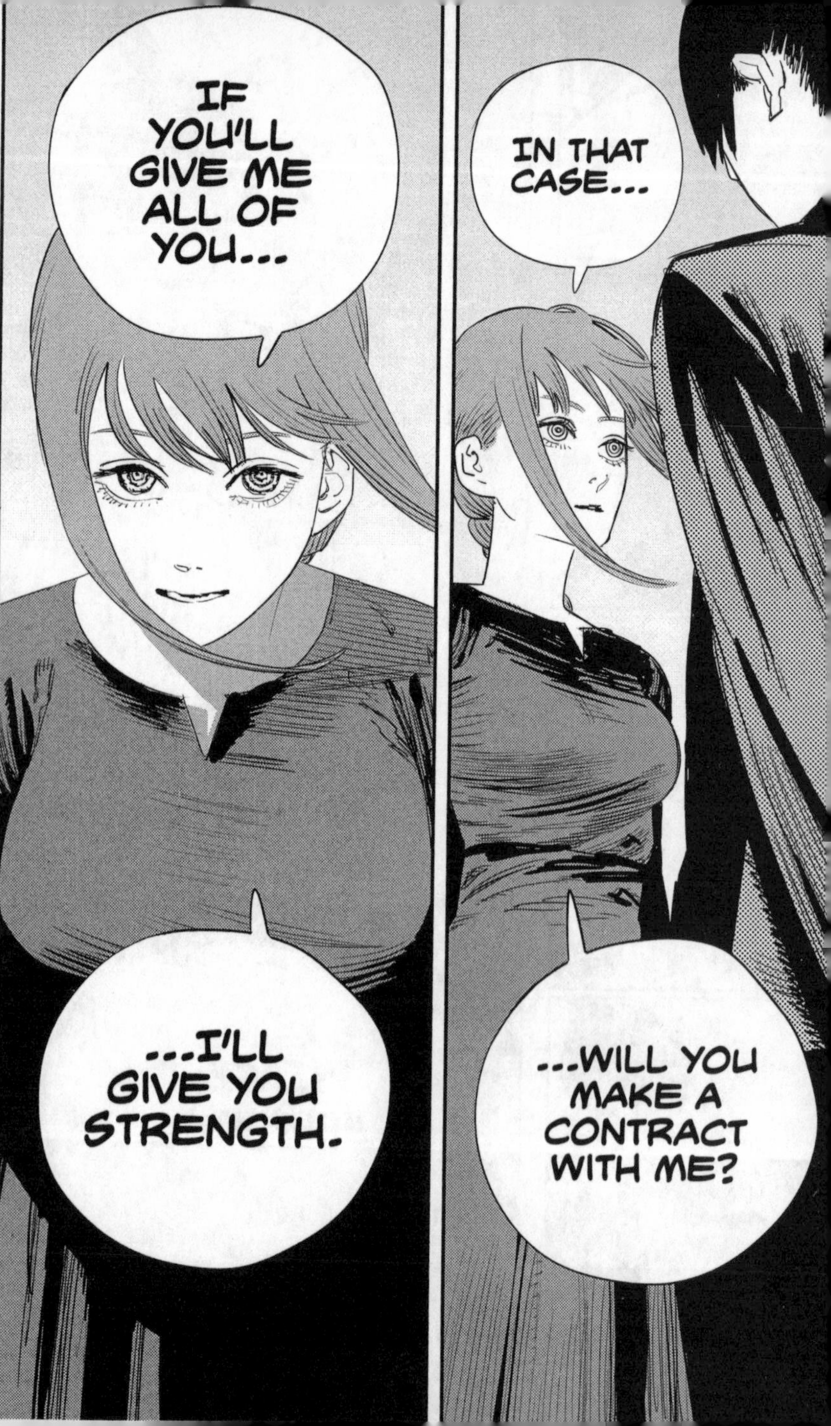
IN THAT CASE...
...WILL YOU MAKE A CONTRACT WITH ME?
IF YOU'LL GIVE ME ALL OF YOU...
...I'LL GIVE YOU STRENGTH.

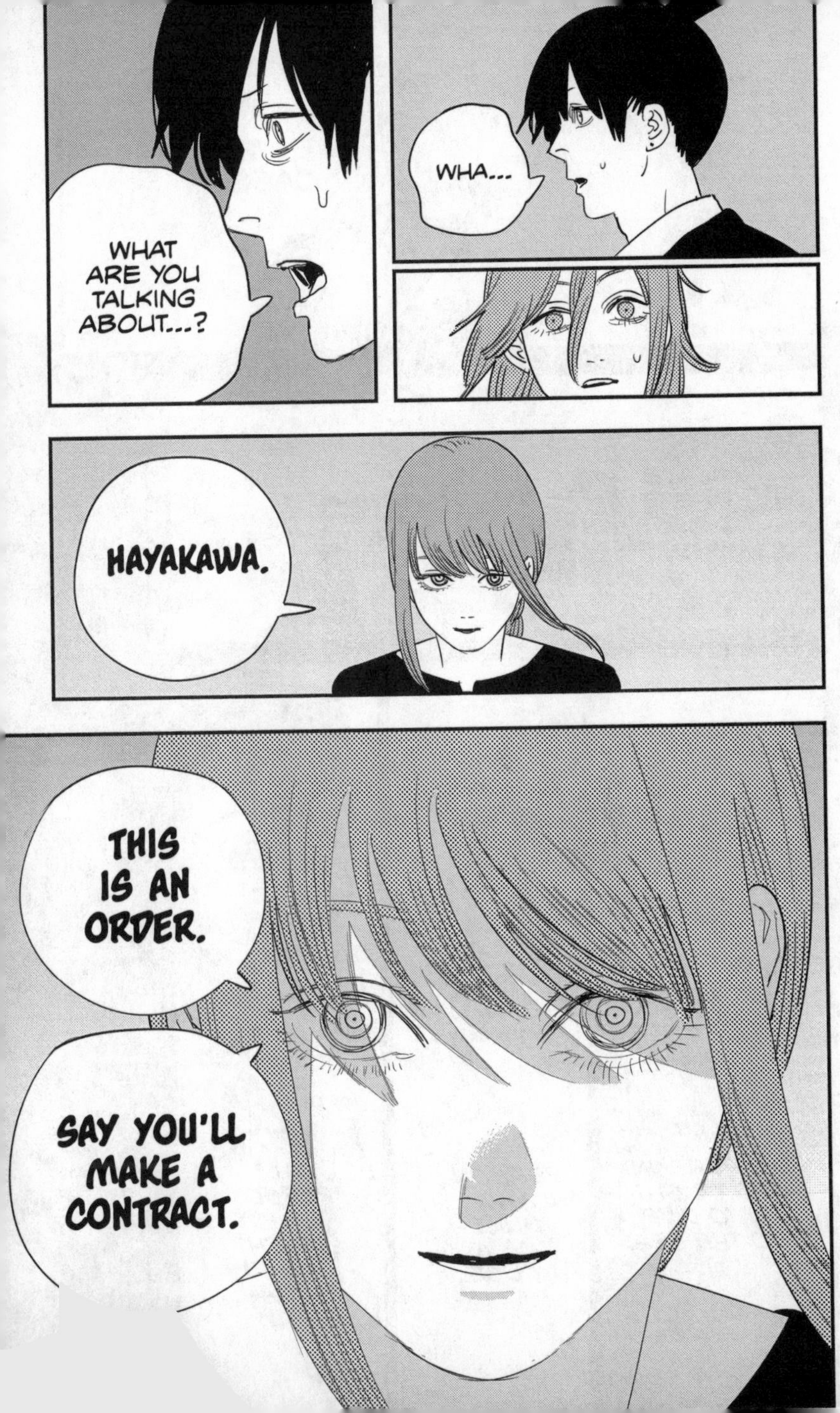
WHA...
WHAT ARE YOU TALKING ABOUT...?
HAYAKAWA.
THIS IS AN ORDER.
SAY YOU'LL MAKE A CONTRACT.

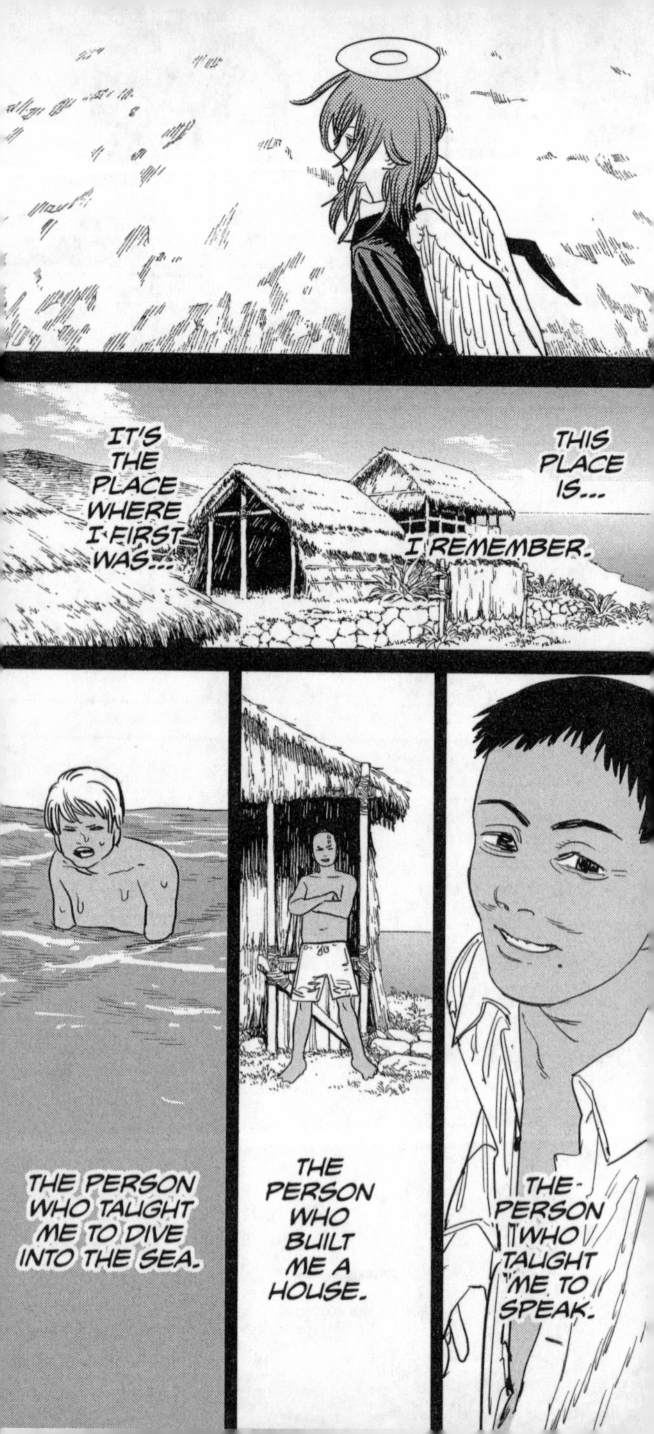
THIS PLACE IS...
I REMEMBER.
IT'S THE PLACE WHERE I FIRST WAS...
THE PERSON WHO TAUGHT ME TO SPEAK.
THE PERSON WHO BUILT ME A HOUSE.
THE PERSON WHO TAUGHT ME TO DIVE INTO THE SEA.

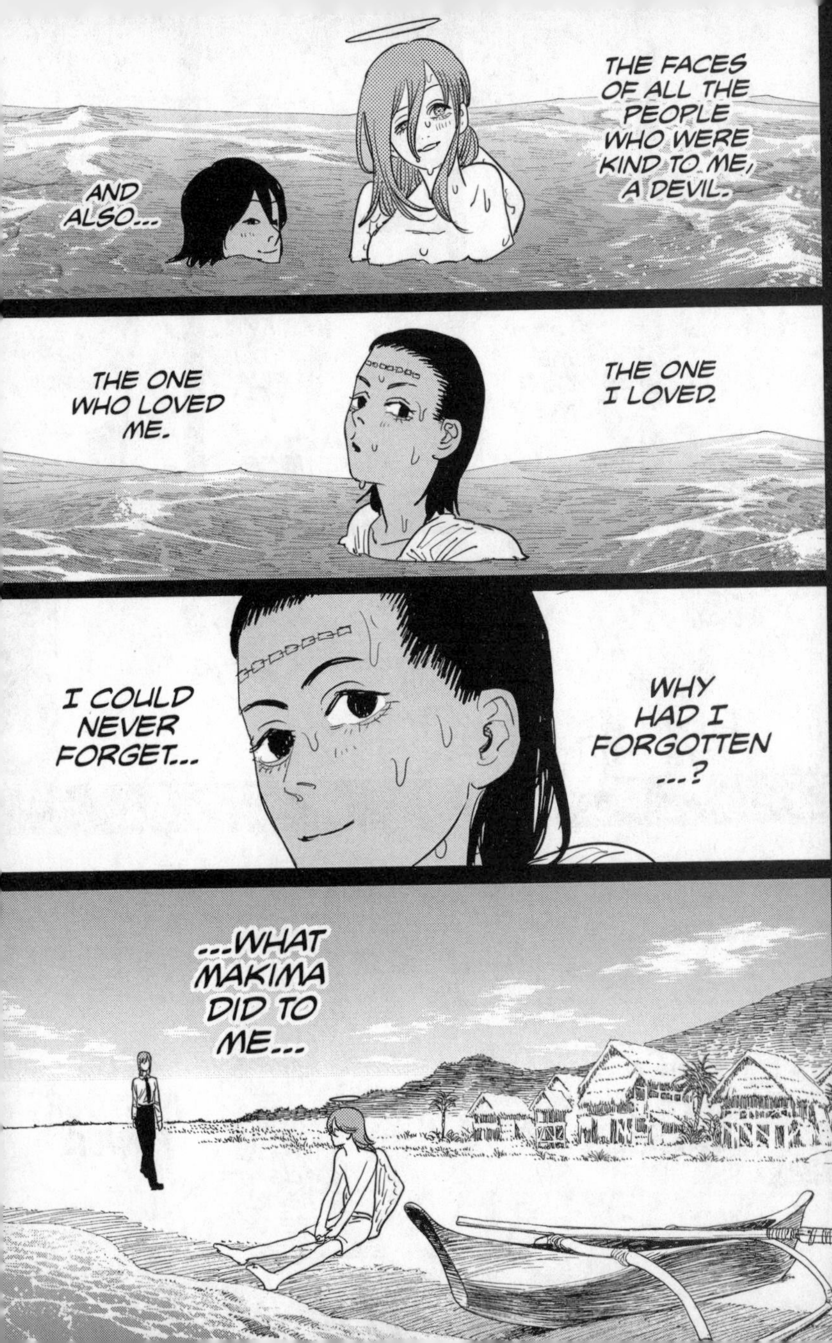
THE FACES OF ALL THE PEOPLE WHO WERE KIND TO ME, A DEVIL.
AND ALSO...
THE ONE I LOVED.
THE ONE WHO LOVED ME.
WHY HAD I FORGOTTEN ...?
I COULD NEVER FORGET...
...WHAT MAKIMA DID TO ME...

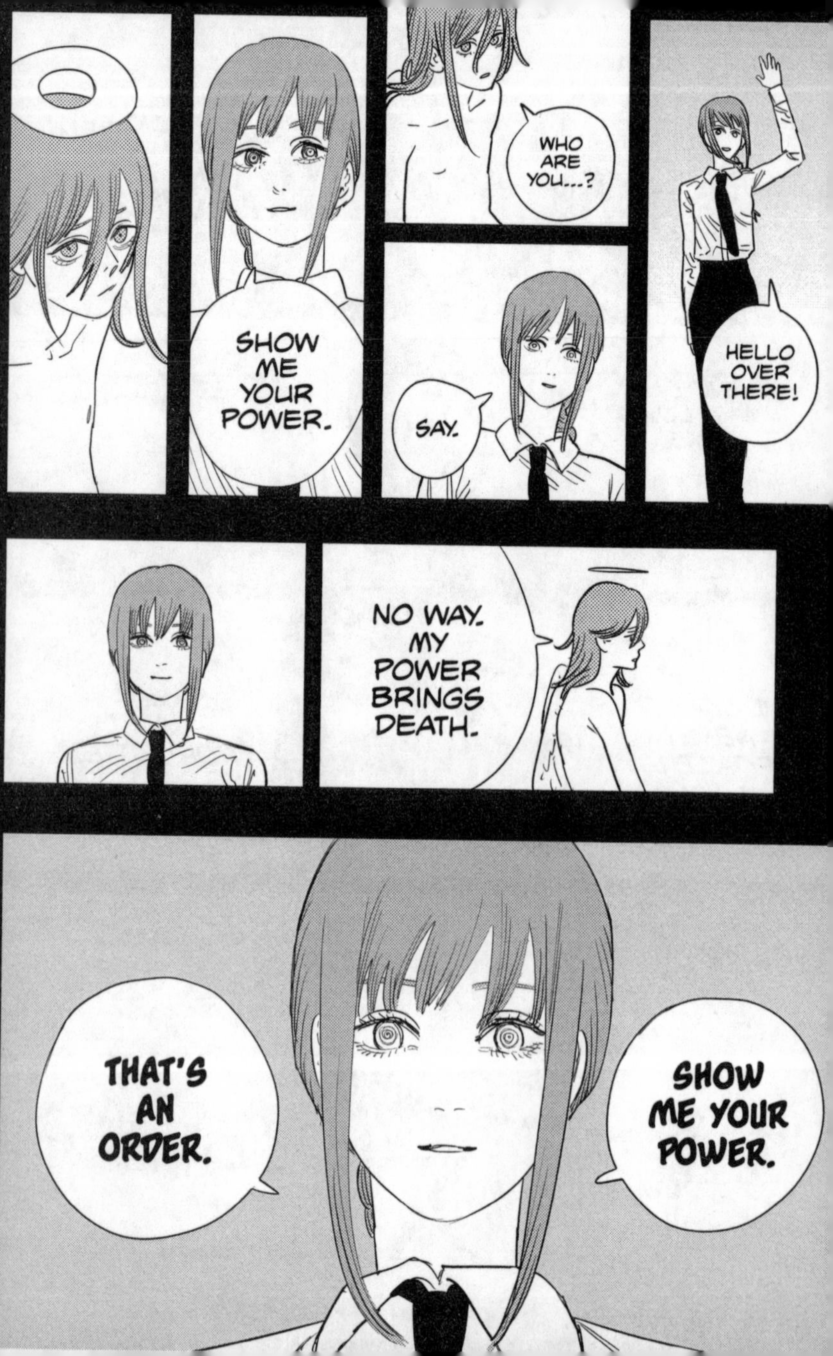
HELLO OVER THERE!
WHO ARE YOU...?
SAY.
SHOW ME YOUR POWER.
NO WAY. MY POWER BRINGS DEATH.
SHOW ME YOUR POWER.
THAT'S AN ORDER.

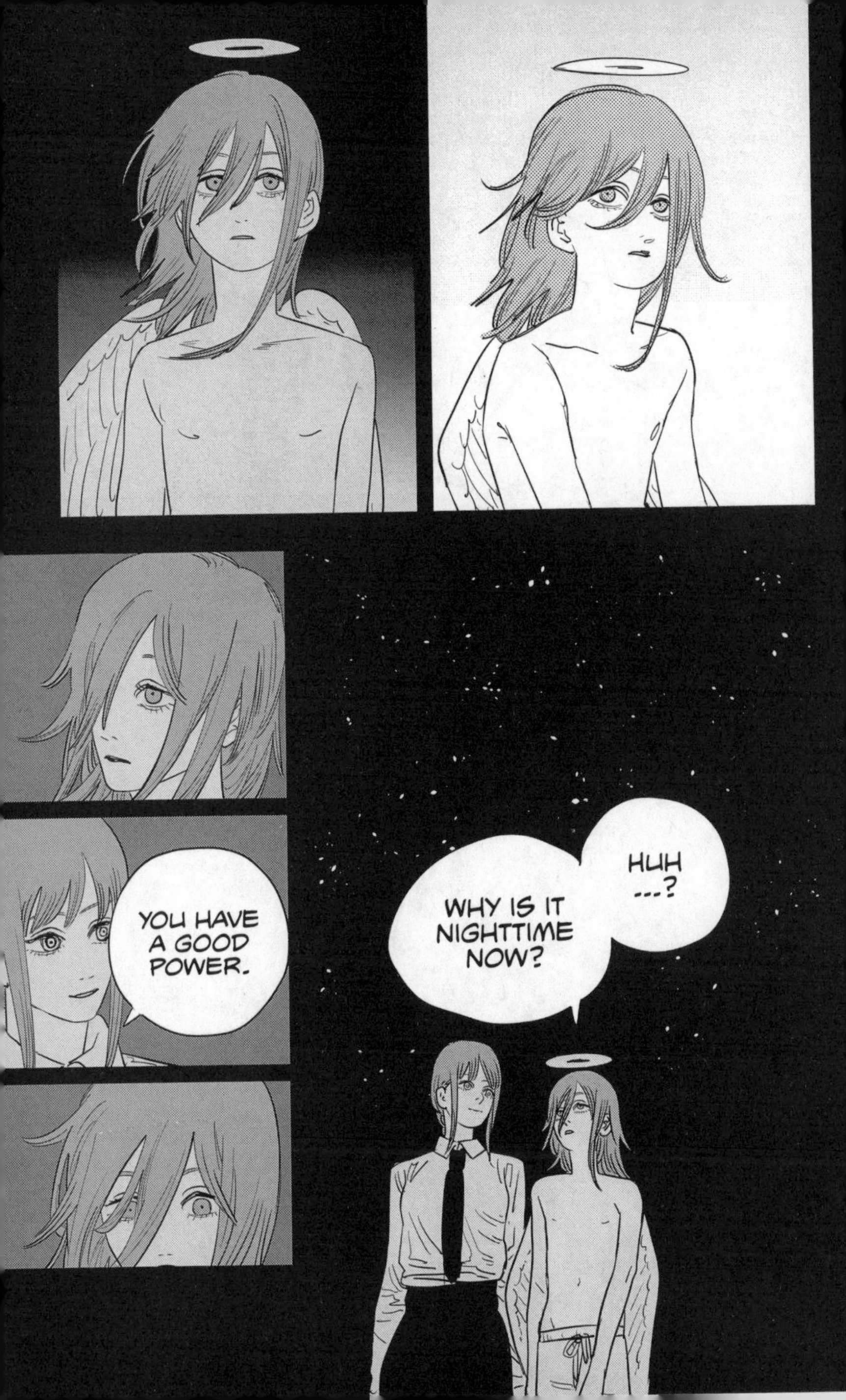
HUH ...?
WHY IS IT NIGHTTIME NOW?
YOU HAVE A GOOD POWER.

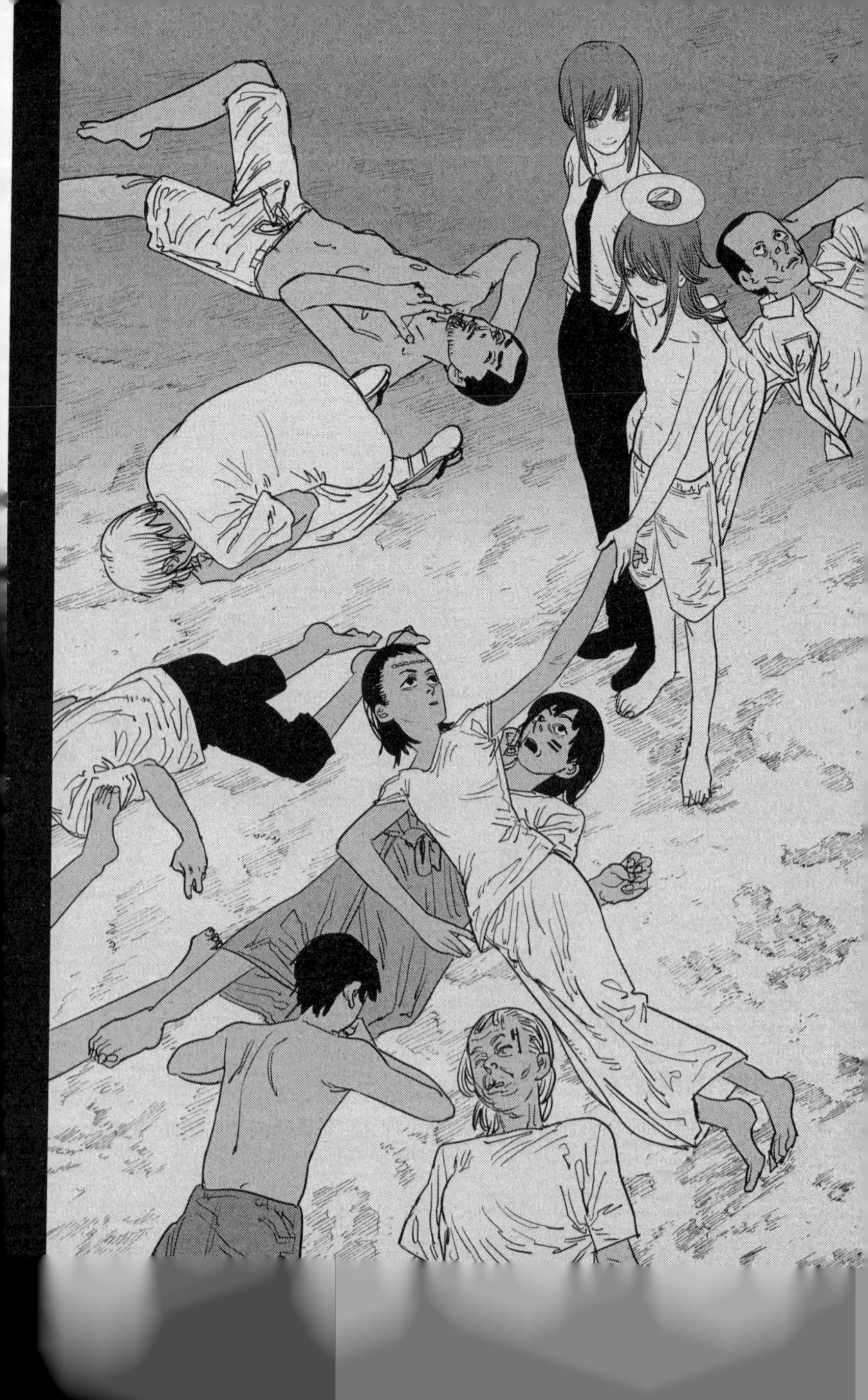

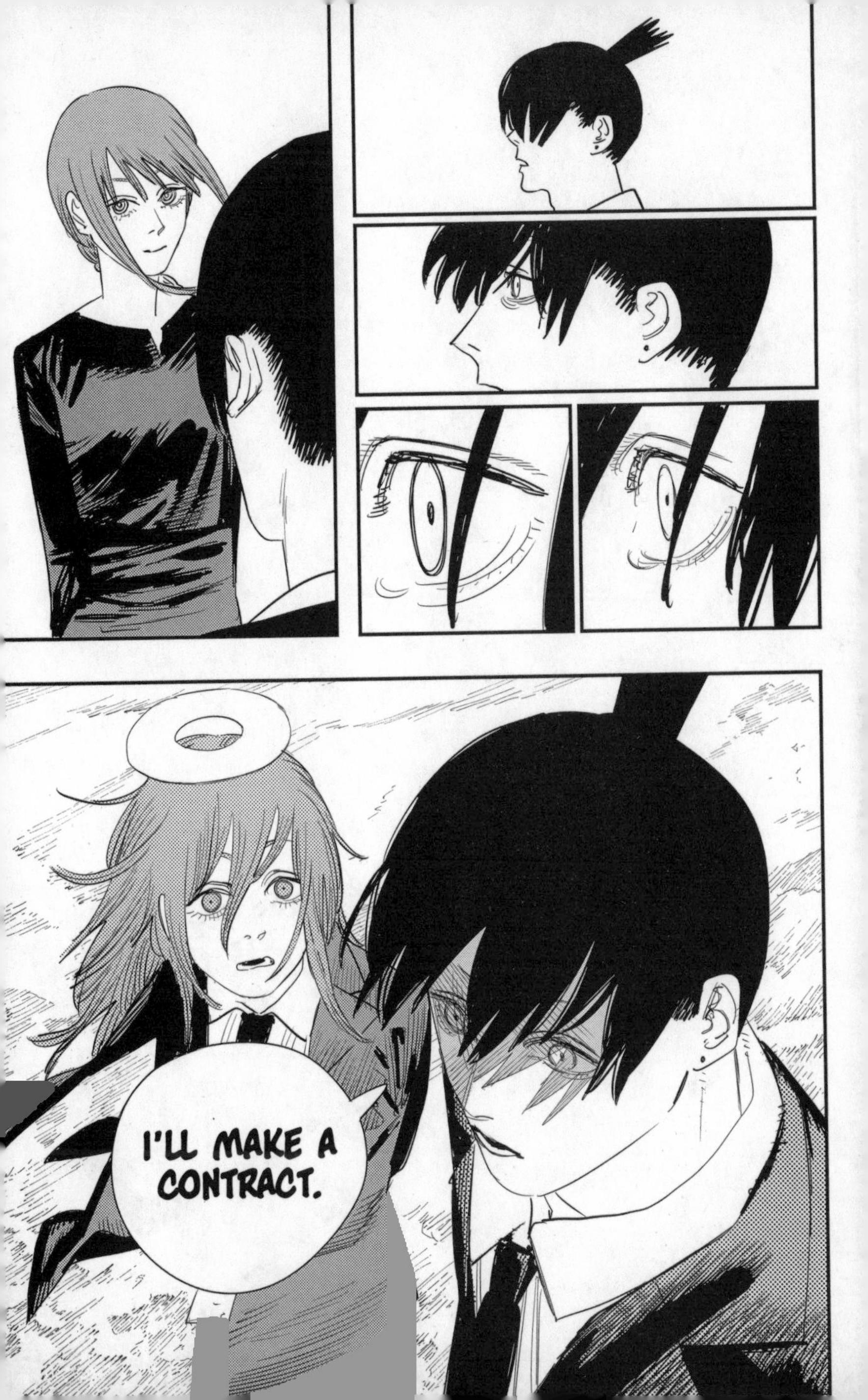
I'LL MAKE A CONTRACT.

chain saw man

Chapter 75: 9.12

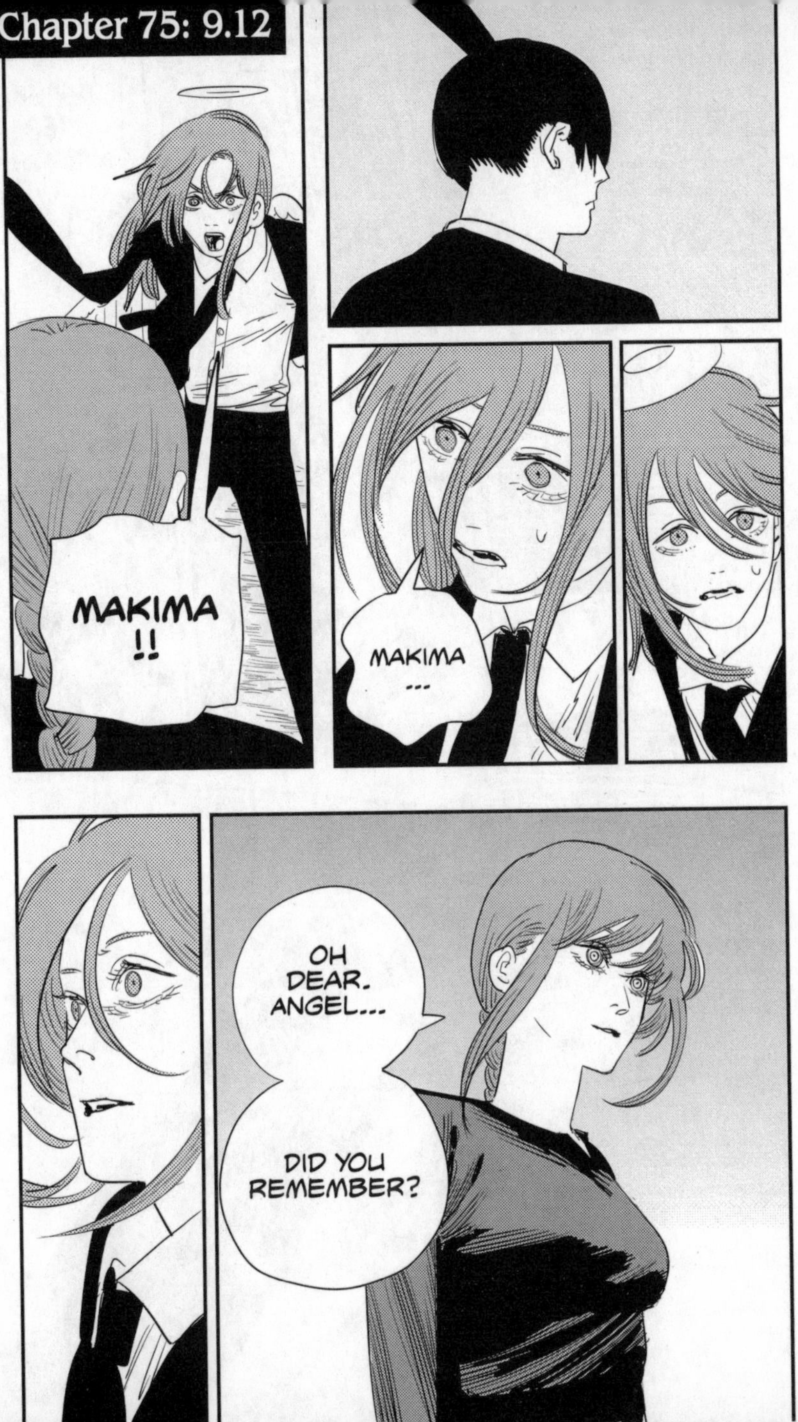
MAKIMA ...
MAKIMA !!
OH DEAR. ANGEL...
DID YOU REMEMBER?

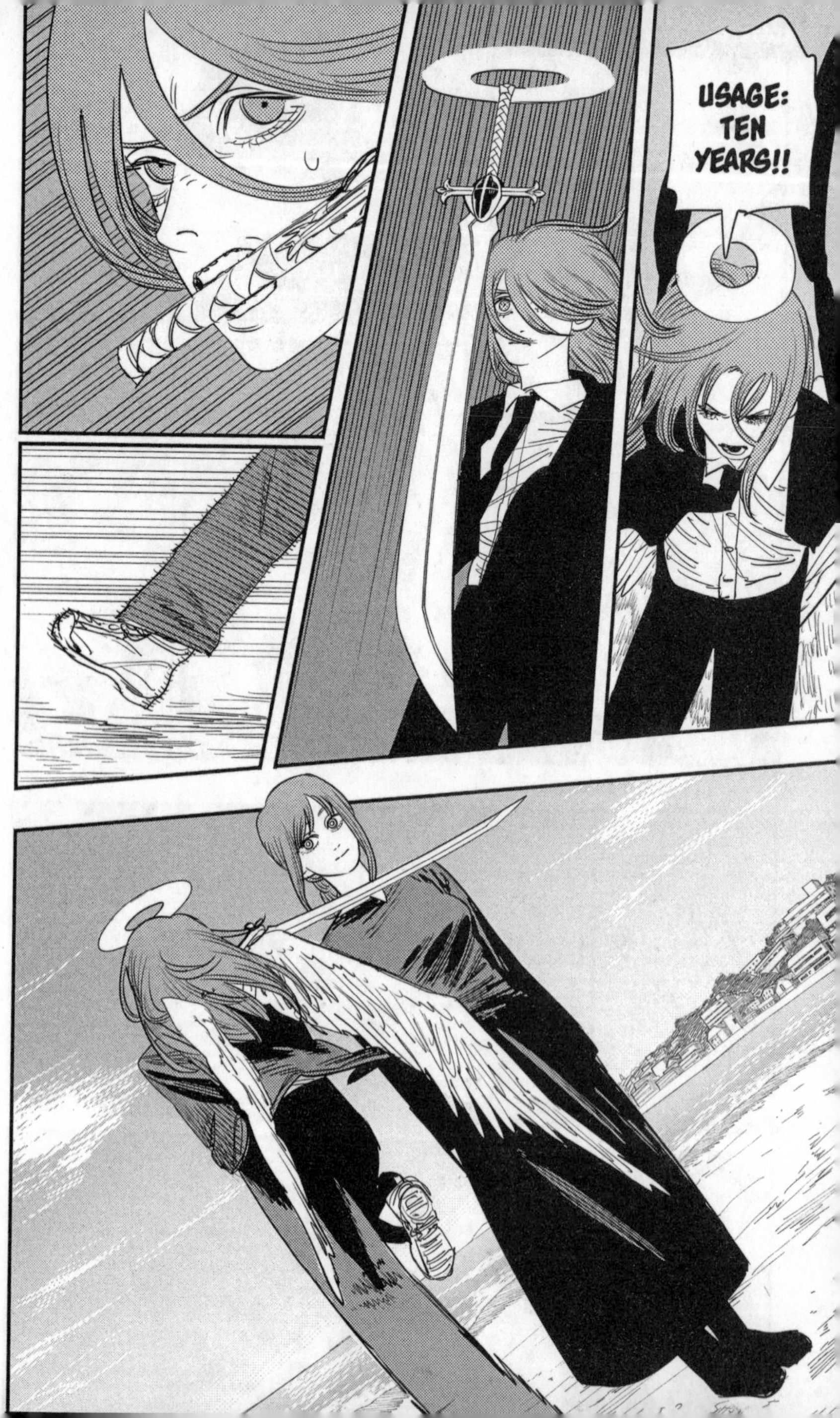
USAGE: TEN YEARS!!

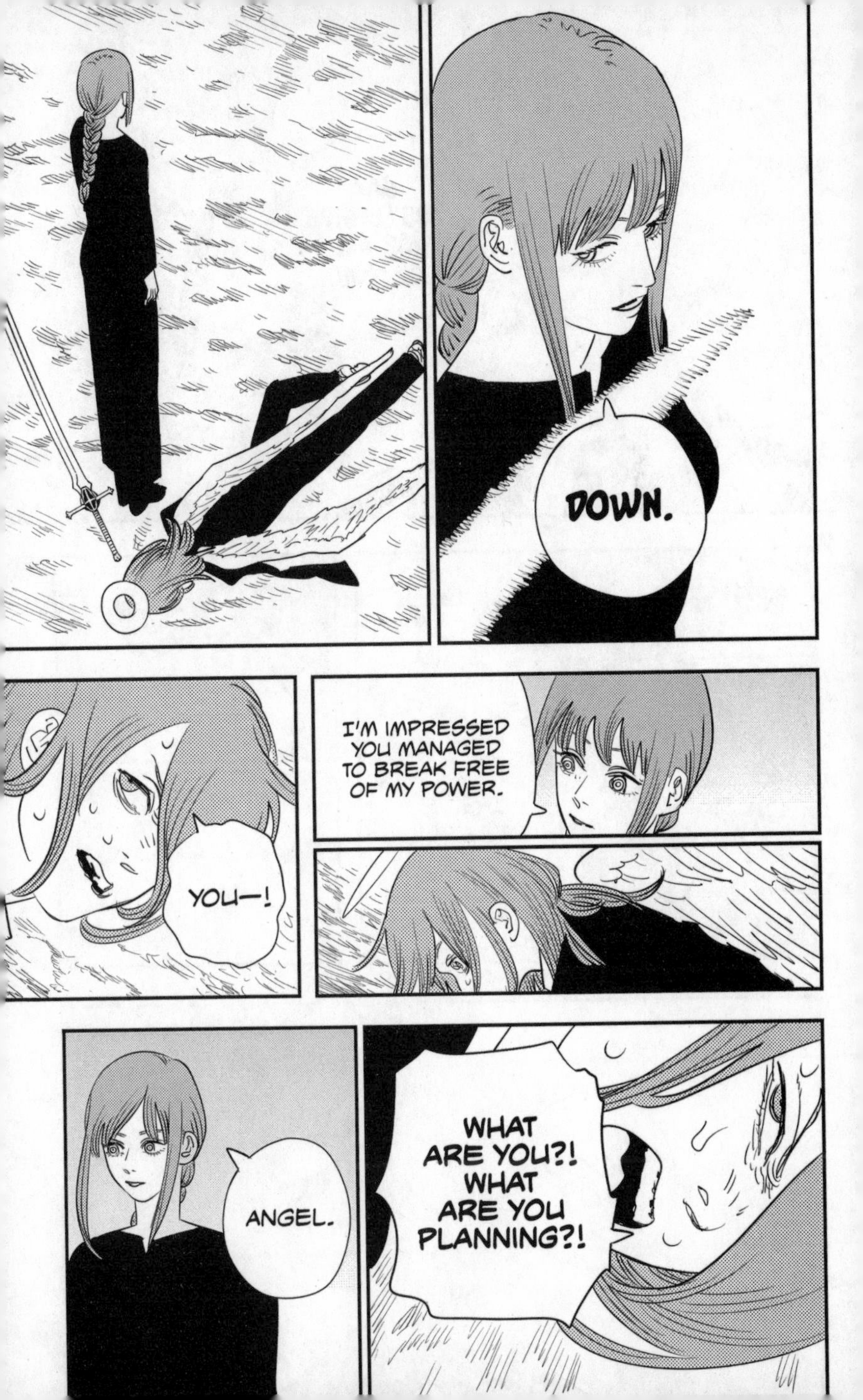
DOWN.
I'M IMPRESSED YOU MANAGED TO BREAK FREE OF MY POWER.
YOU—!
WHAT ARE YOU?! WHAT ARE YOU PLANNING?!
ANGEL.

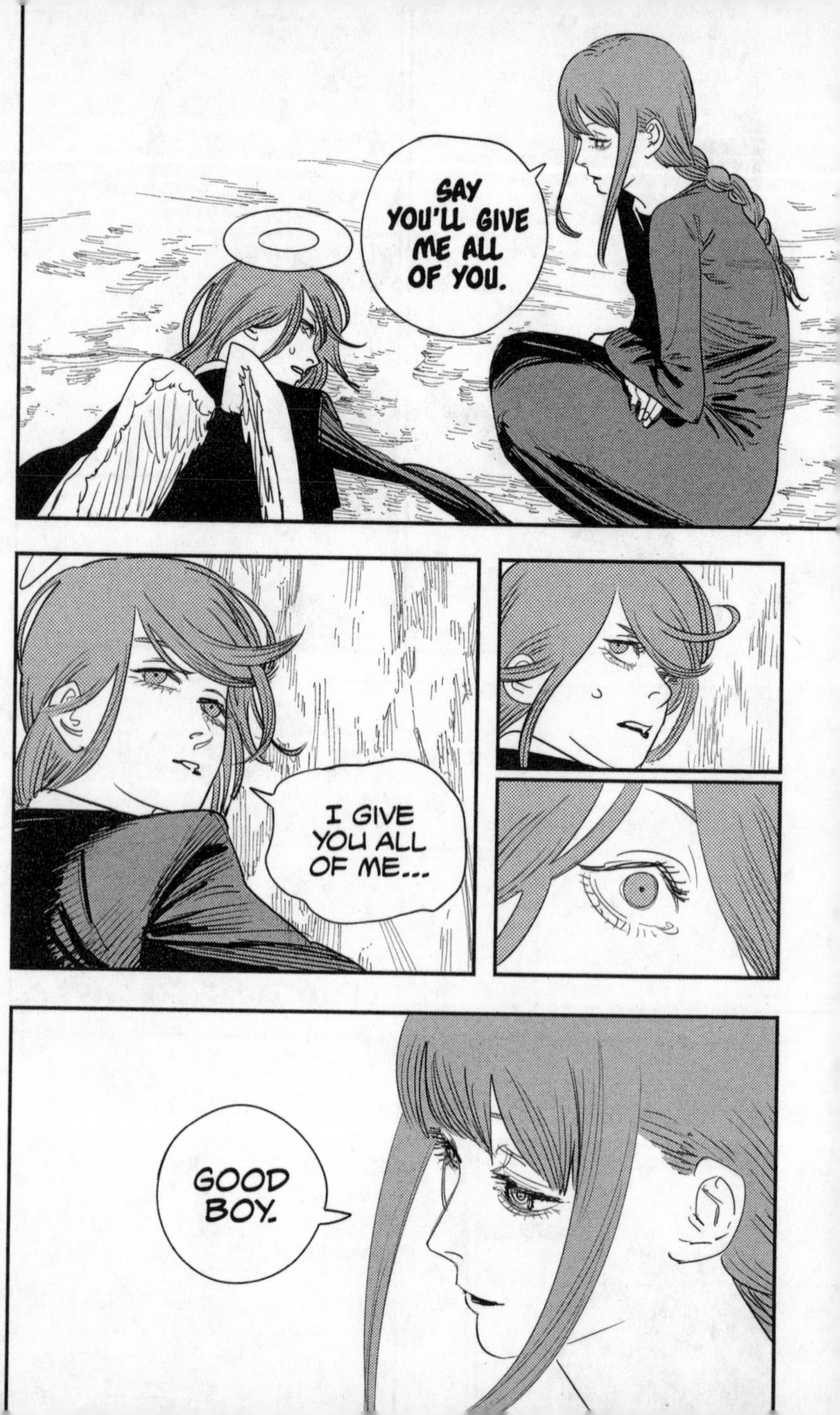
SAY YOU'LL GIVE ME ALL OF YOU.
I GIVE YOU ALL OF ME...
GOOD BOY.

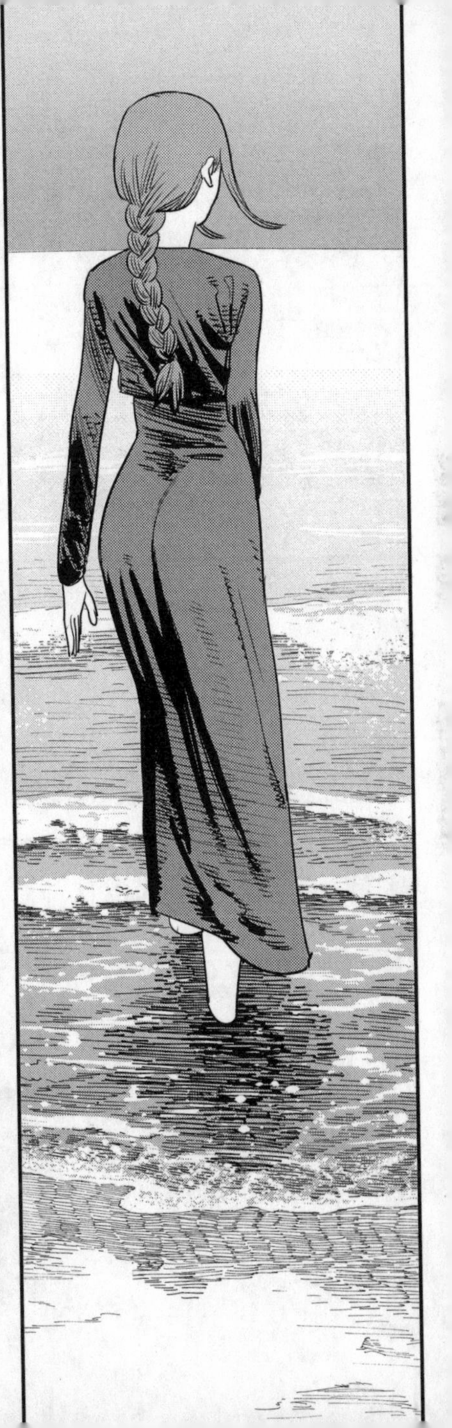

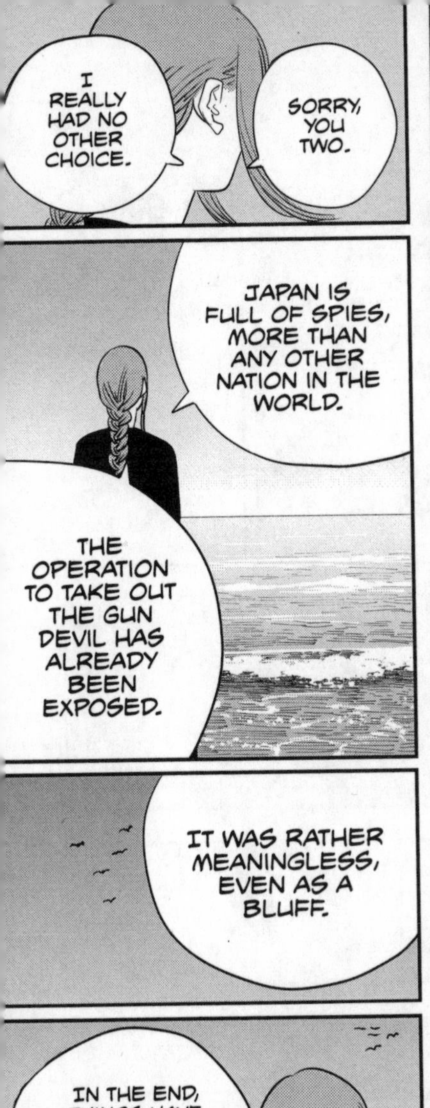
SORRY, YOU TWO.
I REALLY HAD NO OTHER CHOICE.
JAPAN IS FULL OF SPIES, MORE THAN ANY OTHER NATION IN THE WORLD.
THE OPERATION TO TAKE OUT THE GUN DEVIL HAS ALREADY BEEN EXPOSED.
IT WAS RATHER MEANINGLESS, EVEN AS A BLUFF.
IN THE END, THINGS HAVE TAKEN THE COURSE THAT WILL CAUSE THE GREATEST DAMAGE. THAT'S UNFORTUNATE.

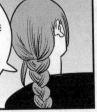

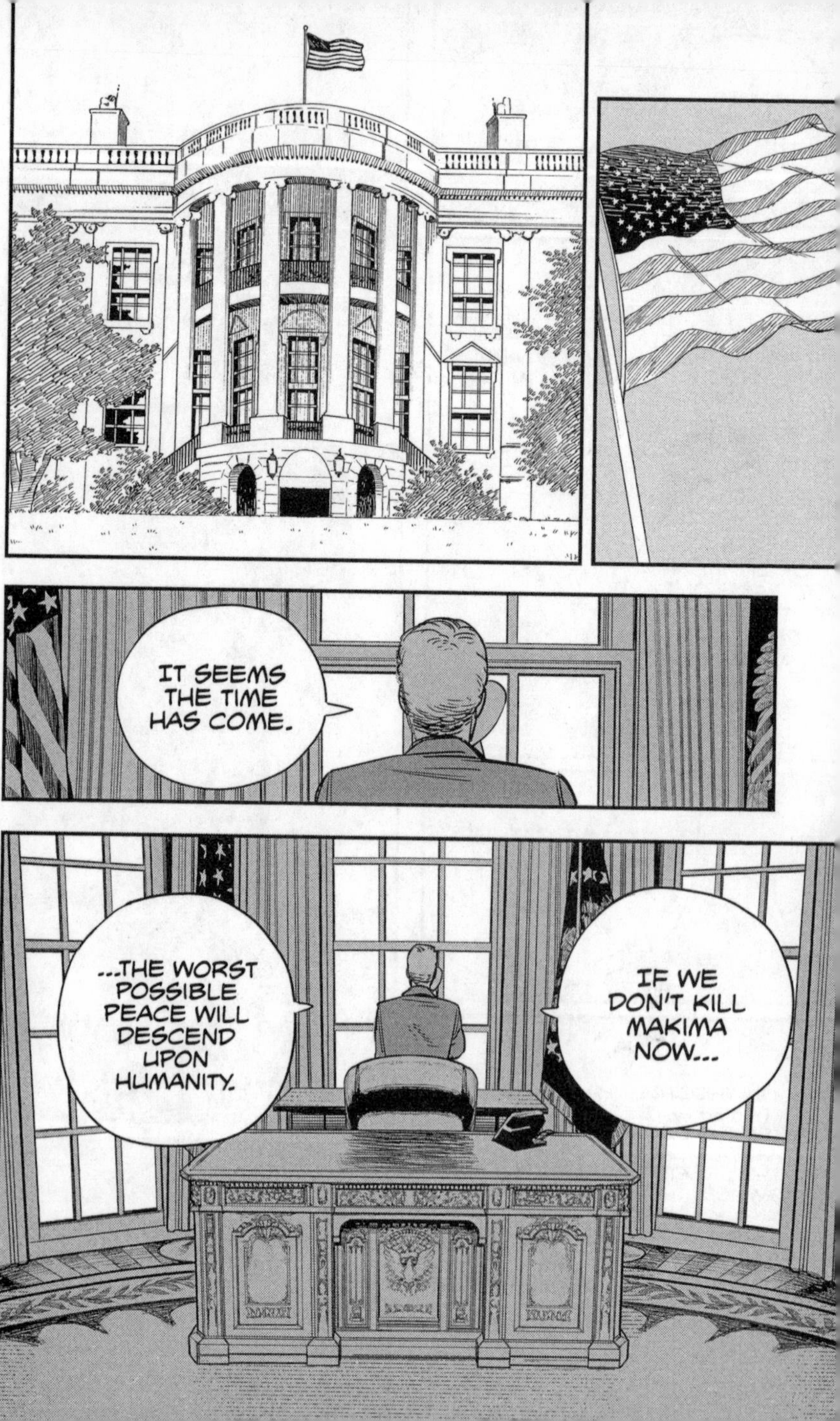
IT SEEMS THE TIME HAS COME.
IF WE DON'T KILL MAKIMA NOW...
...THE WORST POSSIBLE PEACE WILL DESCEND UPON HUMANITY.

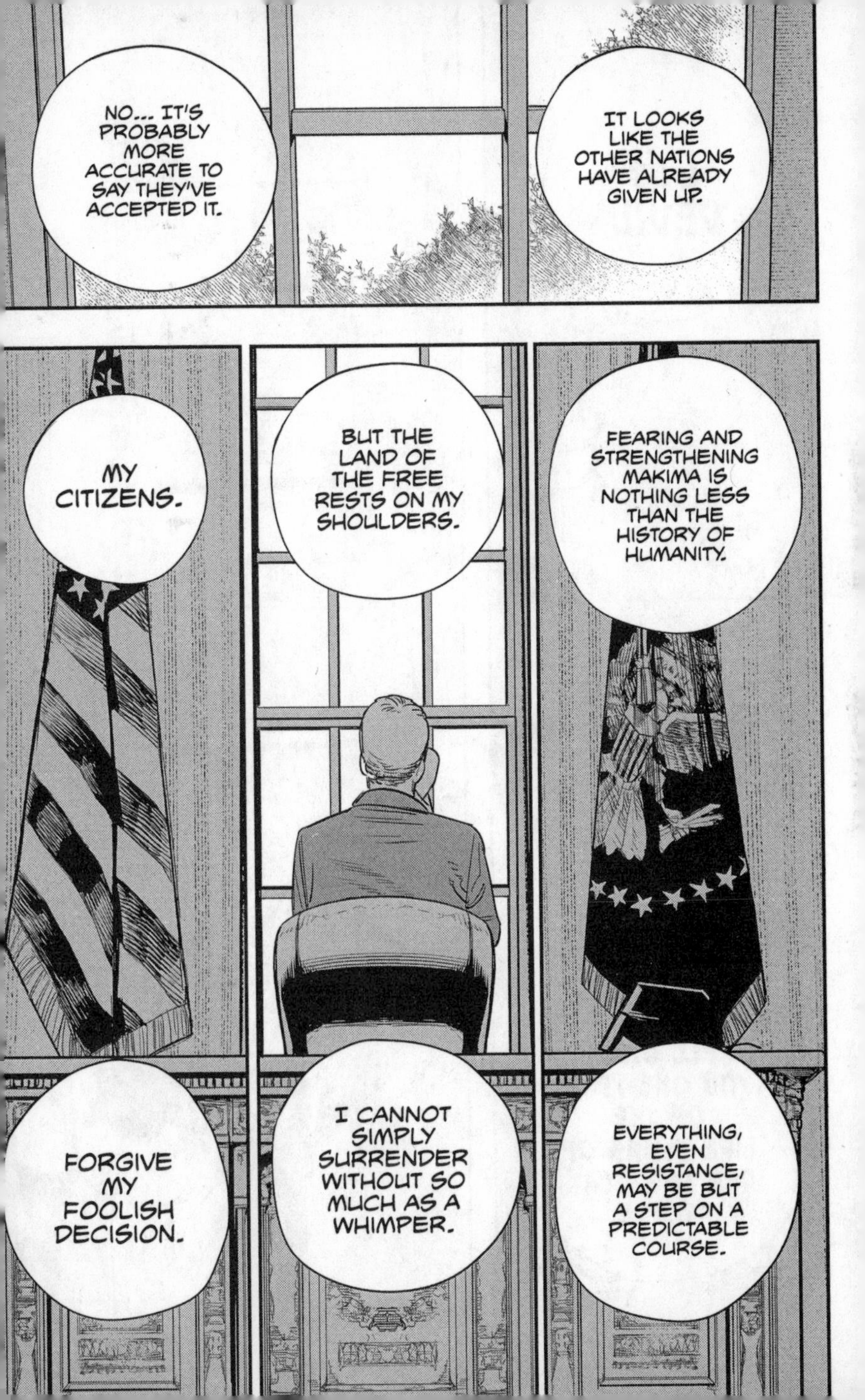
IT LOOKS LIKE THE OTHER NATIONS HAVE ALREADY GIVEN UP.
NO... IT'S PROBABLY MORE ACCURATE TO SAY THEY'VE ACCEPTED IT.
FEARING AND STRENGTHENING MAKIMA IS NOTHING LESS THAN THE HISTORY OF HUMANITY.
EVERYTHING, EVEN RESISTANCE, MAY BE BUT A STEP ON A PREDICTABLE COURSE.
BUT THE LAND OF THE FREE RESTS ON MY SHOULDERS.
I CANNOT SIMPLY SURRENDER WITHOUT SO MUCH AS A WHIMPER.
MY CITIZENS.
FORGIVE MY FOOLISH DECISION.

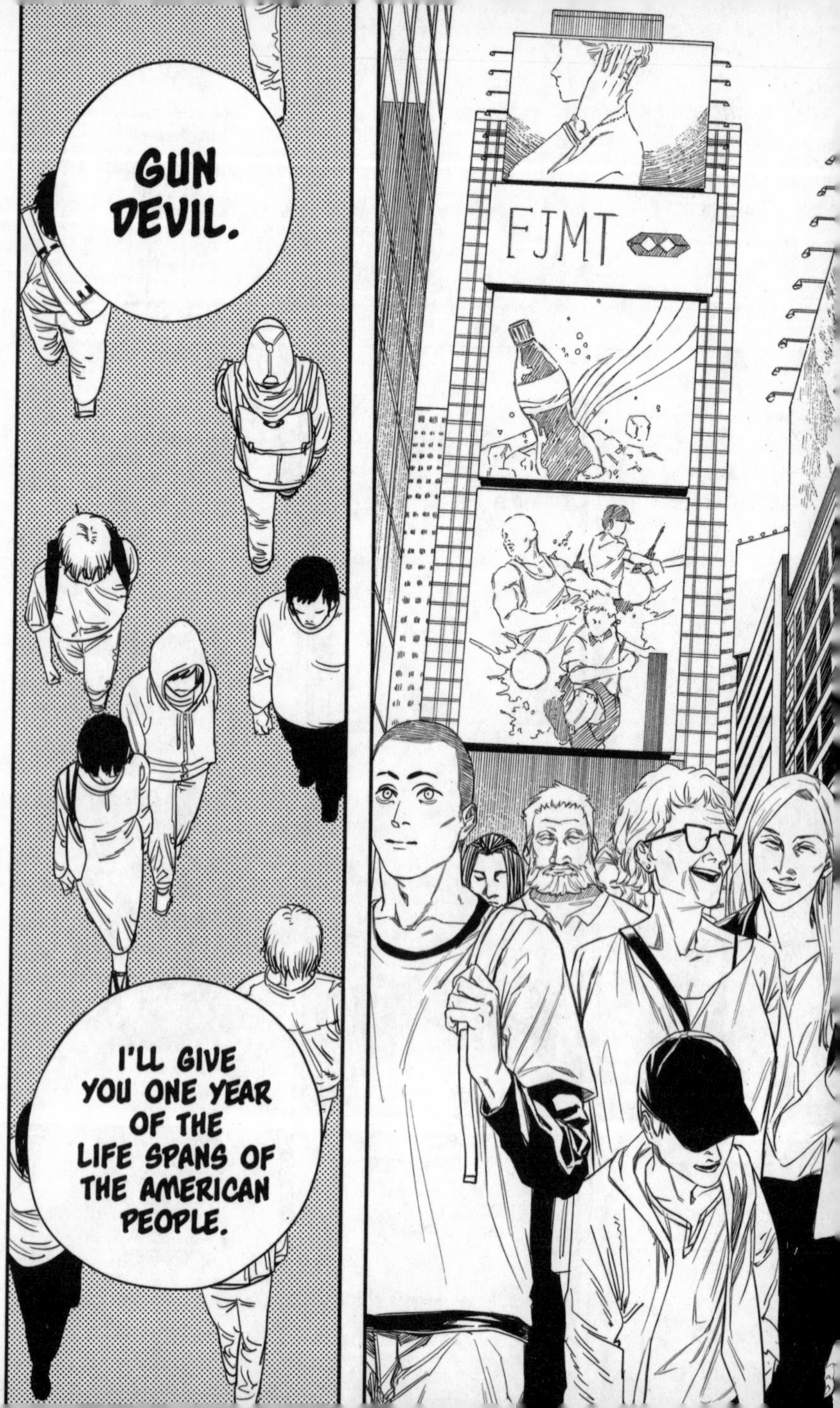
FJMT
GUN DEVIL.
I'LL GIVE YOU ONE YEAR OF THE LIFE SPANS OF THE AMERICAN PEOPLE.

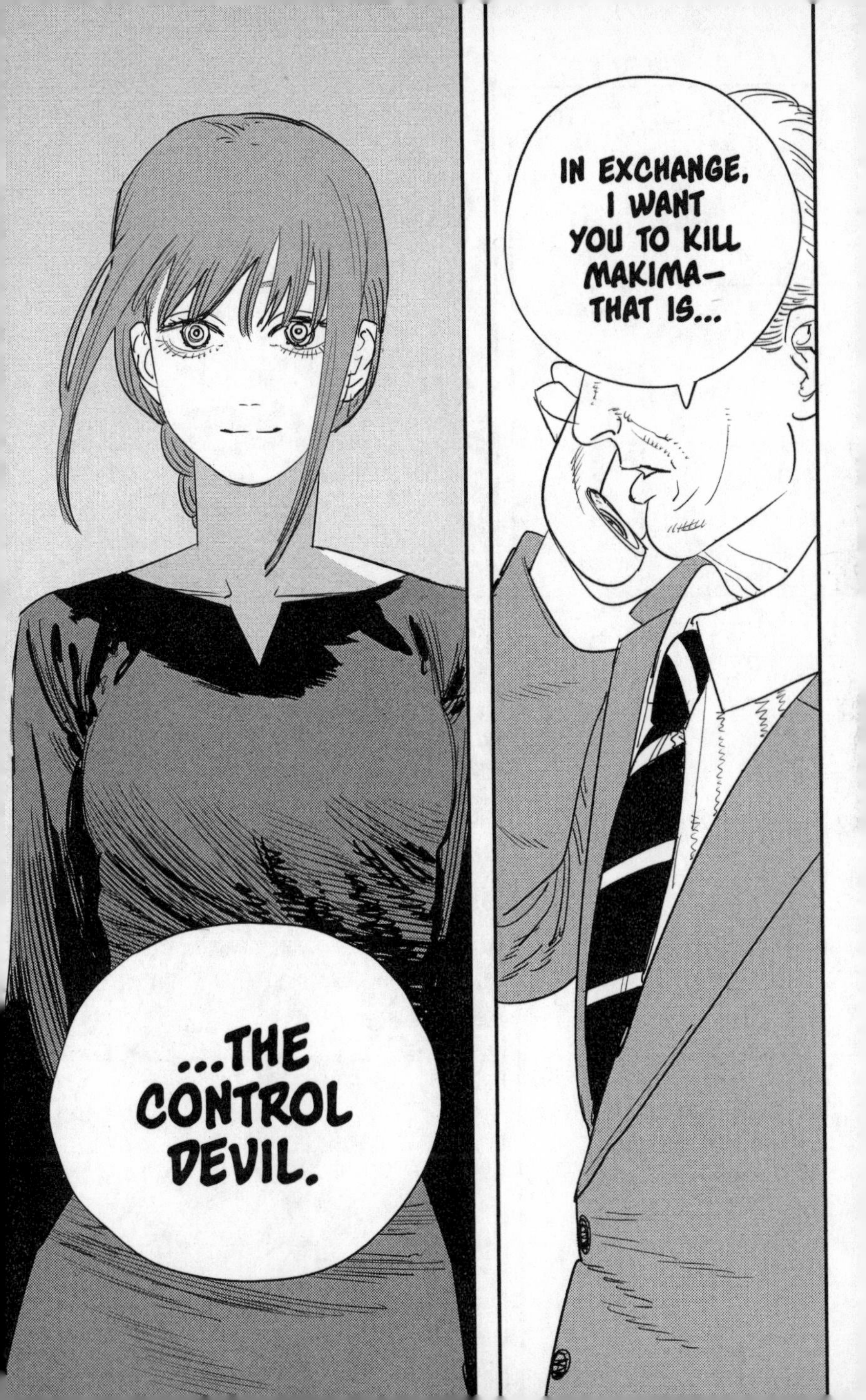
IN EXCHANGE, I WANT YOU TO KILL MAKIMA— THAT IS...
...THE CONTROL DEVIL.

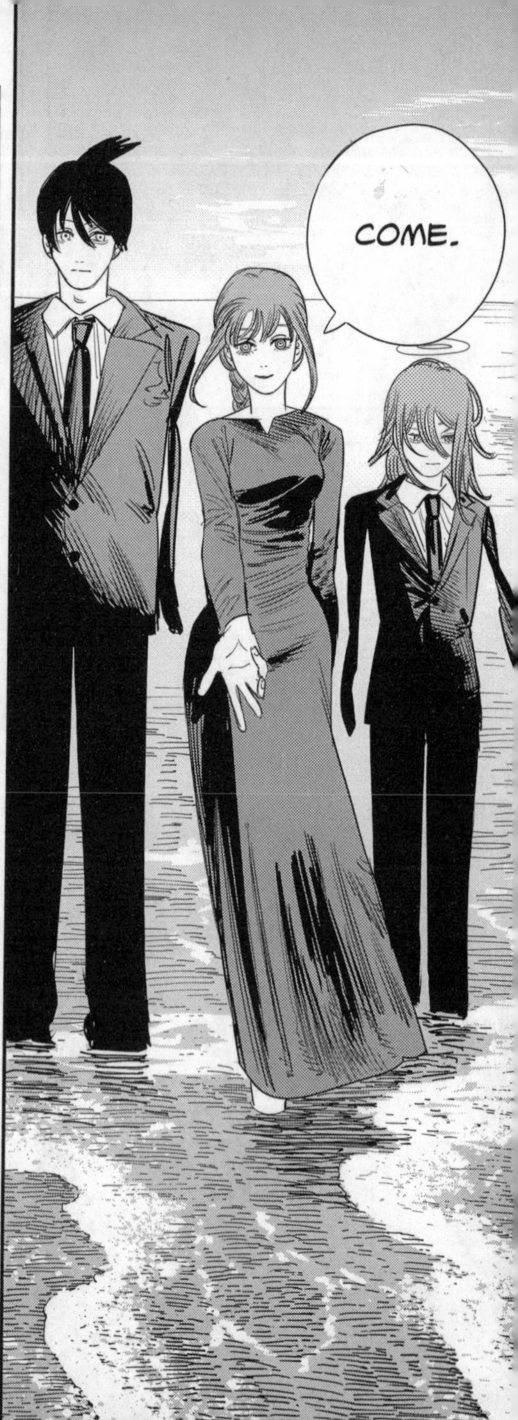
COME.
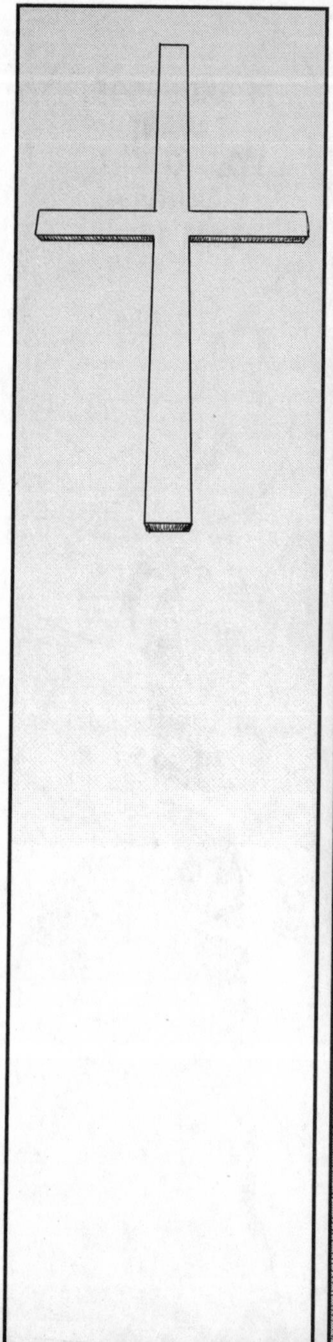

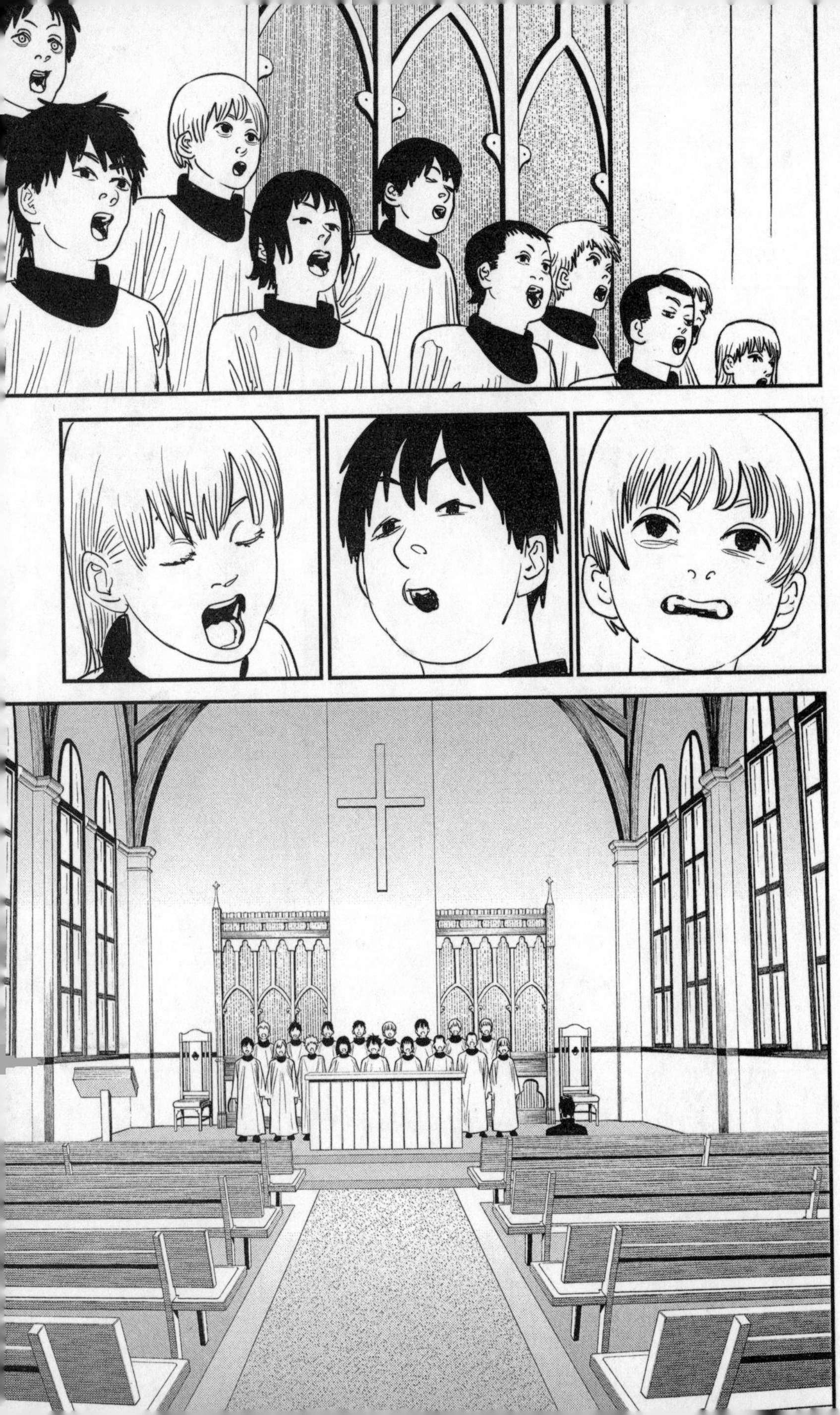

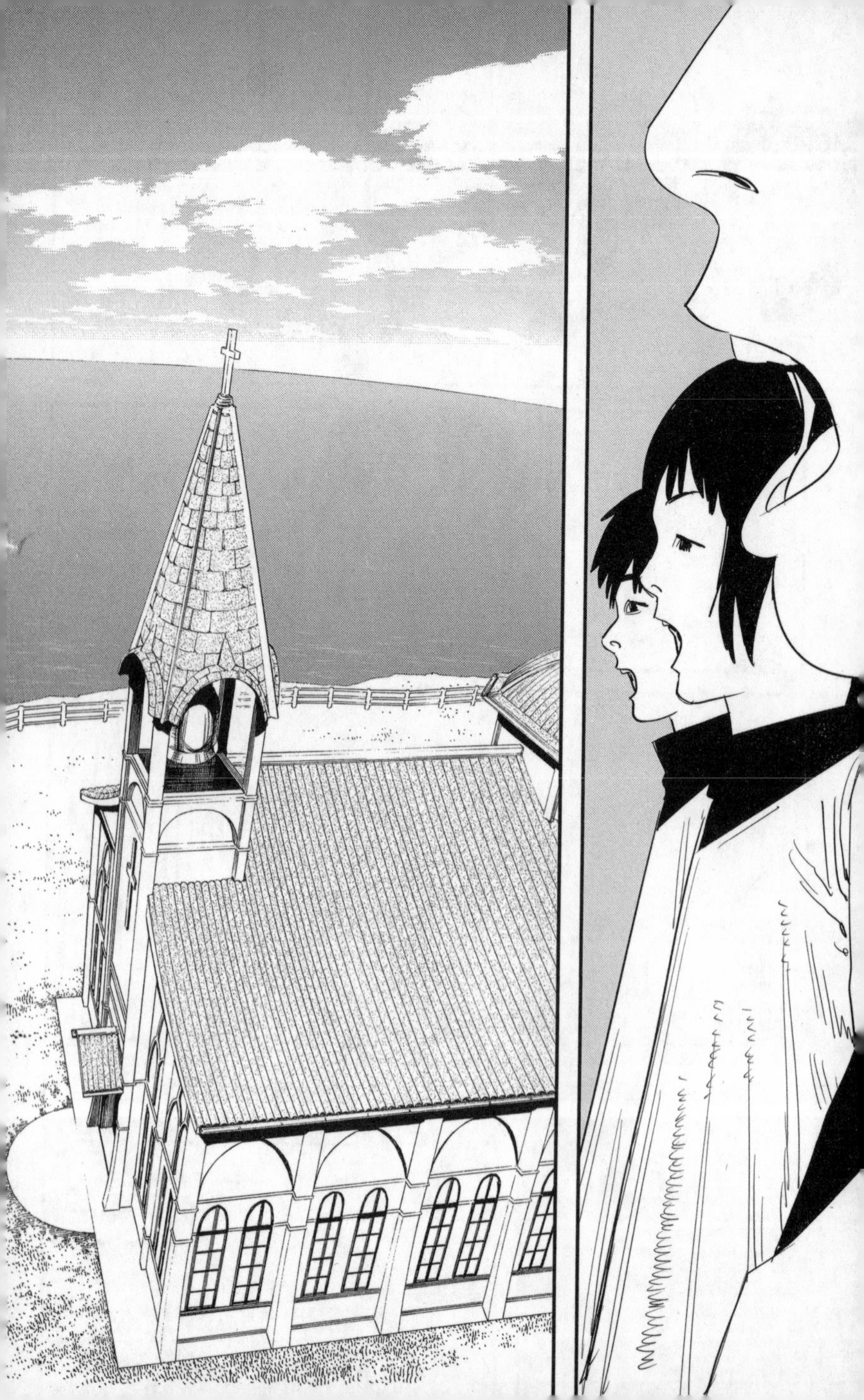

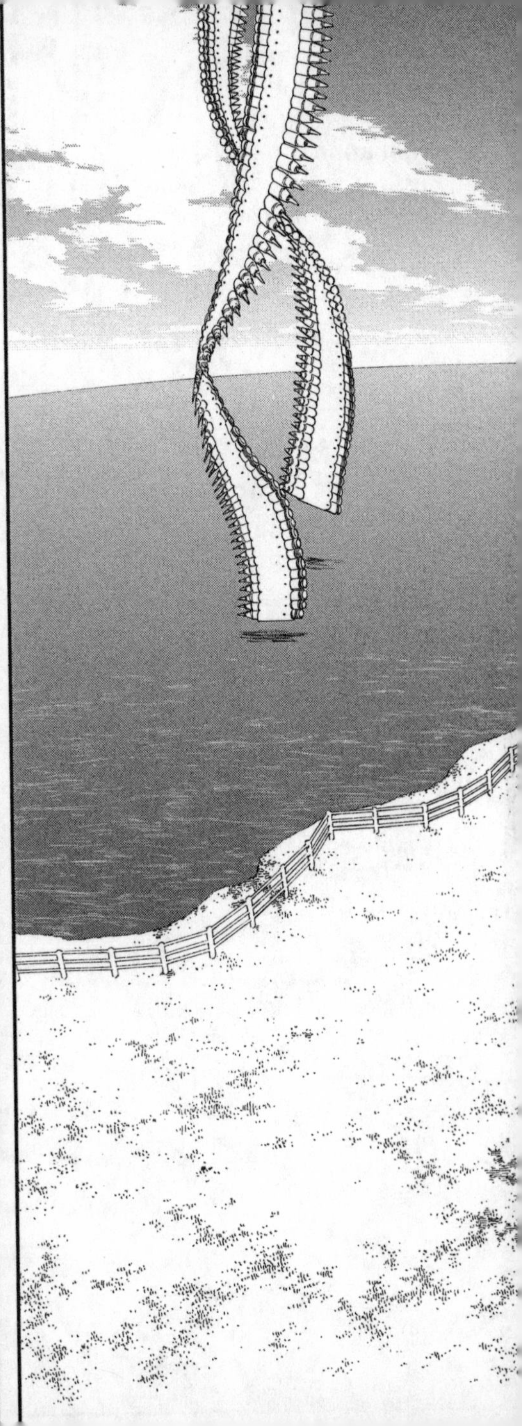

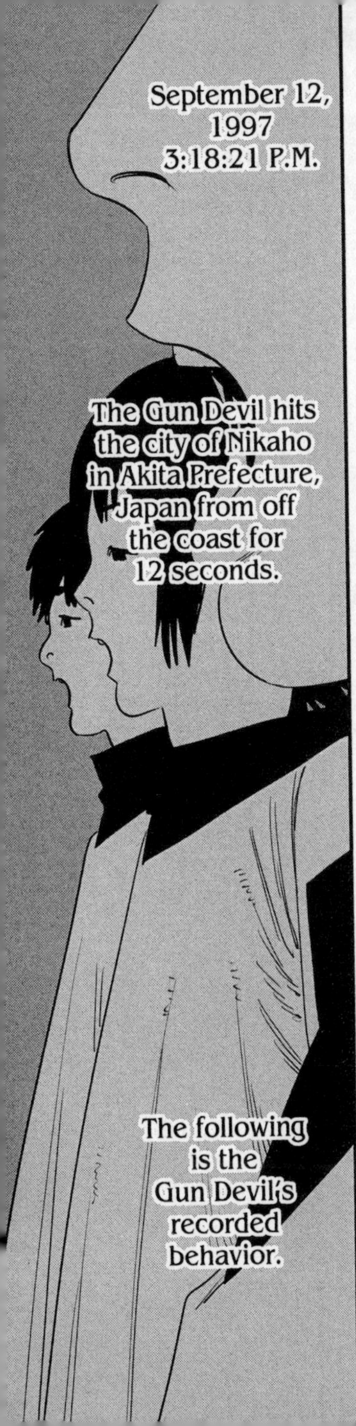
September 12, 1997 3:18:21 P.M.
The Gun Devil hits the city of Nikaho in Akita Prefecture, Japan from off the coast for 12 seconds.
The following is the Gun Devil's recorded behavior.

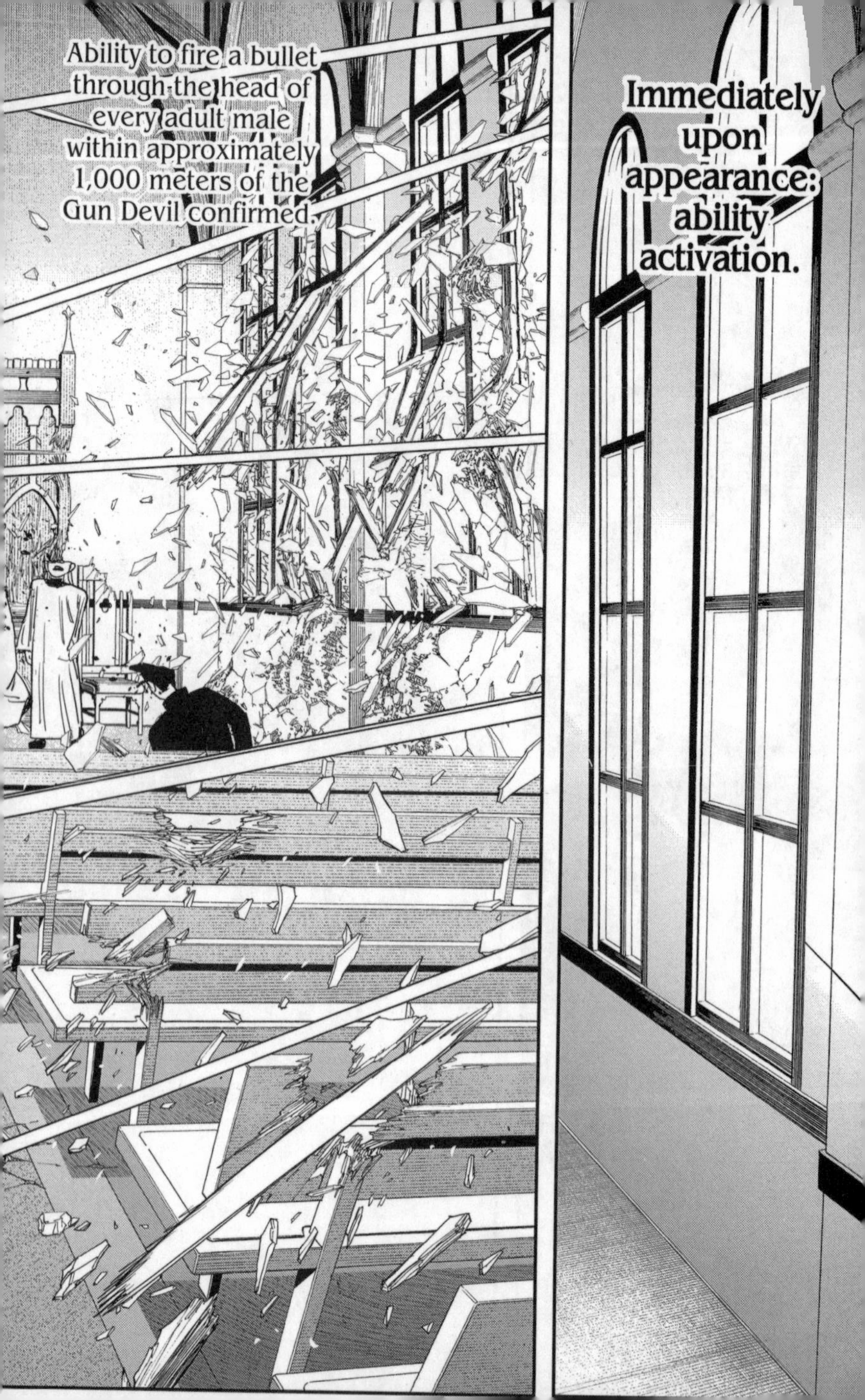
Immediately upon appearance: ability activation.
Ability to fire a bullet through the head of every adult male within approximately 1,000 meters of the Gun Devil confirmed.

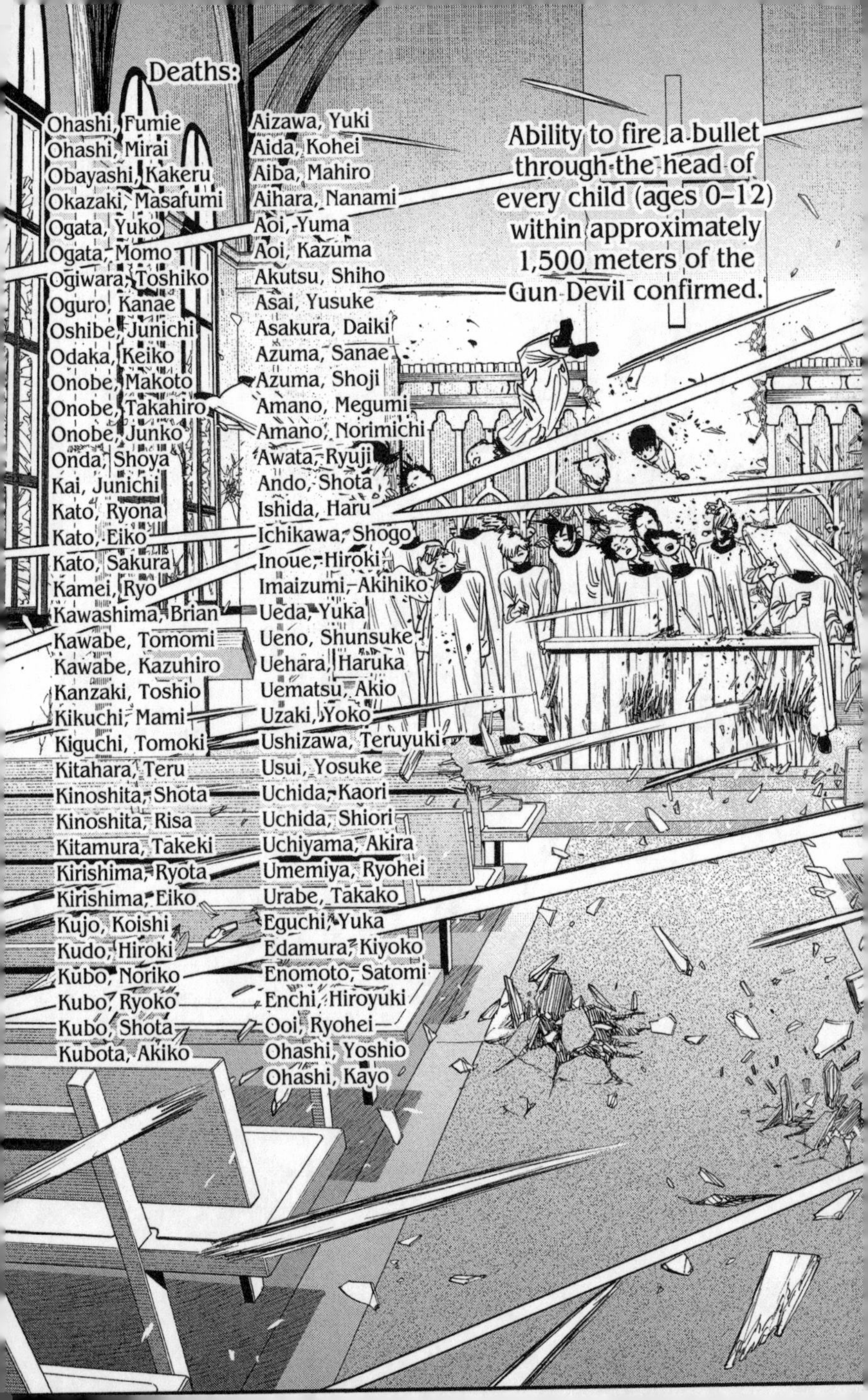
Ability to fire a bullet through the head of every child (ages 0–12) within approximately 1,500 meters of the Gun Devil confirmed.
Deaths:
Aizawa, Yuki
Aida, Kohei
Aiba, Mahiro
Aihara, Nanami
Aoi, Yuma
Aoi, Kazuma
Akutsu, Shiho
Asai, Yusuke
Asakura, Daiki
Azuma, Sanae
Azuma, Shoji
Amano, Megumi
Amano, Norimichi
Awata, Ryuji
Ando, Shota
Ishida, Haru
Ichikawa, Shogo
Inoue, Hiroki
Imaizumi, Akihiko
Ueda, Yuka
Ueno, Shunsuke
Uehara, Haruka
Uematsu, Akio
Uzaki, Yoko
Ushizawa, Teruyuki
Usui, Yosuke
Uchida, Kaori
Uchida, Shiori
Uchiyama, Akira
Umemiya, Ryohei
Urabe, Takako
Eguchi, Yuka
Edamura, Kiyoko
Enomoto, Satomi
Enchi, Hiroyuki
Ooi, Ryohei
Ohashi, Yoshio
Ohashi, Kayo
Ohashi, Fumie
Ohashi, Mirai
Obayashi, Kakeru
Okazaki, Masafumi
Ogata, Yuko
Ogata, Momo
Ogiwara, Toshiko
Oguro, Kanae
Oshibe, Junichi
Odaka, Keiko
Onobe, Makoto
Onobe, Takahiro
Onobe, Junko
Onda, Shoya
Kai, Junichi
Kato, Ryona
Kato, Eiko
Kato, Sakura
Kamei, Ryo
Kawashima, Brian
Kawabe, Tomomi
Kawabe, Kazuhiro
Kanzaki, Toshio
Kikuchi, Mami
Kiguchi, Tomoki
Kitahara, Teru
Kinoshita, Shota
Kinoshita, Risa
Kitamura, Takeki
Kirishima, Ryota
Kirishima, Eiko
Kujo, Koishi
Kudo, Hiroki
Kubo, Noriko
Kubo, Ryoko
Kubo, Shota
Kubota, Akiko

Kubota, Chizuru
Kumano, Kiyomichi
Kurashige, Sohei
Kurahashi, Meiko
Kurihara, Daisuke
Kurihara, Risa
Kurihara, Yukari
Keshino, Akiko
Komoto, Yohei
Koga, Julia
Koga, Koji
Sato, Koji
Sato, Kaho
Sato, Tetsuro
Sato, Harue
Sato, Shinichi
Sawabe, Reina
Shimabara, Noriko
Shimamura, Rie
Shimamura, Yusuke
Shimizu, Katsuji
Shimizu, Mayumi
Shimura, Yasuo
Shimura, Tamae
Shimura, Takane
Shimooka, Yohei
Shirouchi, Moeka
Shirouchi, Shota
Shirouchi, Koki
Shiroishi, Kaho
Shinkai, Midori
Shindo, Masumi
Shindo, Mei
Shindo, Yuichi
Jinnai, Tetsuro
Sugano, Tsunehiro
Sugimoto, Shinichi
Sugimoto, Shinji
Soyama, Noboru
Takada, Koji

Takada, Ryosuke
Takahata, Harumi
Takahashi, Tsuneo
Takahashi, Hiroko
Takahashi, Yui
Takahashi, Karin
Takeuchi, Tetsuro
Takara, Kanami
Takei, Shinsuke
Takei, Nobuyo
Tadano, Koki
Tamura, Chinatsu
Chikamatsu, Momoe
Chikamatsu, Saki
Tsukamoto, Hikari
Tsukamoto, Yuri
Tsukishima, Hiroshi
Tsugehara, Kosuke
Tsuji, Yoko
Tsudamoto, Junpei
Tsuchida, Soichi
Tsuchida, Kayoko
Tsuboi, Yoshiyuki
Tsurui, Kanami
Tegoshi, Katsuyo
Tezuka, Tamotsu
Terasawa, Tomoe
Terasawa, Matsu

Terui, Haruko
Tendo, Shoichi
Toi, Rin
Todo, Miyoshi
Todo, Yoshiyuki
Tono, Yuko
Togawa, Hisae
Tokita, Kyoichi
Tokumaru, Shota
Tokumaru, Takami
Nagae, Yuya
Nakai, Yoshinobu

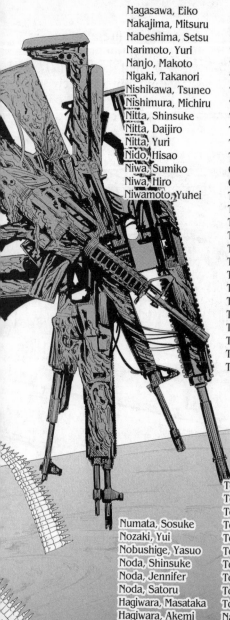

Nagasawa, Eiko
Nakajima, Mitsuru
Nabeshima, Setsu
Narimoto, Yuri
Nanjo, Makoto
Nigaki, Takanori
Nishikawa, Tsuneo
Nishimura, Michiru
Nitta, Shinsuke
Nitta, Daijiro
Nitta, Yuri
Nido, Hisao
Niwa, Sumiko
Niwa, Hiro
Niwamoto, Yuhei

Numata, Sosuke
Nozaki, Yui
Nobushige, Yasuo
Noda, Shinsuke
Noda, Jennifer
Noda, Satoru
Hagiwara, Masataka
Hagiwara, Akemi
Hagiwara, Yu

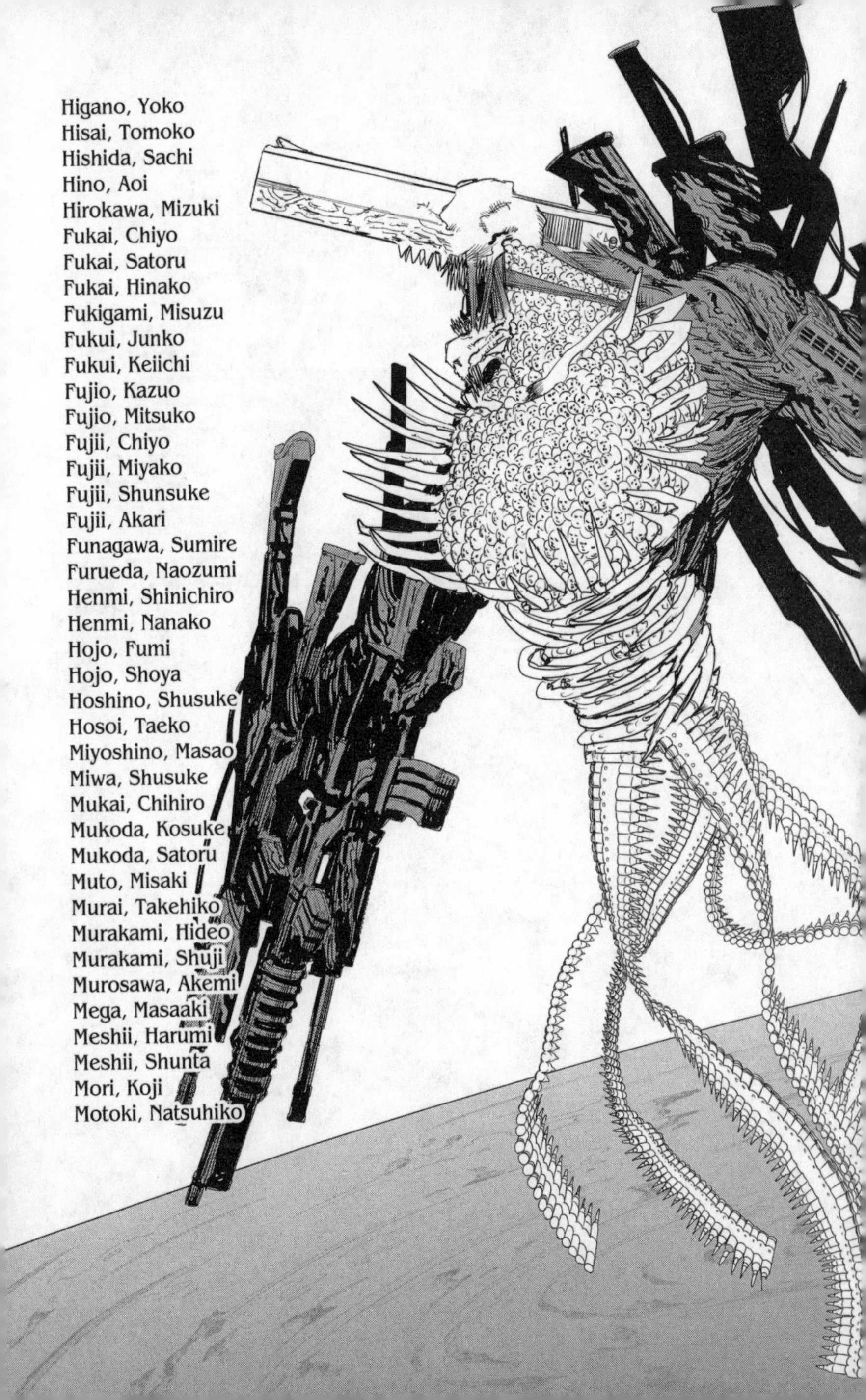
Higano, Yoko
Hisai, Tomoko
Hishida, Sachi
Hino, Aoi
Hirokawa, Mizuki
Fukai, Chiyo
Fukai, Satoru
Fukai, Hinako
Fukigami, Misuzu
Fukui, Junko
Fukui, Keiichi
Fujio, Kazuo
Fujio, Mitsuko
Fujii, Chiyo
Fujii, Miyako
Fujii, Shunsuke
Fujii, Akari
Funagawa, Sumire
Furueda, Naozumi
Henmi, Shinichiro
Henmi, Nanako
Hojo, Fumi
Hojo, Shoya
Hoshino, Shusuke
Hosoi, Taeko
Miyoshino, Masao
Miwa, Shusuke
Mukai, Chihiro
Mukoda, Kosuke
Mukoda, Satoru
Muto, Misaki
Murai, Takehiko
Murakami, Hideo
Murakami, Shuji
Murosawa, Akemi
Mega, Masaaki
Meshii, Harumi
Meshii, Shunta
Mori, Koji
Motoki, Natsuhiko

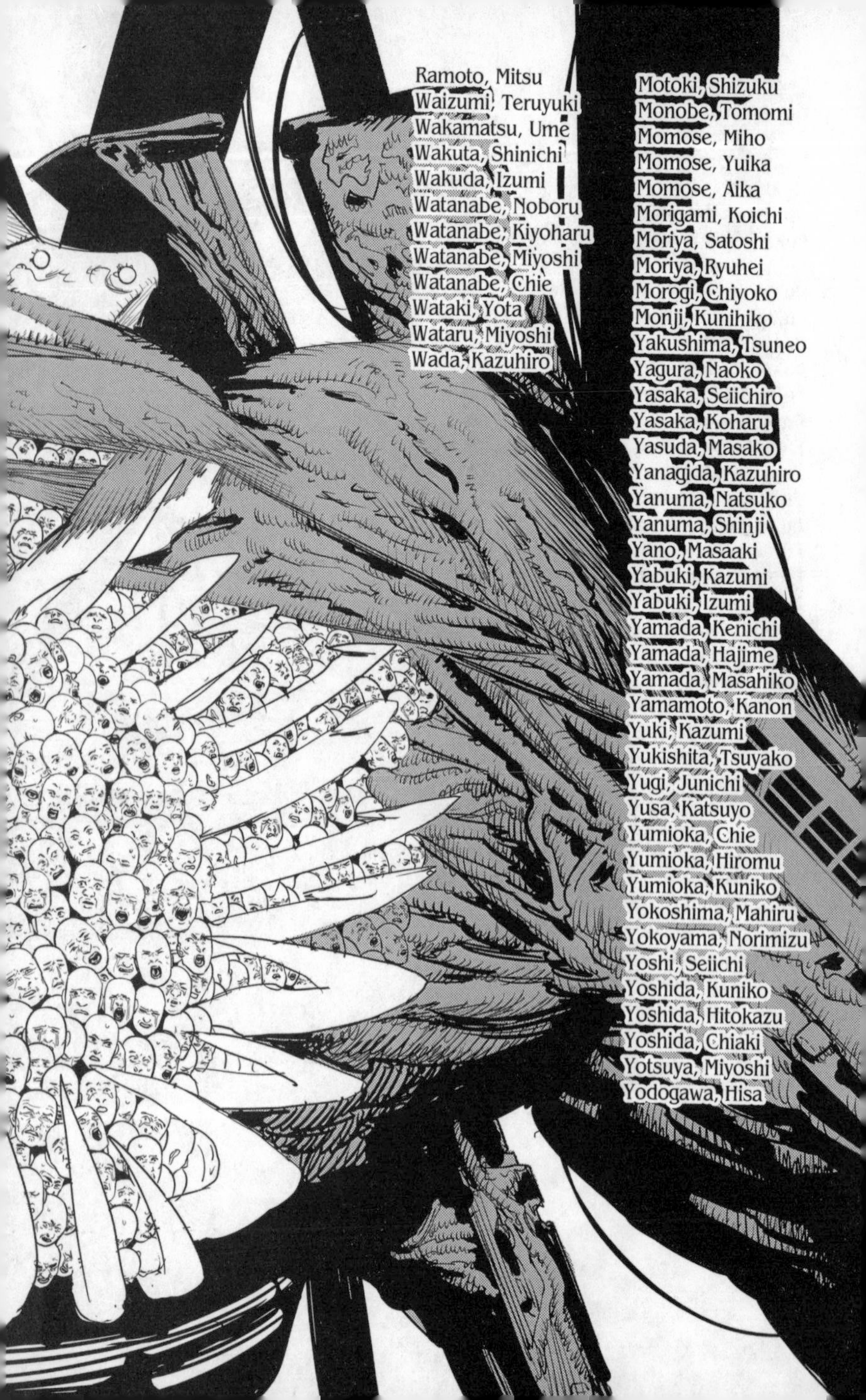
Motoki, Shizuku
Monobe, Tomomi
Momose, Miho
Momose, Yuika
Momose, Aika
Morigami, Koichi
Moriya, Satoshi
Moriya, Ryuhei
Morogi, Chiyoko
Monji, Kunihiko
Yakushima, Tsuneo
Yagura, Naoko
Yasaka, Seiichiro
Yasaka, Koharu
Yasuda, Masako
Yanagida, Kazuhiro
Yanuma, Natsuko
Yanuma, Shinji
Yano, Masaaki
Yabuki, Kazumi
Yabuki, Izumi
Yamada, Kenichi
Yamada, Hajime
Yamada, Masahiko
Yamamoto, Kanon
Yuki, Kazumi
Yukishita, Tsuyako
Yugi, Junichi
Yusa, Katsuyo
Yumioka, Chie
Yumioka, Hiromu
Yumioka, Kuniko
Yokoshima, Mahiru
Yokoyama, Norimizu
Yoshi, Seiichi
Yoshida, Kuniko
Yoshida, Hitokazu
Yoshida, Chiaki
Yotsuya, Miyoshi
Yodogawa, Hisa
Ramoto, Mitsu
Waizumi, Teruyuki
Wakamatsu, Ume
Wakuta, Shinichi
Wakuda, Izumi
Watanabe, Noboru
Watanabe, Kiyoharu
Watanabe, Miyoshi
Watanabe, Chie
Wataki, Yota
Wataru, Miyoshi
Wada, Kazuhiro

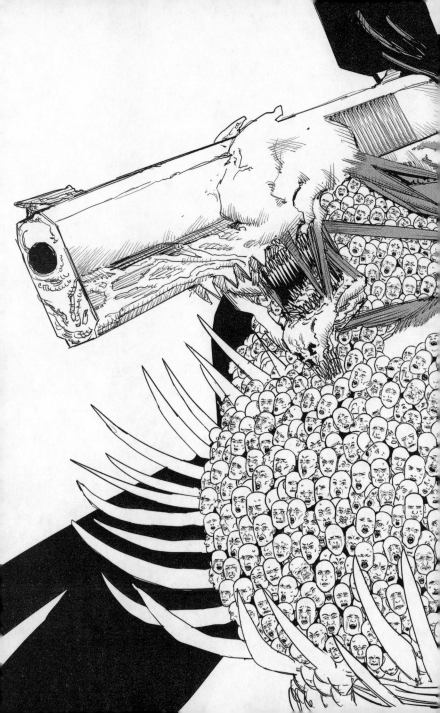

Chain saw man

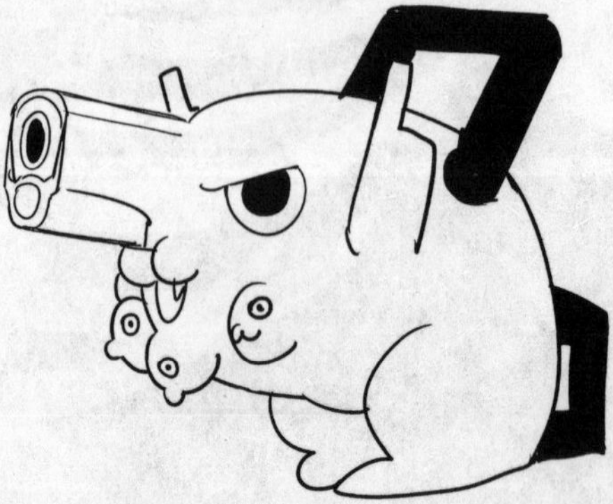

Chapter 76: Don't Open It

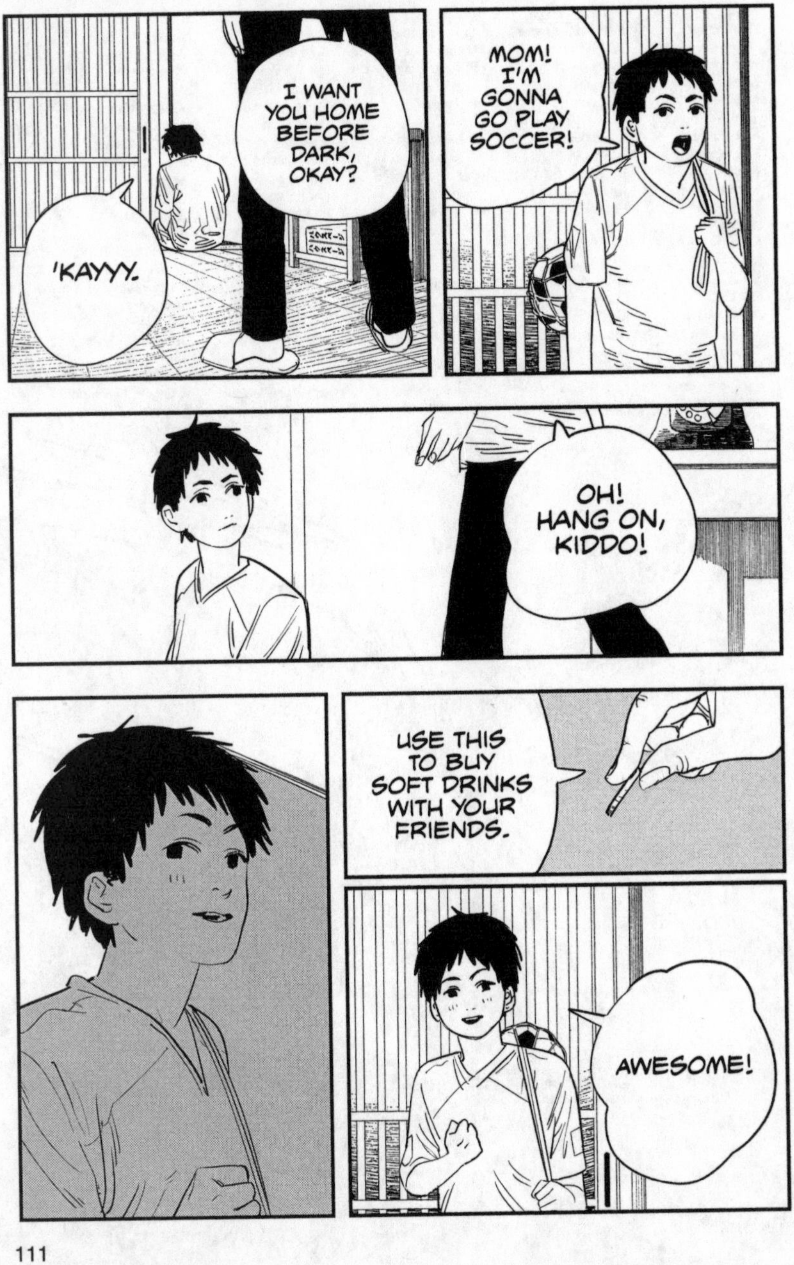
MOM! I'M GONNA GO PLAY SOCCER!
I WANT YOU HOME BEFORE DARK, OKAY?
'KAYYY.
OH! HANG ON, KIDDO!
USE THIS TO BUY SOFT DRINKS WITH YOUR FRIENDS.
AWESOME!

3:18:22
The Gun Devil advances toward Makima.

Deaths:
Aikawa, Kazuki
Aiba, Keiichi
Aono, Setsu
Aono, Daichi
Akashi, Takumi
Agari, Ayaka
Akikawa, Kosuke
Akita, Daisuke
Akui, Koji
Asagami, Rumiko
Asami, Shu
Ajima, Kaori
Adachi, Harumi
Adachi, Ryoichi
Atsugi, Hisao
Atsuta, Koki
Abe, Kozo
Abe, Futa
Amae, Daiki
Amaki, Sayuri
Amashiro, Tamohisa
Ayai, Shoko
Ayai, Natsumi
Ikawa, Koki
Ikuta, Akari
Ikuta, Daichi
Igusa, Kohei
Ikeuchi, Chihiro
Ikeda, Kazumasa
Ikeda, Noboru
Ikeda, Minori
Izawa, Haruka
Ishii, Atsumi
Isoda, Kazuyo
Ichikawa, Shogo
Ichikawa, Yasuko
Ichikawa, Ryohei
Itodagawa, Reiko
Inauchi, Yuki
Inauchi, Ai
Iwai, Akihiro
Uesato, Subaru
Ueshiba, Rinko
Uozumi, Yuichi
Uchiyama, Francois
Utsugi, Jun
Utsugi, Reiji
Ubayama, Yuichi
Urabe, Atsumi
Eikawa, Teruhisa
Ezaki, Teppei
Enosawa, Karin
Erikawa, Shoji
Oikawa, Hiroyuki
Oimatsu, Akiyo
Oashi, Keisuke
Ooi, Shuichi
Ooi, Miho
Ooi, Naoka
Oizumi, Shizuko
Okatake, Shuichi
Otokura, Takeru
Onizuka, Mio
Onoguchi, Misuzu
Obata, Masahiro
Kaizuka, Naoki
Kaido, Shuichi
Kaga, Erika
Kagami, Ichiro
Kagawa, Kazuyo
Kakikawa, Kazumasa
Kakiguchi, Makio
Kakiguchi, Miyuki
Kasagawa, Aya
Kajii, Saki
Kasuga, Nobuyo
Kano, Moe
Kamata, Yuichi
Kayama, Kazuko
Kayama, Masashi
Kikukawa, Sae
Kigure, Kenichi
Kishie, Tetsu
Kishie, Atsuko
Kishie, Asuka
Kitakura, Shizumi
Kirii, Yutaro
Kusunoki, Kumiko
Kunisaki, Masashi
Kunisaki, Aya
Kurai, Yuichi
Kemoto, Kunihiko
Kemoto, Asumi
Kenzaki, Koji
Gejo, Taeko
Koide, Yoshisa
Kosaka, Fumio
Koji, Yukie
Kono, Yoshitake
Kono, Shizumi
Kono, Aya
Kosakai, Koji
Kojima, Sayuri
Kojima, Isamu
Komori, Tomonori
Saida, Junichi
Saegusa, Kazuho
Sakai, Ayako
Sakai, Eiji
Sakai, Ai
Sakaki, Yuria
Sakiyama, Tomoko
Sakura, Tomonori
Sawabe, Yuichi
Sawabe, Seiko

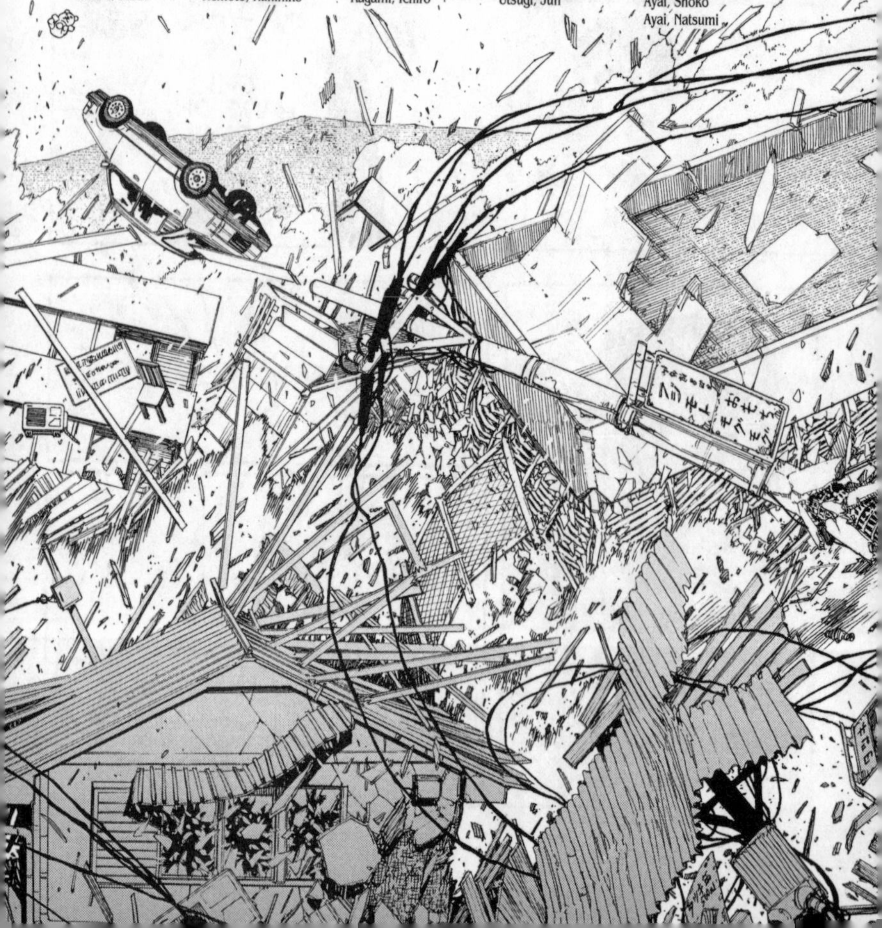

Shigemori, Akihiro
Shizuta, Tsuyoshi
Shinozaki, Daniel
Shibayama, Satoru
Shibayama, Mika
Shibayama, Isamu
Shimada, Yae
Shimojima, Ayame
Shimojima, Soichi
Sugawara, Shizuko
Sugiue, Mana
Sukemoto, Kentaro
Suzugaki, Wakana
Suzugaki, Yuki
Sumikawa, Mika
Sumida, Misayo
Segawa, Satoru
Sekio, Kiku
Sekio, Iwao
Senga, Koji
Senda, Ayako
Soda, Masaru
Sotoura, Misa

Sotoura, Kirara
Sonohara, Kayo
Tauchi, Susumu
Takaura, Ayano
Takagi, Kozo
Takagi, Ren
Takiuchi, Mizuho
Takei, Harue
Takemoto, Masakazu
Takemoto, Kozue
Takemoto, Mahime
Tagoshi, Nobuhisa
Chikamatsu, Misono
Chigasaki, Masanobu
Chigasaki, Masaaki
Chigasaki, Minami
Chikuma, Misayo
Chujo, Shuya
Chiyoda, Koki
Chiyoda, Otoha
Tsukishiro, Tsubasa
Tsugemoto, Keisuke
Tsugemoto, Shizuku

Tsujii, Takahito
Tsuchimori, Tamotsu
Tsuchimoto, Ayano
Tsuchimoto, Saya
Tsutsumi, Shoichi
Tsuruoka, Nariyuki
Terai, Shoho
Terai, Tsubaki
Terumoto, Yutaka
Terai, Isamu
Terai, Shino
Terumoto, Takaki
Toma, Hiroshige
Tokida, Fumika
Togi, Reon
Tokuoka, Shigeru
Tokuoka, Natsuko
Tokuoka, Kaho
Totsuka, Nao
Tonari, Shoichi
Tonari, Rinako
Tonari, Miu
Tobita, Shigeru

Fujii, Naoto
Fushiki, Atsushi
Fushiki, Nanase
Fuchigami, Kazuo
Funada, Futoshi
Funada, Kazuya
Funada, Hiromi
Fuyuki, Kozue
Furui, Takahiro
Hirajima, Kunio
Herai, Asami
Betta, Hitomi
Betta, Sho
Hoki, Kazumasa
Hogi, Satoru
Hoshikawa, Naoya
Hoshikawa, Mari
Hoshikawa, Sekai
Hozumi, Yosuke
Hosoki, Tsutomu
Horiuchi, Asa
Horiuchi, Takaaki
Maizuru, Misaki

Maki, Masayuki
Makishima, Kaneyo
Makishima, Keiko
Makimura, Shunsuke
Maguchi, Takaharu
Maguchi, Sanami
Yukimura, Kenichi
Maguchi, Rina
Masakawa, Satoru
Mashiba, Kaoru
Mase, Yoshiharu
Matashige, Yoko
Matashige, Saki
Machida, Miu
Miura, Takashi
Mikazaki, Yoshiharu
Miki, Toshiaki
Miki, Keiko
Miki, Yuka
Migishima, Etsuko
Misaka, Satoru
Yusa, Kaneyo
Yumisaki, Haruna

Mochida, Ayami
Motoi, Fusao
Momoi, Shoya
Momoi, Reina
Mori, Shunsuke
Moro, Kenji
Moro, Soara
Moromoto, Kinue
Yaka, Keiko
Yaka, Koichi
Yaka, Manami
Yakushige, Ryosuke
Yakeshiro, Yuna
Yashima, Fusao
Yasukata, Kengo
Yasukata, Ayana
Yabata, Takahiro
Yamakura, Nazuna
Yui, Yuto
Yuda, Maria
Yugami, Zenichi
Yugami, Kumiko
Yugami, Manami

Yokogawa, Shino
Yokota, Rokusuke
Yoshii, Kimie
Yoshii, Natsuki
Yoshii, Shota
Yoshikawa, Takahiro
Yoshizaki, Mion
Rakuno, Zenichi
Rakuno, Misako
Rikawa, Yuichi
Rida, Ryosei
Ryutaku, Kenji
Rinno, Hisao
Rinno, Kota
Rinno, Churi
Rekimoto, Shigeko
Renpo, Kazuro
Rokuma, Sakie
Wai, Kumiko
Wakahara, Mizuki
Wagata, Keisuke
Wagatsuma, Kaito
Wakuta, Kunihasa

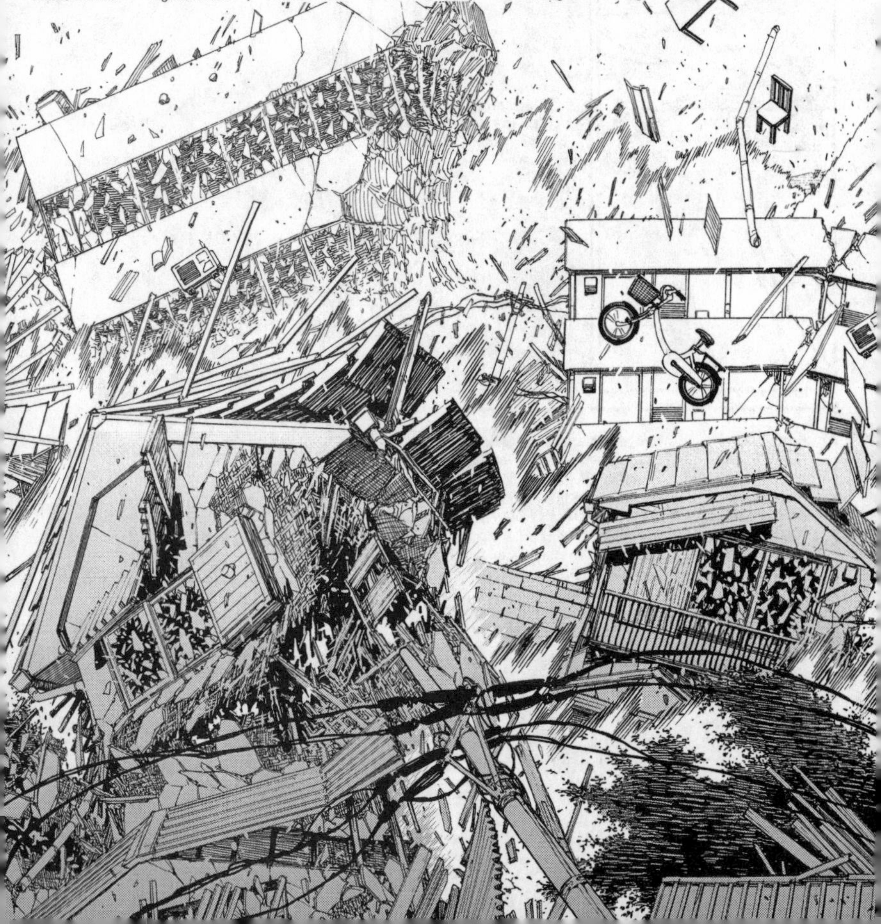

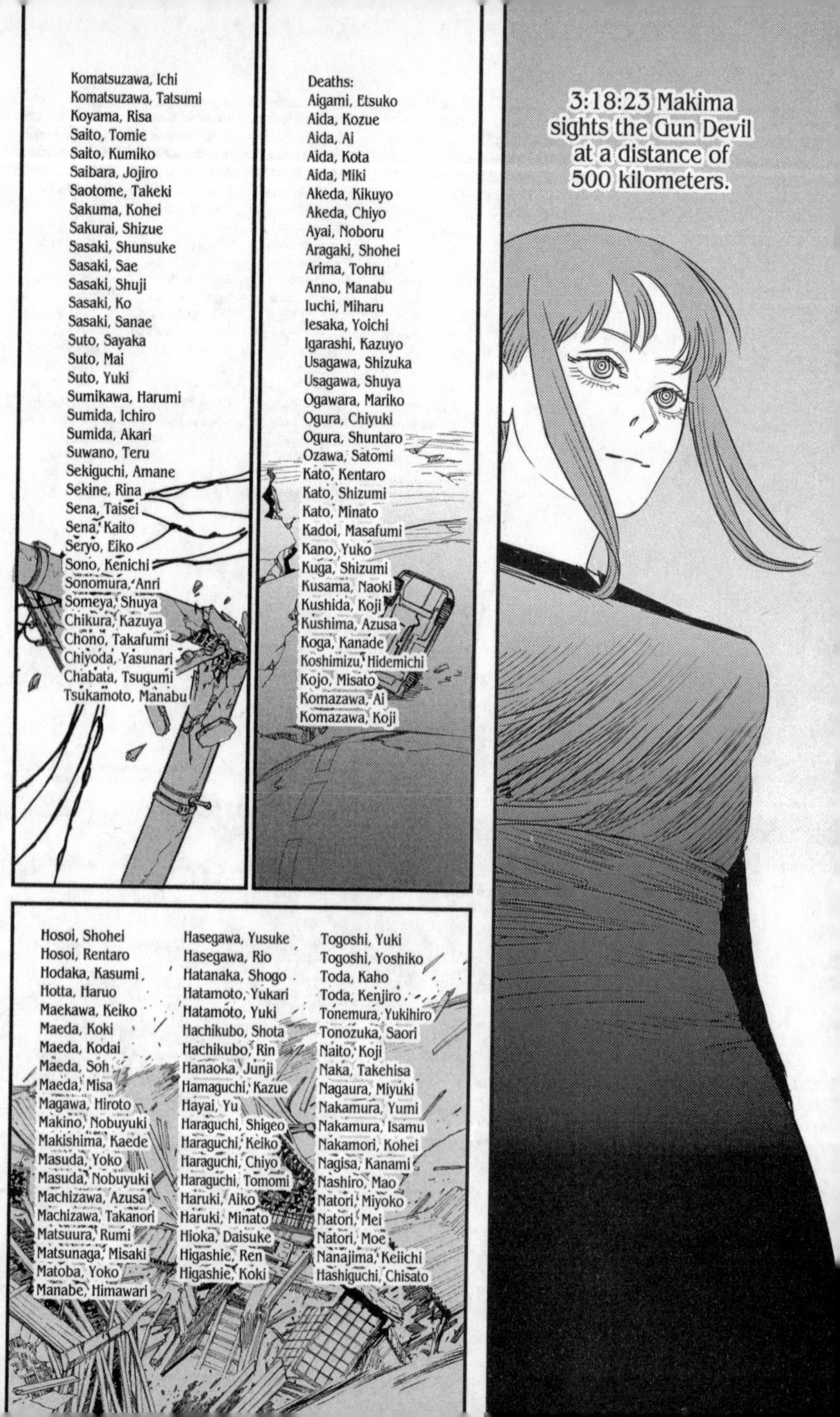

3:18:23 Makima sights the Gun Devil at a distance of 500 kilometers.
Deaths:
Aigami, Etsuko
Aida, Kozue
Aida, Ai
Aida, Kota
Aida, Miki
Akeda, Kikuyo
Akeda, Chiyo
Ayai, Noboru
Aragaki, Shohei
Arima, Tohru
Anno, Manabu
Iuchi, Miharu
Iesaka, Yoichi
Igarashi, Kazuyo
Usagawa, Shizuka
Usagawa, Shuya
Ogawara, Mariko
Ogura, Chiyuki
Ogura, Shuntaro
Ozawa, Satomi
Kato, Kentaro
Kato, Shizumi
Kato, Minato
Kadoi, Masafumi
Kano, Yuko
Kuga, Shizumi
Kusama, Naoki
Kushida, Koji
Kushima, Azusa
Koga, Kanade
Koshimizu, Hidemichi
Kojo, Misato
Komazawa, Ai
Komazawa, Koji
Komatsuzawa, Ichi
Komatsuzawa, Tatsumi
Koyama, Risa
Saito, Tomie
Saito, Kumiko
Saibara, Jojiro
Saotome, Takeki
Sakuma, Kohei
Sakurai, Shizue
Sasaki, Shunsuke
Sasaki, Sae
Sasaki, Shuji
Sasaki, Ko
Sasaki, Sanae
Suto, Sayaka
Suto, Mai
Suto, Yuki
Sumikawa, Harumi
Sumida, Ichiro
Sumida, Akari
Suwano, Teru
Sekiguchi, Amane
Sekine, Rina
Sena, Taisei
Sena, Kaito
Seryo, Eiko
Sono, Kenichi
Sonomura, Anri
Someya, Shuya
Chikura, Kazuya
Chono, Takafumi
Chiyoda, Yasunari
Chabata, Tsugumi
Tsukamoto, Manabu
Togoshi, Yuki
Togoshi, Yoshiko
Toda, Kaho
Toda, Kenjiro
Tonemura, Yukihiro
Tonozuka, Saori
Naito, Koji
Naka, Takehisa
Nagaura, Miyuki
Nakamura, Yumi
Nakamura, Isamu
Nakamori, Kohei
Nagisa, Kanami
Nashiro, Mao
Natori, Miyoko
Natori, Mei
Natori, Moe
Nanajima, Keiichi
Hashiguchi, Chisato
Hasegawa, Yusuke
Hasegawa, Rio
Hatanaka, Shogo
Hatamoto, Yukari
Hatamoto, Yuki
Hachikubo, Shota
Hachikubo, Rin
Hanaoka, Junji
Hamaguchi, Kazue
Hayai, Yu
Haraguchi, Shigeo
Haraguchi, Keiko
Haraguchi, Chiyo
Haraguchi, Tomomi
Haruki, Aiko
Haruki, Minato
Hioka, Daisuke
Higashie, Ren
Higashie, Koki
Hosoi, Shohei
Hosoi, Rentaro
Hodaka, Kasumi
Hotta, Haruo
Maekawa, Keiko
Maeda, Koki
Maeda, Kodai
Maeda, Soh
Maeda, Misa
Magawa, Hiroto
Makino, Nobuyuki
Makishima, Kaede
Masuda, Yoko
Masuda, Nobuyuki
Machizawa, Azusa
Machizawa, Takanori
Matsuura, Rumi
Matsunaga, Misaki
Matoba, Yoko
Manabe, Himawari

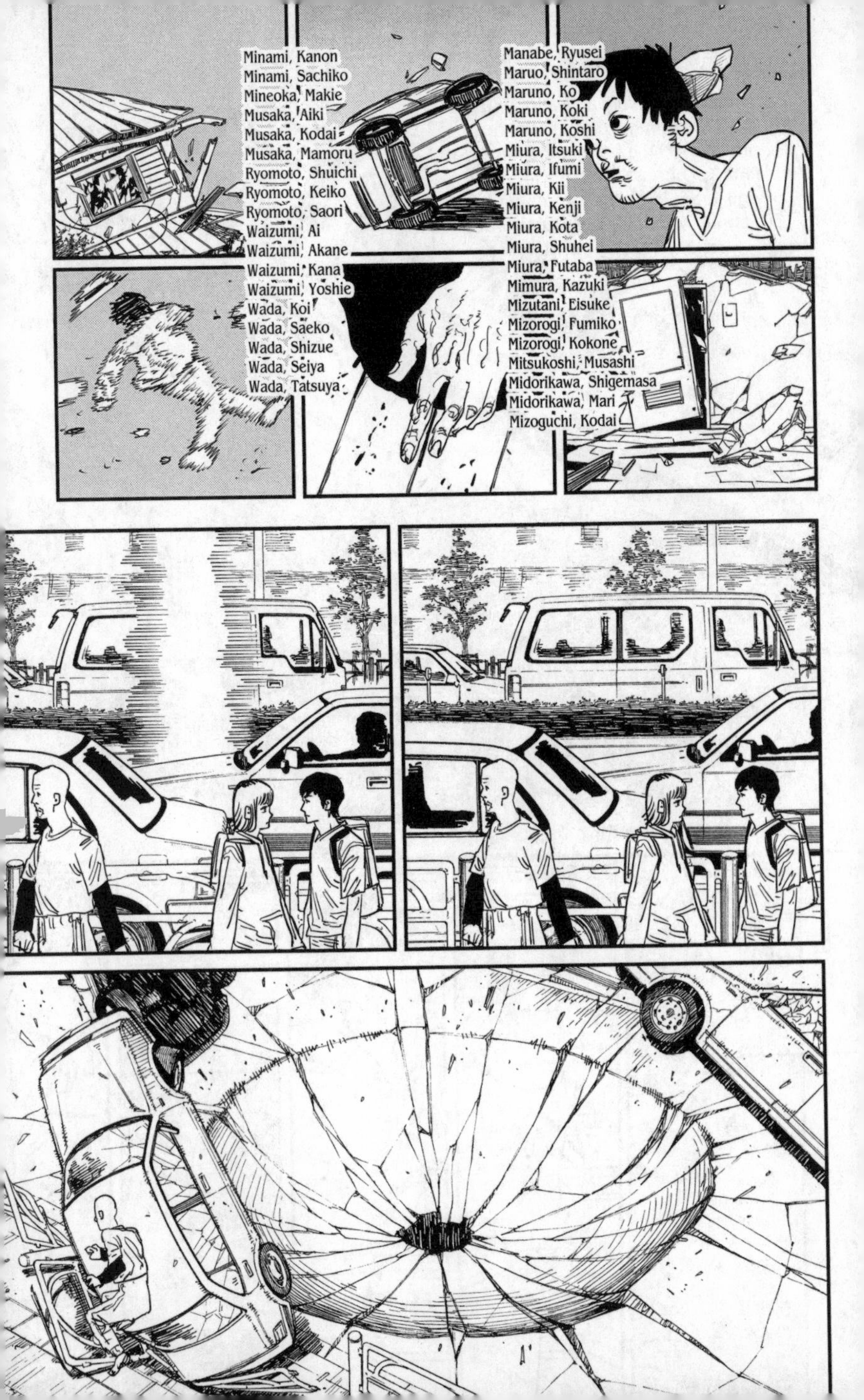
Manabe, Ryusei
Maruo, Shintaro
Maruno, Ko
Maruno, Koki
Maruno, Koshi
Miura, Itsuki
Miura, Ifumi
Miura, Kii
Miura, Kenji
Miura, Kota
Miura, Shuhei
Miura, Futaba
Mimura, Kazuki
Mizutani, Eisuke
Mizorogi, Fumiko
Mizorogi, Kokone
Mitsukoshi, Musashi
Midorikawa, Shigemasa
Midorikawa, Mari
Mizoguchi, Kodai
Minami, Kanon
Minami, Sachiko
Mineoka, Makie
Musaka, Aiki
Musaka, Kodai
Musaka, Mamoru
Ryomoto, Shuichi
Ryomoto, Keiko
Ryomoto, Saori
Waizumi, Ai
Waizumi, Akane
Waizumi, Kana
Waizumi, Yoshie
Wada, Koi
Wada, Saeko
Wada, Shizue
Wada, Seiya
Wada, Tatsuya

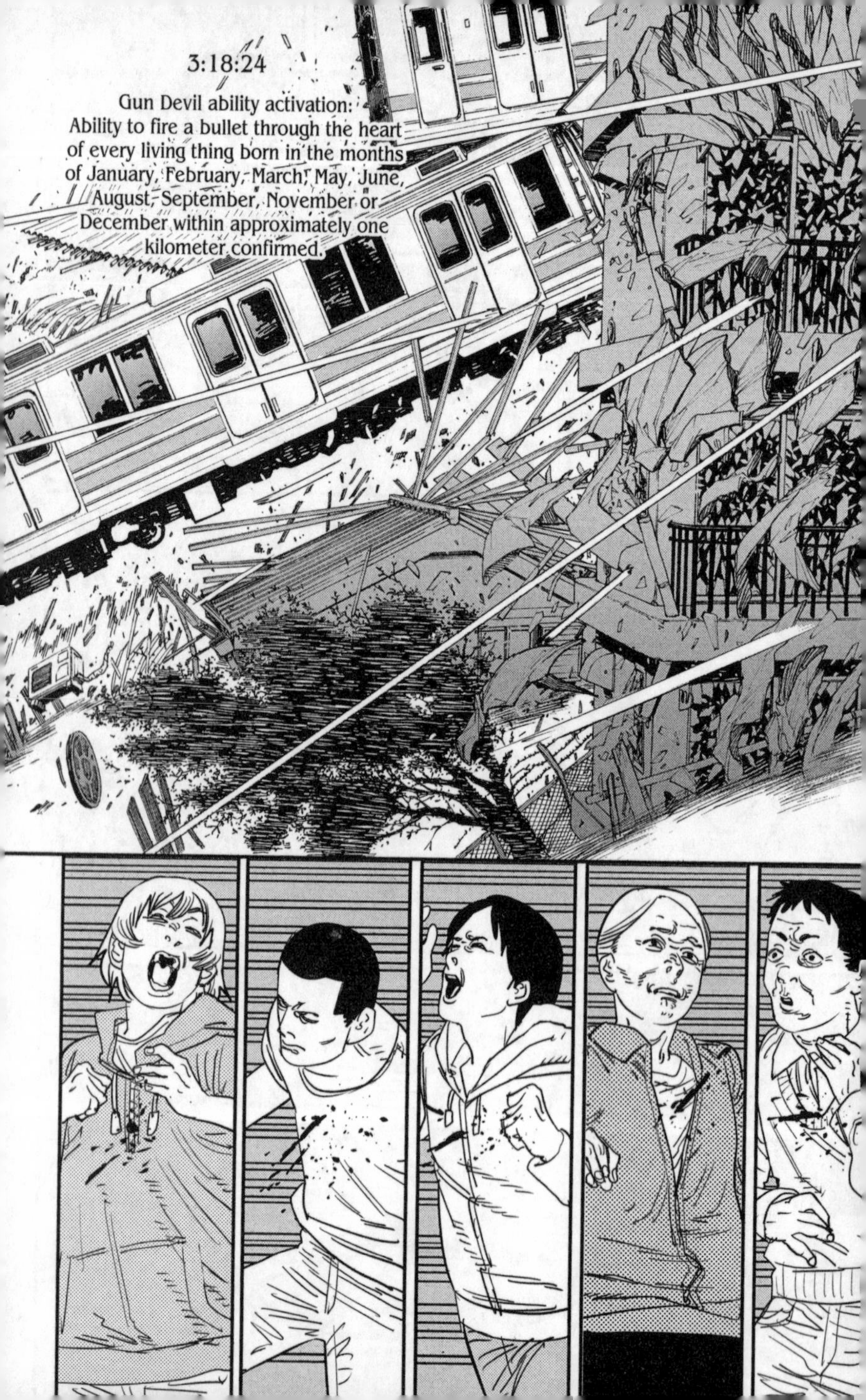
3:18:24
Gun Devil ability activation: Ability to fire a bullet through the heart of every living thing born in the months of January, February, March, May, June, August, September, November or December within approximately one kilometer confirmed.

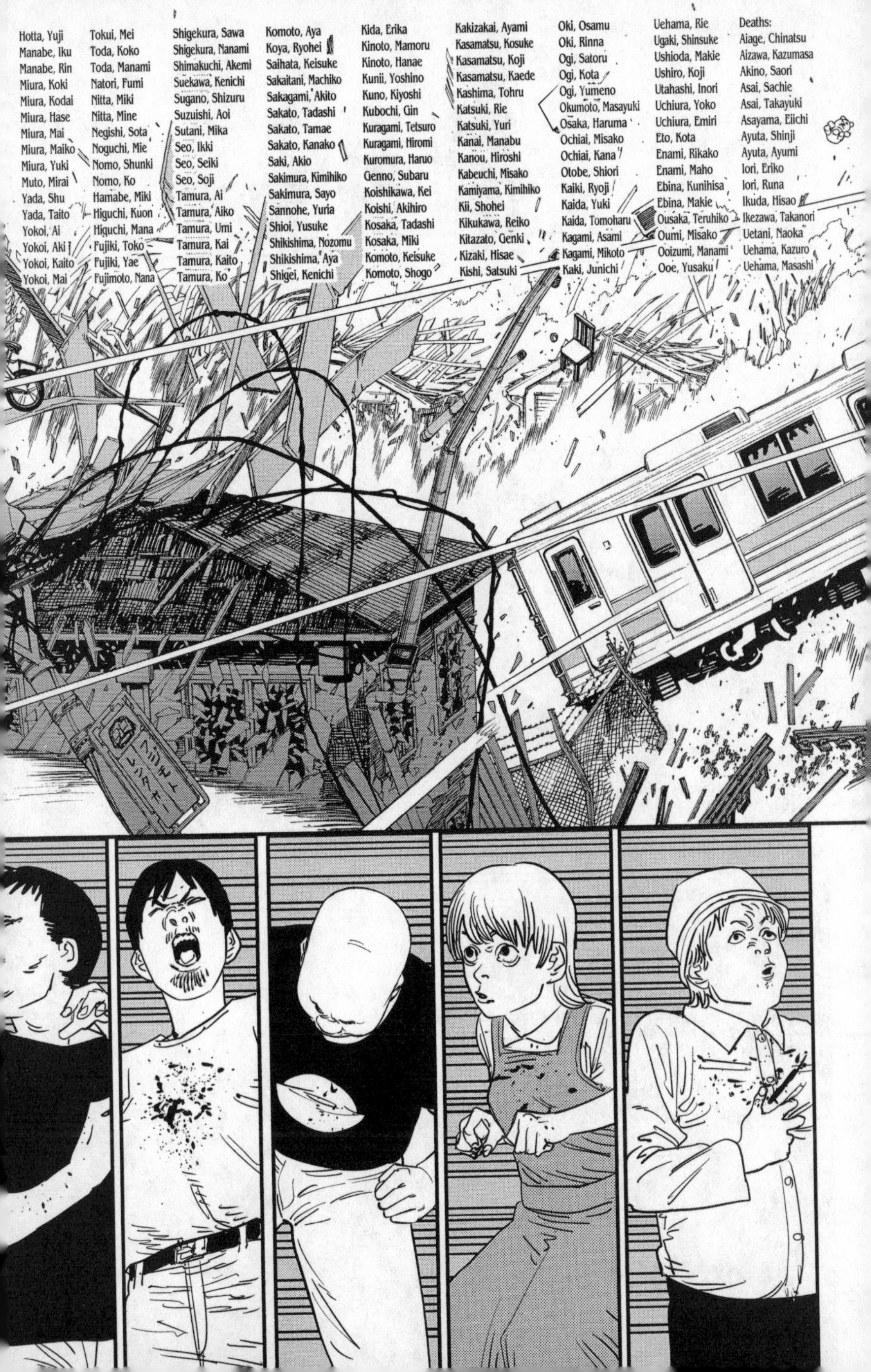
Deaths:
Aiage, Chinatsu
Aizawa, Kazumasa
Akino, Saori
Asai, Sachie
Asai, Takayuki
Asayama, Eiichi
Ayuta, Shinji
Ayuta, Ayumi
Iori, Eriko
Iori, Runa
Ikuda, Hisao
Ikezawa, Takanori
Uetani, Naoka
Uehama, Kazuro
Uehama, Masashi
Uehama, Rie
Ugaki, Shinsuke
Ushioda, Makie
Ushiro, Koji
Utahashi, Inori
Uchiura, Yoko
Uchiura, Emiri
Eto, Kota
Enami, Rikako
Enami, Maho
Ebina, Kunihisa
Ebina, Makie
Ousaka, Teruhiko
Oumi, Misako
Ooizumi, Manami
Ooe, Yusaku
Oki, Osamu
Oki, Rinna
Ogi, Satoru
Ogi, Kota
Ogi, Yumeno
Okumoto, Masayuki
Osaka, Haruma
Ochiai, Misako
Ochiai, Kana
Otobe, Shiori
Kaiki, Ryoji
Kaida, Yuki
Kaida, Tomoharu
Kagami, Asami
Kagami, Mikoto
Kaki, Junichi
Kakizakai, Ayami
Kasamatsu, Kosuke
Kasamatsu, Koji
Kasamatsu, Kaede
Kashima, Tohru
Katsuki, Rie
Katsuki, Yuri
Kanai, Manabu
Kanou, Hiroshi
Kabeuchi, Misako
Kamiyama, Kimihiko
Kii, Shohei
Kikukawa, Reiko
Kitazato, Genki
Kizaki, Hisae
Kishi, Satsuki
Kida, Erika
Kinoto, Mamoru
Kinoto, Hanae
Kunii, Yoshino
Kuno, Kiyoshi
Kubochi, Gin
Kuragami, Tetsuro
Kuragami, Hiromi
Kuromura, Haruo
Genno, Subaru
Koishikawa, Kei
Koishi, Akihiro
Kosaka, Tadashi
Kosaka, Miki
Komoto, Keisuke
Komoto, Shogo
Komoto, Aya
Koya, Ryohei
Saihata, Keisuke
Sakaitani, Machiko
Sakagami, Akito
Sakato, Tadashi
Sakato, Tamae
Sakato, Kanako
Saki, Akio
Sakimura, Kimihiko
Sakimura, Sayo
Sannohe, Yuria
Shioi, Yusuke
Shikishima, Nozomu
Shikishima, Aya
Shigei, Kenichi
Shigekura, Sawa
Shigekura, Nanami
Shimakuchi, Akemi
Suekawa, Kenichi
Sugano, Shizuru
Suzuishi, Aoi
Sutani, Mika
Seo, Ikki
Seo, Seiki
Seo, Soji
Tamura, Ai
Tamura, Aiko
Tamura, Umi
Tamura, Kai
Tamura, Kaito
Tamura, Ko
Tokui, Mei
Toda, Koko
Toda, Manami
Natori, Fumi
Nitta, Miki
Nitta, Mine
Negishi, Sota
Noguchi, Mie
Nomo, Shunki
Nomo, Ko
Hamabe, Miki
Higuchi, Kuon
Higuchi, Mana
Fujiki, Toko
Fujiki, Yae
Fujimoto, Nana
Hotta, Yuji
Manabe, Iku
Manabe, Rin
Miura, Koki
Miura, Kodai
Miura, Hase
Miura, Mai
Miura, Maiko
Miura, Yuki
Muto, Mirai
Yada, Shu
Yada, Taito
Yokoi, Ai
Yokoi, Aki
Yokoi, Kaito
Yokoi, Mai

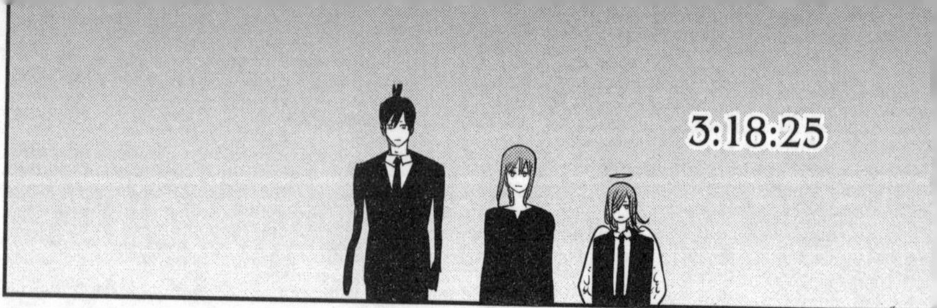
3:18:25
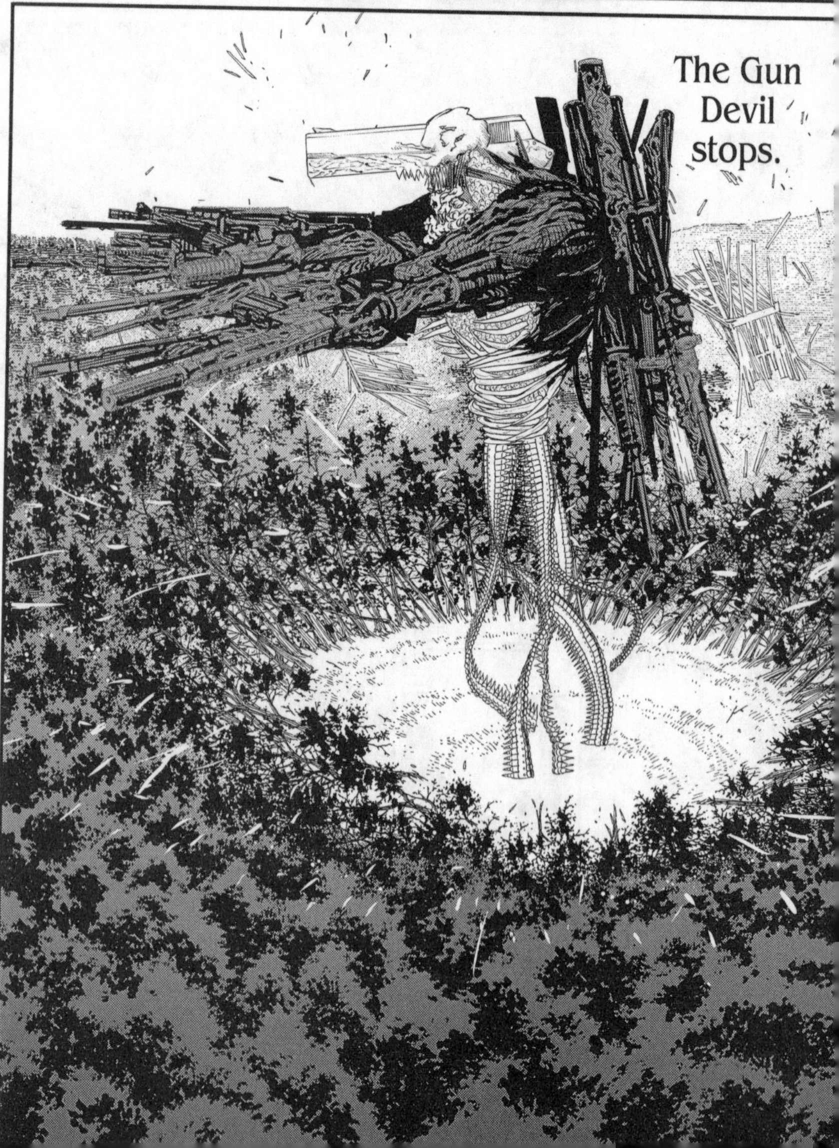
The Gun Devil stops.

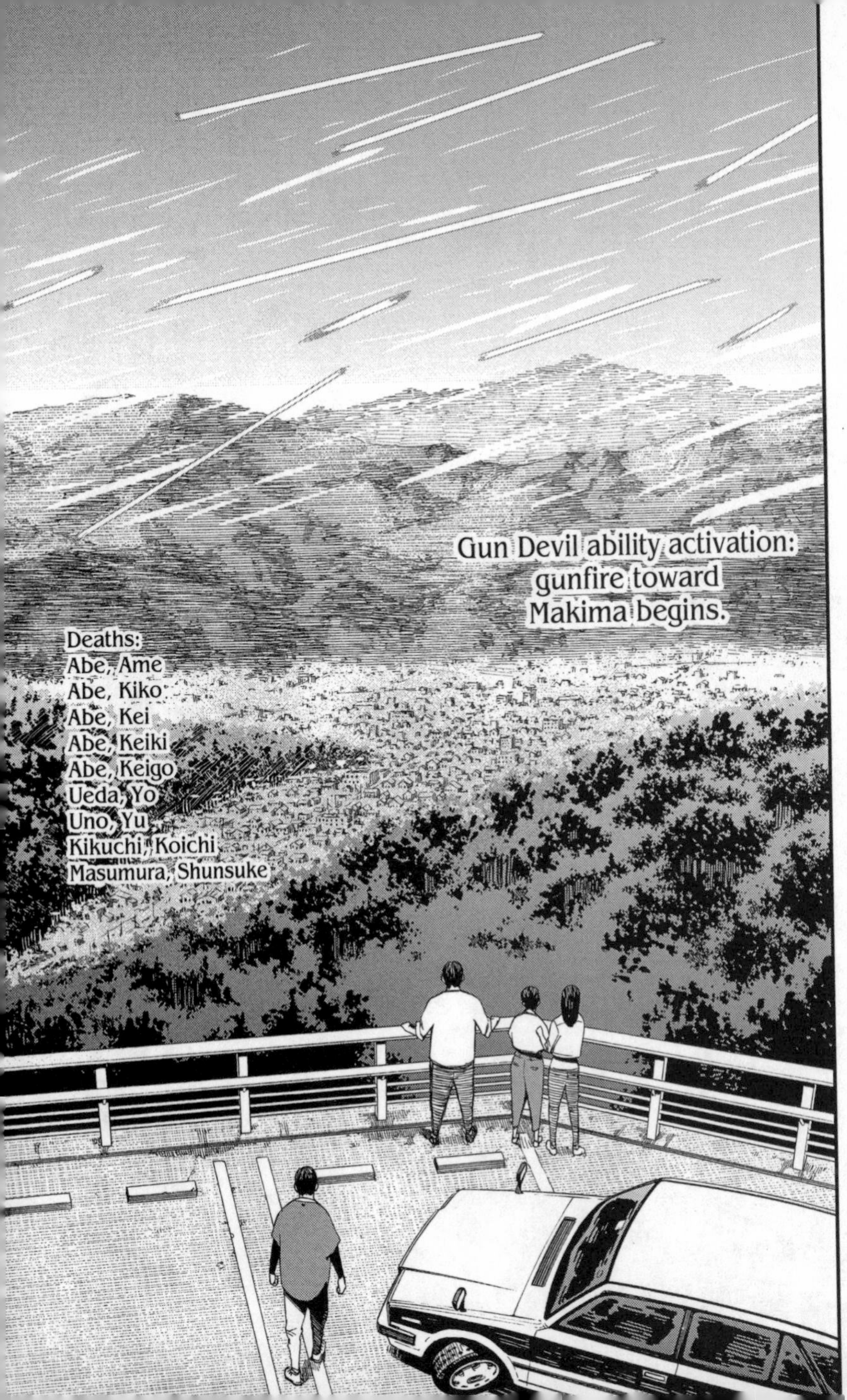
Gun Devil ability activation: gunfire toward Makima begins.
Deaths:
Abe, Ame
Abe, Kiko
Abe, Kei
Abe, Keiki
Abe, Keigo
Ueda, Yo
Uno, Yu
Kikuchi, Koichi
Masumura, Shunsuke

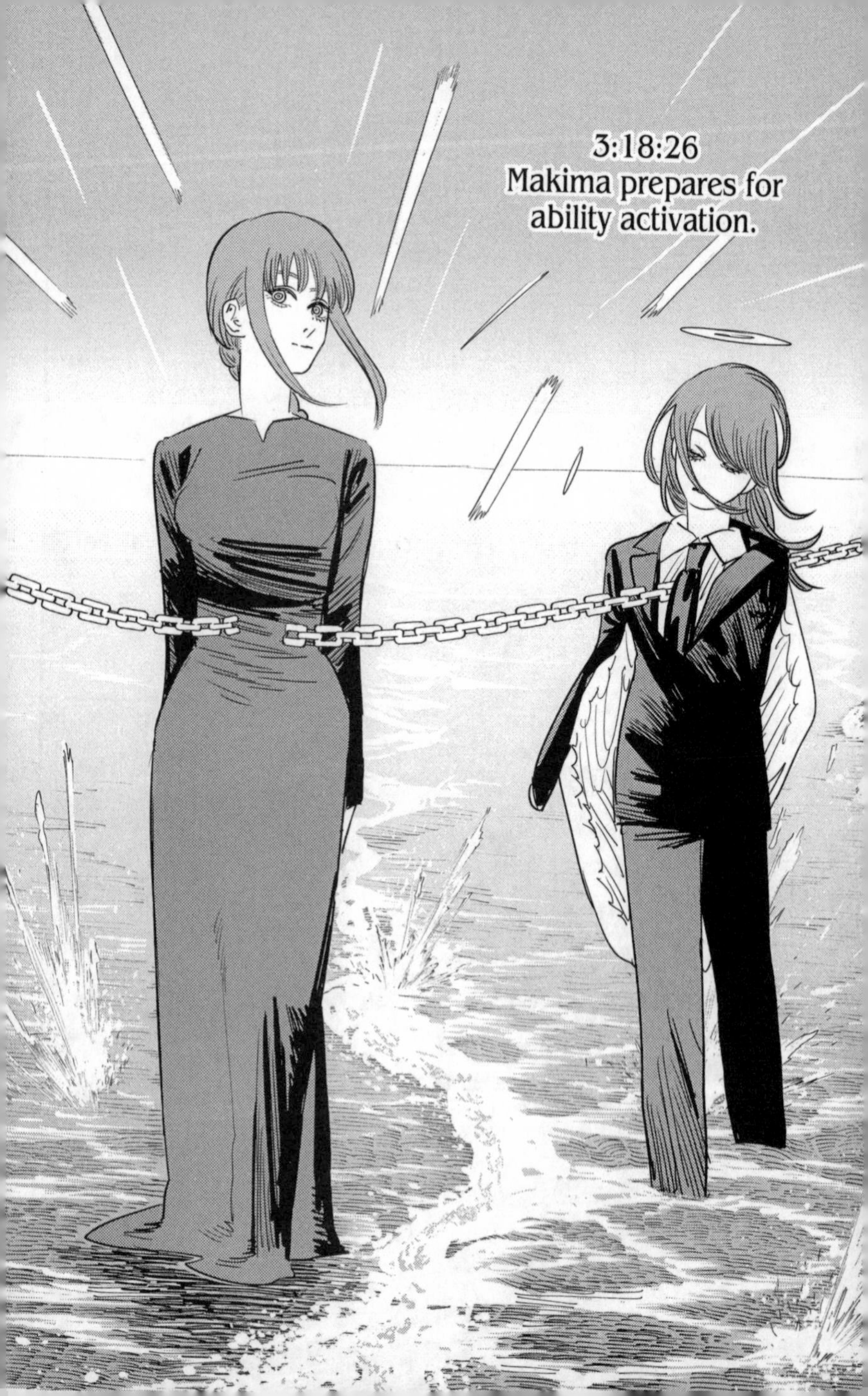
3:18:26
Makima prepares for ability activation.

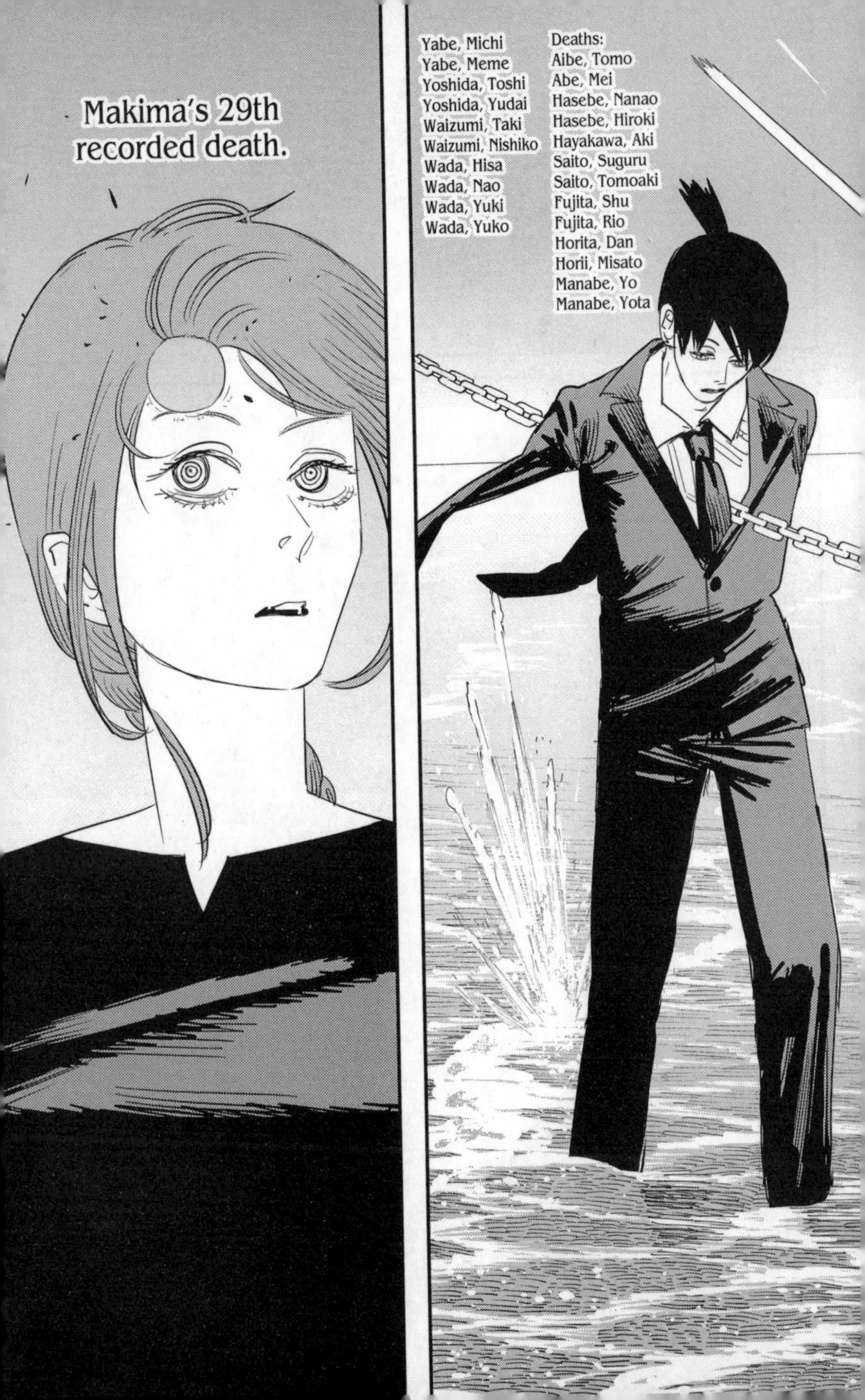
Deaths:
Aibe, Tomo
Abe, Mei
Hasebe, Nanao
Hasebe, Hiroki
Hayakawa, Aki
Saito, Suguru
Saito, Tomoaki
Fujita, Shu
Fujita, Rio
Horita, Dan
Horii, Misato
Manabe, Yo
Manabe, Yota
Yabe, Michi
Yabe, Meme
Yoshida, Toshi
Yoshida, Yudai
Waizumi, Taki
Waizumi, Nishiko
Wada, Hisa
Wada, Nao
Wada, Yuki
Wada, Yuko
Makima's 29th recorded death.

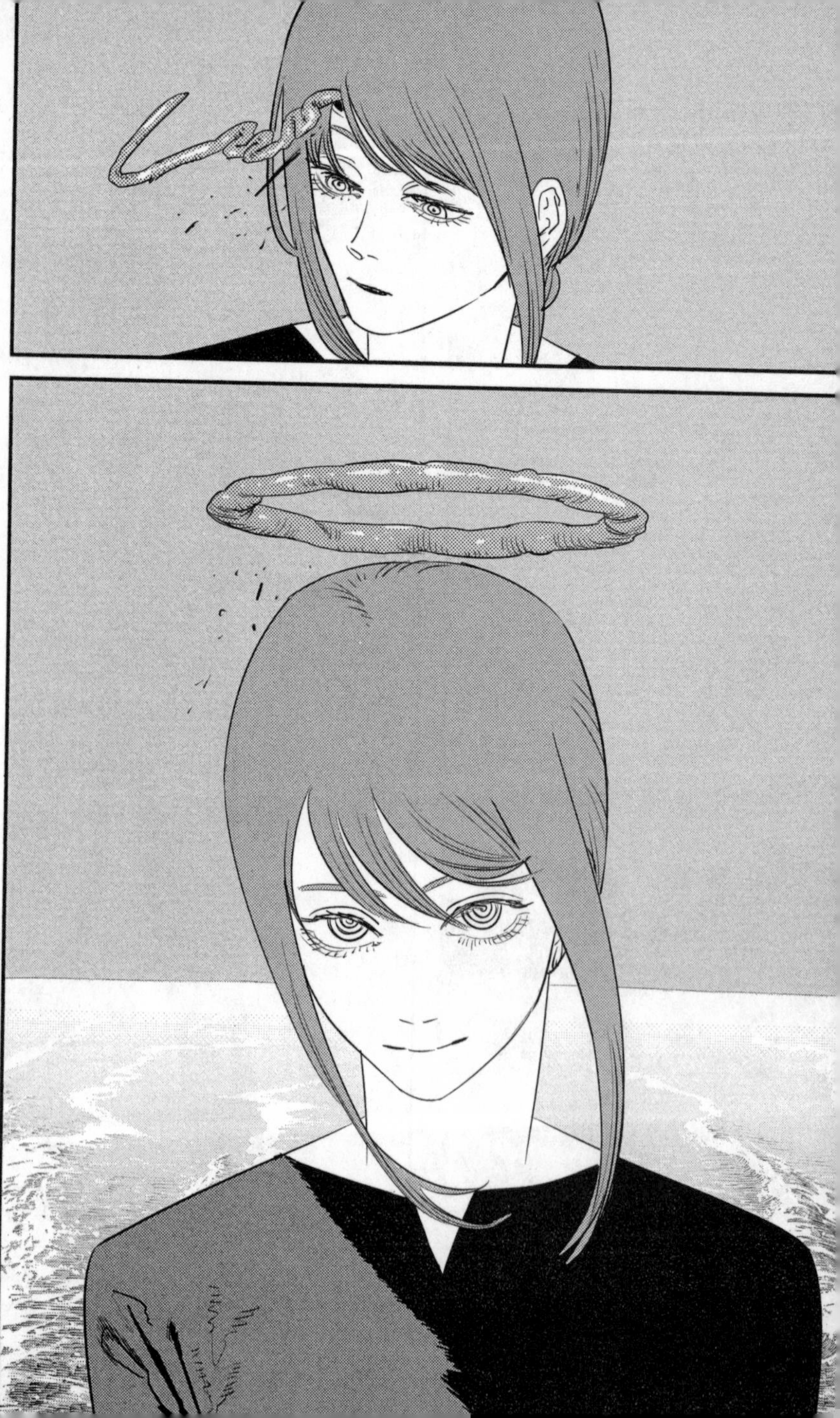

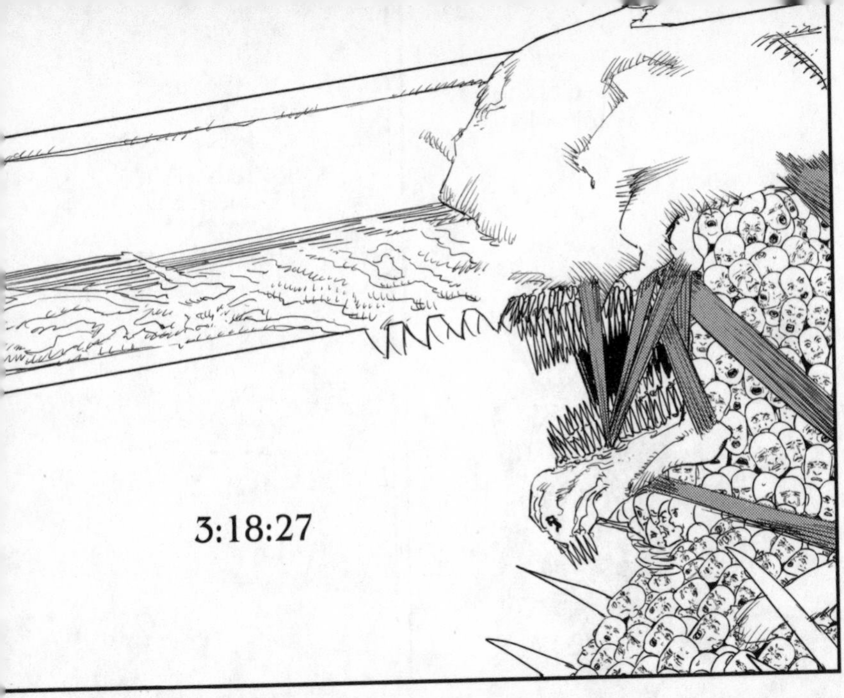
3:18:27

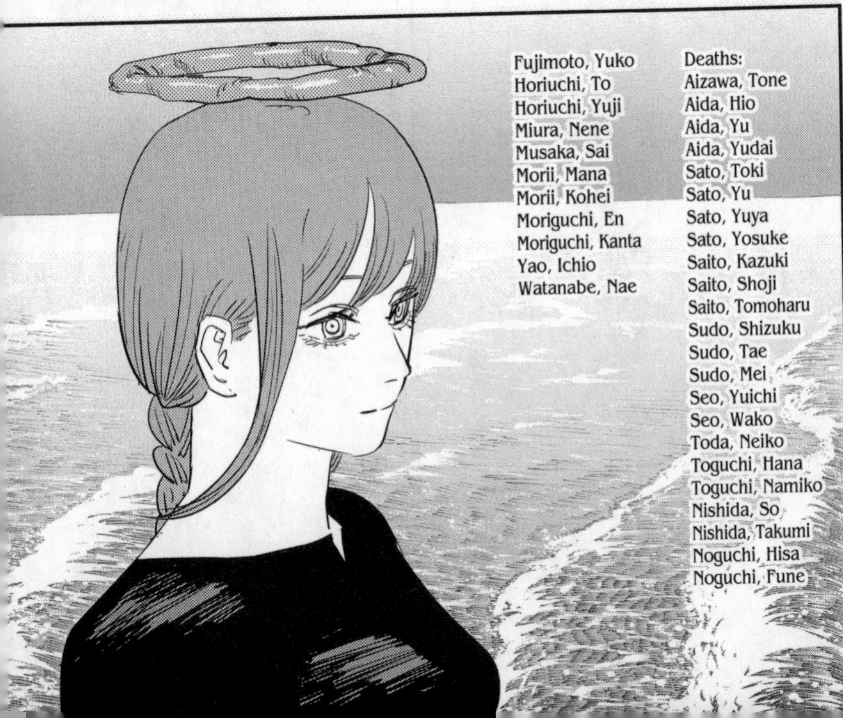
Deaths:
Aizawa, Tone
Aida, Hio
Aida, Yu
Aida, Yudai
Sato, Toki
Sato, Yu
Sato, Yuya
Sato, Yosuke
Saito, Kazuki
Saito, Shoji
Saito, Tomoharu
Sudo, Shizuku
Sudo, Tae
Sudo, Mei
Seo, Yuichi
Seo, Wako
Toda, Neiko
Toguchi, Hana
Toguchi, Namiko
Nishida, So
Nishida, Takumi
Noguchi, Hisa
Noguchi, Fune
Fujimoto, Yuko
Horiuchi, To
Horiuchi, Yuji
Miura, Nene
Musaka, Sai
Morii, Mana
Morii, Kohei
Moriguchi, En
Moriguchi, Kanta
Yao, Ichio
Watanabe, Nae

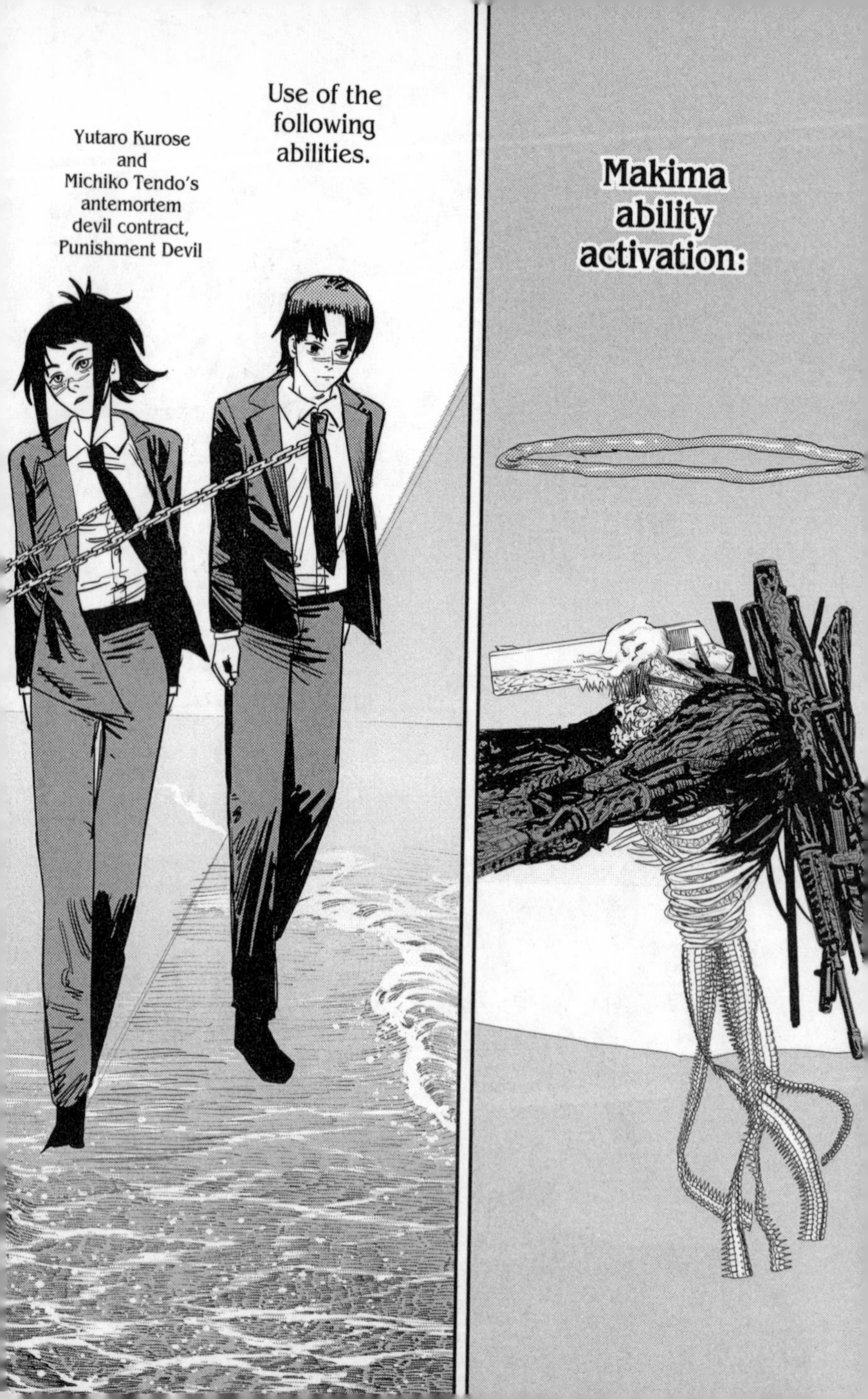
Makima ability activation:
Use of the following abilities.
Yutaro Kurose and Michiko Tendo's antemortem devil contract, Punishment Devil

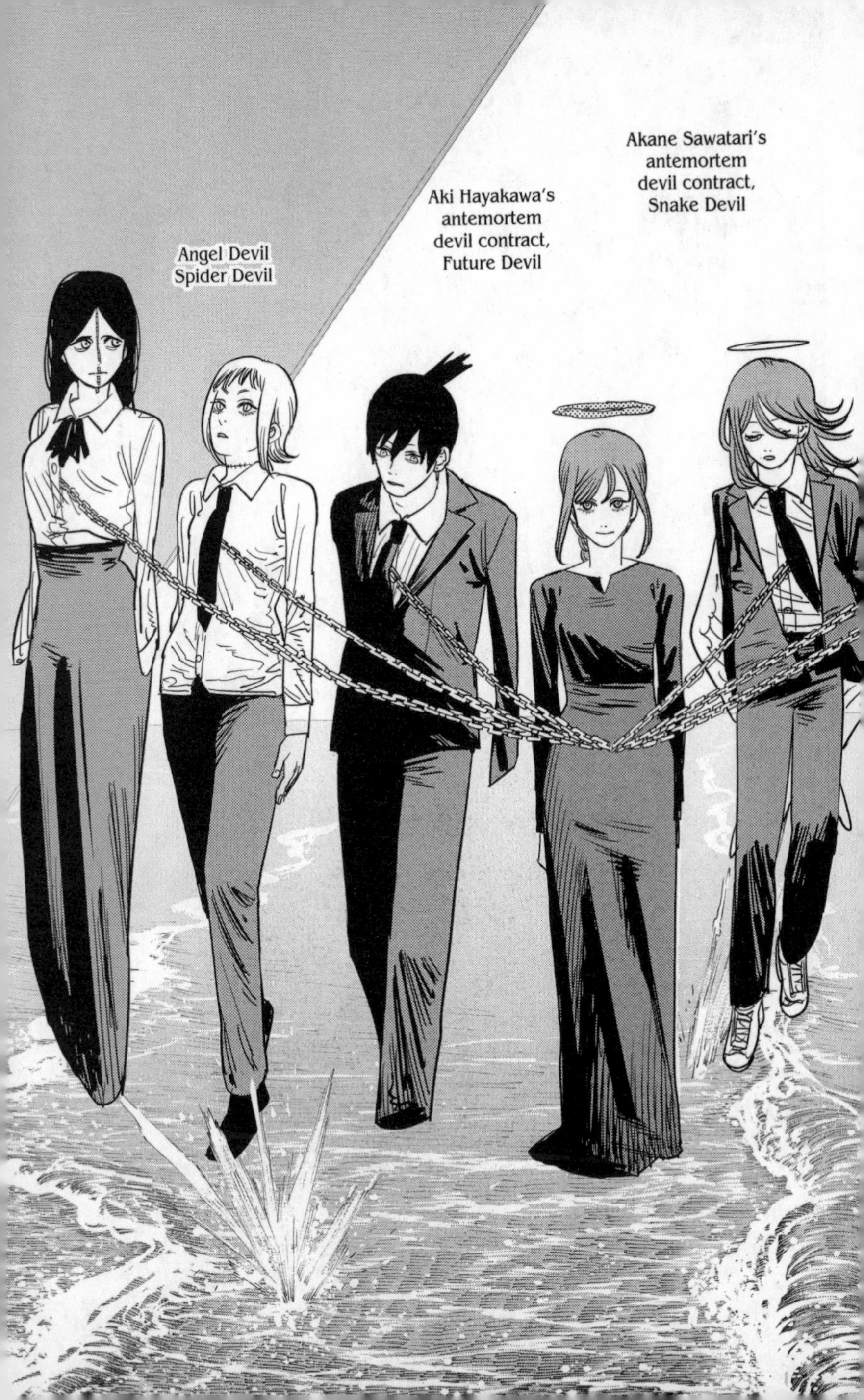
Akane Sawatari's antemortem devil contract, Snake Devil
Aki Hayakawa's antemortem devil contract, Future Devil
Angel Devil
Spider Devil

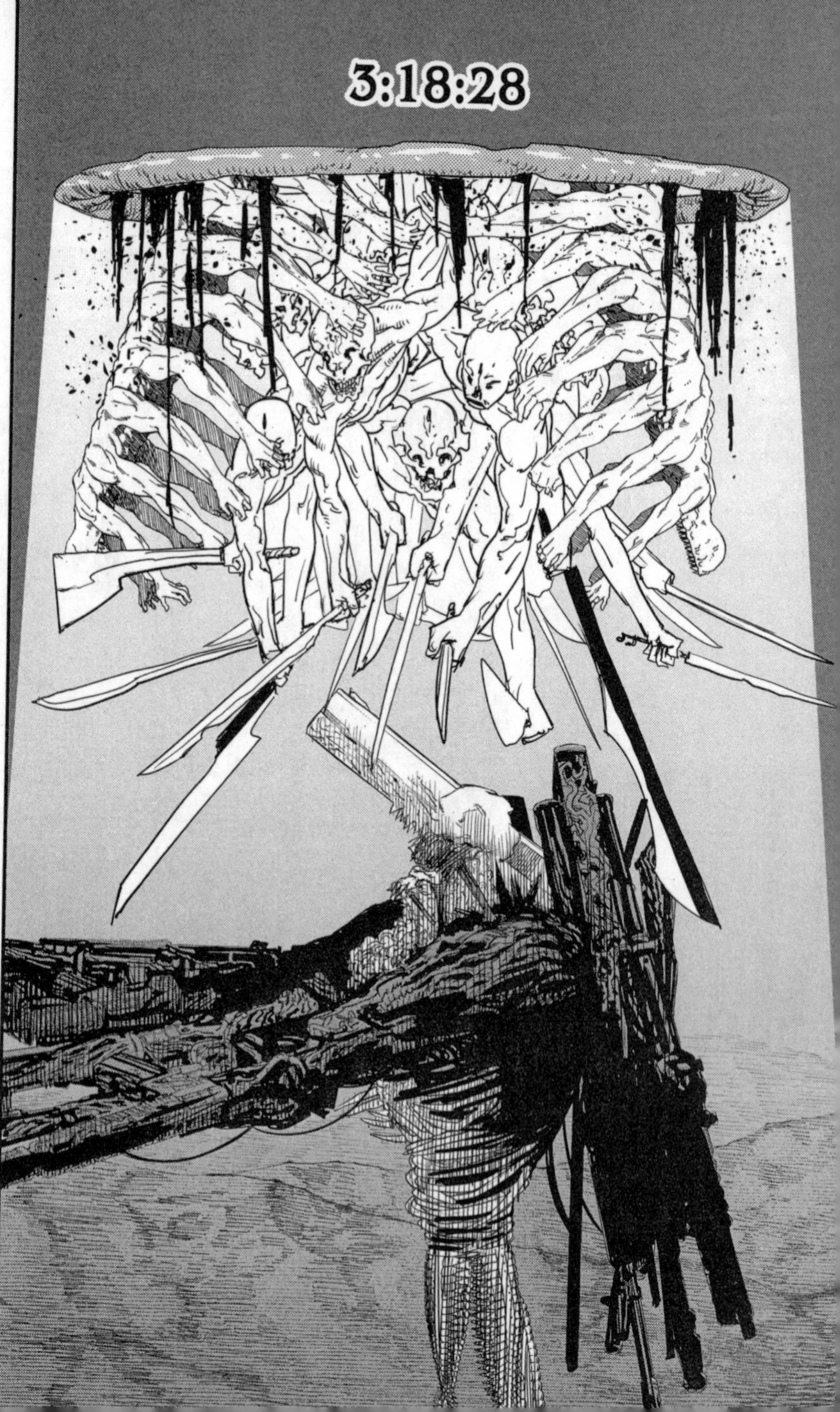
3:18:28

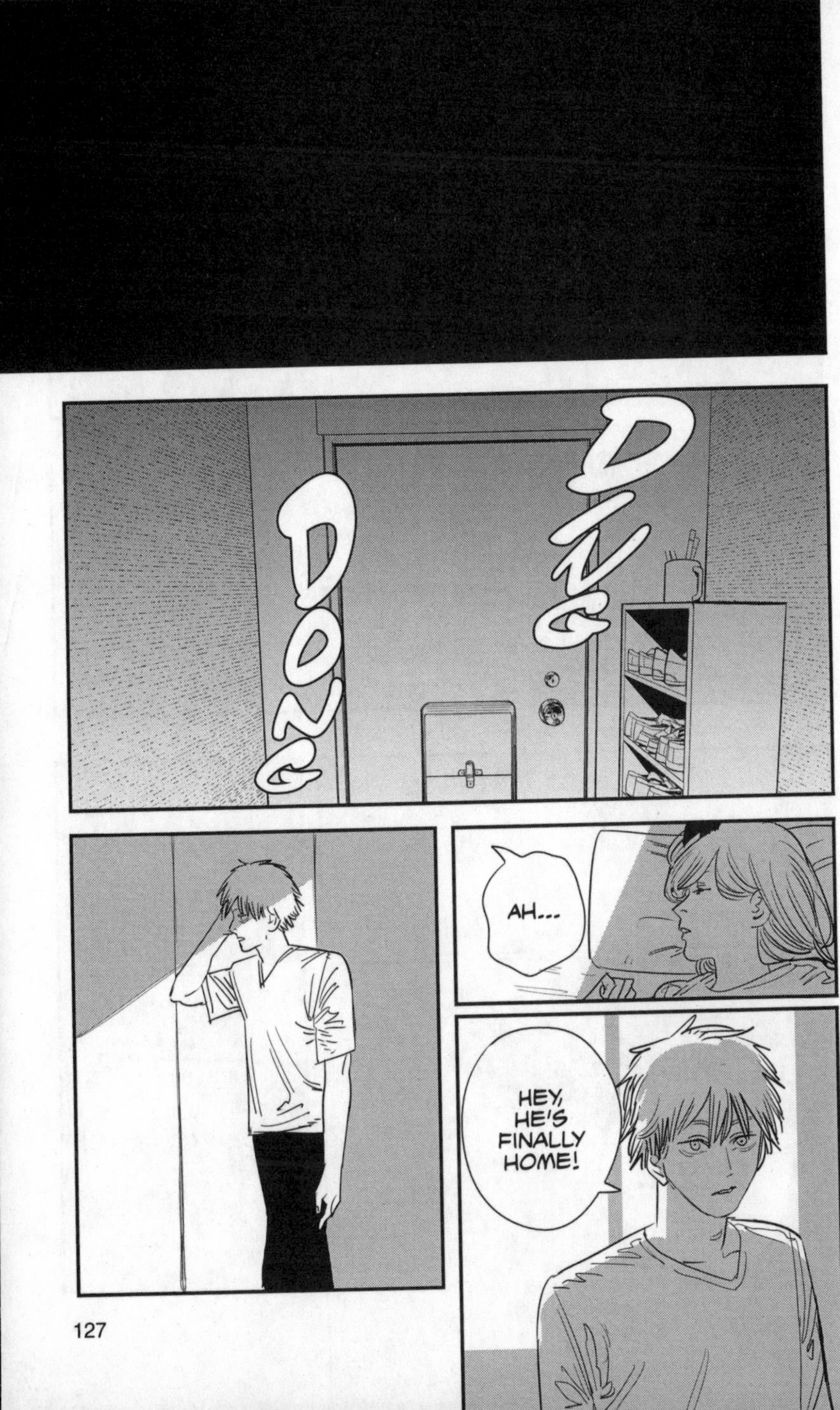
DING
DONG
AH...
HEY, HE'S FINALLY HOME!

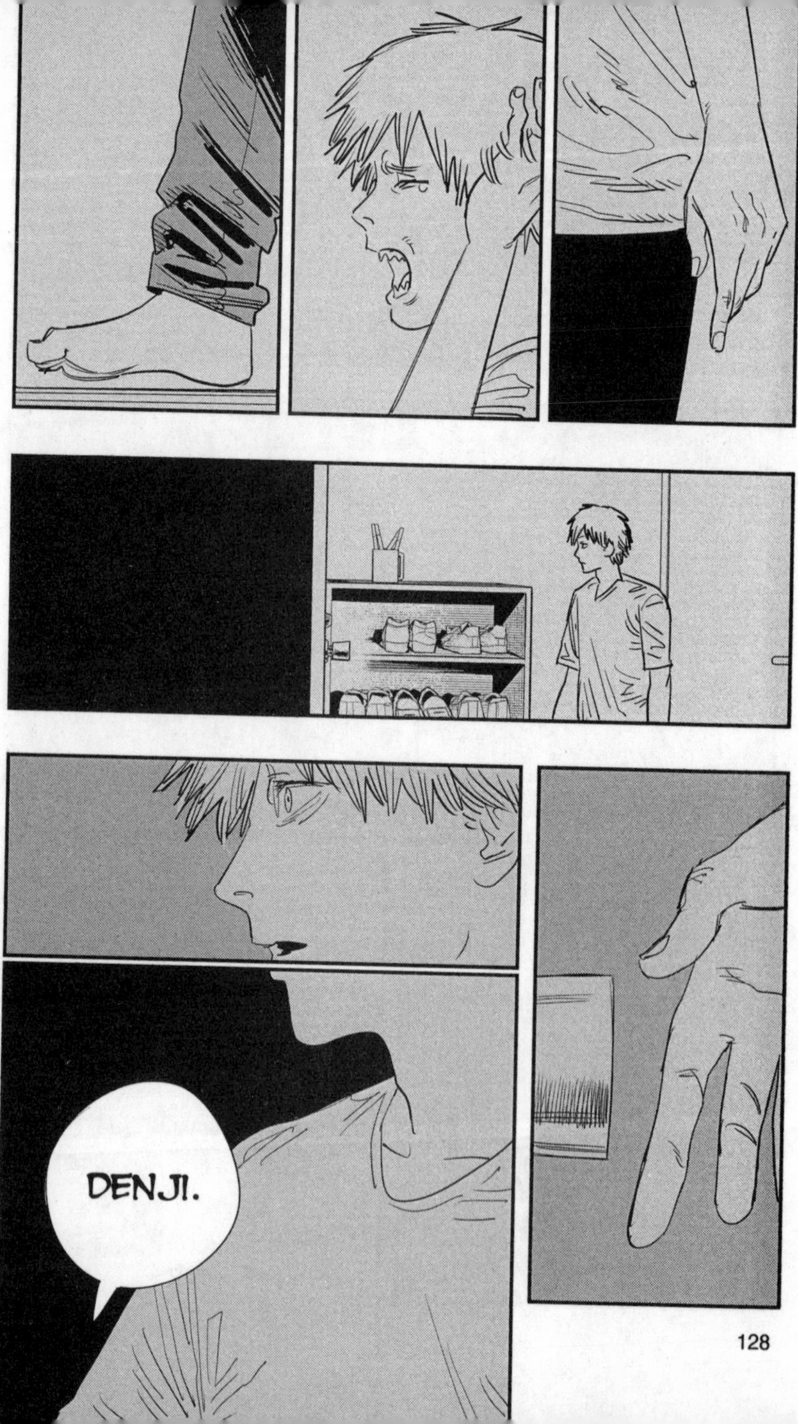
DENJI.

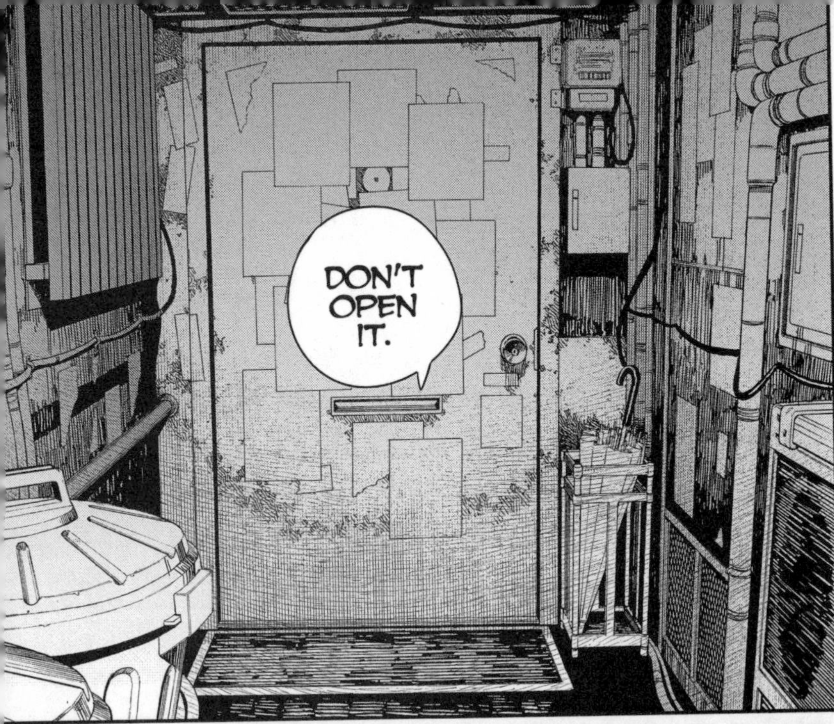
DON'T OPEN IT.

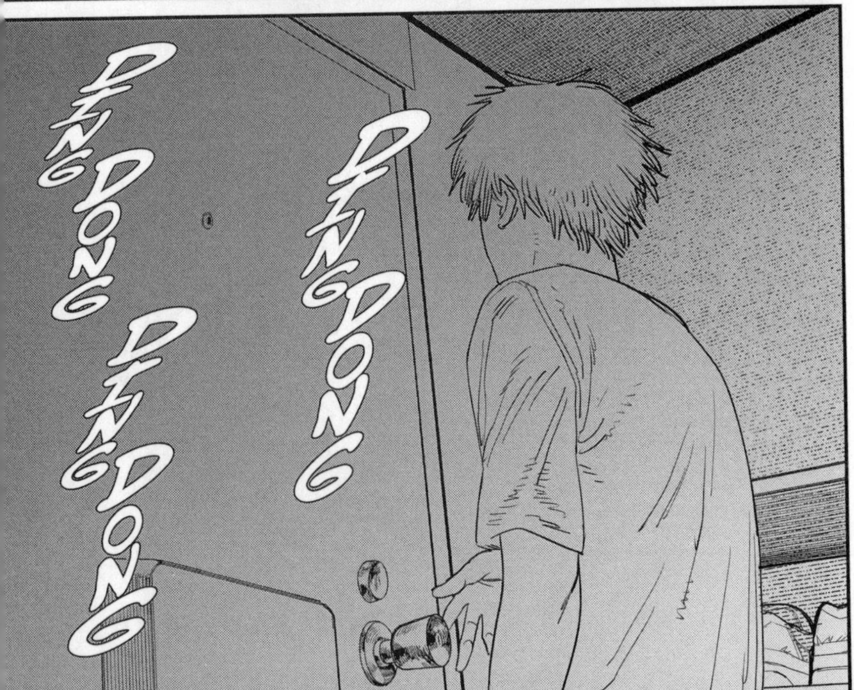
DING DONG
DING DONG
DING DONG

Chain saw man

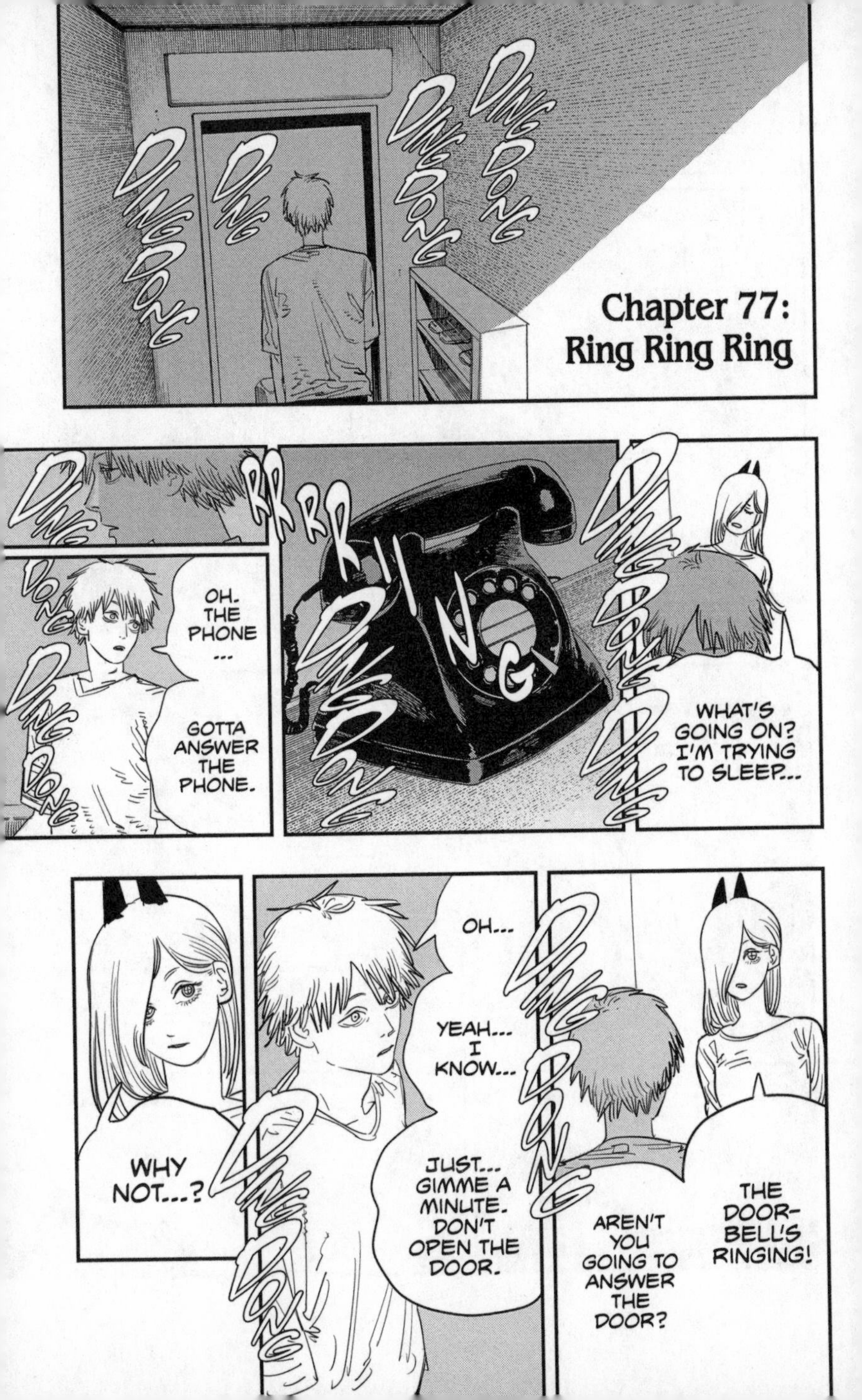

Chapter 77:
Ring Ring Ring
DING DONG
DING DONG
DING
DING DONG
DING DONG DING
WHAT'S GOING ON? I'M TRYING TO SLEEP...
RRRR RIIING
DING DONG
DING DONG DING DONG
OH. THE PHONE...
GOTTA ANSWER THE PHONE.
DING DONG
THE DOOR-BELL'S RINGING!
AREN'T YOU GOING TO ANSWER THE DOOR?
OH...
YEAH... I KNOW...
JUST... GIMME A MINUTE. DON'T OPEN THE DOOR.
DING DONG
WHY NOT...?

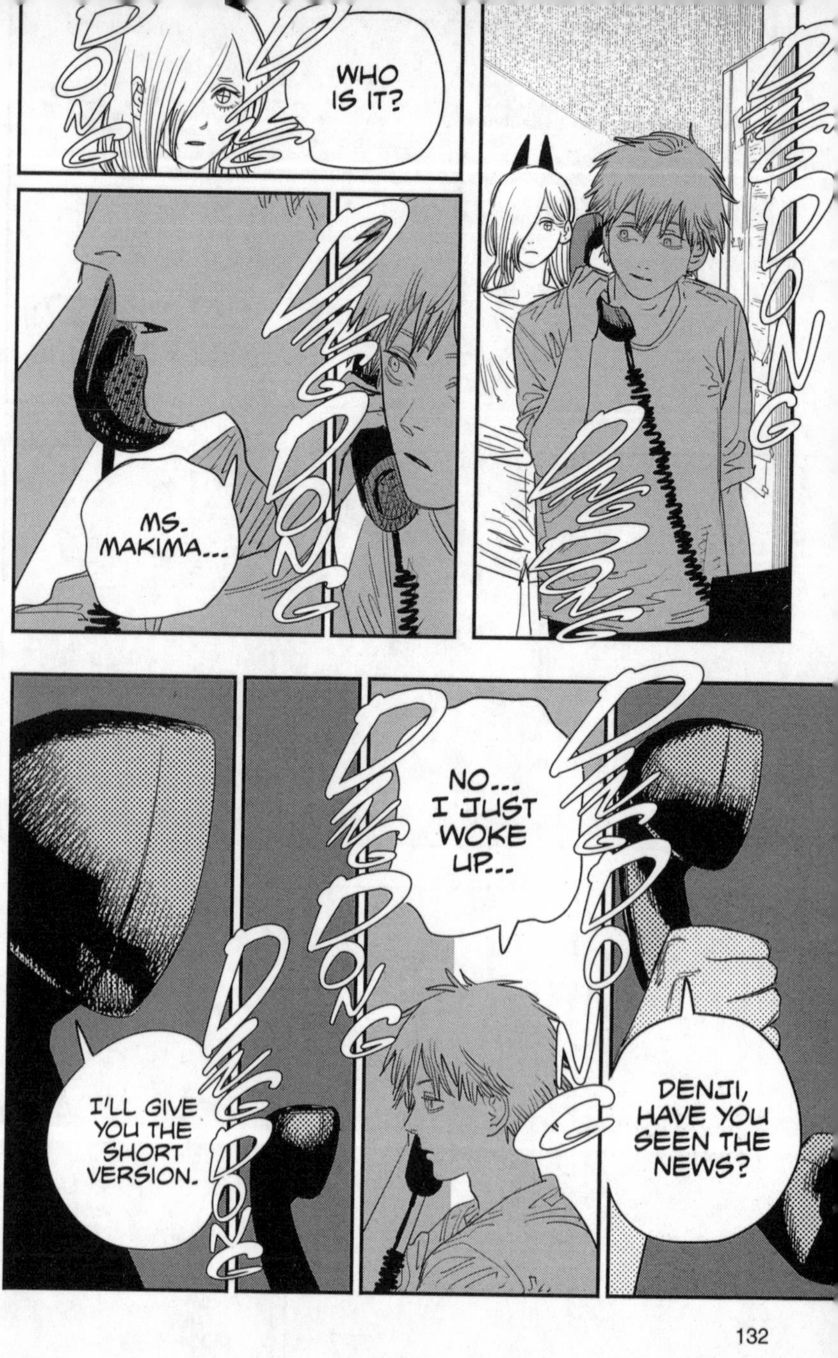
DING DONG
DING DONG
DING DONG
WHO IS IT?
DING DONG
MS. MAKIMA...
DING DONG
DENJI, HAVE YOU SEEN THE NEWS?
NO... I JUST WOKE UP...
DING DONG
DING DONG
I'LL GIVE YOU THE SHORT VERSION.

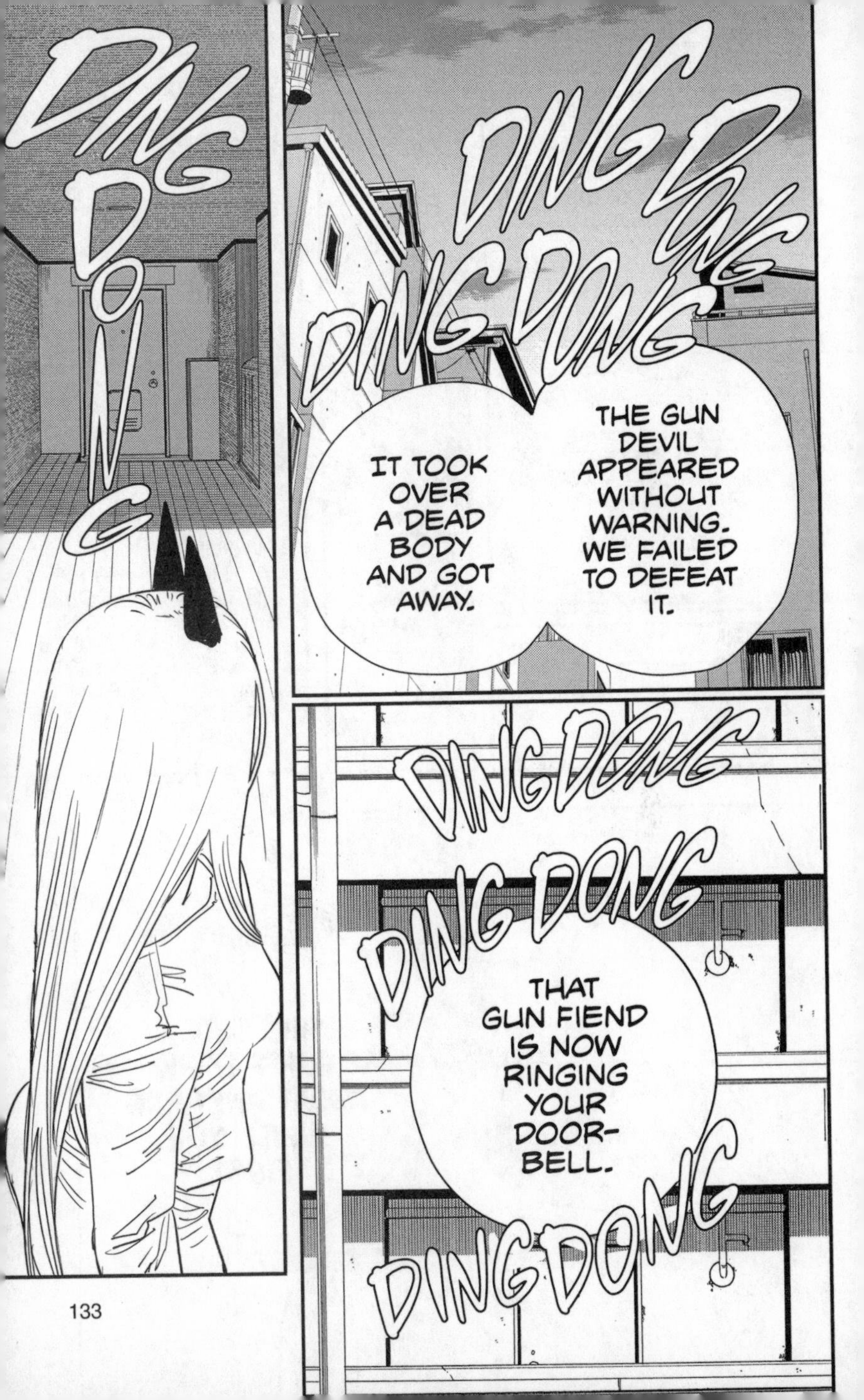
DING DONG
DING DONG
THE GUN DEVIL APPEARED WITHOUT WARNING. WE FAILED TO DEFEAT IT.
IT TOOK OVER A DEAD BODY AND GOT AWAY.
DING DONG
DING DONG
THAT GUN FIEND IS NOW RINGING YOUR DOOR-BELL.
DING DONG
DING DONG

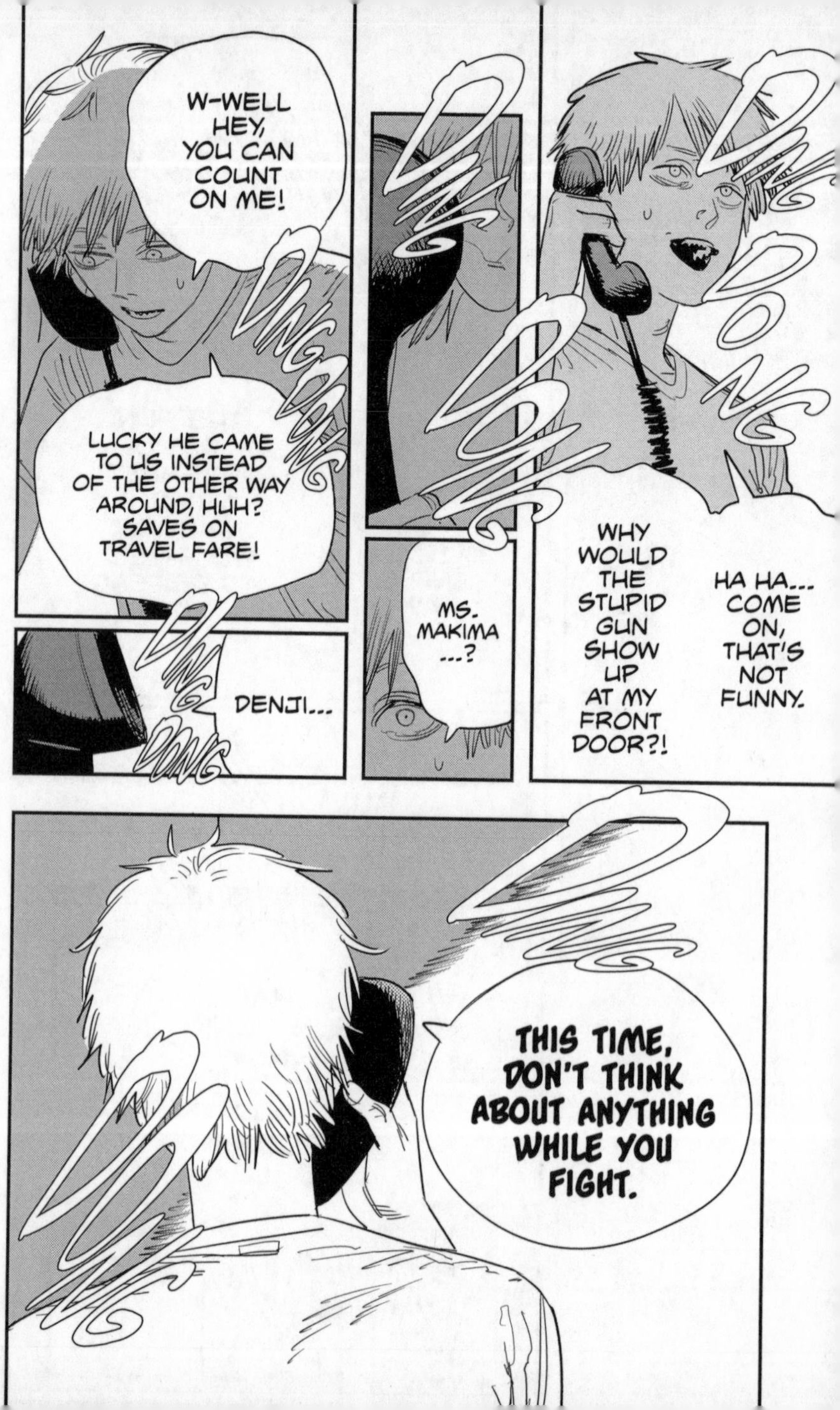
DING DONG
HA HA... COME ON, THAT'S NOT FUNNY.
WHY WOULD THE STUPID GUN SHOW UP AT MY FRONT DOOR?!
DING DONG
MS. MAKIMA...?
W-WELL HEY, YOU CAN COUNT ON ME!
DING DONG
LUCKY HE CAME TO US INSTEAD OF THE OTHER WAY AROUND, HUH? SAVES ON TRAVEL FARE!
DING DONG
DENJI...
DING DONG
THIS TIME, DON'T THINK ABOUT ANYTHING WHILE YOU FIGHT.

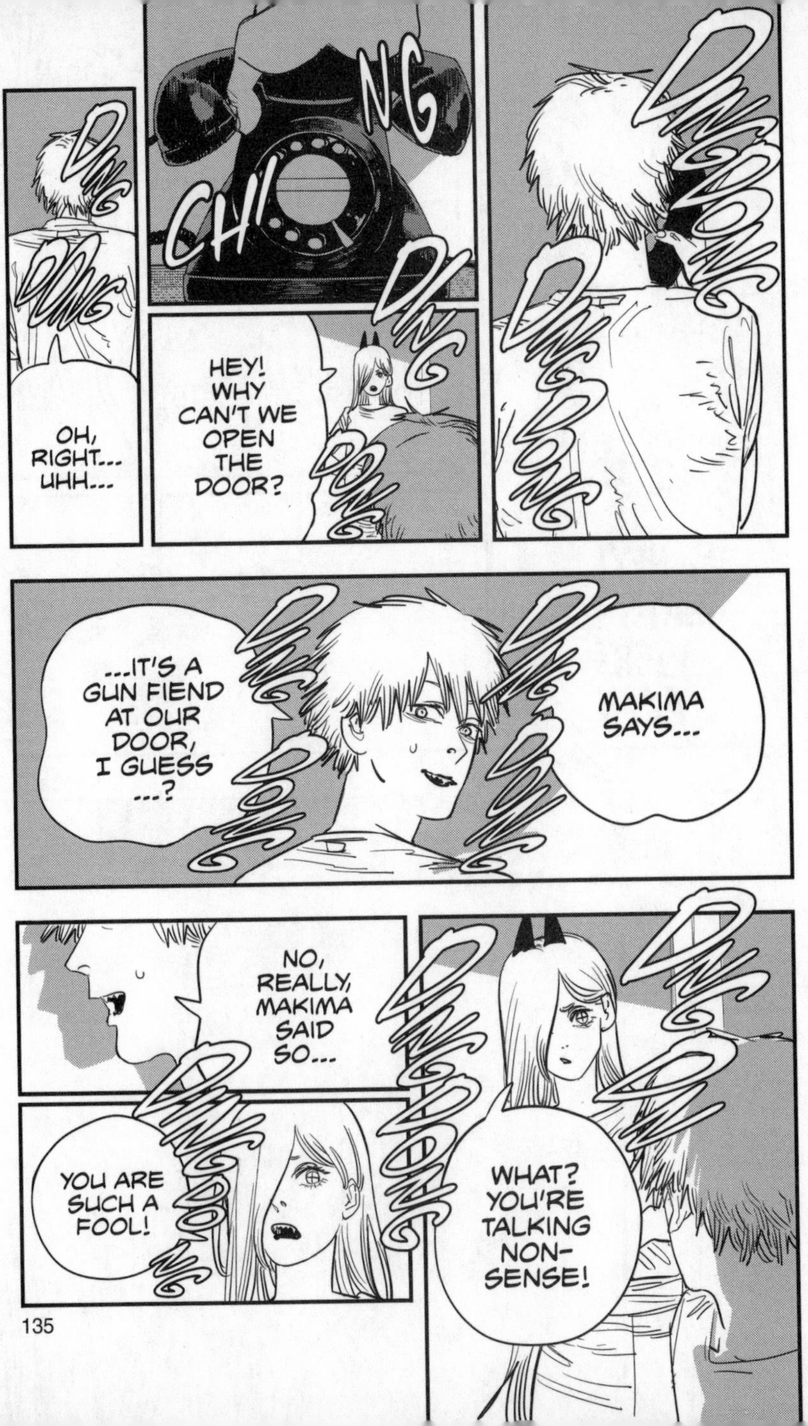
DINGDONG
DINGDONG
CHING
DING DONG
HEY! WHY CAN'T WE OPEN THE DOOR?
DING DONG
OH, RIGHT... UHH...
MAKIMA SAYS...
...IT'S A GUN FIEND AT OUR DOOR, I GUESS...?
WHAT? YOU'RE TALKING NON-SENSE!
NO, REALLY, MAKIMA SAID SO...
YOU ARE SUCH A FOOL!

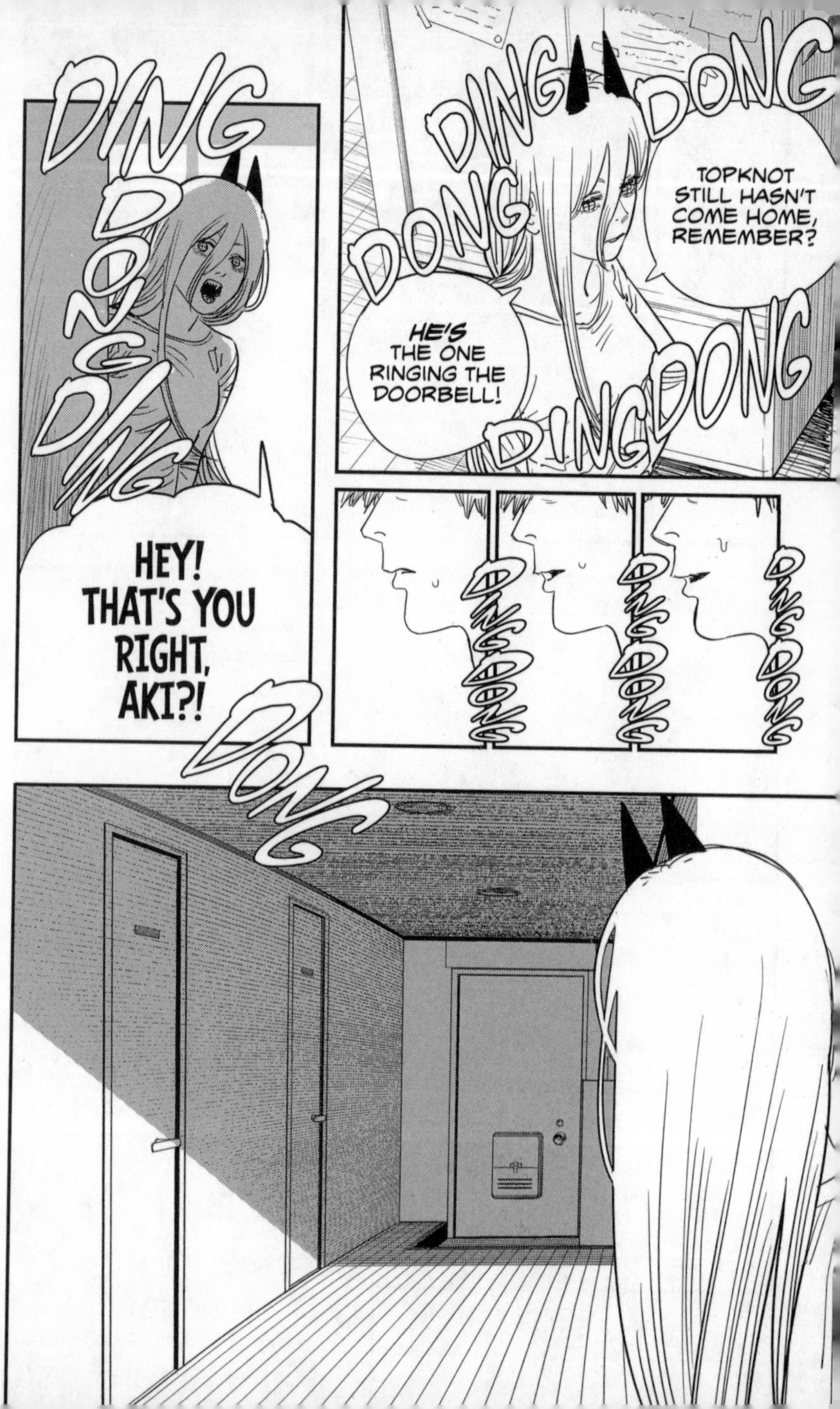
DING DONG
DING DONG
TOPKNOT STILL HASN'T COME HOME, REMEMBER?
HE'S THE ONE RINGING THE DOORBELL!
DING DONG
DING DONG
DING DONG
DING DONG
DING DONG DING
HEY! THAT'S YOU RIGHT, AKI?!
DONG

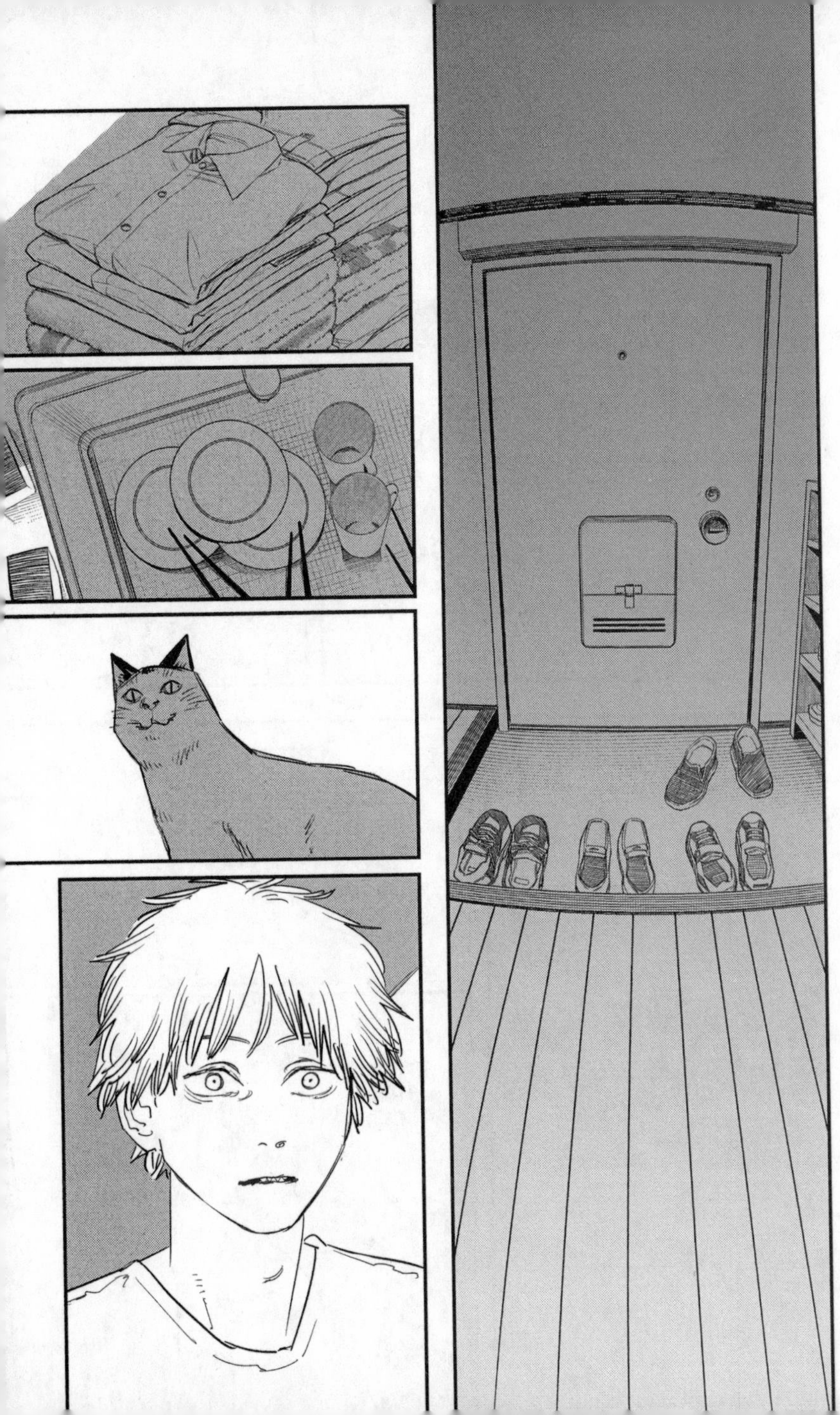

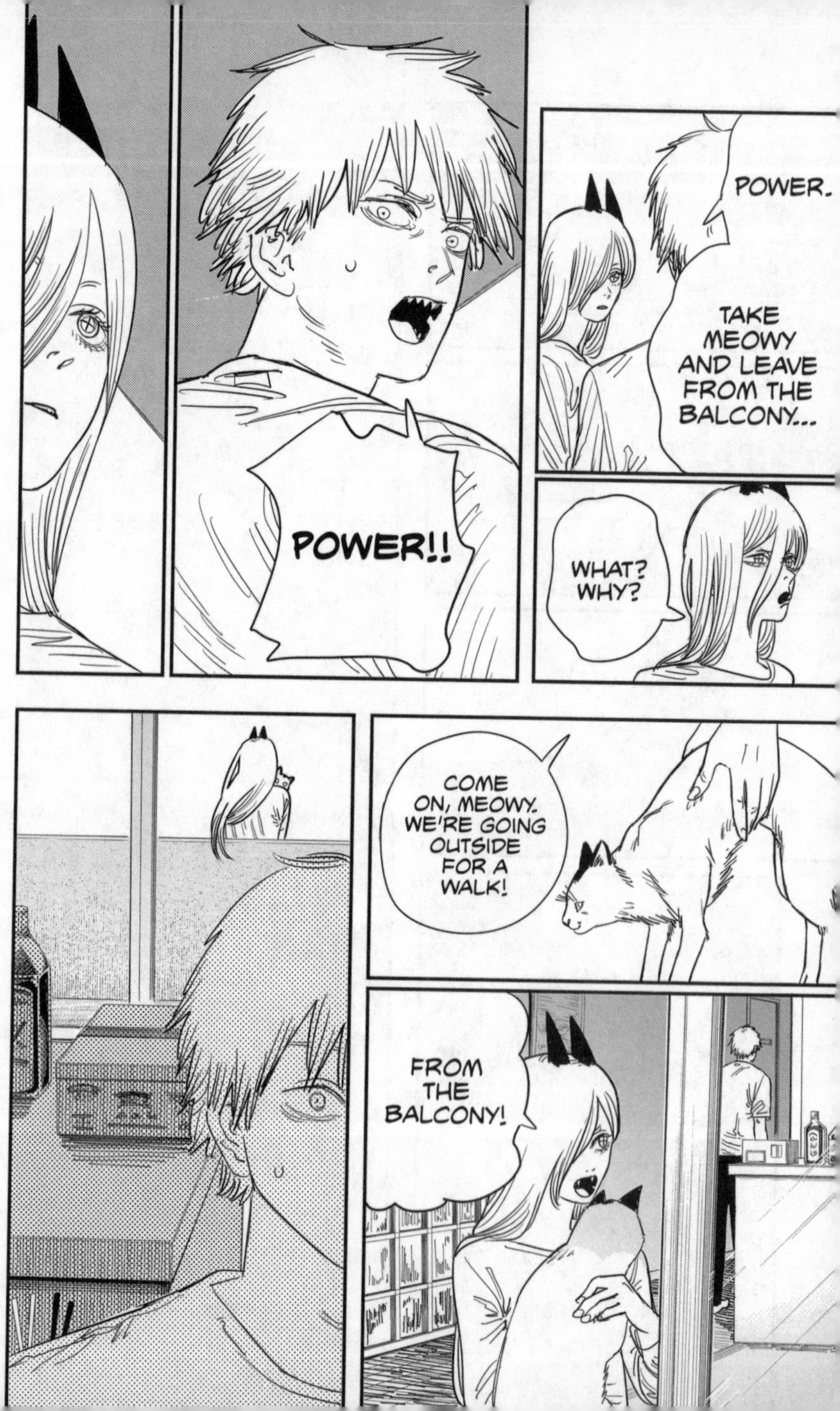
POWER.
TAKE MEOWY AND LEAVE FROM THE BALCONY...
WHAT? WHY?
POWER!!
COME ON, MEOWY. WE'RE GOING OUTSIDE FOR A WALK!
FROM THE BALCONY!

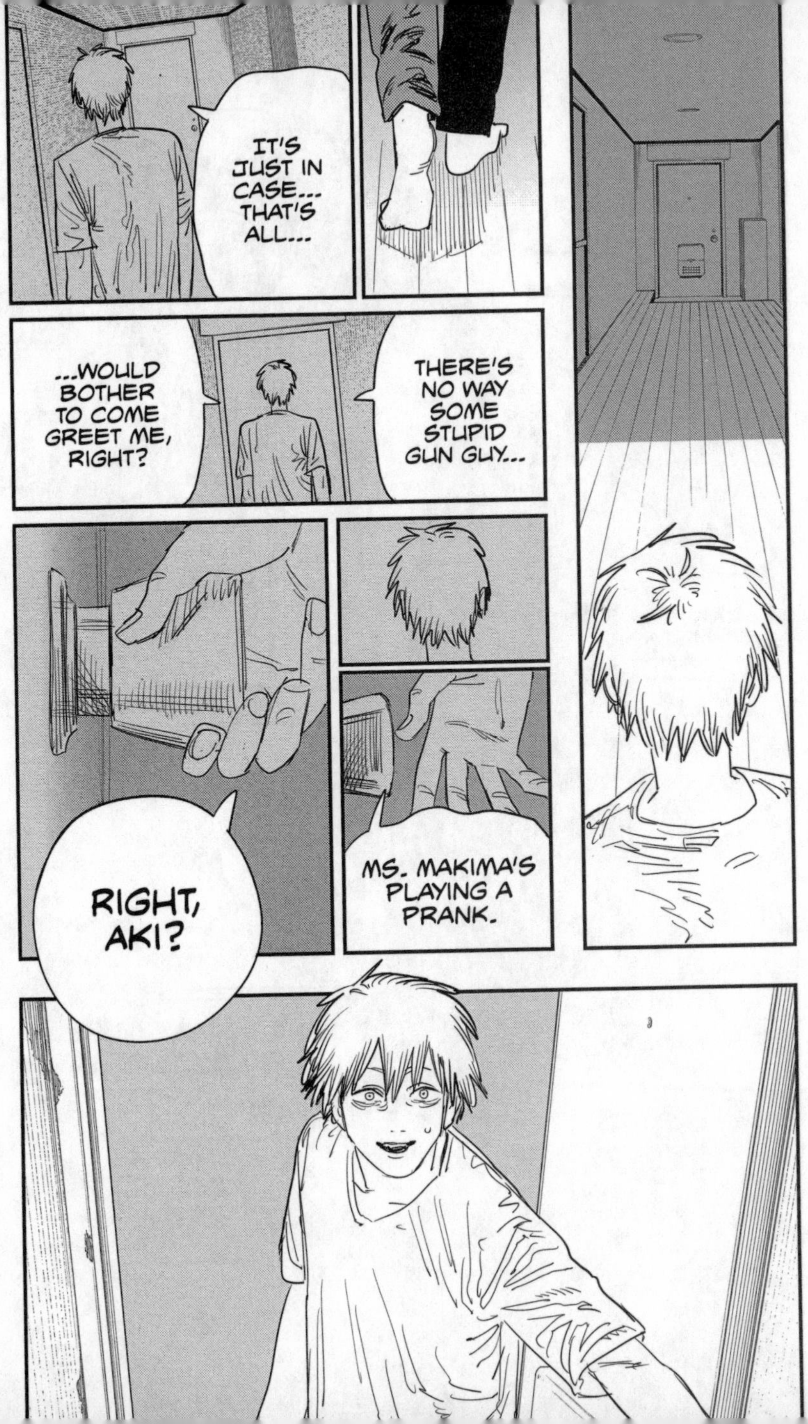
IT'S JUST IN CASE... THAT'S ALL...
THERE'S NO WAY SOME STUPID GUN GUY...
...WOULD BOTHER TO COME GREET ME, RIGHT?
MS. MAKIMA'S PLAYING A PRANK.
RIGHT, AKI?

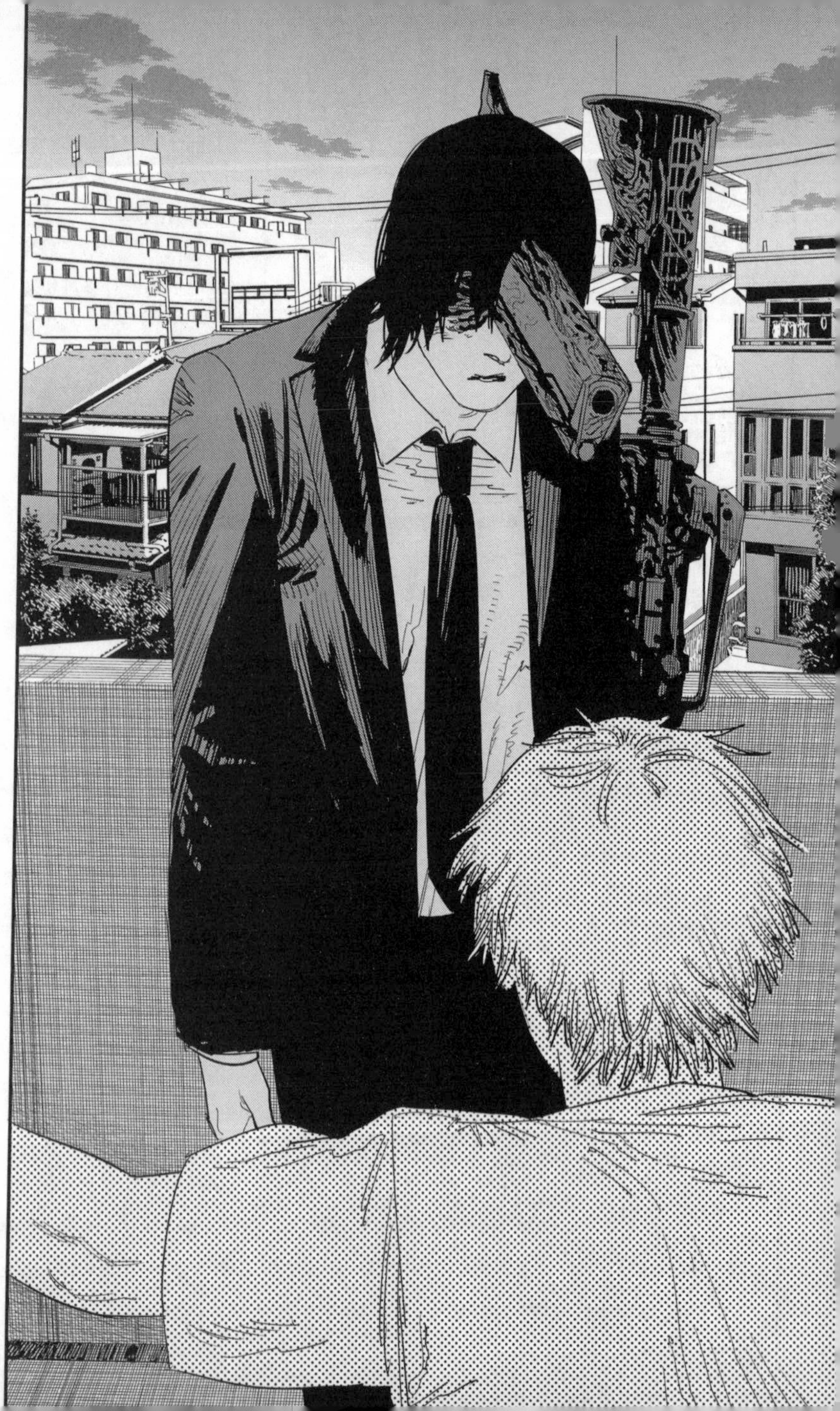

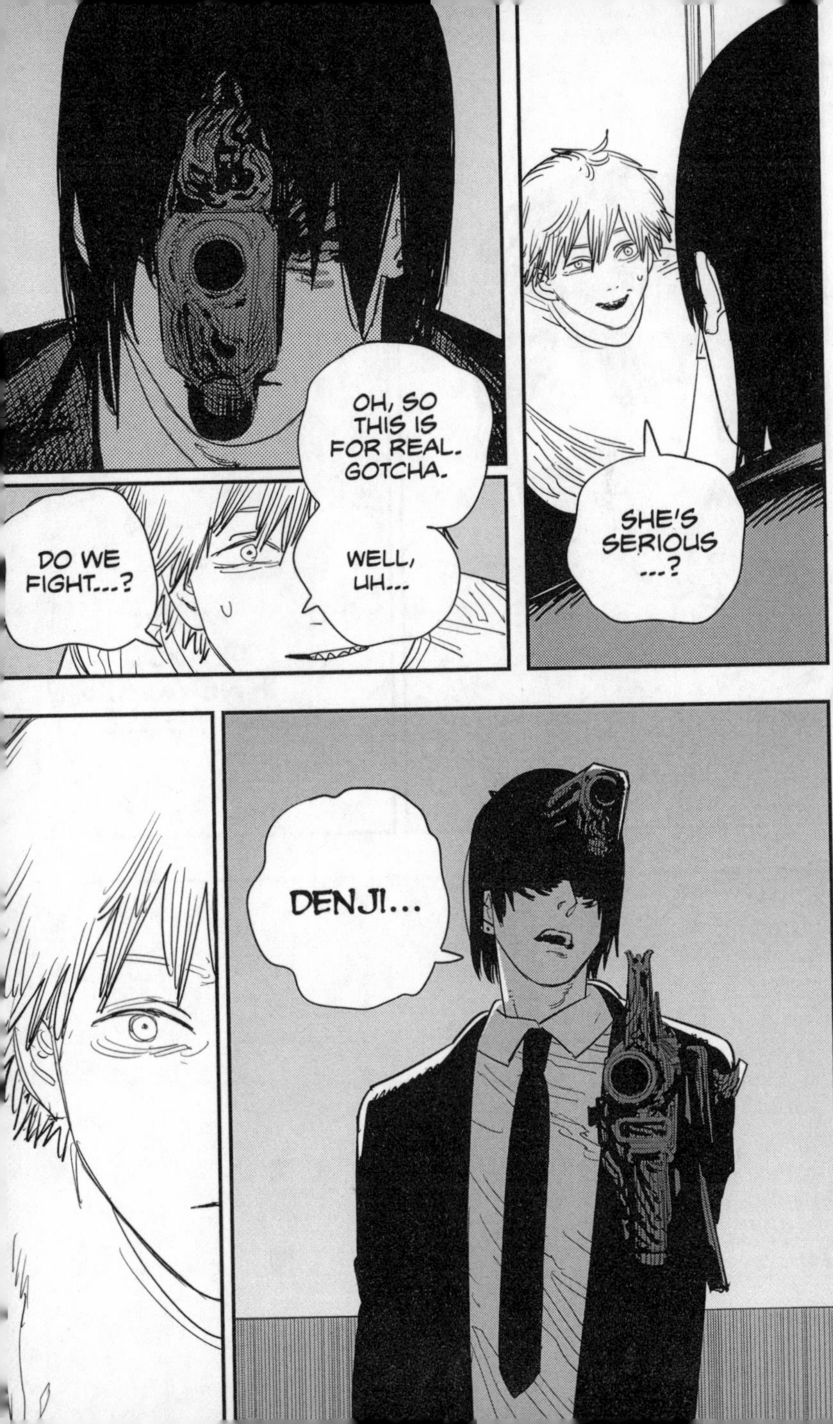
SHE'S SERIOUS...?
OH, SO THIS IS FOR REAL. GOTCHA.
WELL, UH...
DO WE FIGHT...?
DENJI...

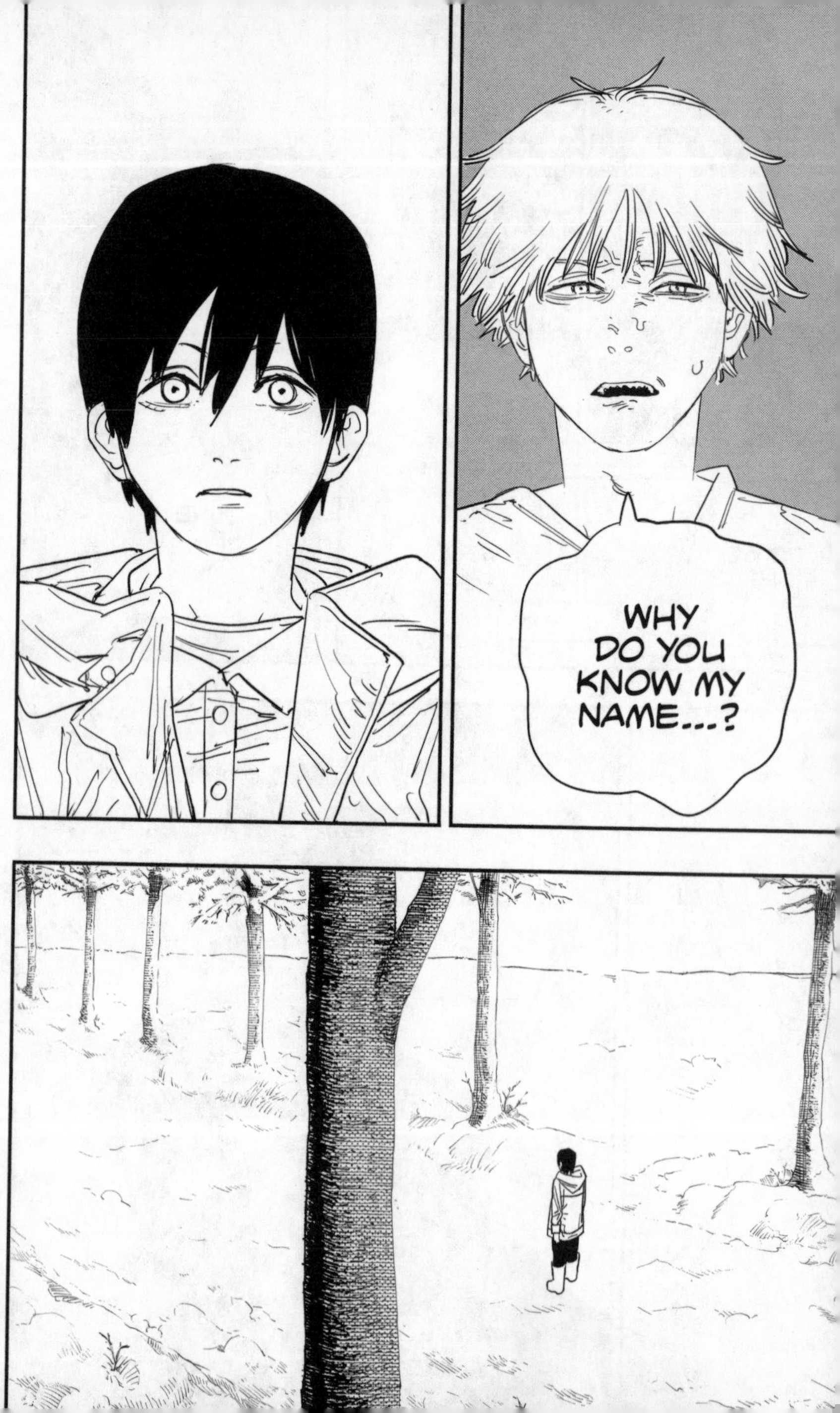
WHY DO YOU KNOW MY NAME...?

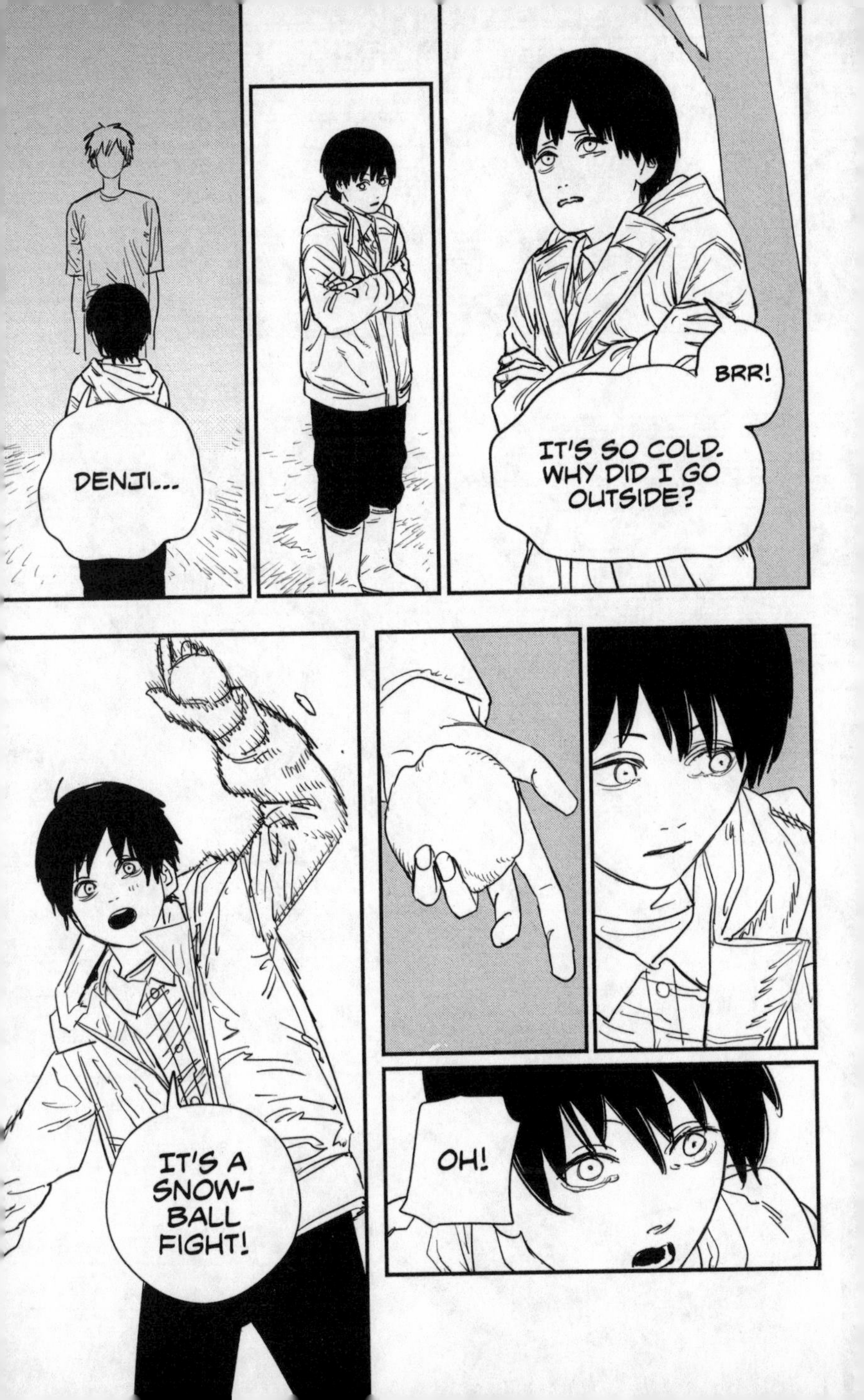
BRR!
IT'S SO COLD. WHY DID I GO OUTSIDE?
DENJI...
OH!
IT'S A SNOW-BALL FIGHT!

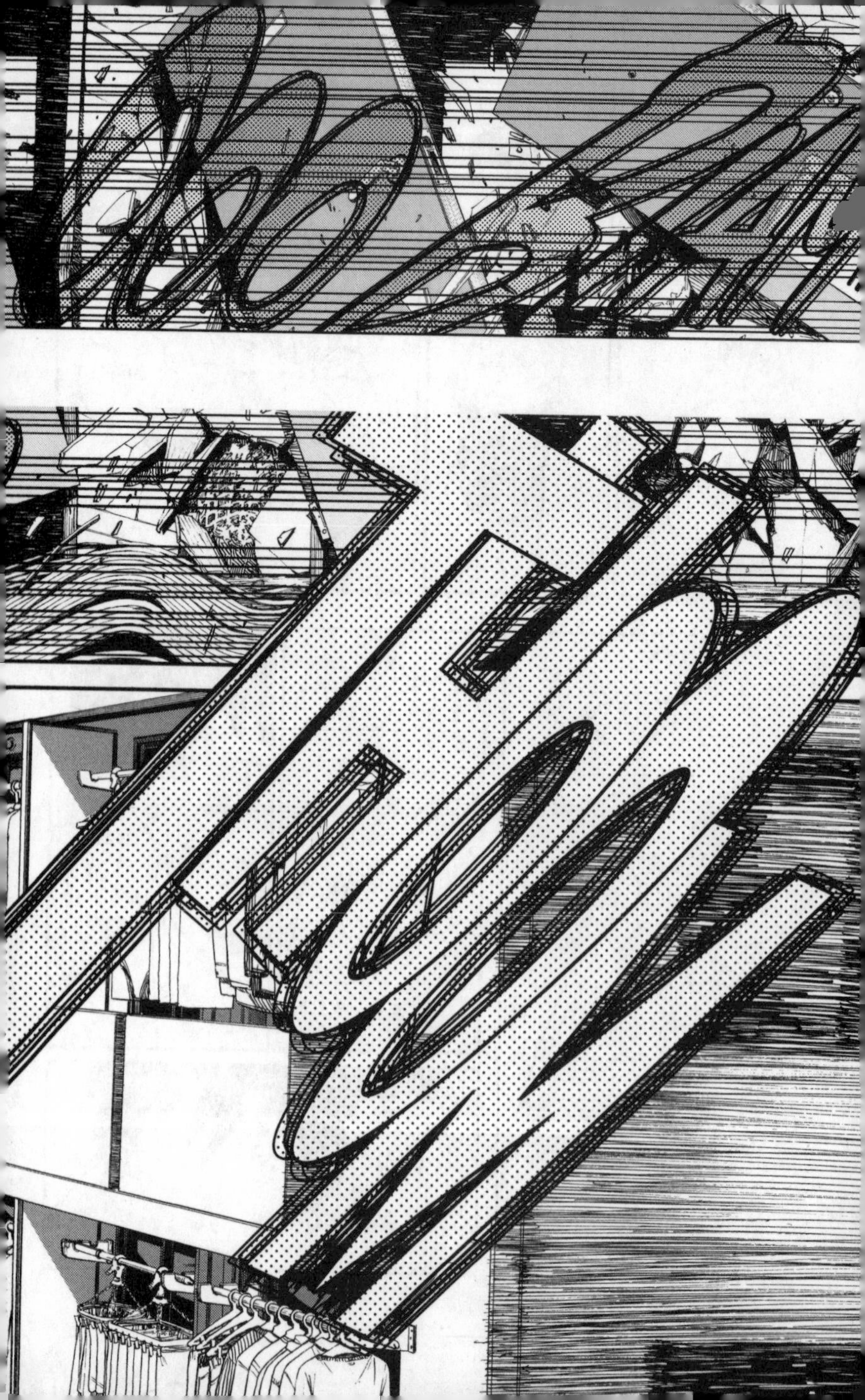

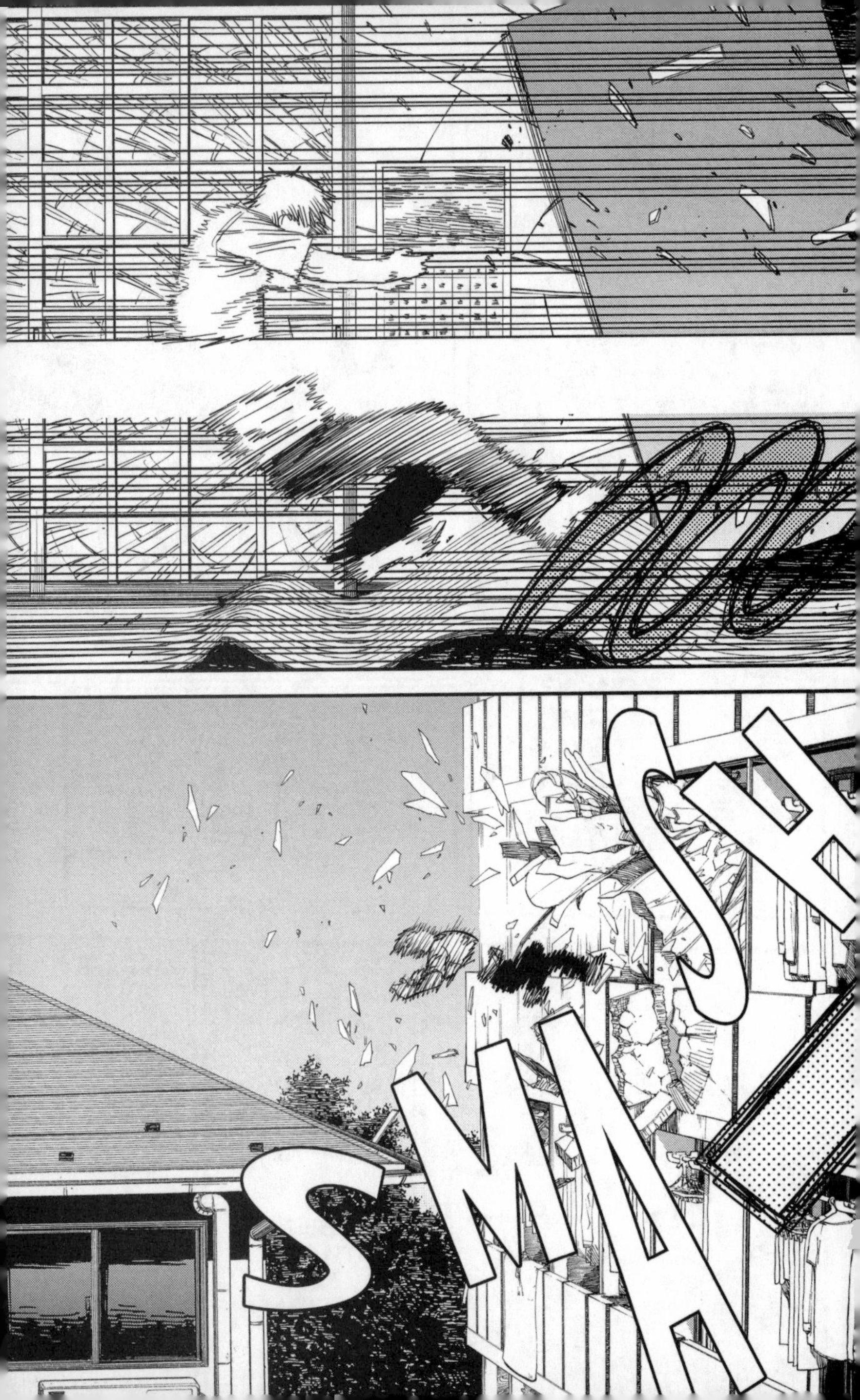
SMASH

BDRM

POWER!! HIDE!! IT WAS A GUN FIEND AFTER ALL!

I'LL TAKE CARE OF 'IM!

MY APART- MENT!

AH! DENJI?!

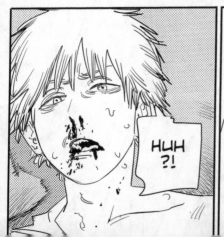

HUH ?!

BUT THAT'S NOT POSSIBLE!!

GUN FIEND ---?

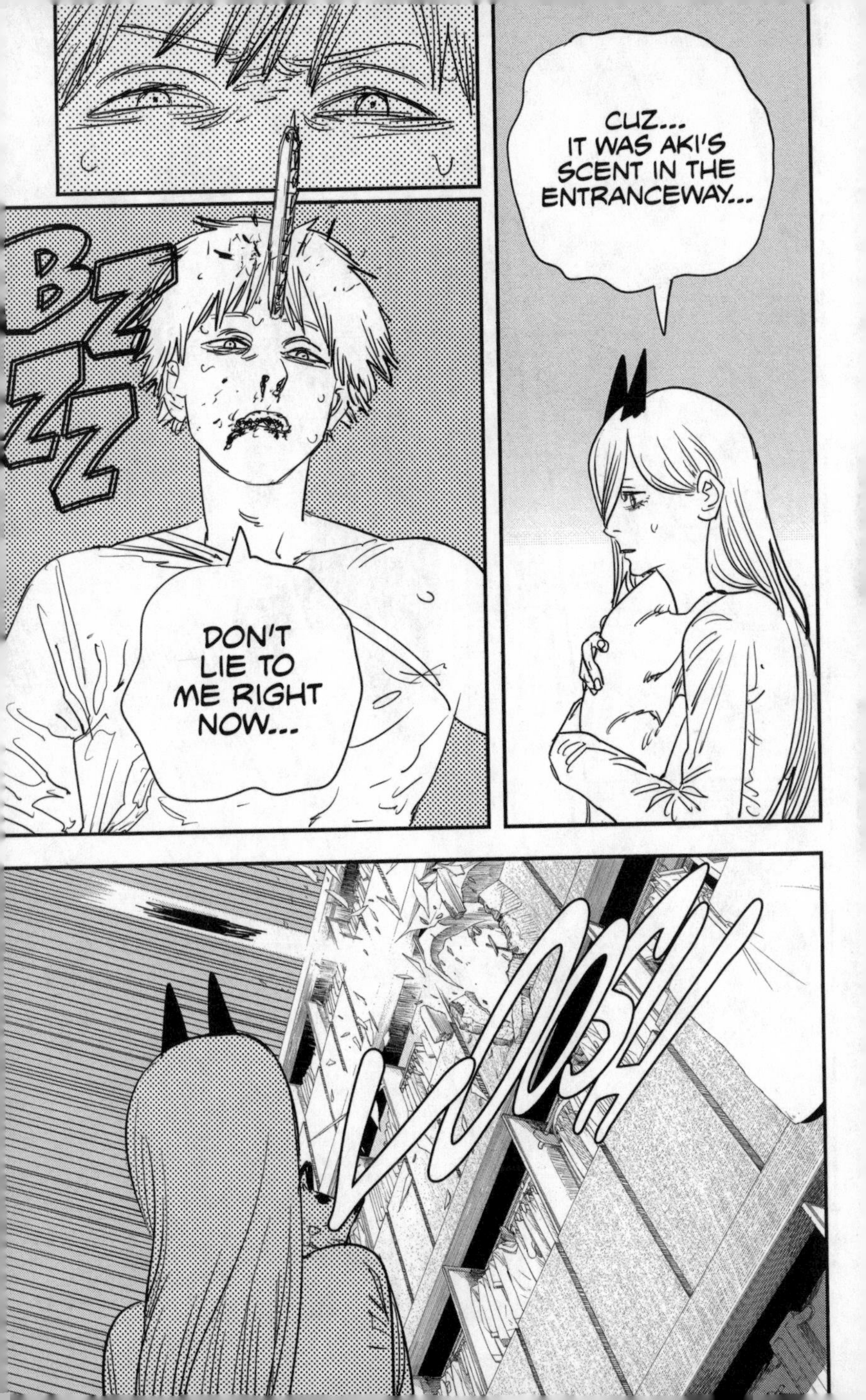
CUZ... IT WAS AKI'S SCENT IN THE ENTRANCEWAY...
DON'T LIE TO ME RIGHT NOW...

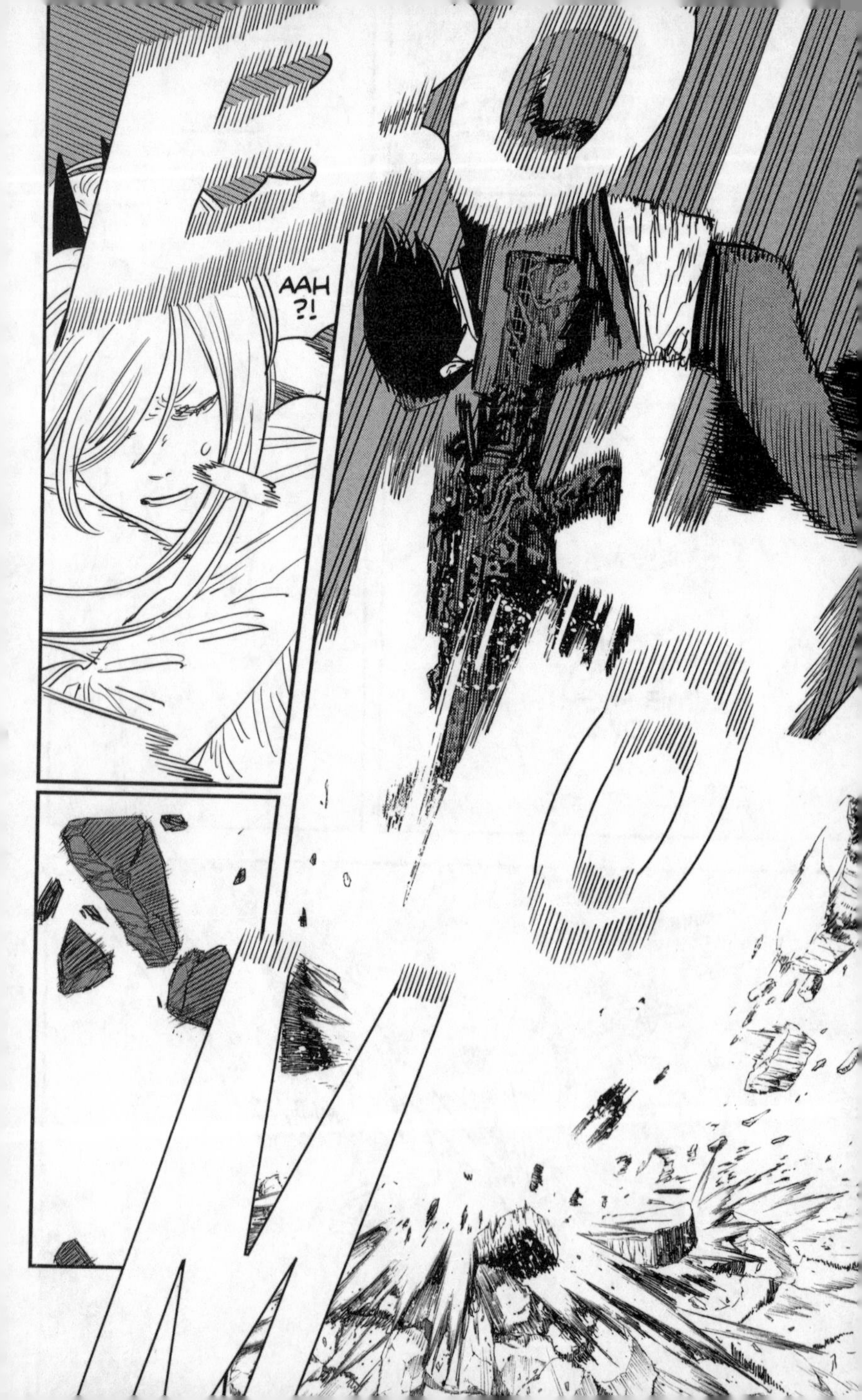
AAH ?!

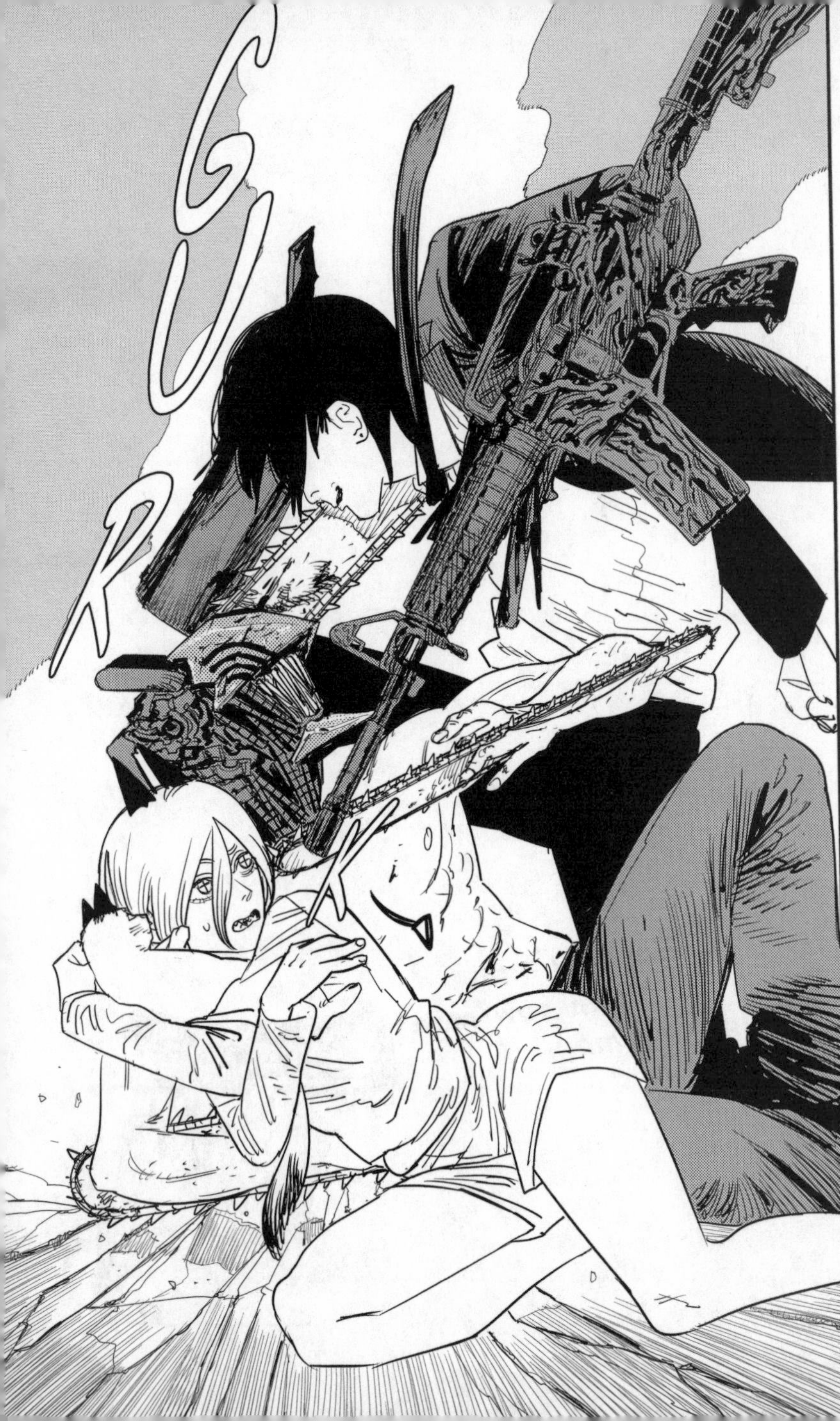

Chain saw man
Chain saw man
Chain saw man

Chapter 78: Snowball Fight

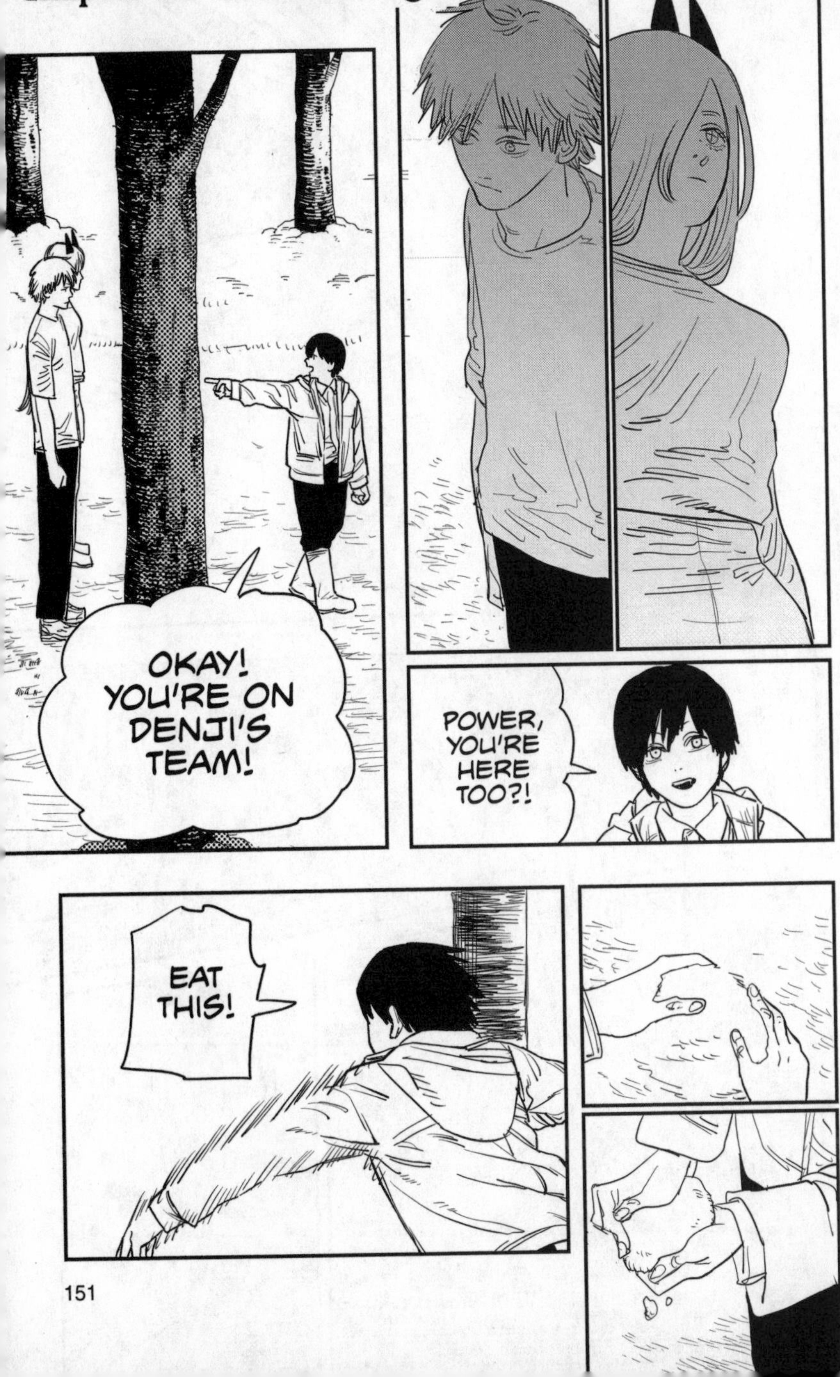
POWER, YOU'RE HERE TOO?!
OKAY! YOU'RE ON DENJI'S TEAM!
EAT THIS!

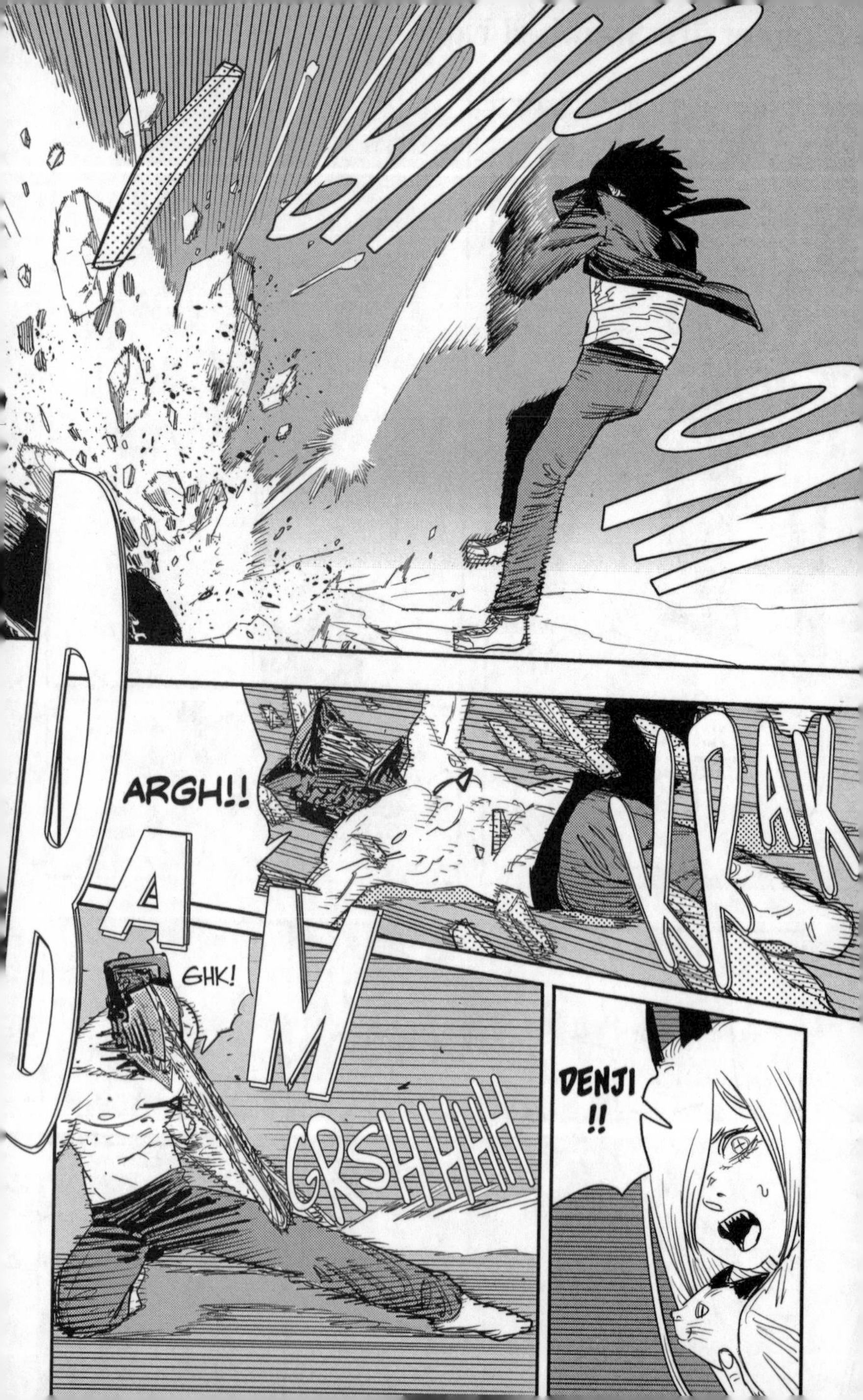

BWOOOM
KRAK
ARGH!!
BAM
DENJI !!
GHK!
GRSHHHH

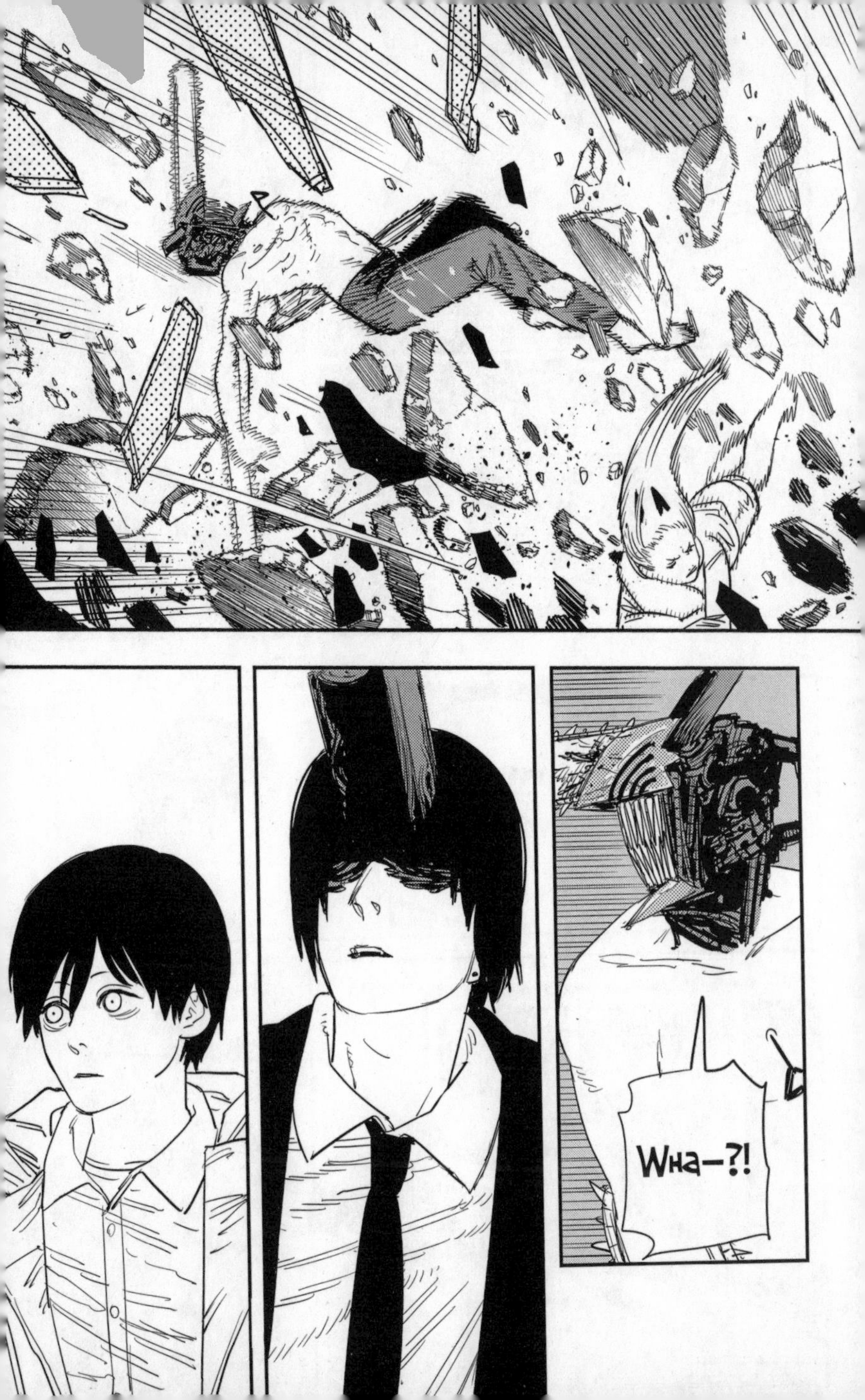
Wha-?!

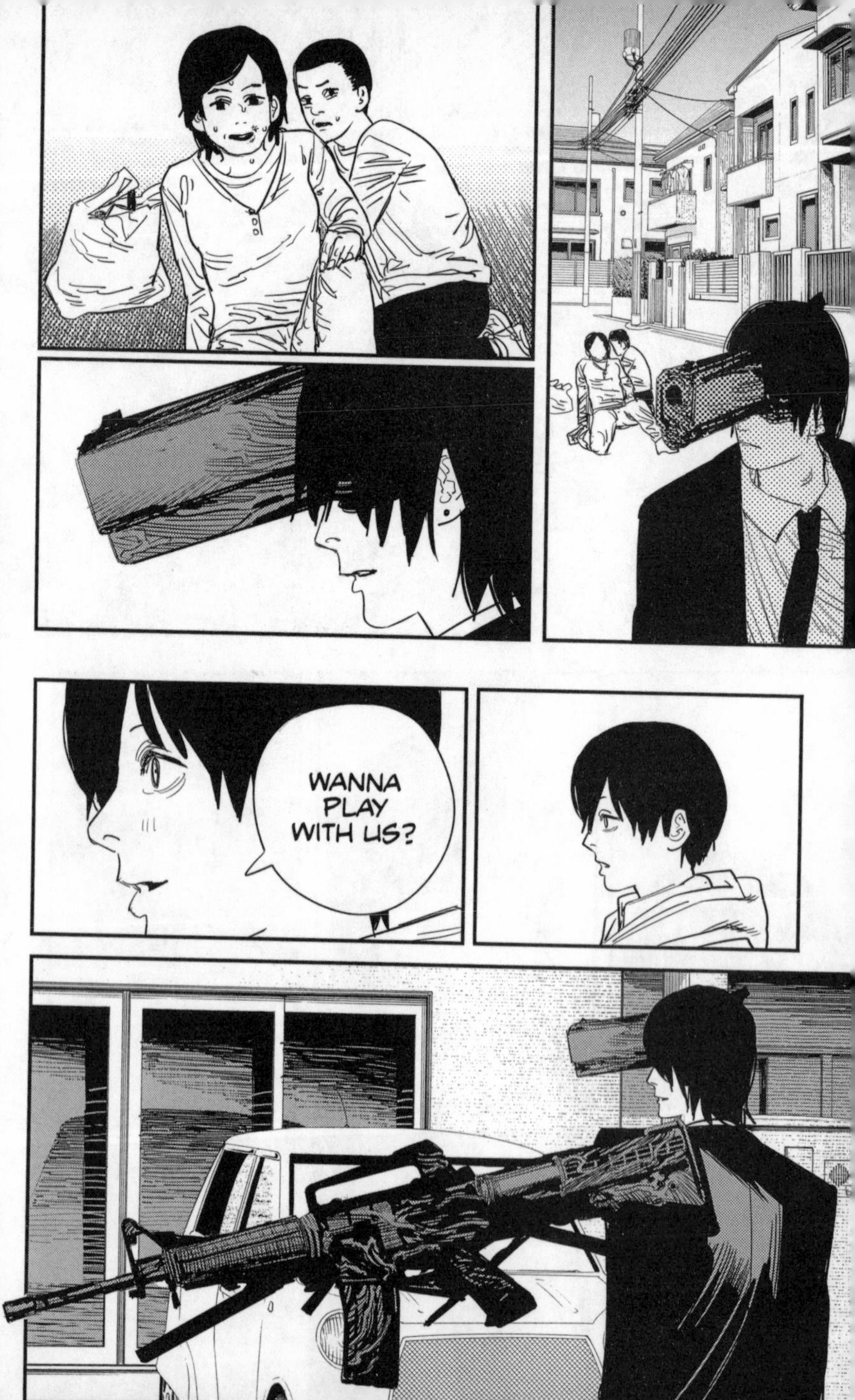
WANNA PLAY WITH US?

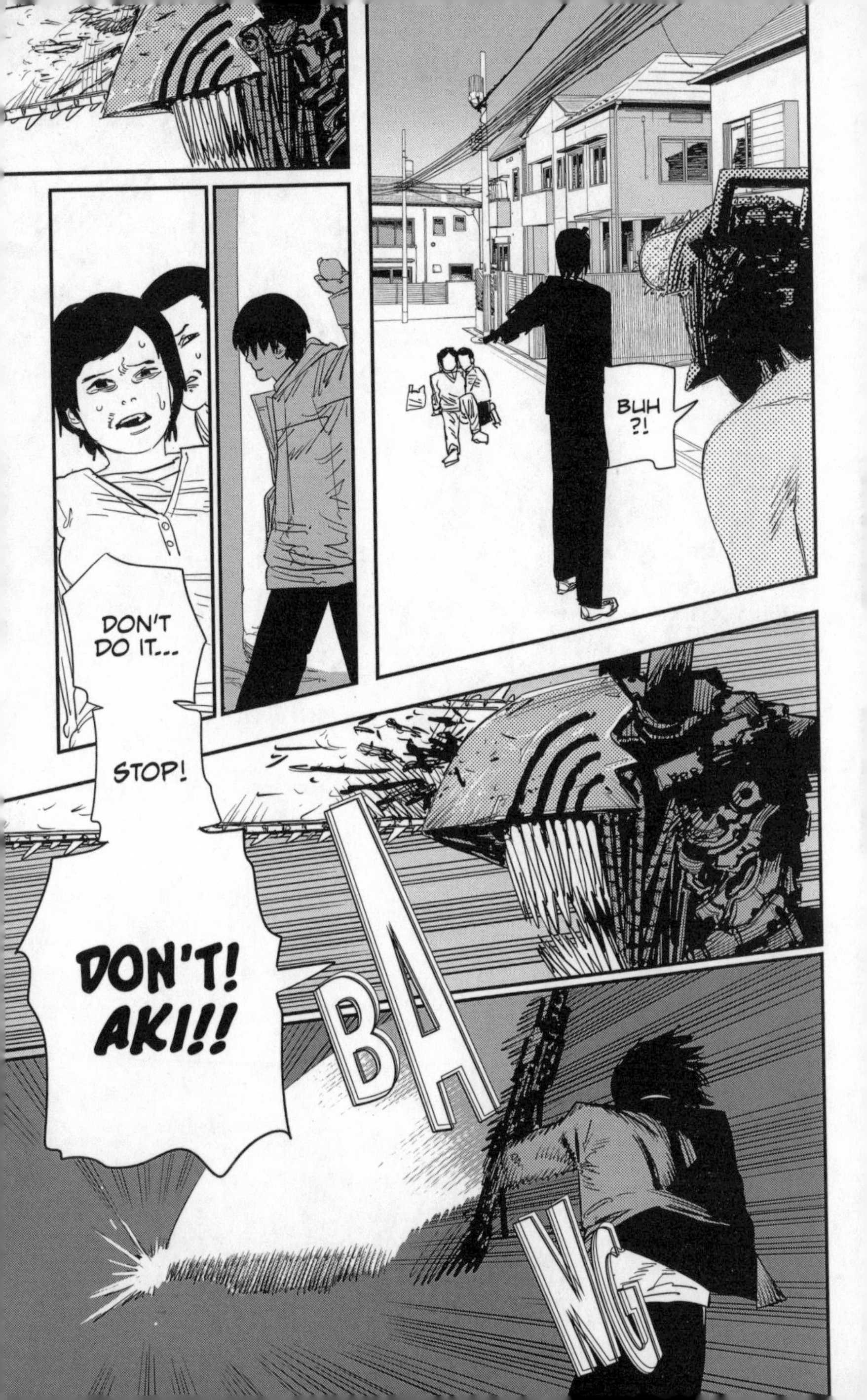
BUH ?!
DON'T DO IT...
STOP!
DON'T! AKI!!
BANG

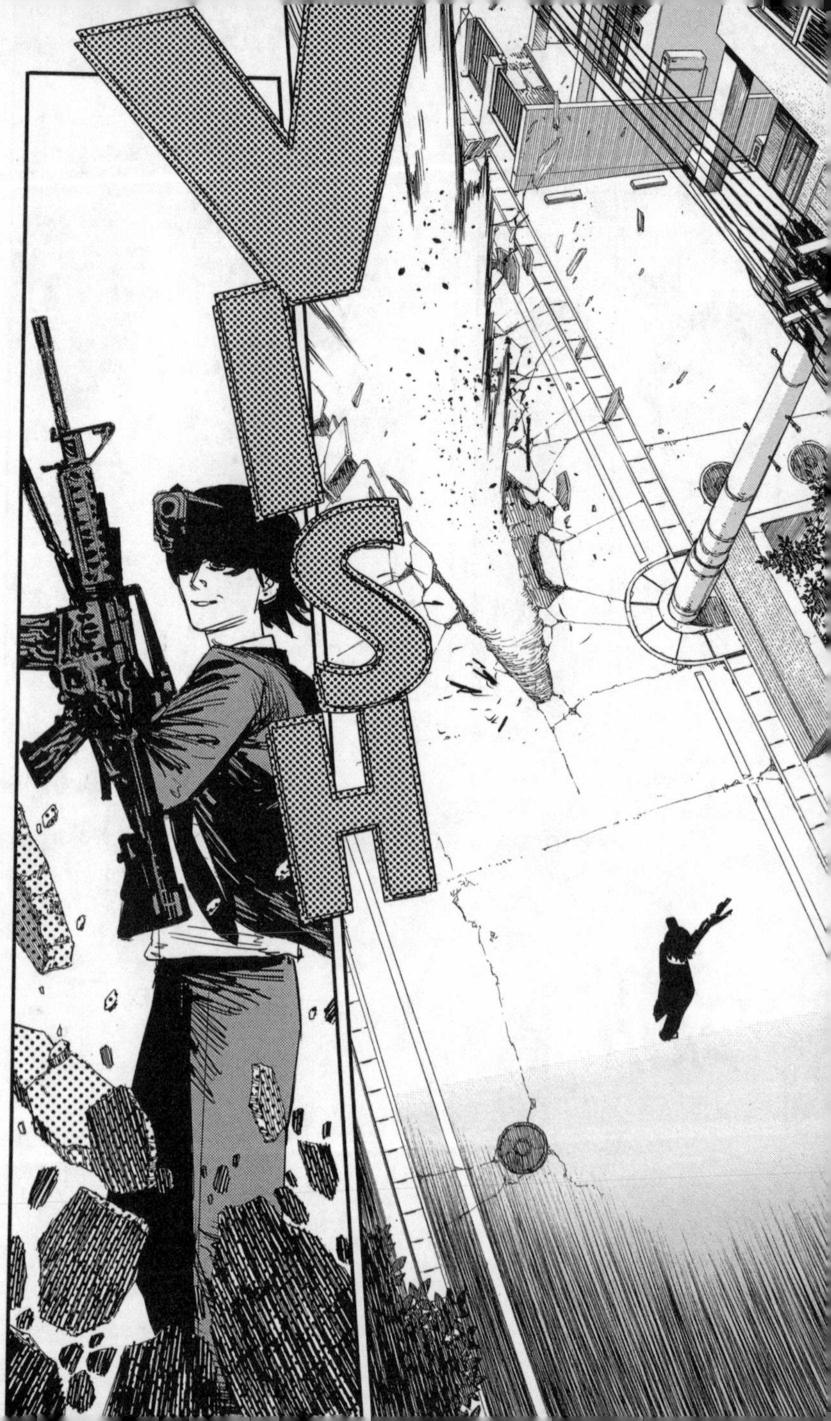
VISH

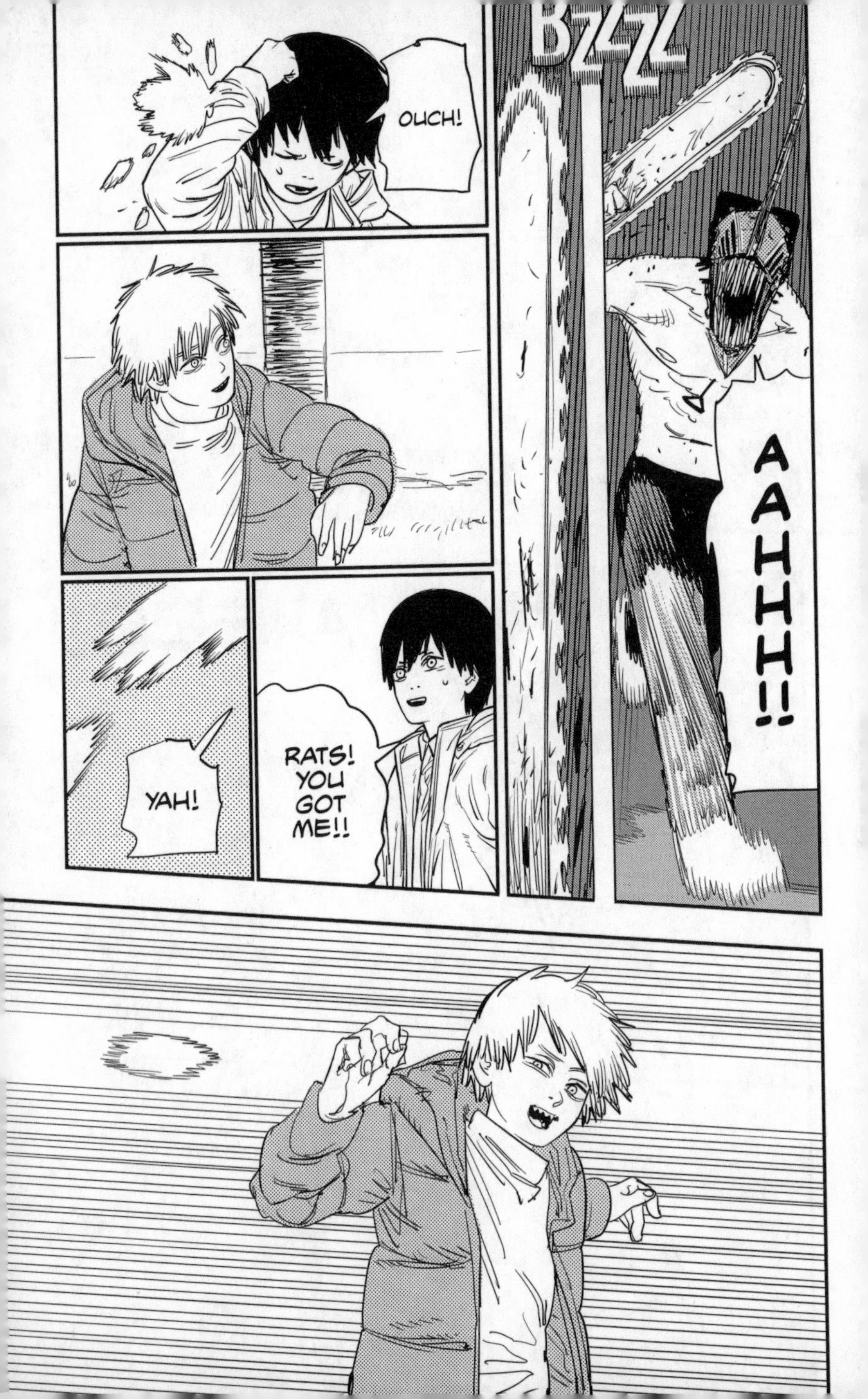
BZZZ
AAHHH!!
OUCH!
RATS! YOU GOT ME!!
YAH!

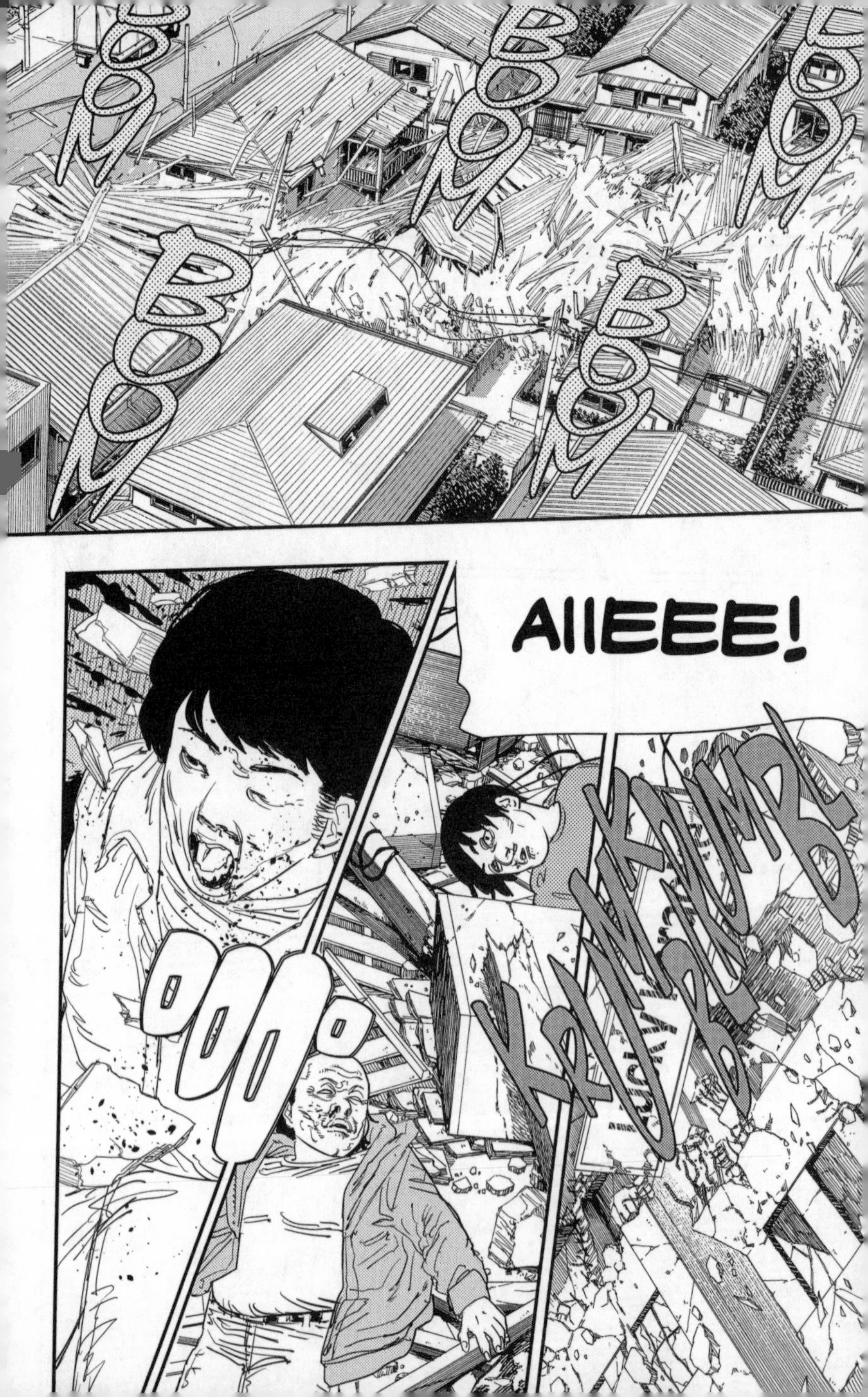
BOOM
BOOM
BOOM
BOOM
BOOM
AIIEEE!
OOO

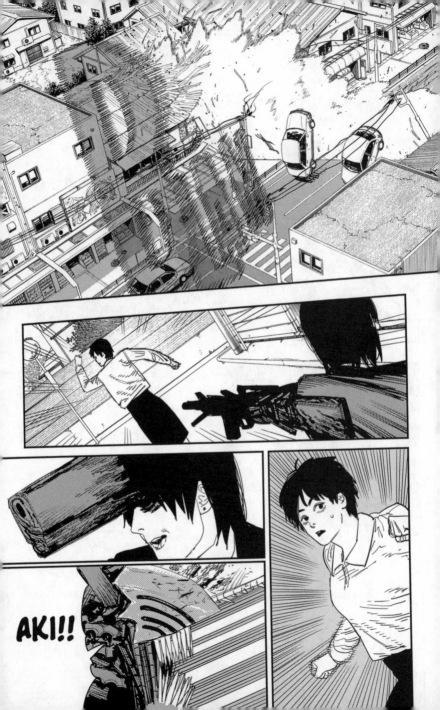

AKI!!

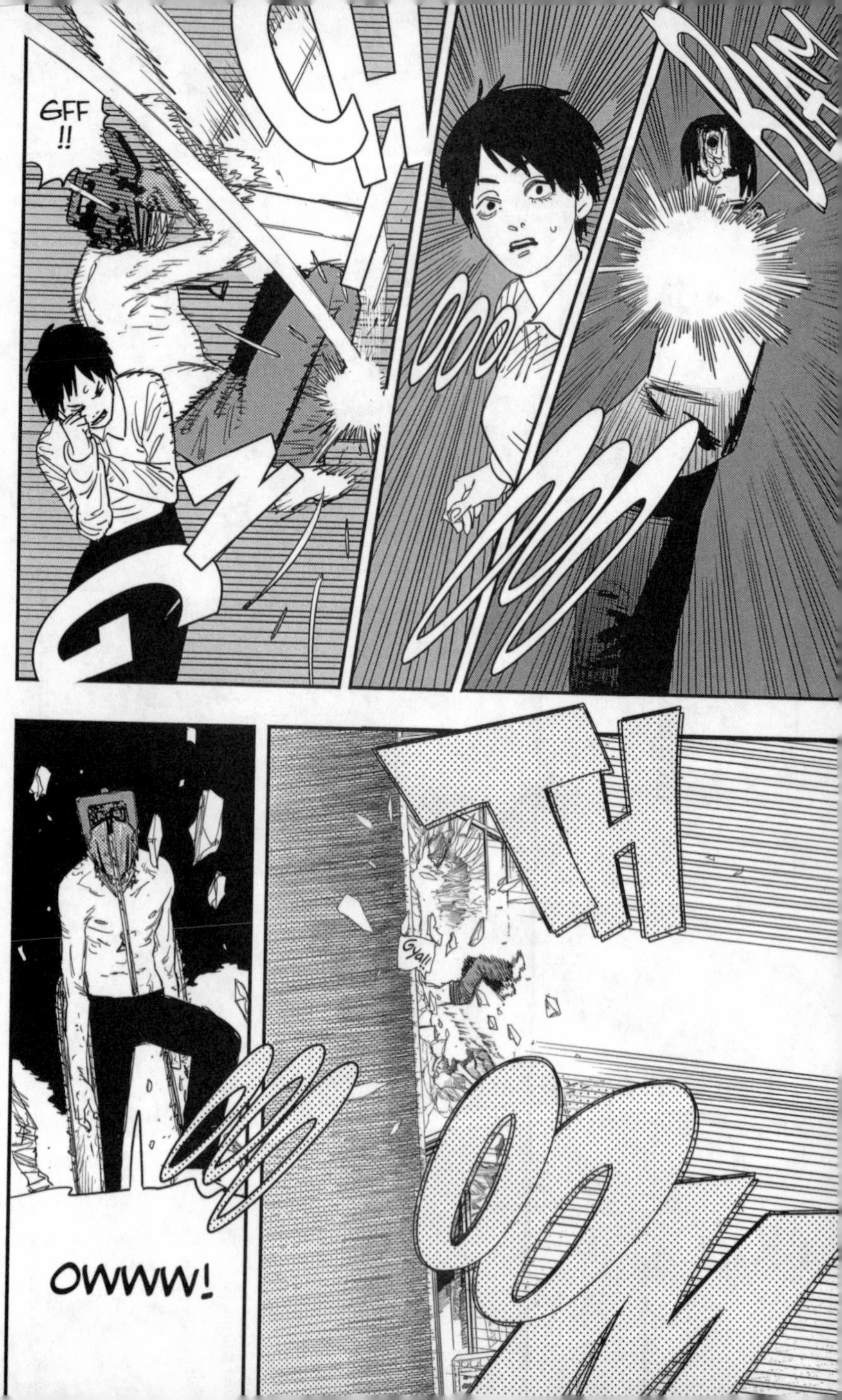
BAM
GFF !!
THOOM
Gya!!
OWWW!

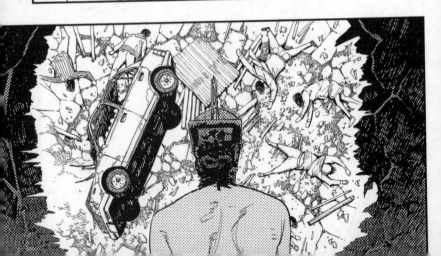

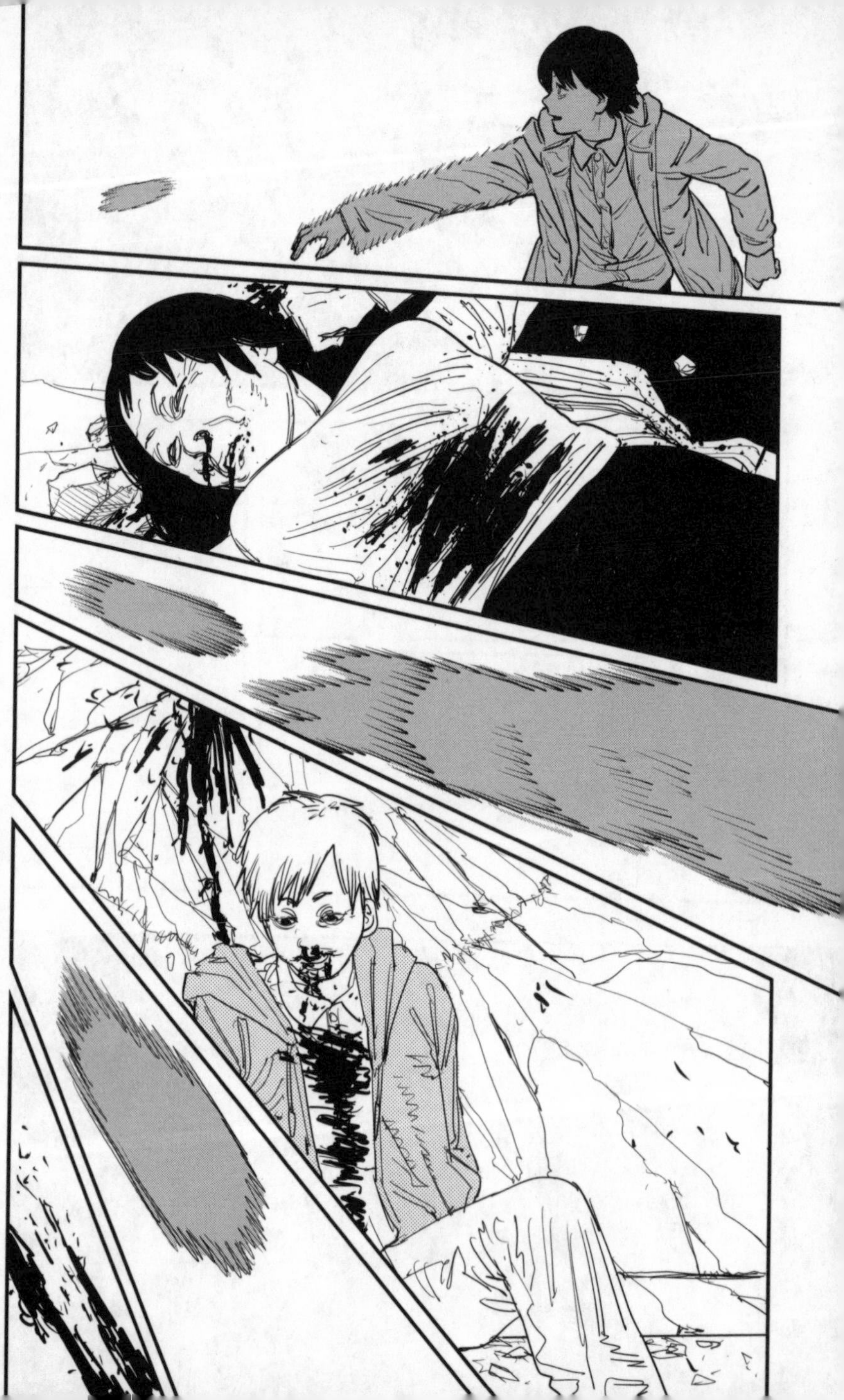

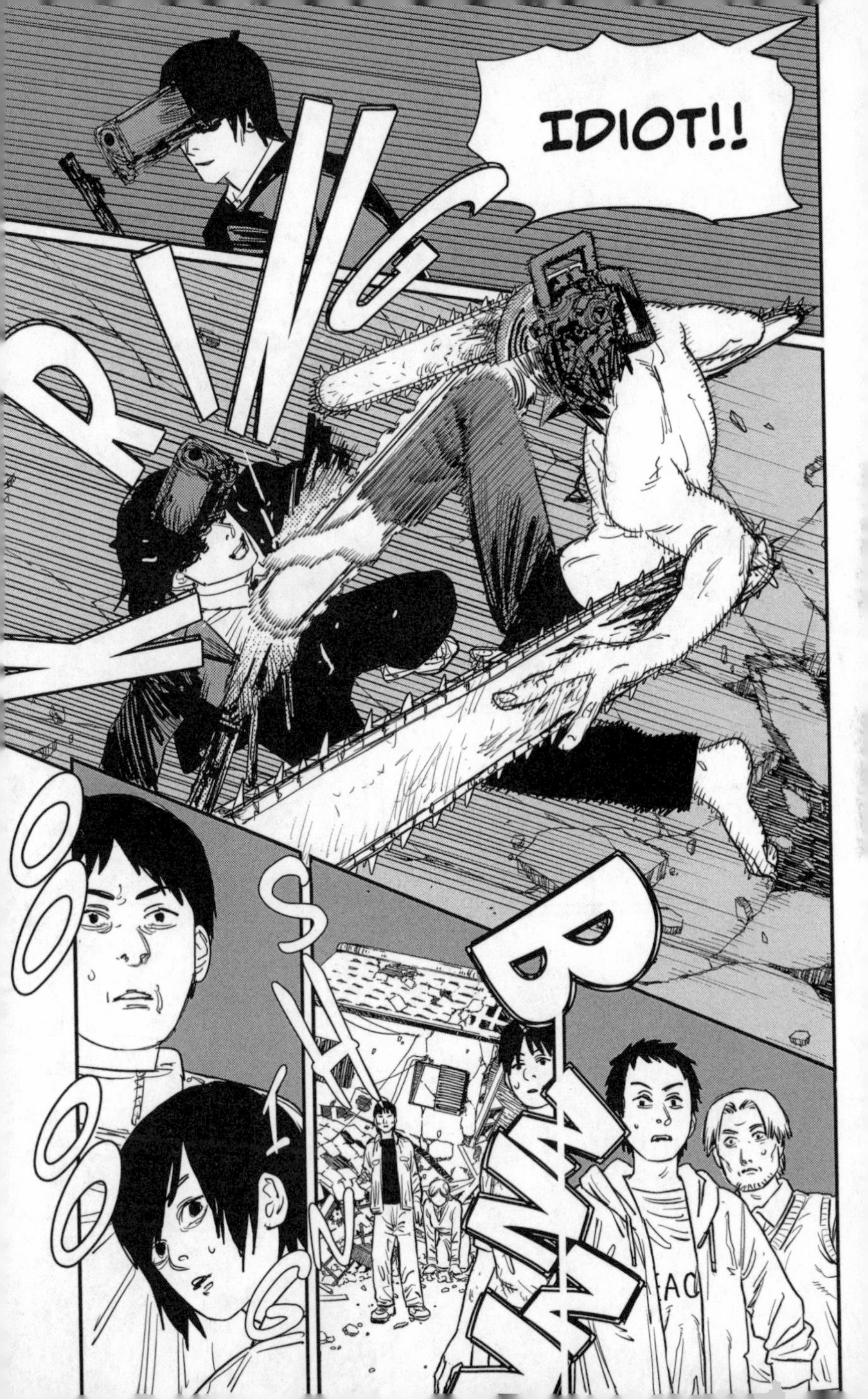
IDIOT!!

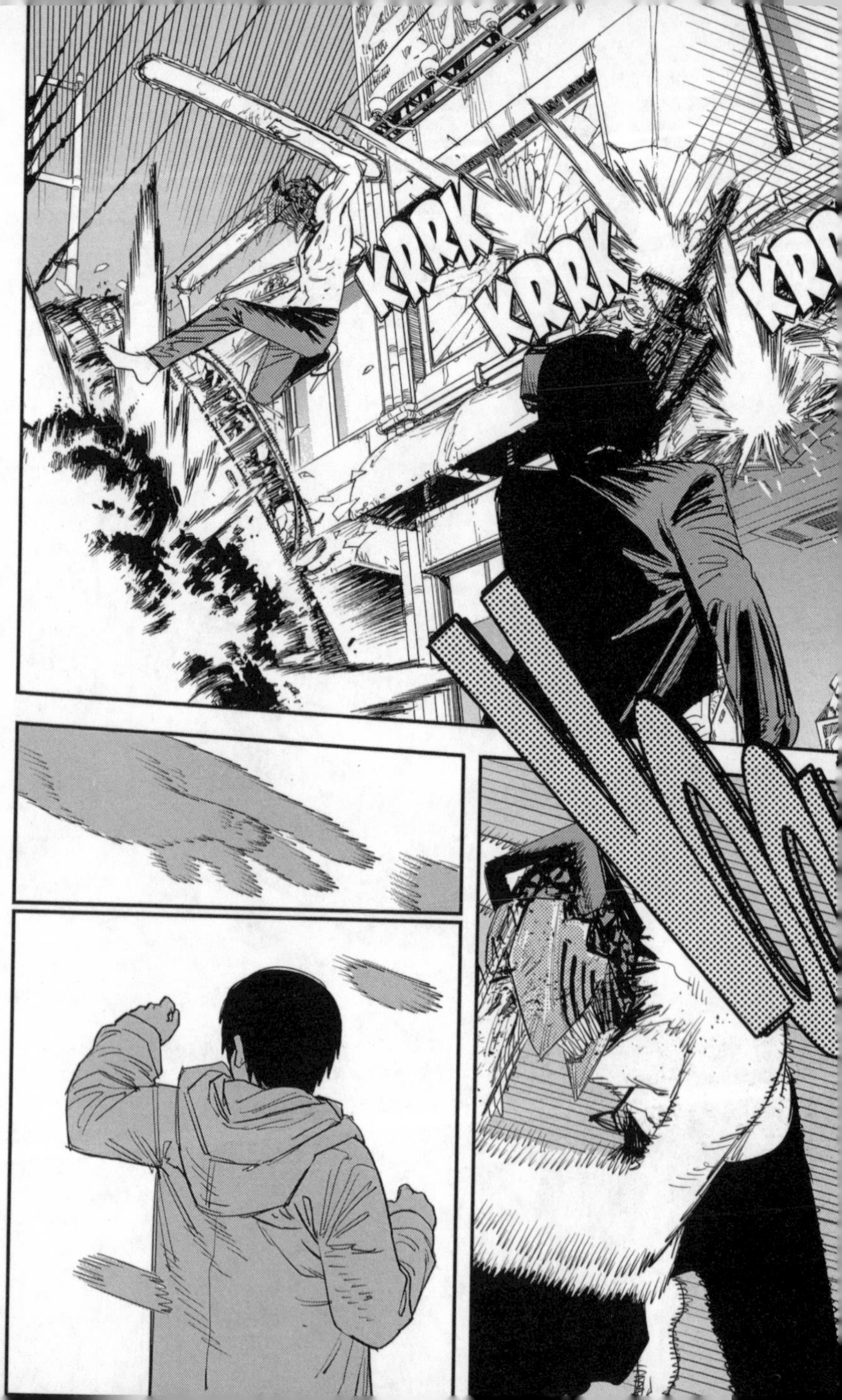
KRRK
KRRK

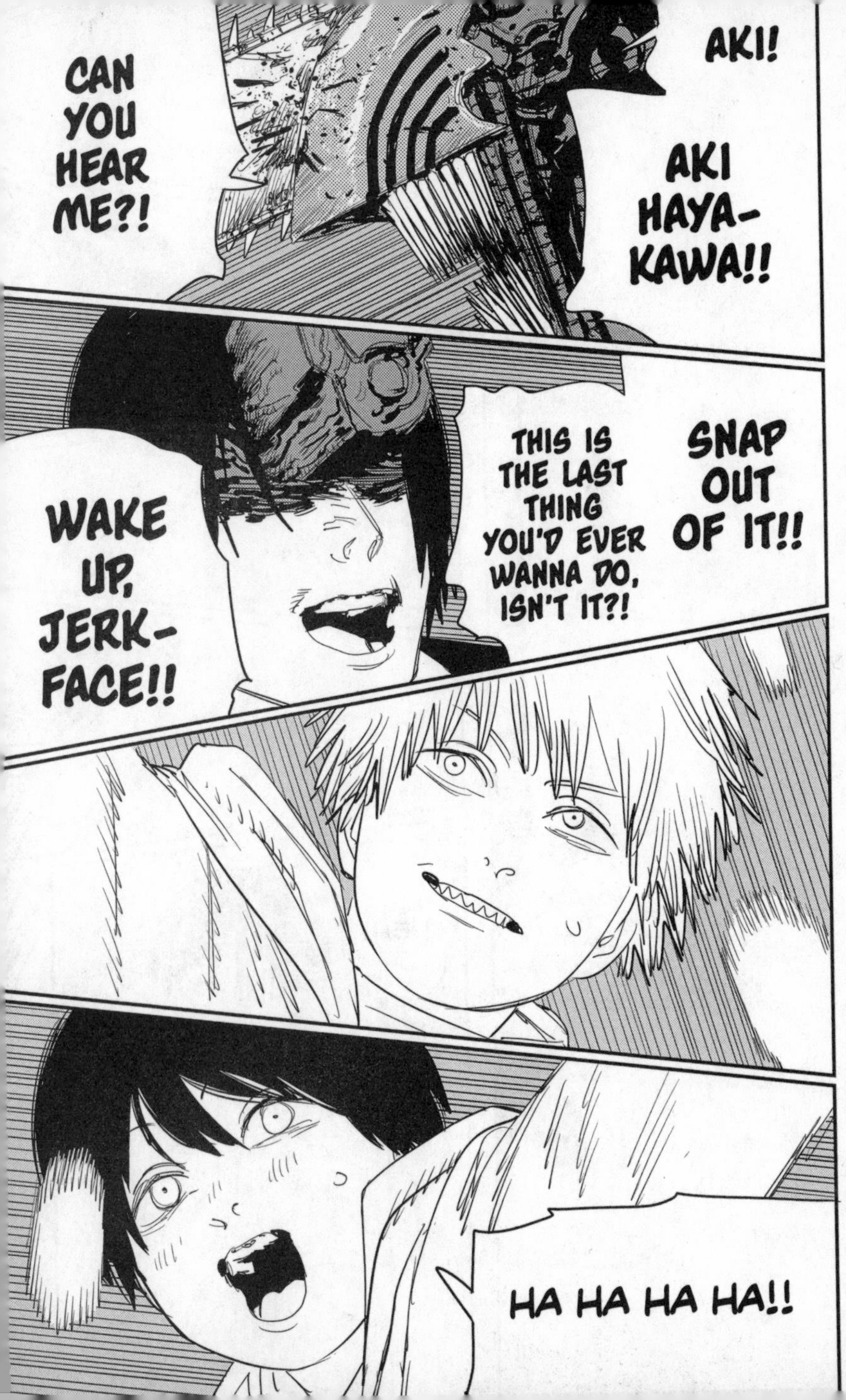
AKI!
AKI HAYA-KAWA!!
CAN YOU HEAR ME?!
SNAP OUT OF IT!!
THIS IS THE LAST THING YOU'D EVER WANNA DO, ISN'T IT?!
WAKE UP, JERK-FACE!!
HA HA HA HA HA!!

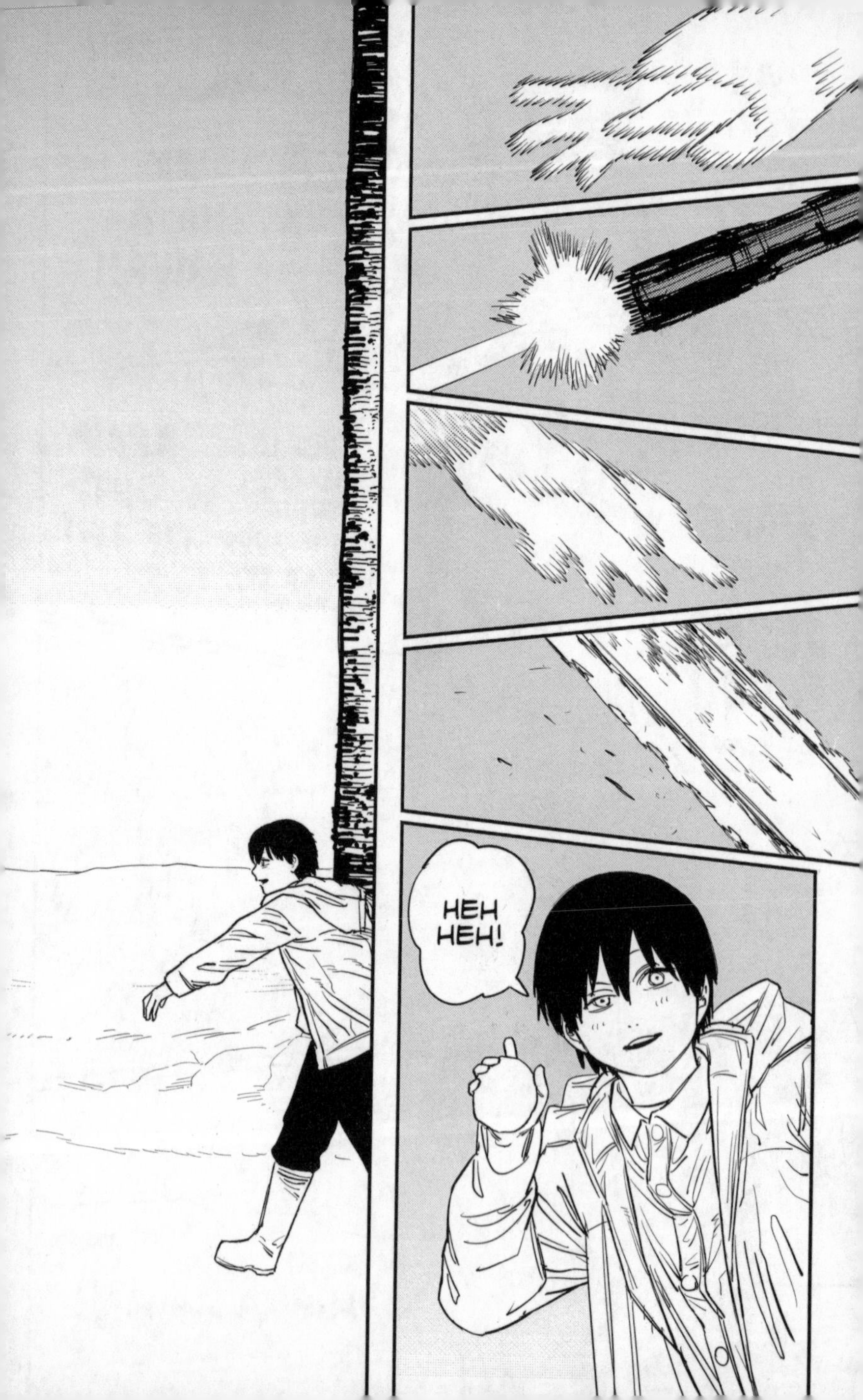
HEH HEH!

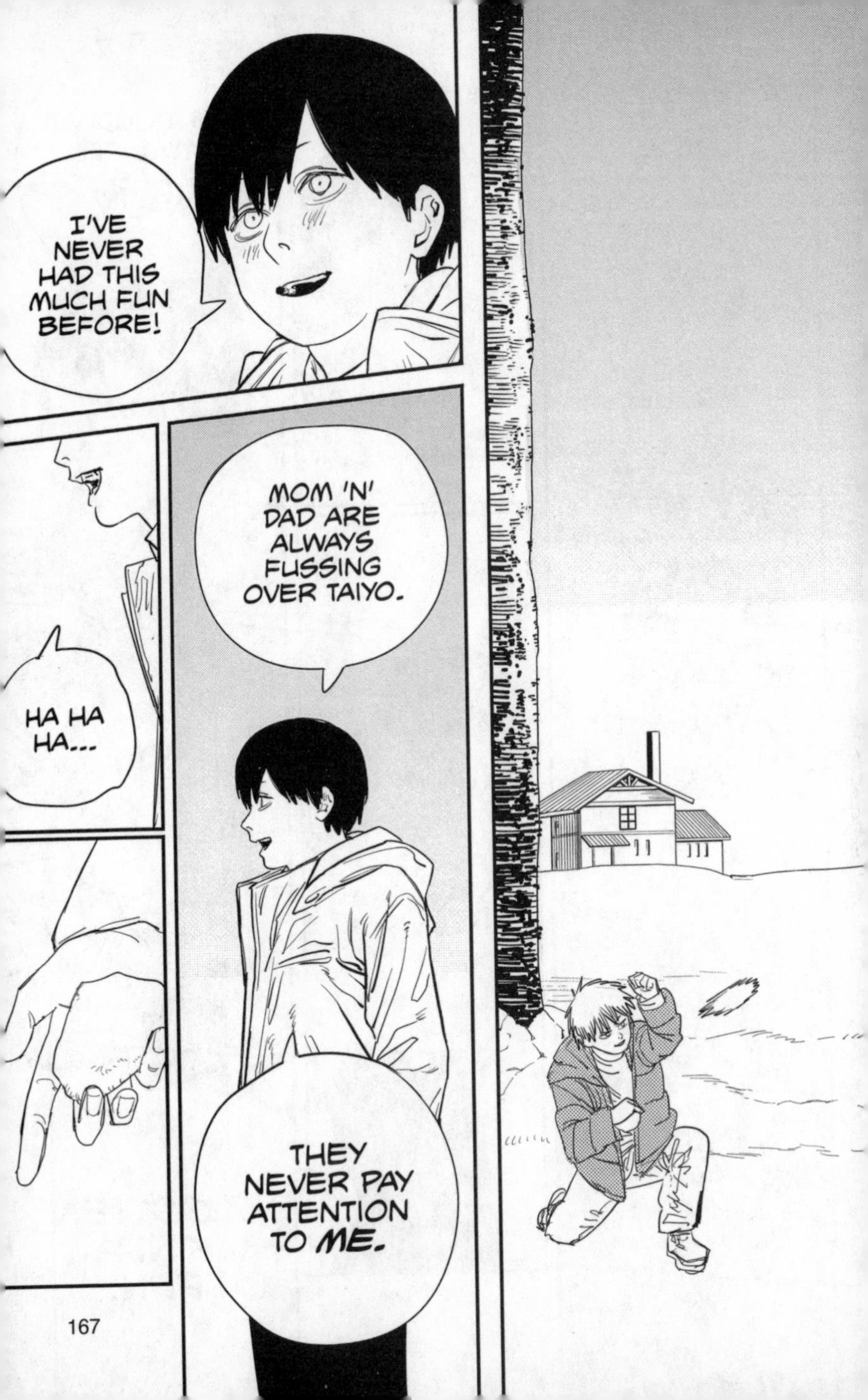
I'VE NEVER HAD THIS MUCH FUN BEFORE!
MOM 'N' DAD ARE ALWAYS FUSSING OVER TAIYO.
THEY NEVER PAY ATTENTION TO *ME*.
HA HA HA...

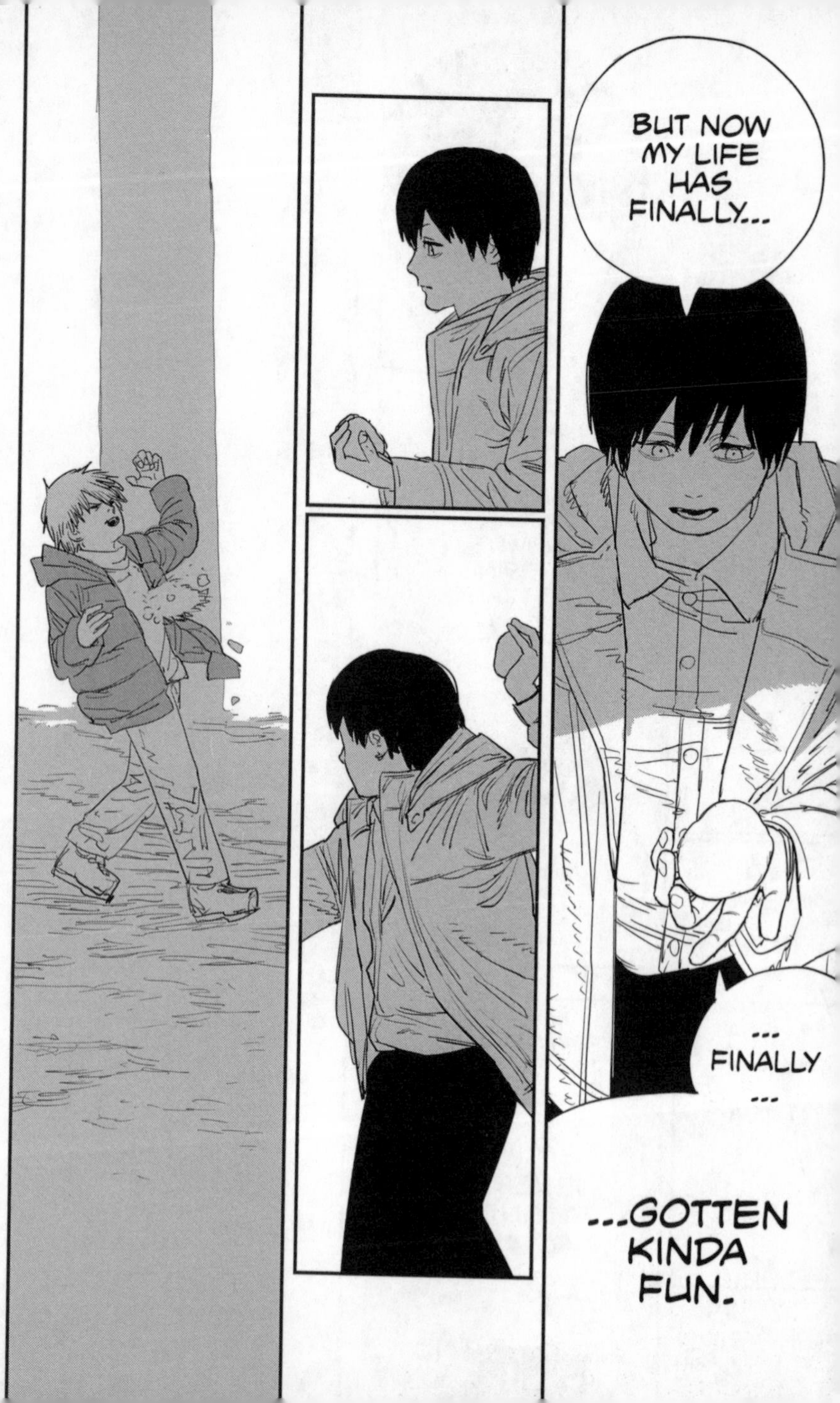
BUT NOW MY LIFE HAS FINALLY...
...FINALLY...
...GOTTEN KINDA FUN.

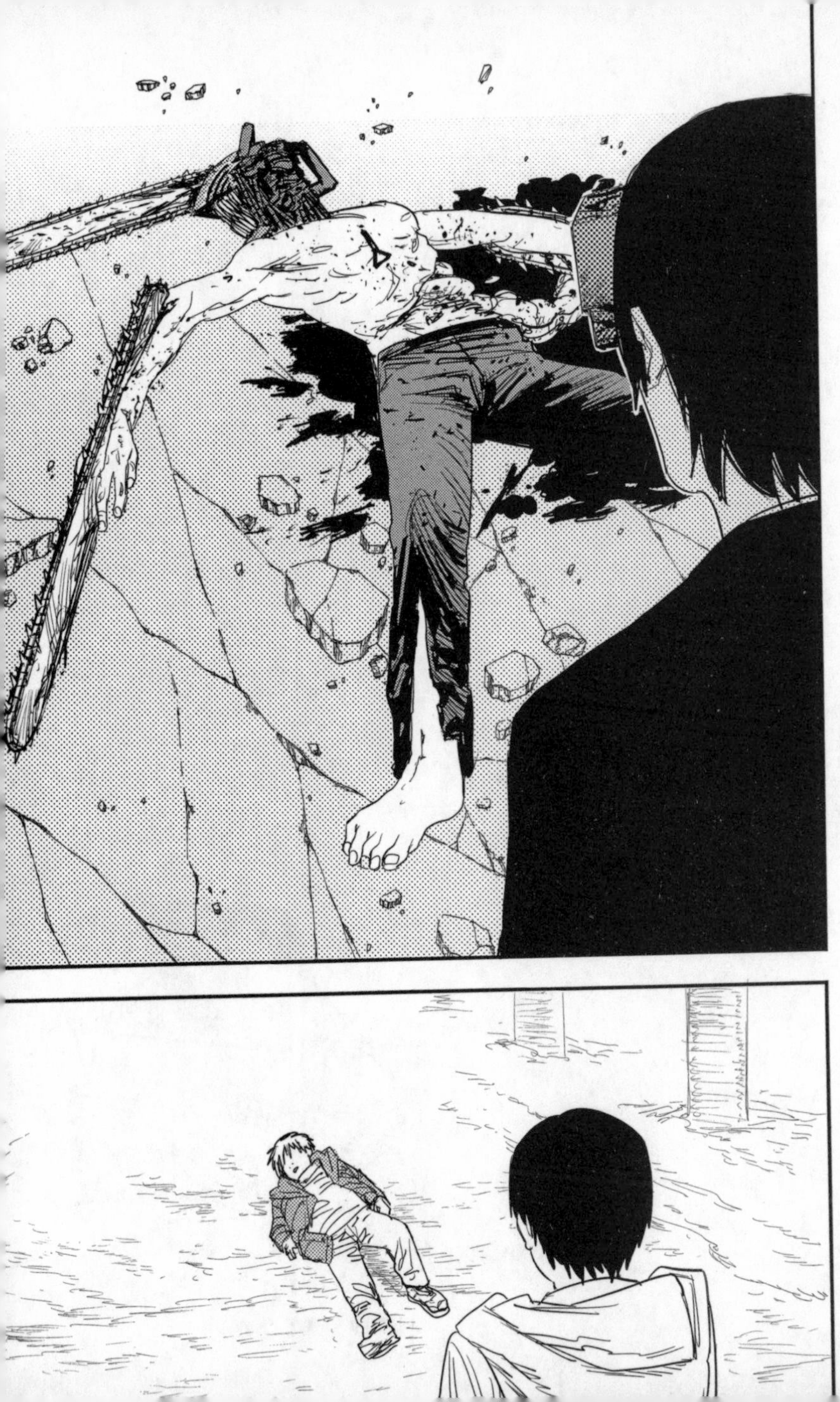

Chain
saw man

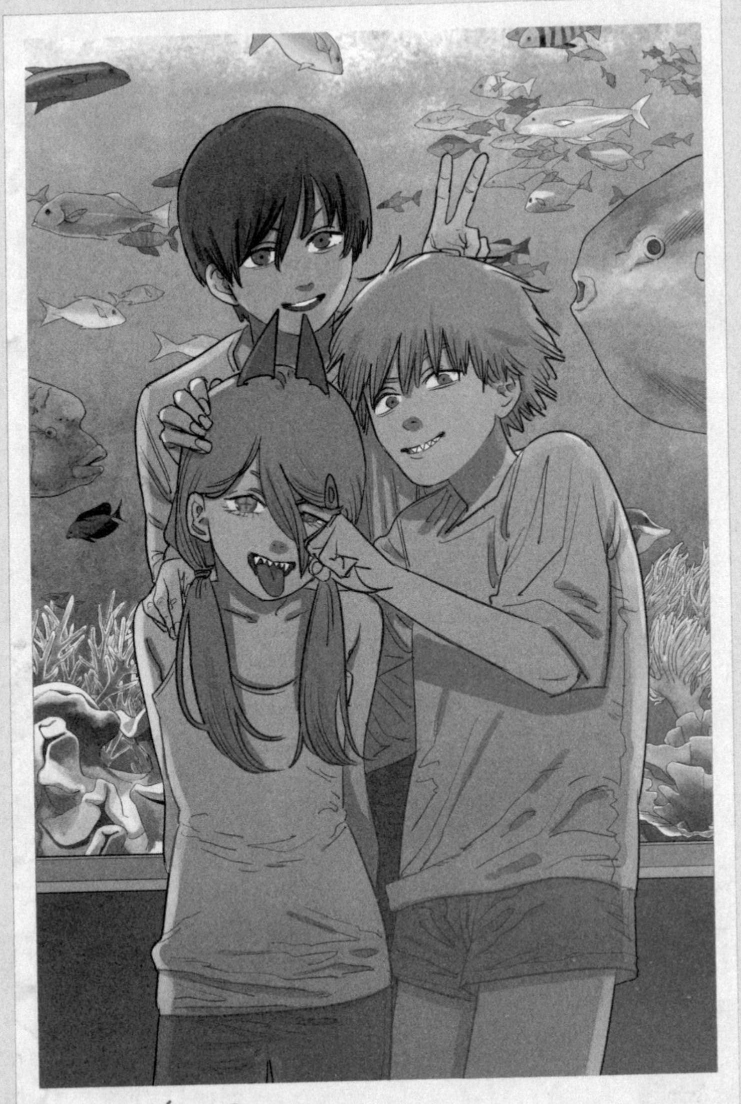
6.12

Chapter 79: Play Catch

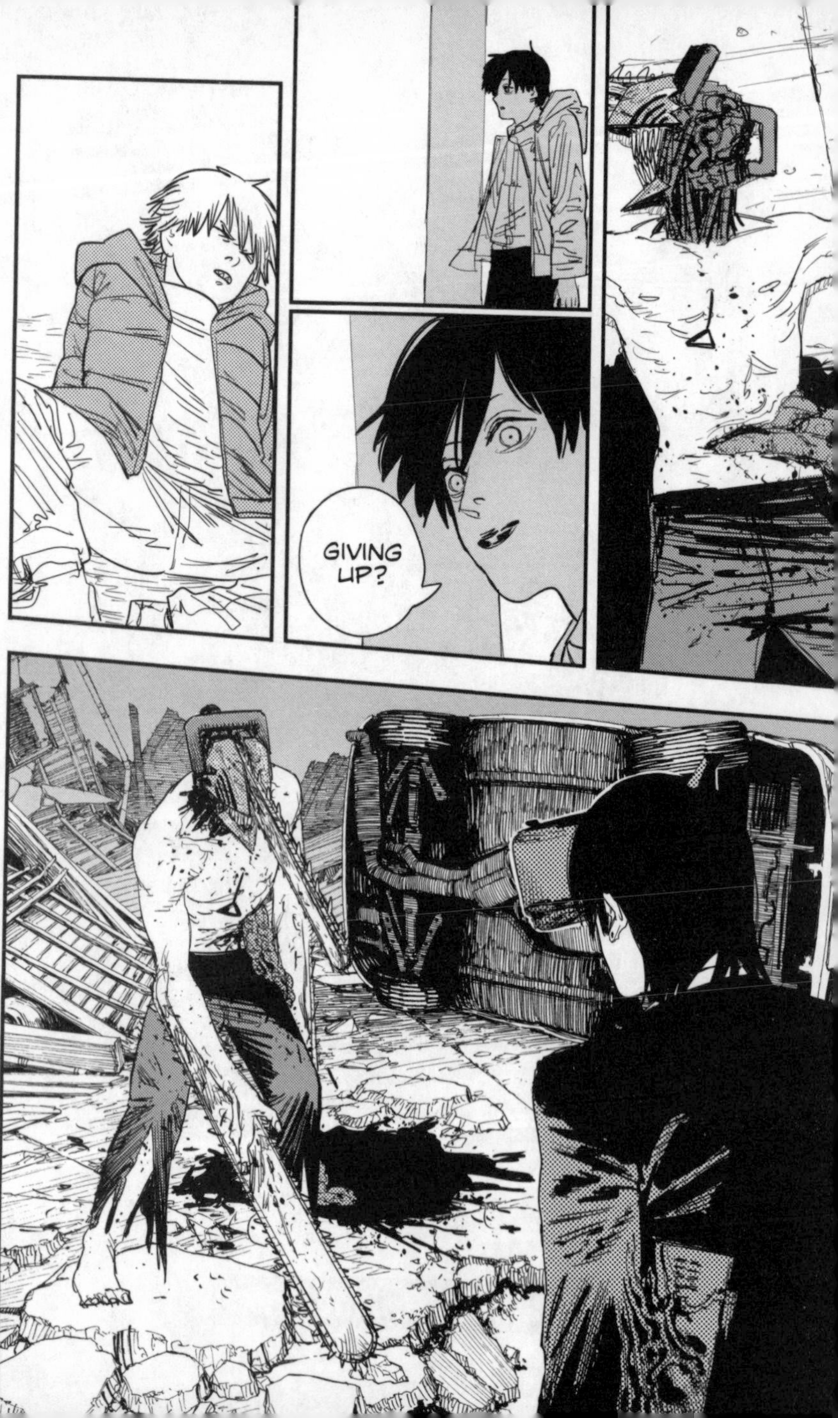
GIVING UP?

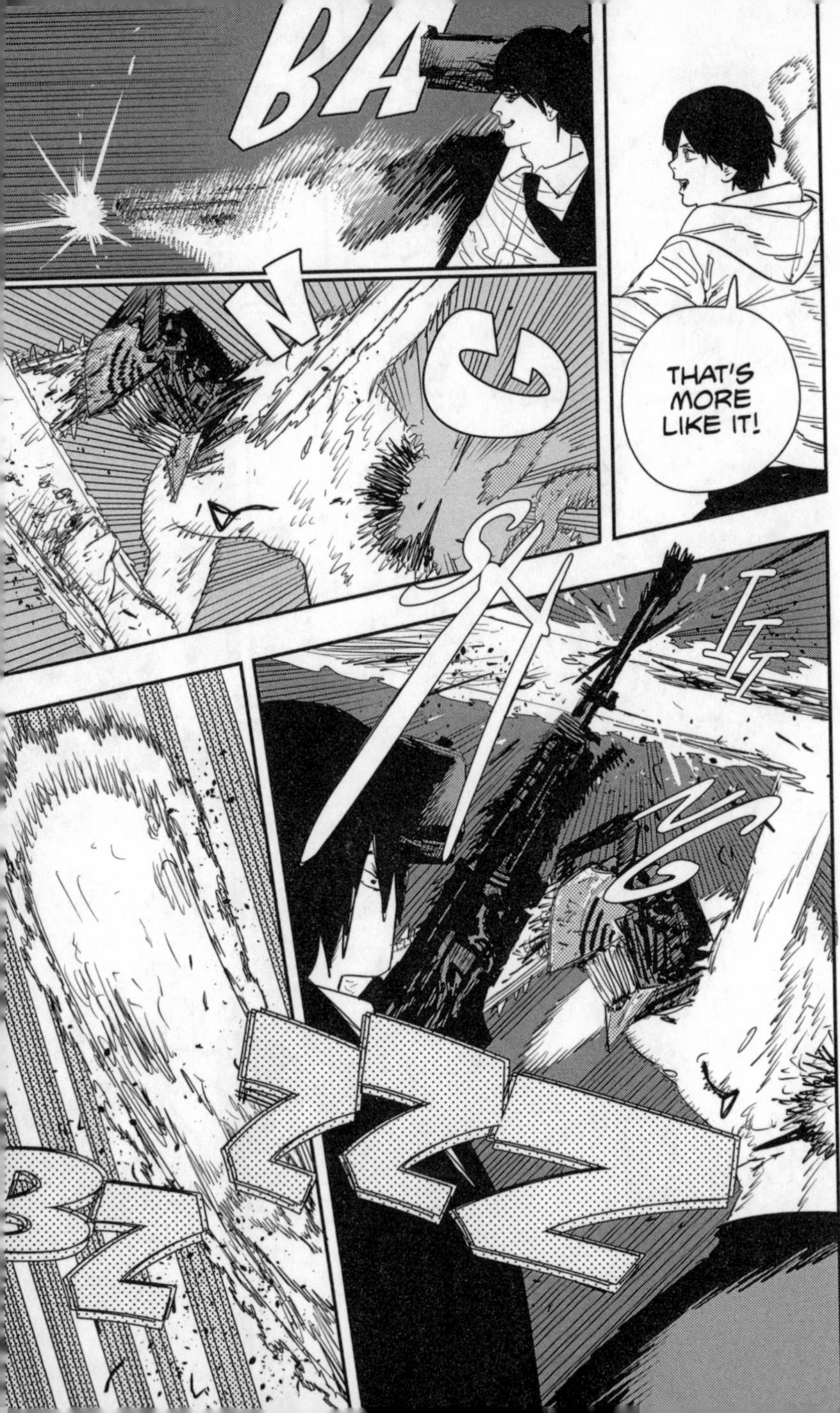
THAT'S MORE LIKE IT!
BANG

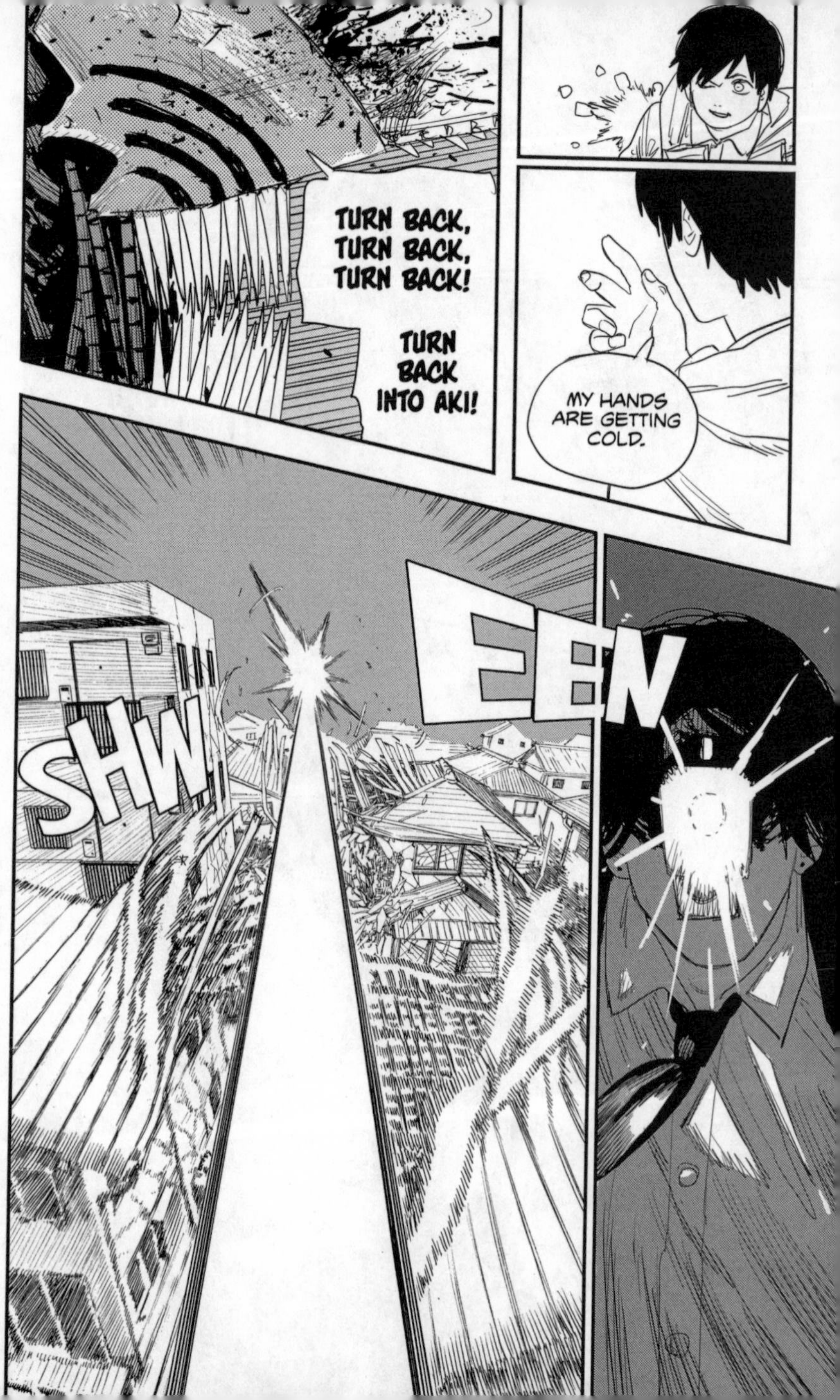
MY HANDS ARE GETTING COLD.
TURN BACK, TURN BACK, TURN BACK!
TURN BACK INTO AKI!
SHW
EEN

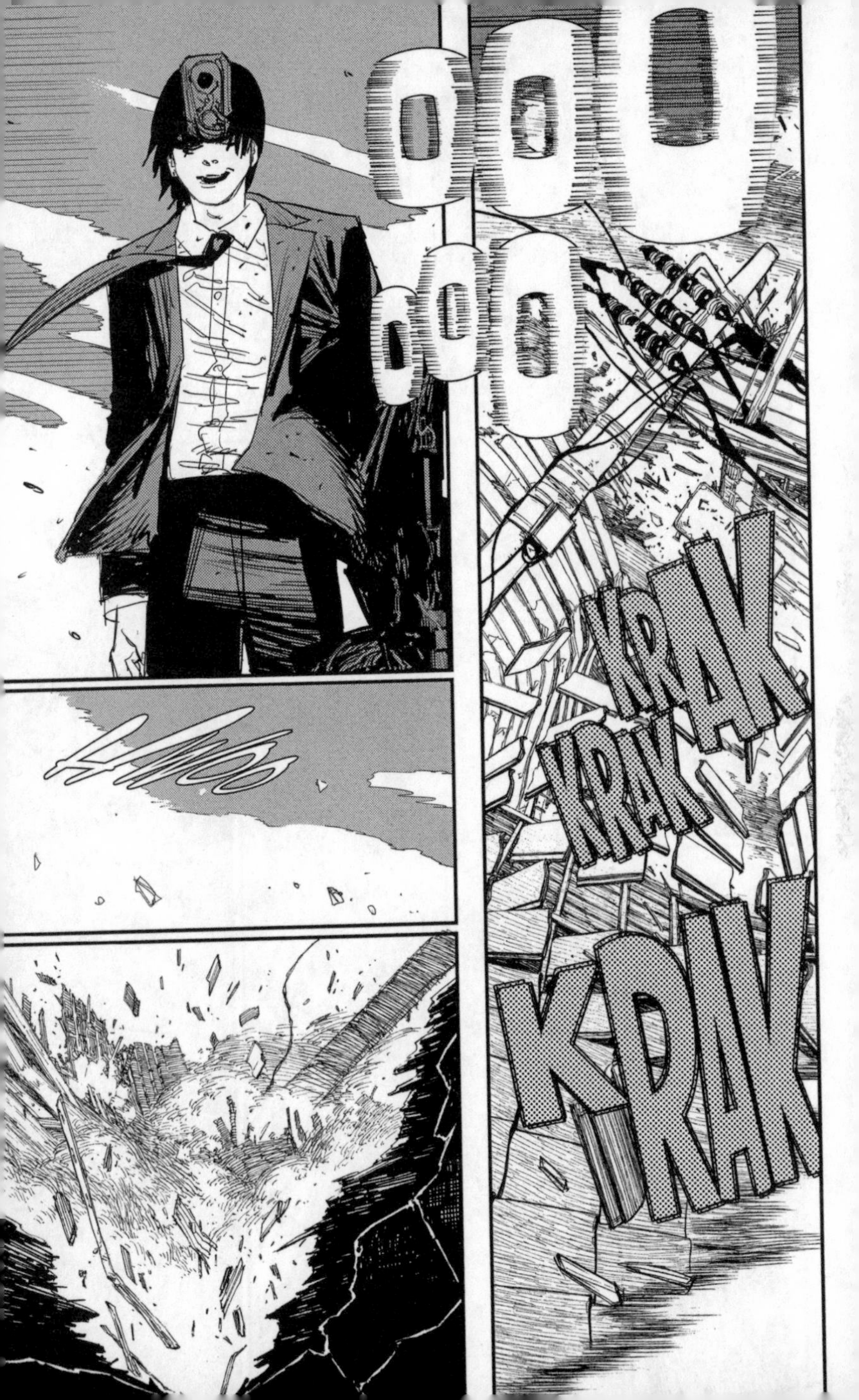
KRAK
KRAK
KRAK
FWOO

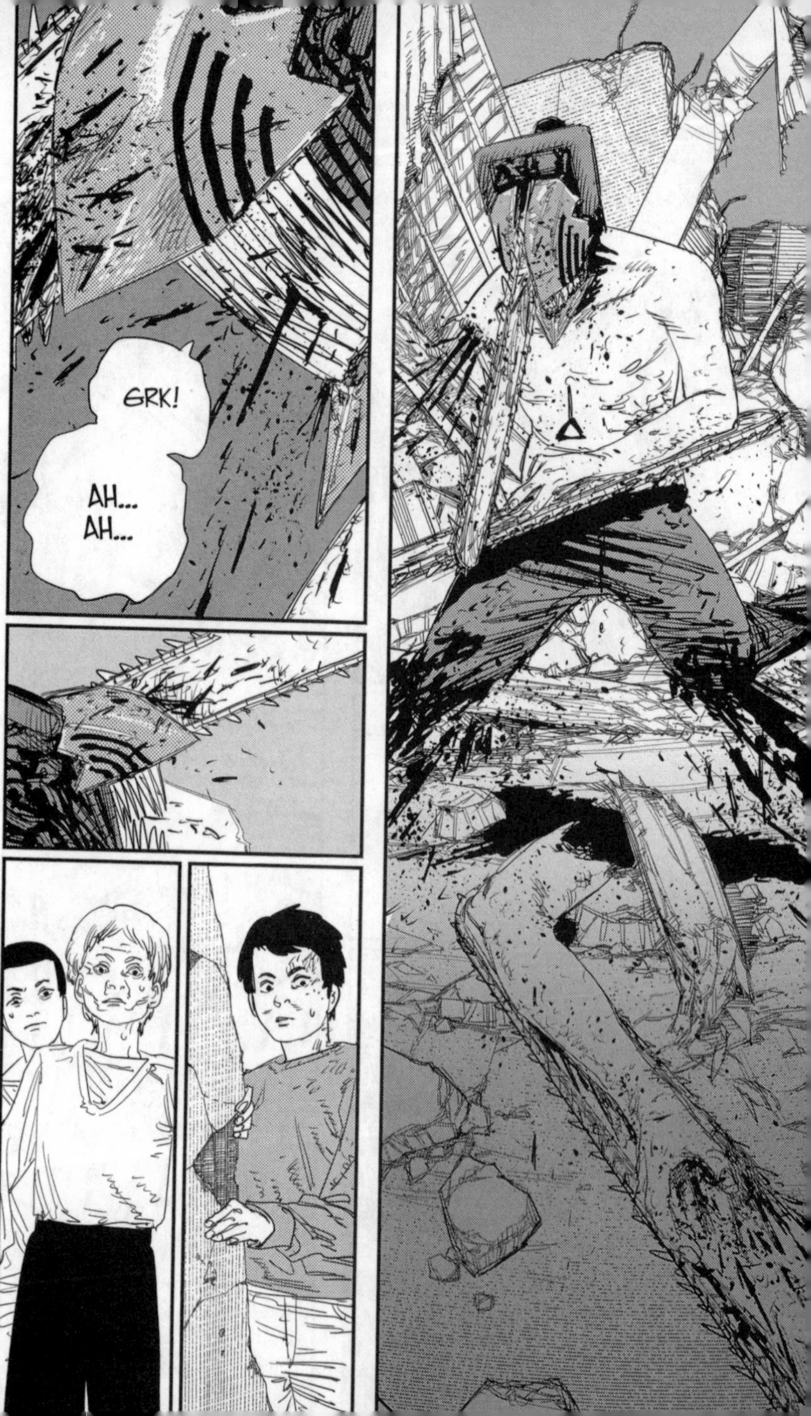
GRK!
AH... AH...

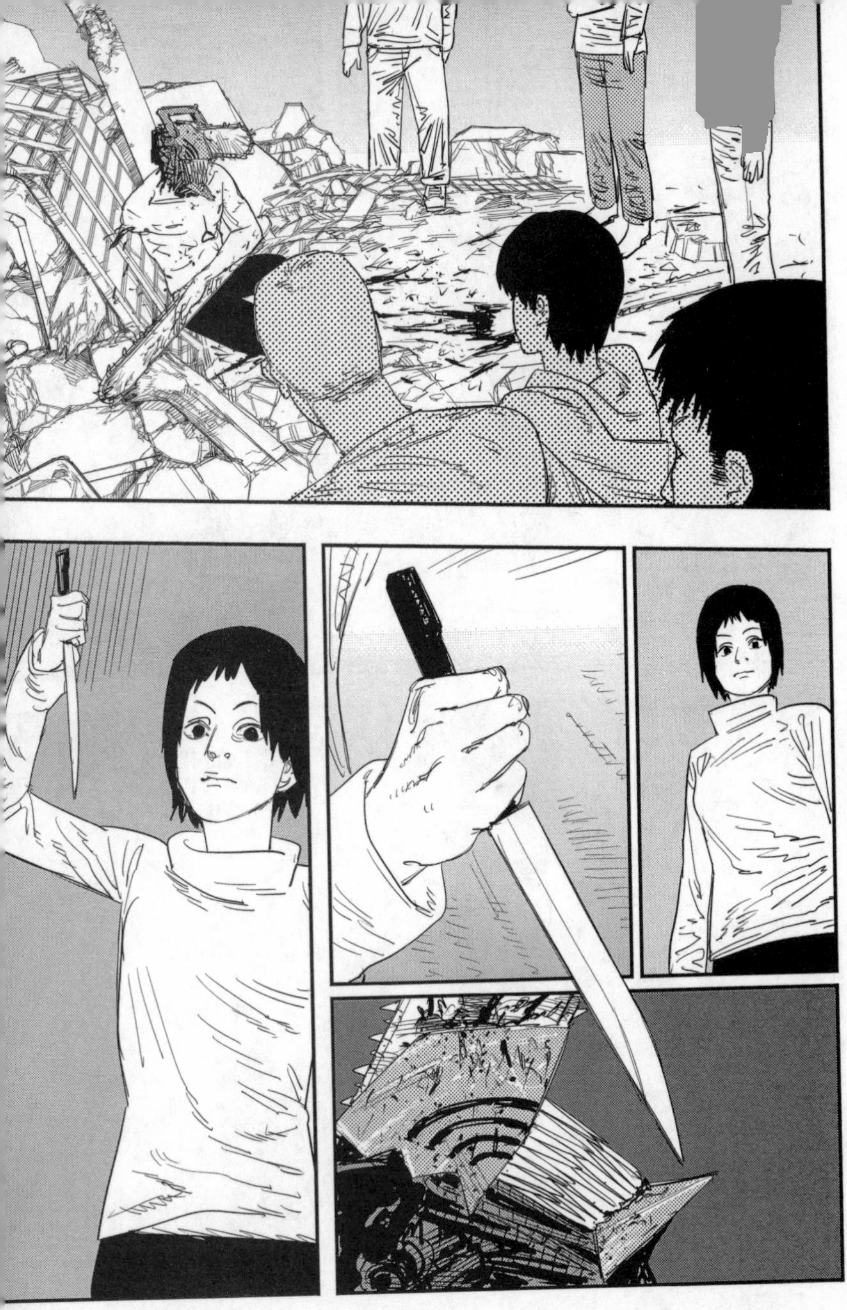

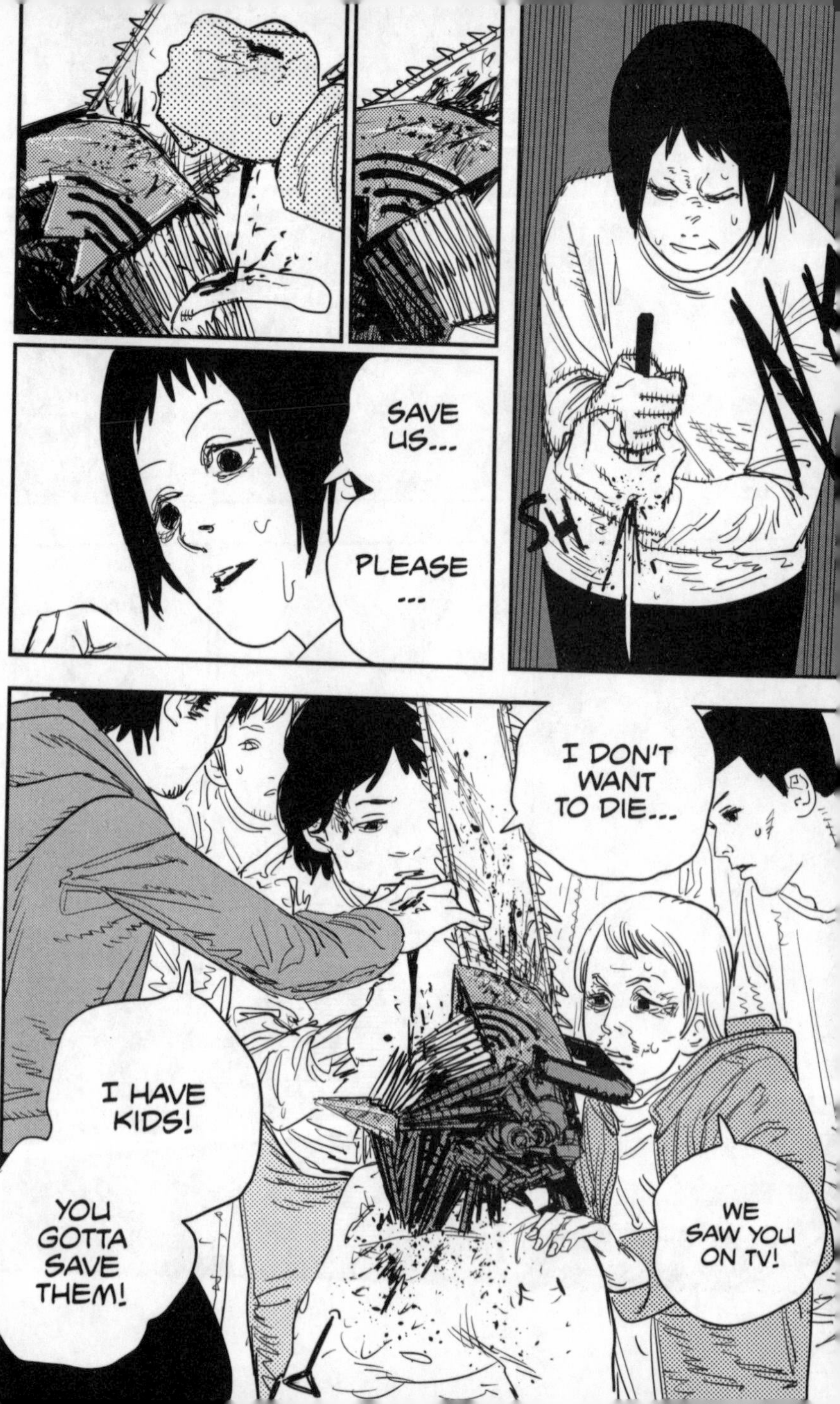
SAVE US...
PLEASE ...
I DON'T WANT TO DIE...
WE SAW YOU ON TV!
I HAVE KIDS!
YOU GOTTA SAVE THEM!

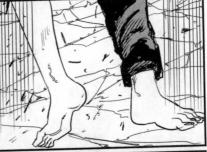

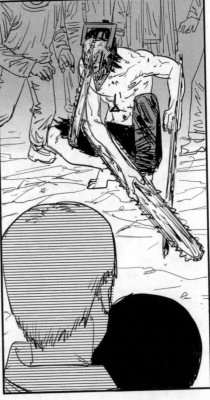

HELP...

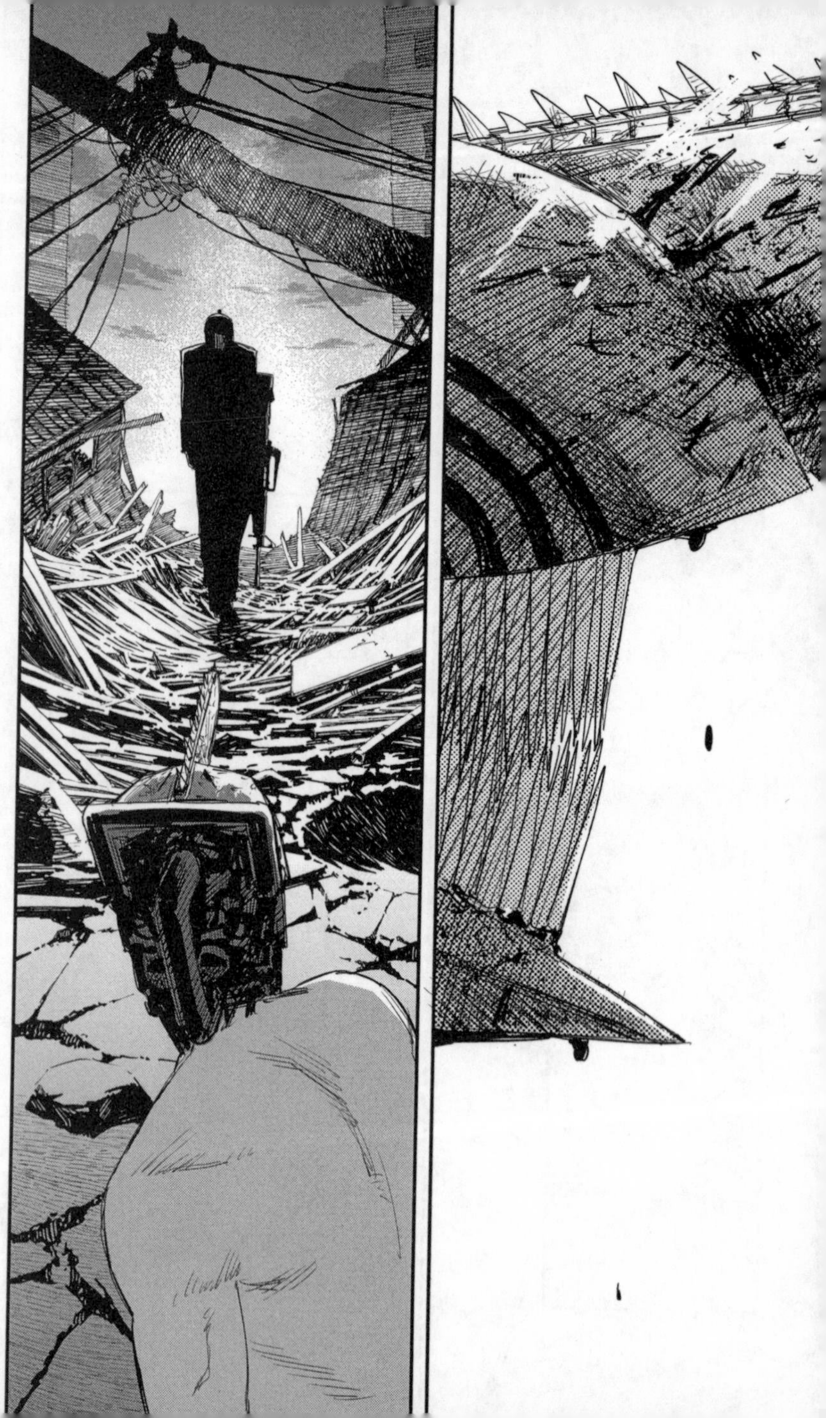

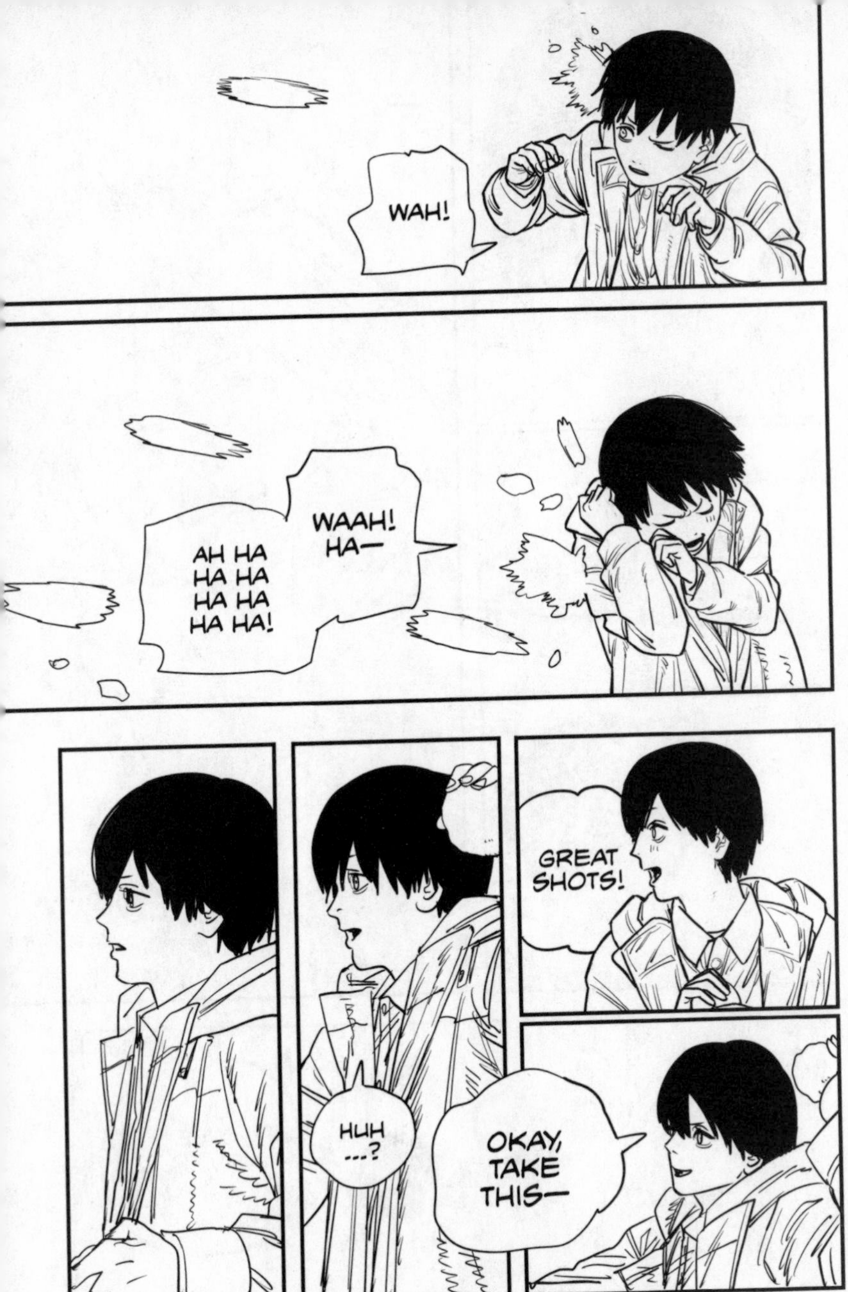
WAH!
WAAH! HA—
AH HA HA HA HA HA HA HA!
GREAT SHOTS!
OKAY, TAKE THIS—
HUH ...?

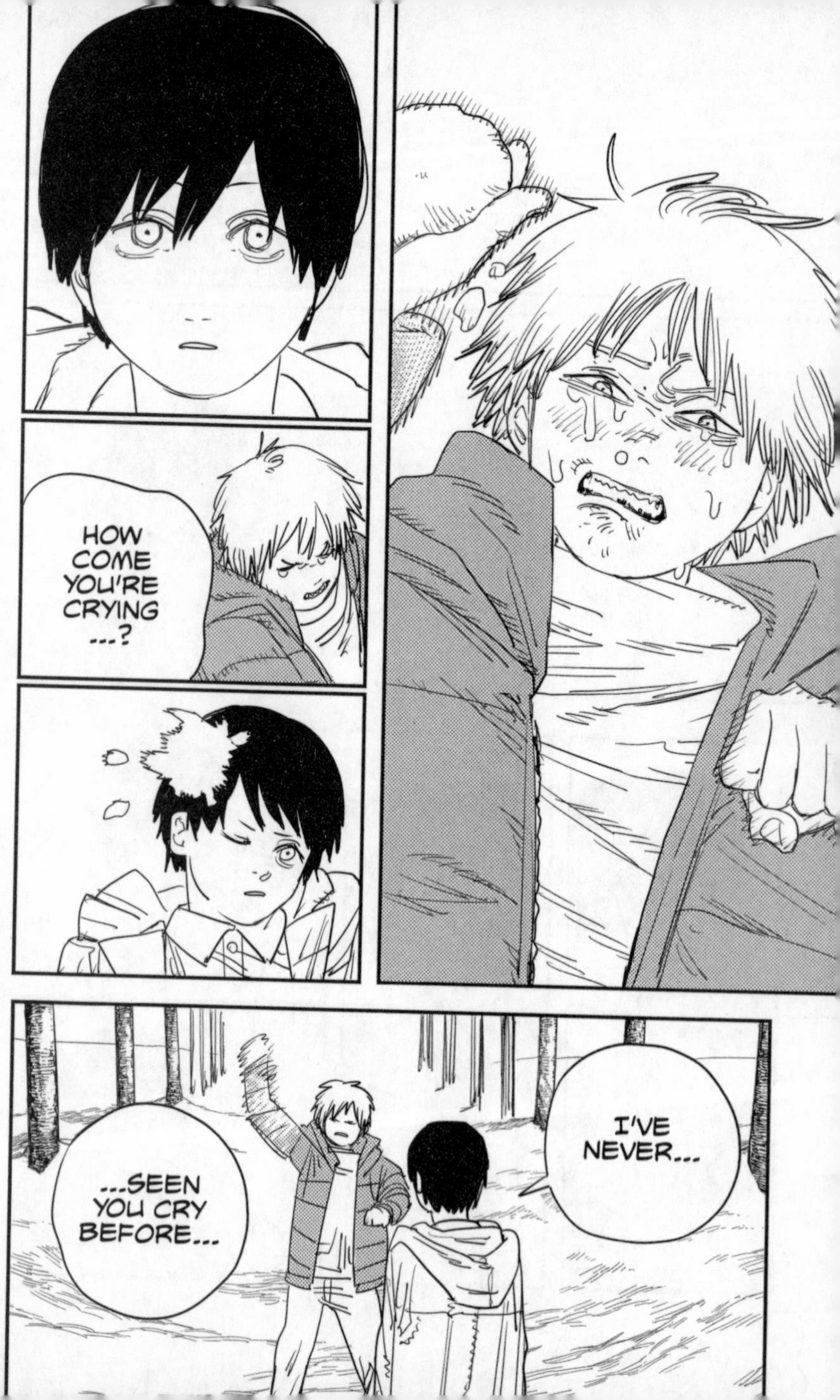
HOW COME YOU'RE CRYING ...?
I'VE NEVER...
...SEEN YOU CRY BEFORE...

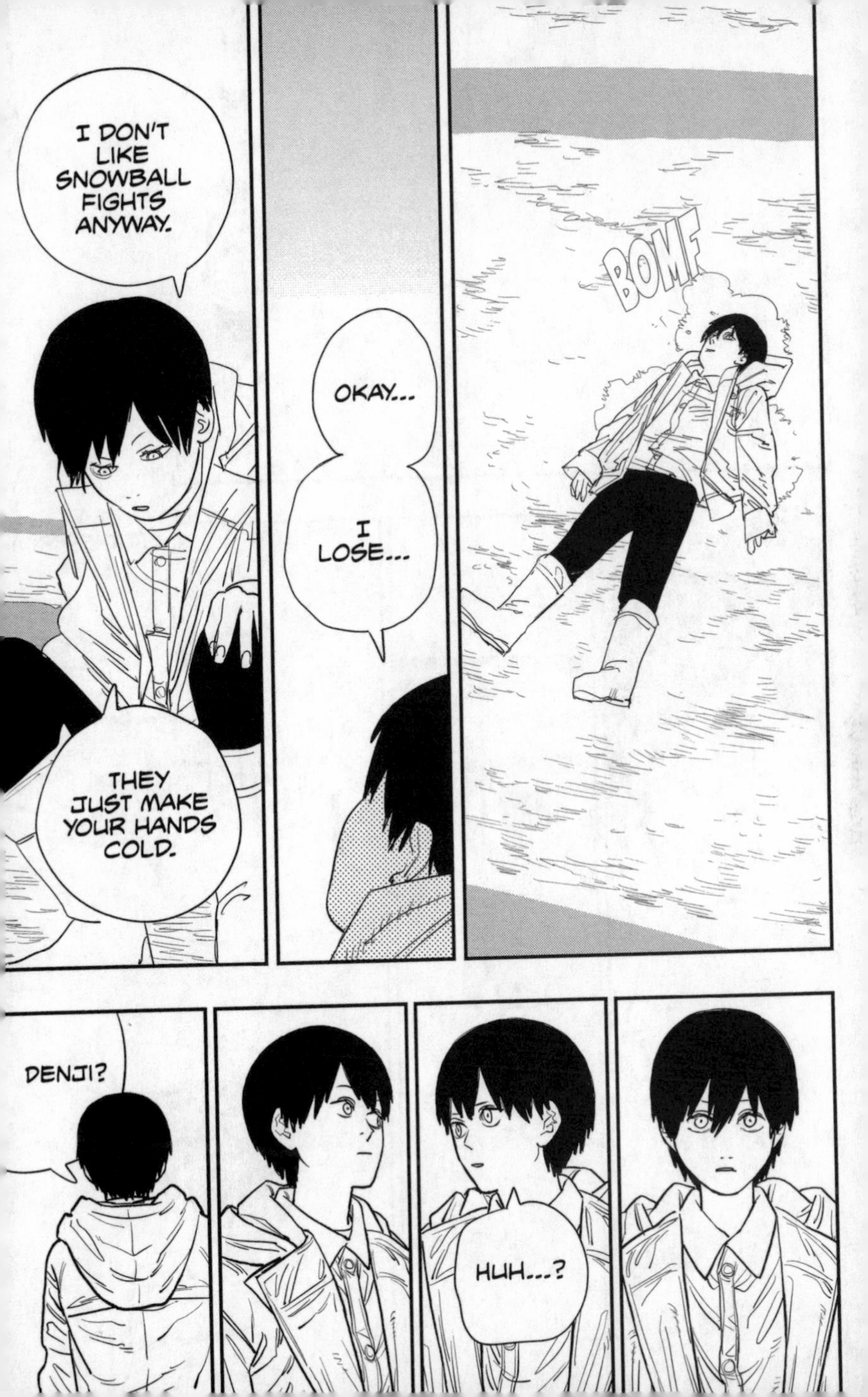
BOMF
OKAY... I LOSE...
I DON'T LIKE SNOWBALL FIGHTS ANYWAY.
THEY JUST MAKE YOUR HANDS COLD.
HUH...?
DENJI?

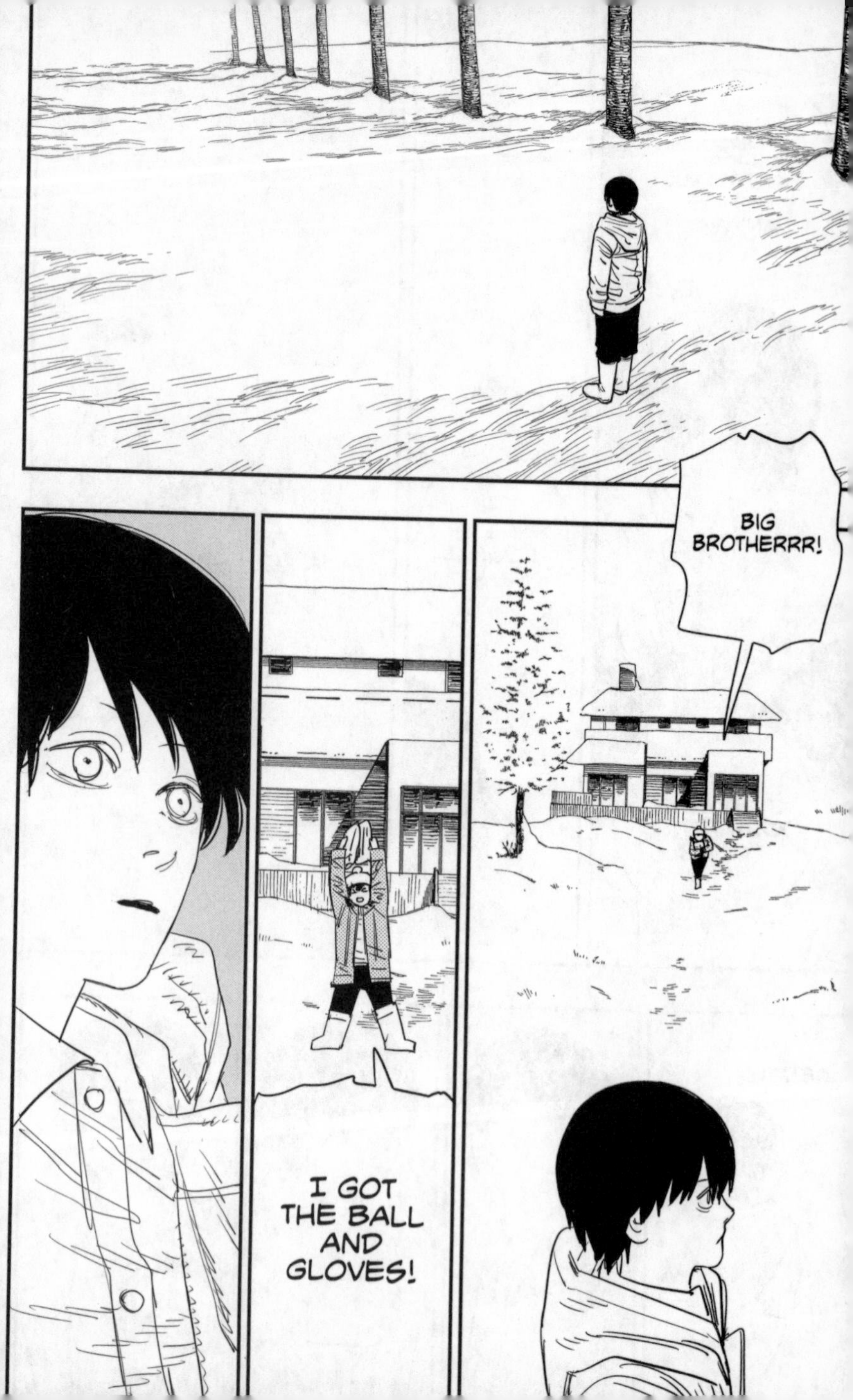
BIG BROTHERRR!
I GOT THE BALL AND GLOVES!

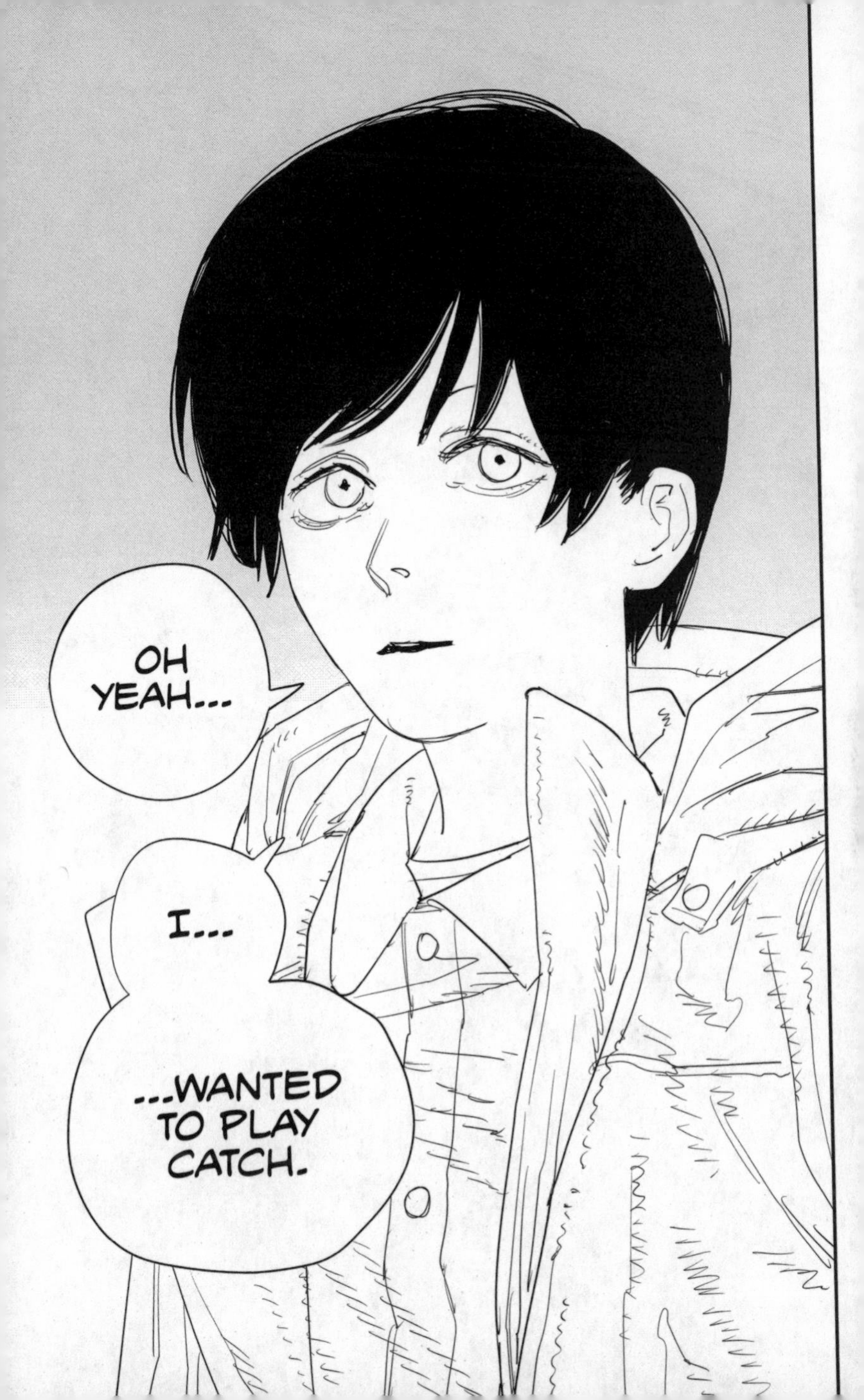
OH YEAH...
I...
...WANTED TO PLAY CATCH.

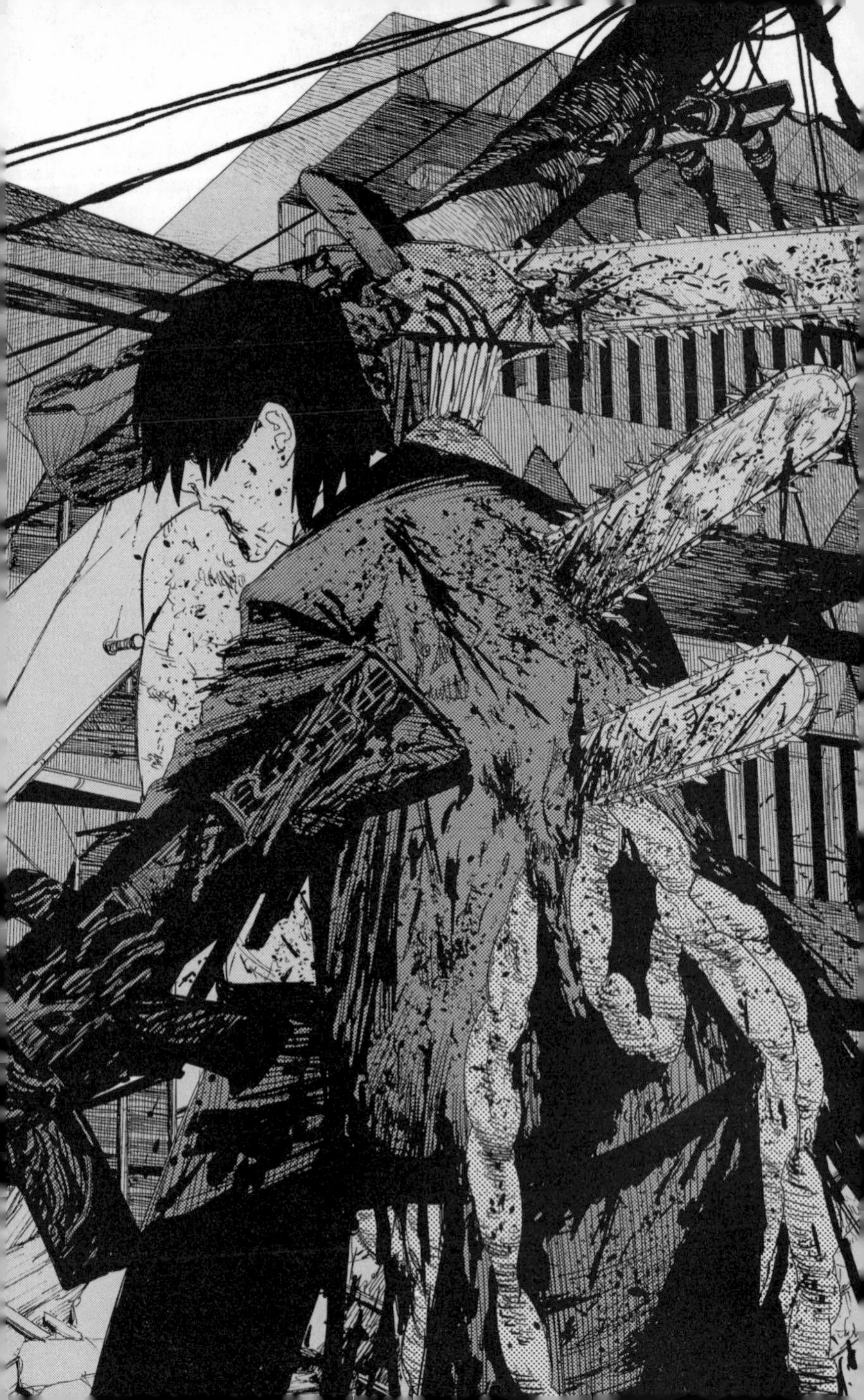

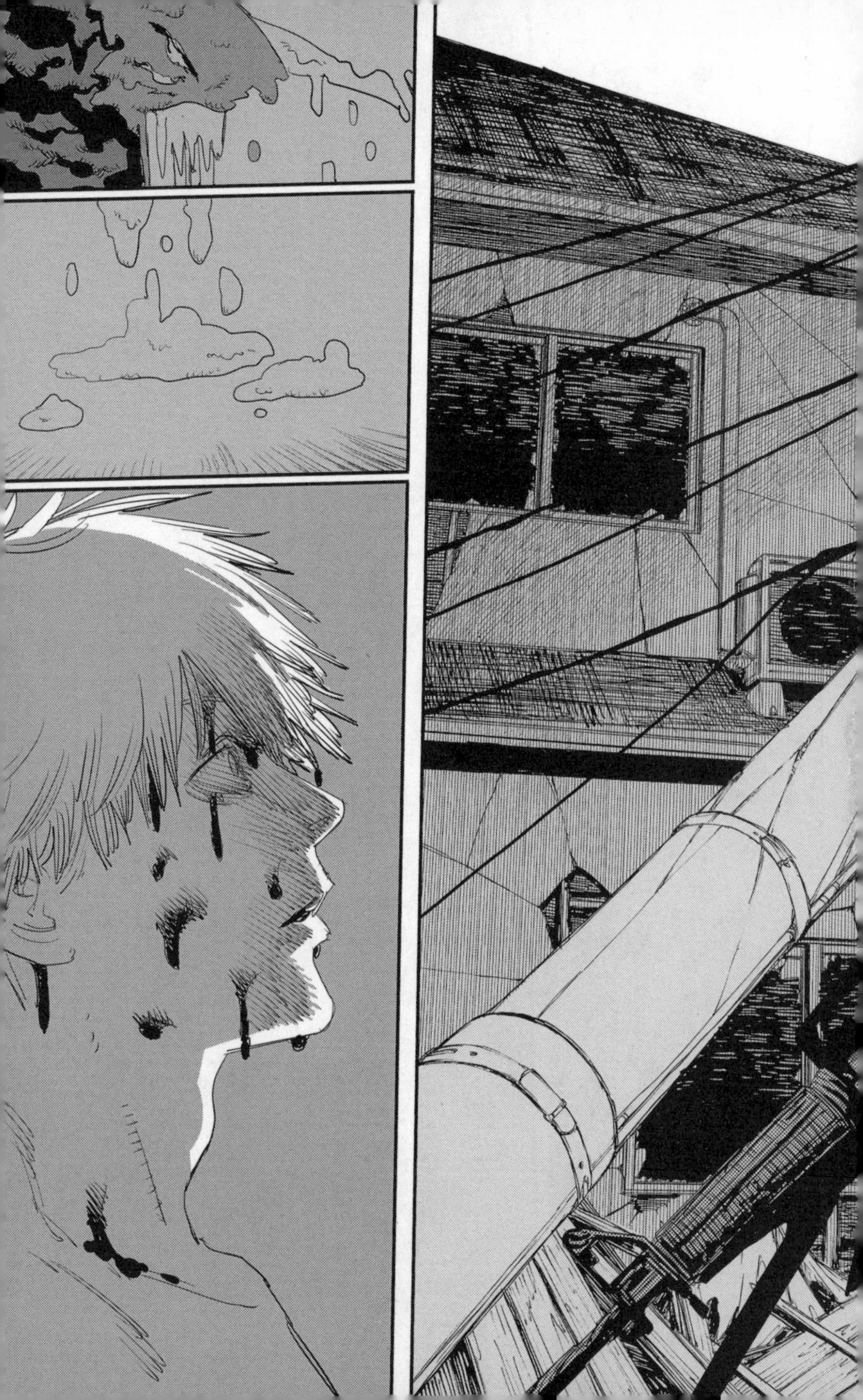

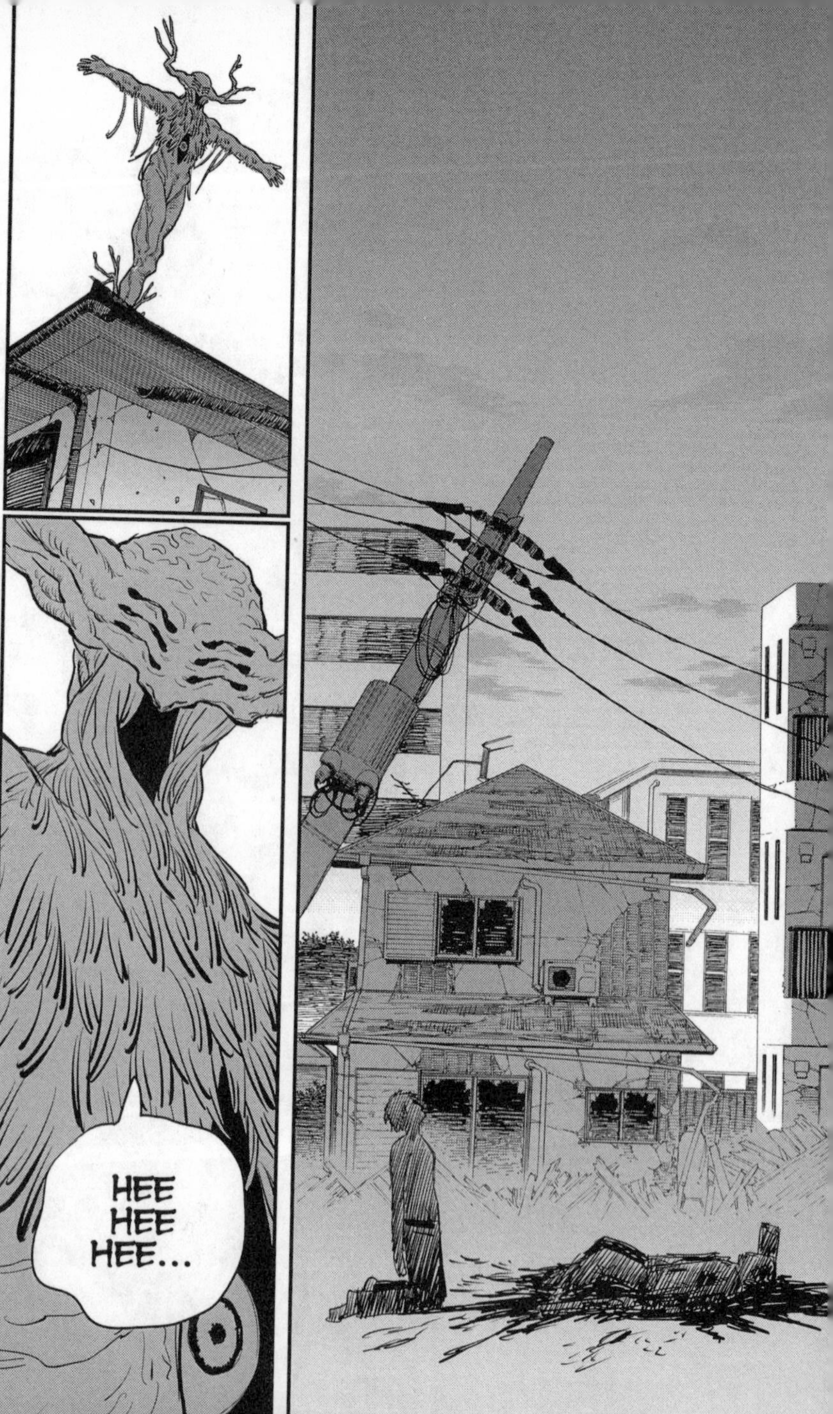
HEE HEE HEE...

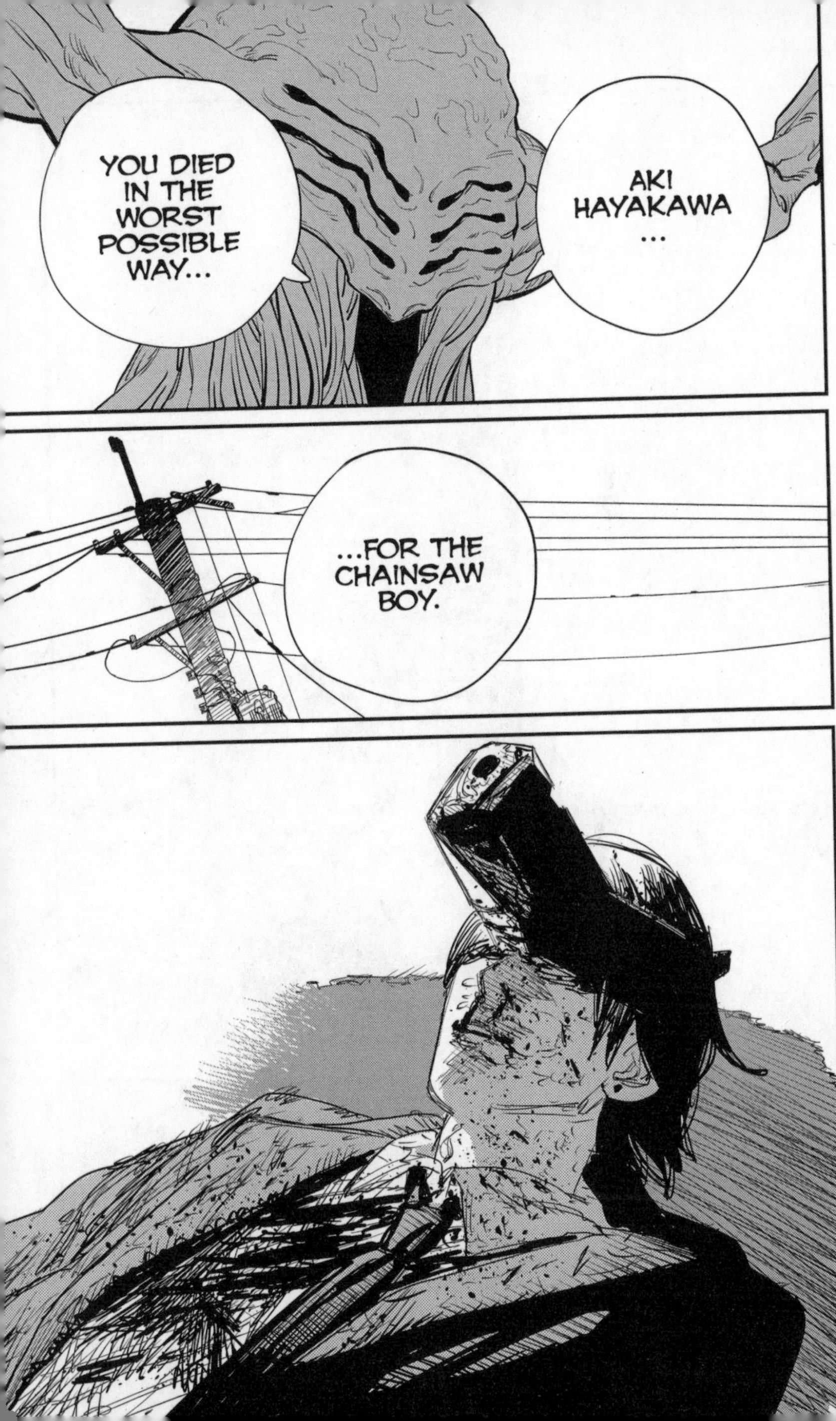
AKI HAYAKAWA ...
YOU DIED IN THE WORST POSSIBLE WAY...
...FOR THE CHAINSAW BOY.

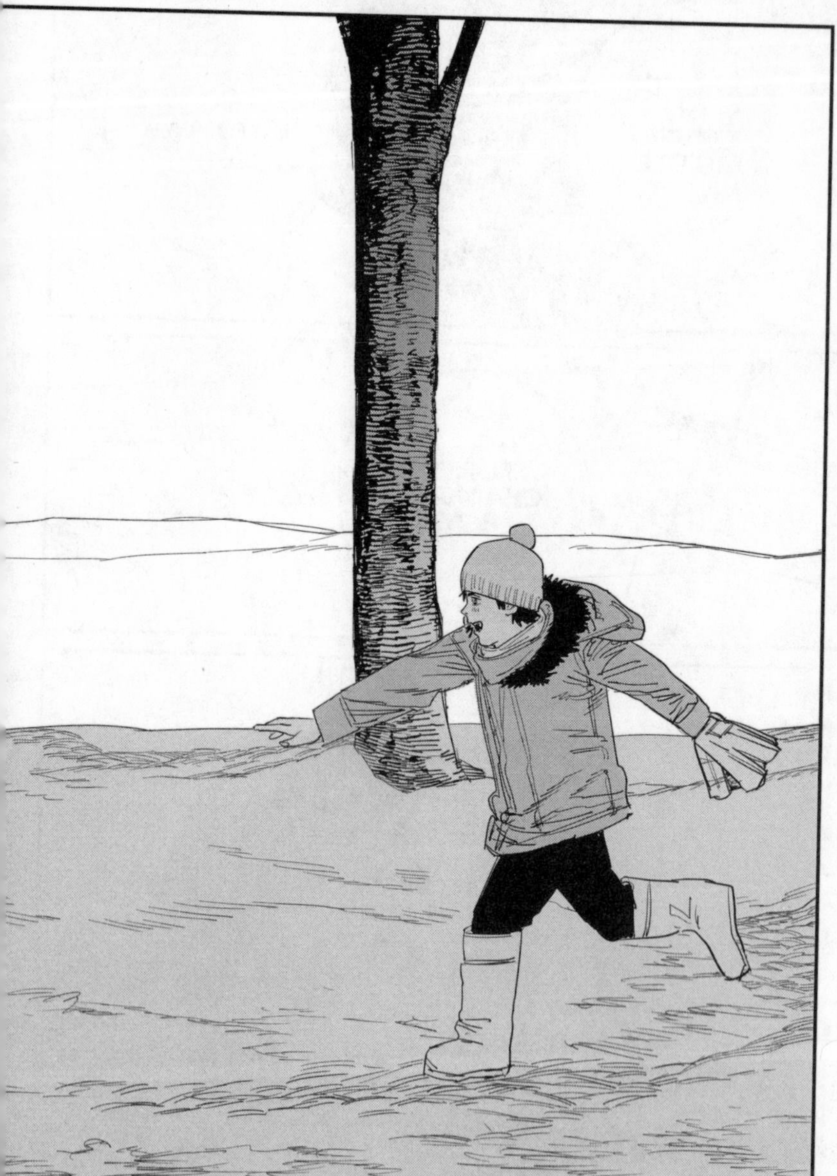

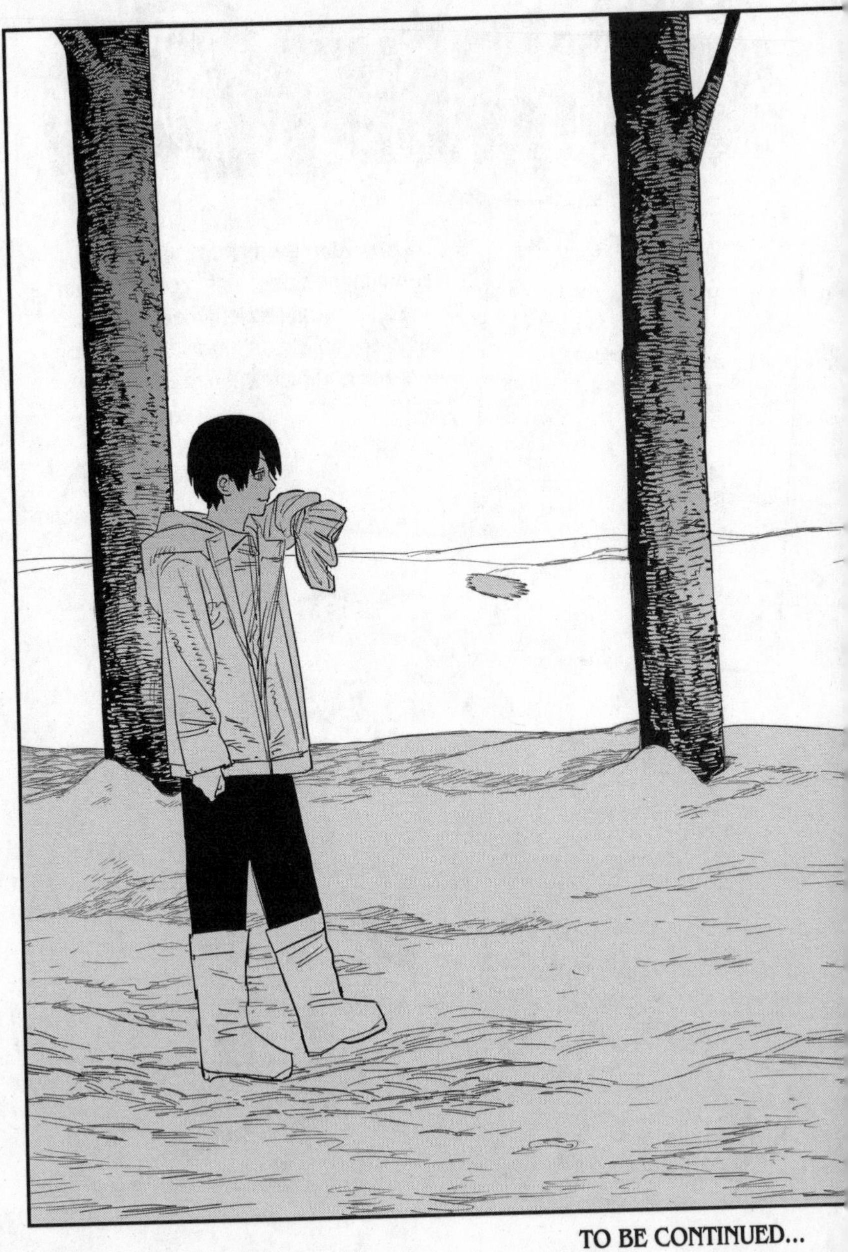

TO BE CONTINUED...

YOU'RE READING THE WRONG WAY!

CHAINSAW MAN

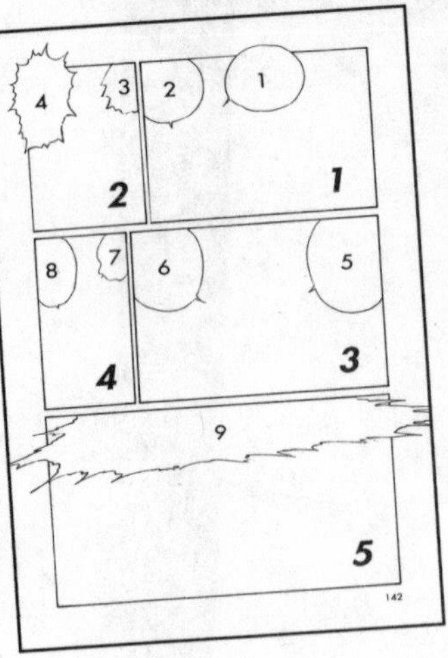
1
2
3
4
5
1
2
3
4
5
6
7
8
9
142

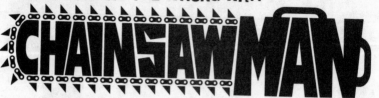

Chainsaw Man reads from right to left, starting in the upper-right corner. Japanese is read from right to left, meaning that action, sound effects, and word-balloon order are completely reversed from English order.

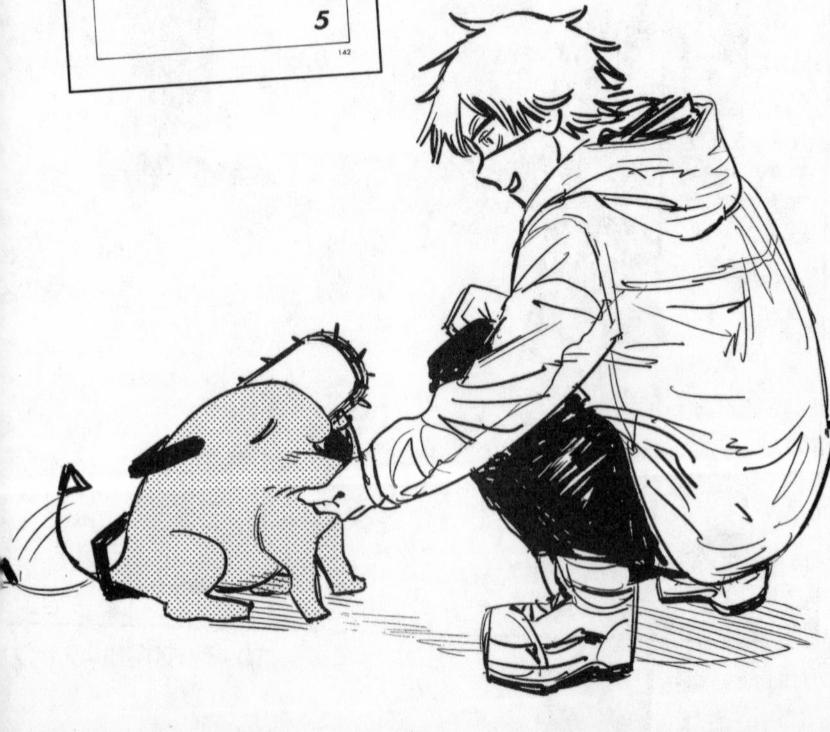